English 3200

with Writing Applications

A PROGRAMMED COURSE IN GRAMMAR AND USAGE

Fourth College Edition

Joseph C. Blumenthal

HEINLE & HEINLE

THOMSON LEARNING

Australia Canada Mexico Singapore Spain United Kingdom United States

HEINLE & HEINLE

THOMSON LEARNING

English 3200 with Writing Applications/Fourth College Edition
A Programmed Course in Grammar and Usage
Joseph C. Blumenthal

Publisher: *Ted Buchholz*
Acquisitions Editor: *Stephen T. Jordan*
Project Editor: *Nancy Lombardi*
Production Manager: *Kelly Donaldson; Erin Gregg*
Cover Designer: *Diana Jean Parks*

Printed in the United States of America
12 13 14 15   06 05 04 03 02

For more information contact Heinle & Heinle, 25 Thomson Place, Boston, MA 02210 USA,
or you can visit our Internet site at http://www.heinle.com

For permission to use material from this text or product contact us:
Tel   1-800-730-2214
Fax   1-800-730-2215
Web   www.thomsonrights.com

ISBN: 0-15-500865-X

Library of Congress Catalog Card Number:
        92-83968

The College Series

English 2200

English 2600

English 3200

TESTS FOR ENGLISH 2200

TESTS FOR ENGLISH 2600

TESTS FOR ENGLISH 3200
Alternate Tests for English 3200

ANSWER KEY FOR EACH TEST BOOK

About the Author

Joseph C. Blumenthal received his A.B. and A.M. degrees from the University of Michigan. He also did graduate work at the University of Chicago and at Columbia University. From 1938 to 1959 he was head of the English Department at Mackenzie High School in Detroit. Among his writings are the *Common Sense English* series, the *English Workshop* series (with John F. Warriner and others), and *The English Language* series (with Louis Zahner and others).

About the Fourth Edition

This edition retains the index that is intended to make *English 3200* more useful to students and instructors by giving them ready access to the entire body of material treated in the text. Each entry is indexed by frame and page numbers to facilitate reference.

New to this edition is a writing applications section, designed to move students from mastering skills to using those skills in real writing situations.

The Test Booklet

The 60-page test booklet designed for use with *English 3200* consists of a Pre-Test, two parallel tests for each of the twelve units, two Halfway Tests, and a Final Test.

PREFACE

English 2200, English 2600, and *English 3200* are the original programmed courses in grammar, usage, sentence-building, capitalization, and punctuation. Since the introduction of the series in colleges in 1963, it has proved effective in teaching the elements of English to more than a million students of all abilities in a wide range of institutions: state and private universities, community, junior, and four-year colleges, vocational and technical institutes, and business colleges.

The Self-Teaching Method

Like their predecessors, the 1994 College Editions of the series are self-pacing, self-correcting, thorough, and flexible. They are programmed to make the learning of grammar and usage a positive, success-oriented experience. Each lesson in *English 2200, English 2600*, and *English 3200* contains twenty to forty sequential learning "frames." Each frame has three elements: an easy-to-understand explanation of a small but significant step in the mastery of the lesson topic; a question or statement about the topic to which the student must respond; and the answer to the preceding frame's question. Students perform and correct their work individually, at their own pace. Correct responses are immediately reinforced and incorrect responses are corrected at once. This step-by-step format, based on decades of in-class testing and refinement, provides the immediate positive reinforcement and encouragement students need to maximize learning.

Three Parallel, Graduated Programs

English 2200, English 2600, and *English 3200* are parallel in approach and design and may therefore be used cumulatively. As their titles indicate, they vary in length according to the number of frames, and they vary in emphasis. *English 2200* and *English 2600* focus on the parts of speech and how they are combined into correctly punctuated sentences. In *English 2200*, students are introduced to words that make up and enrich sentences. In *English 2600*, they expand on this knowledge by studying the function of verbs, subjects, and modifiers, as well as the patterns of simple sentences. *English 3200* guides students directly from one unit on the simple sentence to six units on more sophisticated ways of handling sentences. It treats compound and complex sentences, devices of subordination, and techniques for writing sentences with variety and smoothness.

Pedagogical Flexibility

College instructors have found that the cumulative programmed format of the series offers an extraordinary degree of pedagogical flexibility. They have used the same book as a basic text for an entire class, as an independent course of study for individuals, as a review for groups outside the classroom, and as a remedial text for individuals or groups. These last two uses have made the series especially attractive to writing laboratories and learning centers. Further, because the three programs in the series cover the same principles of grammar and usage, they may be used sequentially in three graduated courses or even together in a single class. For example, using the results of the diagnostic Pre-Test for *English 2600*, instructors may assign students either *English 2200*, *English 2600*, or *English 3200*. Instead of spending many class hours on details of grammar and usage, instructors assigning these self-teaching programs are free to devote more time to the teaching of writing, vocabulary, spelling, and other skills.

The Writing Applications

The writing applications in the second part of this book correspond to the units on grammar, sentence-building, usage, and punctuation in the first part. They are designed to complement the programmed instruction so that students can use the information already learned in their writing. The writing applications give students the opportunity to apply directly the principles of grammar and usage mastered in the first part of the book.

Each writing application asks the student to write about a topic, using a six-stage process, called the *writing process*. Learning to use the writing process will enable the student to plan, compose, and revise more quickly, easily, and accurately.

Indexes

A detailed index, useful to both instructors and students, follows each programmed course. Every entry in the index is followed by the frame number and the page, in parentheses, on which the frame appears. The frames indexed are those containing key concepts, definitions, or illustrations. For example, under the entry "fragment" in the index to *English 3200* are eleven subentries; these entries direct students to various kinds of fragments, as well as to methods for correcting them. Students may turn to particular entries to answer their own questions about specific points of grammar and usage. Besides offering a handy reference, however, the index is a useful aid for planning remedial and review exercises. When students reveal that they have not yet mastered a particular concept, the instructor, by consulting the index, can guide them to review the appropriate frames. Students who require help in correcting specific errors when revising a composition may be alerted to frames that show them how to identify and remedy those errors.

Test Booklets and Answer Keys

A 60- or 64-page test booklet for each volume in the series is provided free to college instructors in class quantities, one booklet for each textbook ordered. Additional copies of the test booklets are sold separately and may be ordered from the publisher. An alternate test booklet, parallel in form and content to the original, is available for *English 3200*. When placing orders for *English 3200*, instructors should indicate whether they wish the original or the alternate test booklets. In addition, an Answer Key for each of the test booklets is available to instructors.

Each test booklet contains a diagnostic Pre-Test, two parallel Mastery Tests (labeled A and B) for each unit in the textbook, two parallel Halfway Tests, and a Final Test.

This testing apparatus considerably enhances the flexibility of the series. Whether a test is given to individual students or to an entire class at the same time depends on how the textbook itself is used. If students proceed at their own rate until they complete the entire book, individual testing will be necessary. If the class waits until all students complete a given unit before proceeding to the next unit, the class may be tested simultaneously. The Pre-Test enables instructors to determine a student's overall grasp of fundamentals, to identify his or her strengths and weaknesses, and to plan an individualized program while avoiding material the student has already mastered.

The inclusion of parallel Mastery Tests offers flexibility in meeting the needs of a specific class in providing for various classroom situations. For example:

1. Test A may be used as a pre-test for every unit and Test B as a final test.

2. Test A may serve as a practice test and Test B as the official test.

3. Test A or B may be used as a makeup test for students who did not achieve satisfactory scores on their first test.

4. Tests A and B may be used with different classes or with alternate rows in the same classroom.

No matter how the tests are used, one idea, basic to the method of programmed learning, should be kept in mind: a response should have an immediate reinforcement.

To the Student

English 3200, Fourth Edition, is a programmed course in grammar, sentence-building, usage, and punctuation designed to provide a quick recapitulation of the elements of language. A very substantial part of this programmed text deals with devices of sentence construction and types of subordination. The book also has lessons on the placing of modifiers, dangling construction, parallelism, the reference of pronouns, and other grammatical concepts.

If this should be your first experience with a programmed textbook, you will be interested in knowing why programmed instruction is regarded as a major advance in education. Programmed texts are making rapid headway as a teaching method for the following reasons:

1. When a course is programmed, it is broken down into very minute and carefully arranged steps—approximately 3,200 in the case of the present book—through which you reason your way, one small step at a time. There is no separation, as in conventional textbooks, between explanation and exercises; the two are woven tightly together. Every step—or frame—calls for a written response, which requires both *thinking* and *concentration*. Thinking your way, step by step, through a program is like following a very gradual path up a steep mountain. Without becoming winded or losing your footing, you suddenly discover that you have reached the top.

2. Programs are constructed on the principle of "errorless learning." The steps are so small and their order is so logical that, with reasonable concentration, you are not likely to make many mistakes. Should you, now and then, write the wrong answer, you are corrected immediately—before the error can become established. It is as though a watchful teacher were constantly looking over your shoulder, ready to put you back on the track the moment you wander off. Using a programmed textbook is the nearest approach to having a private tutor.

3. With the usual language textbook, you first study the explanation, which you may or may not understand thoroughly. Next, you apply what you have studied to the exercises in the text—often with a feeling of uncertainty. Usually, it is not until the next day that you discover whether or not you did the exercises correctly.

With *English 3200*, however, as soon as you turn the page you find out whether your reasoning was right. At this point something very important happens. The instant you find out that your answer is right, all doubt disappears and the idea "takes root," so to speak, in your brain.

The psychologists who developed programming call this *reinforcement*, and it is a most important factor in learning. The more often reinforcement takes place and the more quickly it follows the writing of your answer, the better you learn.

4. With programmed instruction, you can progress at your own best rate. Many students have completed entire courses in a fraction of the time required by the traditional textbook method and have demonstrated a better mastery of the subject matter. With programmed instruction, your mind is constantly in high gear. You lose no time waiting for other students to recite, correcting other students' papers, or listening to a discussion of other students' mistakes. In the rapidly developing world of today, education is becoming a longer and longer road. The time you save by this new scientific method can be used to advance yourself in literature, composition skills, discussion, and creative activities.

Each step, or frame, requires that you perform some operation. For example, in many of the frames you will do one of two things:

1. If there is a blank line, write in the missing word or letter.

    Example: Jones is the name of a *person*.

2. If there are two or more words or letters in parentheses, underline the correct answer.

    Example: Jones is the name of a (*person*, *place*).

(Note: Your instructor will tell you whether to write your answers in the book or write them in a separate notebook or on separate sheets of paper.)

The first work frame is Frame 2 (on page 3). After you complete Frame 2, turn to Frame 3, *in the same position* on the next *right-hand* page (page 5). In the column to the left of Frame 3, you will find the correct answer to Frame 2. If your answer is not correct, turn back and correct it before doing Frame 3. You will always find the answer to a frame in the column to the left of the frame that you are to do next. Thus, you find the answer to Frame 3 to the left of Frame 4, the answer to Frame 4 to the left of Frame 5, and so on.

Go completely through the book, taking only the top colored frame on each *right-hand* page (3, 5, 7, 9, 11, and so on) until you reach the end. When you reach the end of the book, turn back to page 1 and follow the second band—a white one—through the book, still working only on the *right-hand* pages. Then proceed to the third horizontal band, which is colored, going through all the *right-hand* pages. Continue in this way through the fourth, fifth, and sixth bands. When you come to the last white band on the last *right-hand* page (frame 1620), turn back to page 2 and start reading the colored bands at the top of the *left-hand* pages. Continue following each horizontal band through the *left-hand* pages. The last frame is 3232 on page 534.

The alternating colored and white bands will make it easy for you to stay on the same horizontal band as you advance through the book. Since both frame and answer are numbered (each in the lower right corner), you will always know where you are and where to go next.

The Writing Applications

The writing applications in the second part of this book correspond to the units on grammar, sentence-building, usage and punctuation in the first part. They are designed to complement the programmed instruction so that you can use in your writing the information you have already learned. The writing applications give you the opportunity to apply directly the principles of grammar and usage you mastered in the first part of the book.

How to Use the Writing Applications

Preceding the writing applications is a basic introduction to the writing process. Read this information carefully before you complete your first writing application. Then use this section for reference whenever you want to review the basic concepts and stages of the writing process.

Following the introduction to the writing process are the writing applications. There are three writing applications for each unit. Your teacher will tell you exactly which writing applications to complete and when.

Each writing application follows a specific order that will enable you to practice using the stages of the writing process. Each application begins with an introductory paragraph and examples of a particular writing skill that you will be asked to demonstrate. Following this information is a writing assignment, which gives you the opportunity to plan and write your first draft.

Since evaluation is an important stage in the writing process, each writing assignment is followed by an evaluation checklist. The checklist will enable you to analyze your writing for weaknesses. Thus you always have the opportunity to revise your writing before you prepare a final version. The writing applications and the programmed instruction, although different in several ways, are alike in that they have you follow a step-by-step process that enables you to evaluate your own progress.

Each application concludes with steps for revising, proofreading, and writing a final version.

Getting the Most from *English 3200*

1. Whenever you are puzzled for the correct answer to a frame, read the frame very carefully again. Many of the frames contain clues that guide you to the right

answer, although the clues gradually diminish as the lesson advances. You are not likely to make a mistake very often. When you do, look back a few frames and try to straighten out your thinking. When you can't help yourself, consult your instructor. With an ordinary textbook, it is difficult for your instructor to discover where your thinking jumped the track. With a programmed text, your instructor can help you immediately at the precise point where you need assistance.

2. Take as much time as you need in figuring out your answer. But once you write your answer, *lose no time* in turning to the next frame to check its correctness. Scientific experiment has proved that the quicker you check your answer, the better you learn. *Even the lapse of a few seconds makes a big difference.*

3. *English 3200* is designed for students mature enough to want to improve their minds by thinking things through for themselves—the most effective way of learning and remembering. No student has paid a greater compliment to this book than the one who said, "It makes me think too much." Exercising your brain, like exercising your muscles, is sometimes a bit strenuous. But it is this effort that will develop your power to think systematically and to reason logically.

If you use *English 3200* in the mature way, you may discover that you have acquired a better knowledge of grammar and usage—and in a fraction of the usual time. You may find, too, that you have developed your ability to think and to concentrate in a way that will be useful to you in all your studies. You will have profited by the latest and most exciting discoveries of science about how people learn!

Contents

LESSON NUMBER	FRAME NUMBERS	BEGINS ON PAGE

LESSON NUMBER	FRAME NUMBERS	BEGINS ON PAGE

adverb

270

In the following frames, each sentence contains two prepositional phrases in various combinations—two adjective phrases, two adverb phrases, or one of each. Before classifying each phrase, ask yourself, "Does this phrase describe a noun or pronoun, or does it answer a question about the verb?" (*Turn to the next frame.*)

271

---

b

540

I have a friend *who raises tropical fish.*

The adjective clause *who raises tropical fish* modifies the

noun _____.

541

---

b

810

Put a comma after any participial phrase that comes at the beginning of a sentence.

    a. *Thinking the paint was dry* **I sat on the bench.**
    b. **We removed the tree** *shading the flower beds.*

Which sentence requires a comma? _____

811

---

before

1080

a. **His** *strong, calloused* **hands were no strangers to work.**
b. **His hands,** *strong* **and** *calloused,* **were no strangers to work.**

In which sentence are the italicized adjectives given more emphasis? _____

1081

---

pulp. High-grade
or
pulp; high-grade

1350

It was a wonderful party   **the best I have ever attended.**

_____

1351

similar 1620	Try to apply parallel construction whenever you use the co-ordinating conjunctions **and, but,** and **or,** which generally connect words or word groups of the same type. **Edison paid little attention to** *what he ate* **or** *his clothes.* In this sentence does the conjunction **or** connect parallel word groups? (*Yes, No*) 1621
One 1889	Underline the correct verb: **One of these steaks** (*is, are*) **enough for a meal.** 1890
cards 2158	**The dishes** *were laid* **on the sink.** What *were laid* on the sink? _____ 2159
Yes 2427	*GOOD* and *WELL* Always use the adverb **well**—never the adjective **good**—to describe an action. A person eats *well*, plays *well*, or works *well*. a. **This pen writes** *well.* b. **This pen writes** *good.* Which sentence is correct? _____ 2428
their 2696	From here on, write in the pronoun that is appropriate for formal usage: **Nobody was ever more confused about** _____ **rela-tives than I.** 2697
items: 2965	**The Student Council makes suggestions in regard to such matters as lockers, the lunchroom, and homework and Mrs. Roska, the principal, discusses these suggestions with the faculty.** 2966

A sentence is a group of words that gives us a sense of completeness.

a. **The barking dog**
b. **The dog is barking.**

Which group of words is a sentence—*a* or *b*? _____

2

This TV program brings the services (*a*) *of a great university* (*b*) *into your home.*

After each letter, indicate whether the corresponding phrase is an *adjective* or an *adverb* phrase. (Notice that only one of these phrases can be moved to another position.)

(a) _____ *phrase*; (b) _____ *phrase*.   272

---

friend

541

I have a friend *who raises tropical fish.*

An adjective clause signal is nearly always a *pronoun*. This pronoun stands for the noun that the entire clause modifies. In the above sentence, the pronoun *who* stands for the noun _____.

542

---

a

811

Put a comma after any participial phrase that comes at the beginning of a sentence.

a. **We noticed a small dog** *crossing the busy highway.*
b. *Attempting to start a conversation* **I made some remark about the weather.**

Which sentence requires a comma? _____

812

---

b

1081

a. **His** *strong, calloused* **hands were no strangers to work.**
b. **His hands,** *strong* **and** *calloused,* **were no strangers to work.**

The italicized adjectives in sentence *b* are given more emphasis because they (*are, are not*) in their usual position.

1082

---

party, the

1351

There were Mother's sketches   **scattered all over the yard and covered with mud.**

_____

1352

No

1621

a. **Edison paid little attention to** *what he ate* **or** *his clothes.*
b. **Edison paid little attention to** *what he ate* **or** *what he wore.*

In which sentence does the conjunction **or** connect parallel word groups? _____

1622

---

is

1890

Once you state your subject, keep your mind on it until you select your verb. Don't let a noun in a prepositional phrase run away with your verb.

    Our supply of scientific books (*was, were*) **inadequate.**

The noun **supply** is singular; the noun **books** is plural. We choose the verb _____ to agree with the subject _____.

1891

---

dishes

2159

PRESENT	PAST	PAST PARTICIPLE
lie (to rest)	**lay**	**(have) lain**
lay (to put)	**laid**	**(have) laid**

Laid is never a form of **lie.**

Would you ever use **laid** when you mean **rested?** (*Yes, No*)

2160

---

a

2428

      WRONG: **This pen writes** *good.*

This sentence is wrong because the adjective *good* cannot modify the verb _____.

2429

---

his or her

2697

Almost anyone can increase _____ **reading rate considerably.**

2698

---

homework;

2966

Somebody   maybe it was Lenore   had let the cat out of the bag.

2967

The dog is barking.

b

This group of words is a sentence because it gives us a sense of (*completeness, incompleteness*).

2   3

Our mayor is a person (*a*) *with a reputation* (*b*) *for great honesty.*

(a) adjective
(b)   adverb

After each letter, indicate whether the corresponding phrase is an *adjective* or an *adverb* phrase:

(a) _____ *phrase*; (b) _____ *phrase*

272   273

I have a friend *who raises tropical fish.*

friend

The noun that the adjective clause modifies and the noun that the pronoun *who* stands for are (*the same word, different words*).

542   543

When a participial phrase ends a sentence, look for the word it modifies. If it modifies the subject at the other end of the sentence, set it off with a comma.

b

  a. **We found Mr. Ling** *hoeing his garden.*
  b. **Mr. Ling was in the back yard** *hoeing his garden.*

Which sentence requires a comma? _____

812   813

---

a. **The team,** *tired* **and** *discouraged,* **trudged back to the locker room.**
b. **The** *tired* **and** *discouraged* **team trudged back to the locker room.**

are not

In which sentence are the italicized adjectives given more emphasis? _____

1082   1083

The return on a stock is called a dividend   the return on a bond is called interest.

sketches (,)
covered

_____

1352   1353

b	**Ray's trouble is not** *that he doesn't earn enough money* **but** *spending it foolishly.* Does the conjunction **but** connect parallel word groups? (*Yes, No*)
1622	1623

(verb) was (subject) supply	**Several pieces of the puzzle** (*was, were*) **missing.** The noun **pieces** is plural, but the noun **puzzle** is singular. We choose the verb _____ to agree with the subject _____.
1891	1892

No	Underline the correct words. (*Note:* These two sentences are parallel and require the same verb.)
	
	  a. **The tired travelers** (*lay, laid*) **in bed all morning.**
	  b. **My missing wallet** (*lay, laid*) **in the snow all winter.**

2160	2161

writes	Underline the correct word: **Brush your clothes** (*good, well*) **before putting them away.**
2429	2430

his or her	**Both women made the welfare of children _____ chief concern in life.**
2698	2699

Somebody— Lenore—	**Murray is allergic to several foods for example, eggs and chocolate.**
2967	2968

completeness 3	**The dog is barking.** This group of words gives us a sense of completeness because it (1) *names* what we are talking about, and (2) *tells* something about it. Which two words belong to the *naming part* of the sentence? _____ _____ 4
(a) adjective (b) adjective 273	(*a*) *In several states,* **the smoke** (*b*) *from this forest fire could be clearly seen.* (a) _____ *phrase;* (b) _____ *phrase* 274
the same word 543	**I have a friend** *who raises tropical fish.* The pronouns that start adjective clauses are called **relative pronouns** because they *relate* (or *connect*) the adjective clause to the sentence. The clause signal *who* in the above sentence is called a _____ *pronoun.* 544
b 813	a. **The director took us through the museum** *explaining all the important pictures.* b. **The museum sold a guidebook** *explaining all the important pictures.* Which sentence requires a comma because the participial phrase that ends the sentence modifies the subject? _____ 814
a 1083	Underline the word or phrase which is emphasized by a change from its normal position: **For fifty years Grandmother attended the same church.** 1084
dividend. The *or* dividend; the 1353	**Ships are like people each having its own personality.** _____ 1354

No

1623

a. **Ray's trouble is not** *that he doesn't earn enough money* **but** *that he spends it foolishly.*
b. **Ray's trouble is not** *that he doesn't earn enough money* **but** *spending it foolishly.*

In which sentence does the conjunction **but** connect parallel word groups? _____

1624

(verb) were
(subject) pieces

1892

People frequently make errors in subject-verb agreement because they have the mistaken idea that adding an *s* to a verb in the present tense makes it plural.

My shoe hurts.

The subject **shoe** is singular, and the verb **hurts** is singular. The word that ends in *s* is the (*subject, verb*).

1893

---

lay

2161

Fill in the missing forms:

PRESENT	PAST	PAST PARTICIPLE
lay (to put)	_____	**(have)** _____

2162

---

well

2430

Although **good** should not be used as an adverb, **well** may be used as an adjective to mean *in good health, of good appearance,* or *satisfactory.*

    a. **Stir the paint** *well* **before using it.**
    b. **Our dog is now** *well* **again.**

Well is used as an adjective in sentence (*a, b*).

2431

---

their

2699

Everyone has _____ own ideas about what constitutes success in life.

2700

---

foods;
or
foods—

2968

Your letter of application should state these facts   your age, education, and experience.

(Note that this series is preceded by a grammatically complete statement.)

2969

The dog 4	**The dog is barking.** Which two words *tell* something about **the dog** and therefore belong to the *telling part* of the sentence? ———— ———————————— 5
(a) adverb (b) adjective 274	**The invention** (*a*) *of the automobile* **has changed American life** (*b*) *in many ways.* (a) ———————— *phrase;* (b) ———————— *phrase* 275
relative 544	**I have a friend** *who raises tropical fish.* The relative pronoun *who* starts the adjective clause. It also stands for the noun ————————, which the clause modifies. 545
a 814	In this and the following frames, combine each pair of sentences by changing the italicized sentence to a participial phrase. Insert a comma wherever needed. **I read the list of winners.** *I hoped to see my name.* ———————————————————— ———————————————————— 815
For fifty years 1084	Underline the word or phrase which is emphasized by a change from its normal position: **Resign he will not.** 1085
people, each 1354	**O. J. trudged to the sideline wiping the mud from his face.** ———————————————————— 1355

a 1624	Parallel construction is also needed when you use the words **than, as,** and **as well as** to make comparisons. *Writing* **is faster than** *to print.* Are the italicized words parallel? (*Yes, No*) 1625
verb 1893	**My <u>shoes</u> <u>hurt</u>.** Now the subject **shoes** is plural, and the verb **hurt** is plural. The word that ends in *s* is the (*subject, verb*). 1894
laid, (have) laid 2162	In this and the following frames, underline the correct forms of **lie** and **lay:** (*Lay, Lie*) **your books aside and** (*lay, lie*) **down to rest for a while.** 2163
b 2431	Underline the correct words: **When the pressure is** (*good, well*), **the sprinkler works** (*good, well*). 2432
his or her 2700	**If a woman wants to have a family and earn a college degree, _____ can do so.** 2701
facts: 2969	**Practically all the accommodations hotels, motels, and tourist homes were jammed with vacationists.** 2970

is barking

5

a. **The argument was useless.**
b. **A useless argument.**

Which group of words is a sentence because it gives us a sense of completeness—*a* or *b?* _____

6

(a) adjective
(b) adverb

275

(*a*) *At feeding time,* **a large crowd always gathers** (*b*) *around the lions' cage.*

(a) _____ *phrase;* (b) _____ *phrase*

276

---

friend

545

I have a friend *who* *raises* *tropical fish.*

In the above sentence the relative pronoun *who* is the subject of the verb _____.

546

I read the
list of winners,
hoping to see
my name.

815

Continue to follow the directions for the previous frame:

    I read the list of winners. **I hoped to see my name.**

_____

_____

816

Resign

1085

Underline the word or phrase which is emphasized by a change from its normal position:

Of all the cakes I have ever eaten, this was the most delicious.

1086

---

sideline, wiping

1355

Lesson **37** When Does a Sentence End?

[Frames 1357–1387]

No

1625

---

a. *Writing* **is faster than** *printing*.
b. *Writing* **is faster than** *to print*.
c. *To write* **is faster than** *to print*.

Which is the one sentence in which the construction is not parallel? _____

1626

---

subject

1894

SINGULAR: **My shoe hurts.**
PLURAL: **My shoes hurt.**

In either the singular or plural sentence, is there a final *s* on both the subject and the verb? (*Yes, No*).

1895

Lay, lie

2163

PRESENT	PAST	PAST PARTICIPLE
lie (to rest)	**lay**	**(have) lain**
lay (to put)	**laid**	**(have) laid**

I (*laid, lay*) **awake, trying to recall where I had** (*lain, laid*) **my receipt.**

2164

---

good, well

2432

Underline the correct words:

You can't study (*good, well*) **unless the light is** (*good, well*).

2433

---

she

2701

Ask anybody where the Eiffel Tower is and _____ **can tell you.**

2702

---

accommodations—
homes—

2970

The lighter seeds are scattered by the wind   the heavier ones are distributed by squirrels.

2971

a. **Helping his friend.**
b. **With the help of his friend.**
c. **Alonzo helped his friend.**

Which group of words is a sentence because it gives us a sense of completeness—*a, b,* or *c?* _____

7

---

a

6

Some words can be used as either <u>prepositions</u> or <u>adverbs</u>. These words, such as *before, behind, after, past, through, down,* and *around,* generally refer to direction. To decide how such a word is used, look for an *object*. If you find an object, the word in question is a (*preposition, adverb*).

277

(a) adverb
(b) adverb

276

Let's take another look at the adjective clause signals.

RELATIVE PRONOUNS: **who (whose, whom), which, that**

> **The student . . .** *essay wins* **receives a scholarship.**

Which relative pronoun would be appropriate in this sentence? _____

547

---

raises

546

Be sure to change the italicized sentence—not the main statement—to a participial phrase. If you lose your subject in so doing, put it back at the start of the main statement.

> *Fred stood at the window.* **He saw the lightning strike.**

_____

_____

817

Reading the list of winners, I hoped to see my name.

816

---

a. **The Turners had little ready money although they owned a lot of land.**
b. **Although they owned a lot of land, the Turners had little ready money.**

If you had written many sentences with the subject first, which sentence would break the monotony? _____

1087

Of all the cakes I have ever eaten,

1086

Many sentence fragments come about in this way. You start out, for example, by writing—

> **Charles Sifford plays golf.**

Is this a complete sentence? (*Yes, No*)

1357

b

1626

a. **To read a foreign language is easier than to speak it.**
b. **Reading a foreign language is easier than speaking it.**
c. **To read a foreign language is easier than speaking it.**

Which is the one sentence in which the construction is not parallel? _____

1627

No

1895

The <u>window</u> <u>opens</u>.

When you change this sentence to the plural, the final *s* on the verb **opens** (*remains, disappears*).

1896

---

lay, laid

2164

PRESENT	PAST	PAST PARTICIPLE
lie (to rest)	**lay**	**(have) lain**
lay (to put)	**laid**	**(have) laid**

Underline the correct words:

Your books will (*lay, lie*) **there until you** (*lay, lie*) **them somewhere else.**

2165

---

well, good

2433

How do you decide whether to use **good** or **well** after a "sense" verb?

If the "sense" verb means an action, use **well** to describe this action.

Underline the correct word:

    I felt the cloth (*good, well*) **before buying the coat.**

2434

---

he or she

2702

Any person making a telephone call should give _____ **name at once.**

2703

---

wind;

2971

The water was close to the top of the levee   and it was rapidly rising.

(Punctuate so as to make the second idea very forceful.)

2972

c 7	The *naming part* of a sentence is called the **complete subject.** A **complete subject** is usually built around a noun (or pronoun) that is known as the **simple subject.** The **complete subject** is likely to be (*longer, shorter*) than the **simple subject**—or **subject,** as we usually call it. 8
preposition 277	a. **The dog trotted** *behind.* b. **The dog trotted** *behind* **the car.** In which sentence is *behind* a preposition because it is followed by an object? _____ 278
whose 547	**The woman whose car we bumped was very angry.** The adjective clause starts with the relative pronoun *whose* and ends with the word _____. 548
Standing at the window, Fred saw the lightning strike. 817	**Reverend Jesse Jackson stresses education.** *He maintains it is the key to success.* _____ _____ 818
b 1087	a. **When it was first delivered, the Gettysburg Address made little impression.** b. **The Gettysburg Address made little impression when it was first delivered.** If you had written many sentences with the subject first, which sentence would break the monotony? _____ 1088
Yes 1357	**Charles Sifford plays golf.** Because you recognize this as a complete sentence with a subject and a verb, you close it with a _____. (What punctuation mark?) 1358

1627

c

Parallel construction does not mean having a word-for-word match between the parallel word groups. So long as the basic pattern is the same, minor differences do not matter.

Is he really _calling the police_ **or just** _pretending to call them?_

In spite of their difference, the italicized word groups are parallel because _calling_ is matched by _____.

1628

1896

disappears

In the present tense, a verb without a final _s_ may be either singular or plural (_I think, We think_), but with a final _s_ (_he thinks, she thinks_), the verb is _always_ singular.

.?. **thinks.**

Could this verb possibly have a plural subject? (_Yes, No_)

1897

2165

lie, lay

PRESENT	PAST	PAST PARTICIPLE
lie (to rest)	**lay**	**(have) lain**
lay (to put)	**laid**	**(have) laid**

Underline the correct words:

Mother (_laid, lay_) **her glasses where she had usually** (_laid, lain_) **them.**

2166

2434

well

If the "sense" verb is used as a linking verb, as it more often is, follow it with the adjective **good** to modify the subject.

A warm coat _feels_ (= _is_) **good on a chilly day.**

The adjective **good** modifies the subject _____.

2435

2703

his or her

Lesson **75** Review: Pronoun Problems

[Frames 2705–2736]

2972

levee—

We had only one objection to the house   its distance from school.

2973

longer	**The old black dog** wagged its shaggy tail.
	The **complete subject** of this sentence consists of four words—**The old black dog.**
	The **simple subject**, or **subject**, is the one word _____.
8	9

---

	a. **Ralph fell** *down* **the stairs.**
b	b. **Ralph fell** *down.*
	In which sentence is *down* a preposition? _____
278	279

---

bumped	**The woman whose car we bumped was very angry.**
	The woman **was very angry.**
	When we omit the adjective clause, do we have a complete sentence remaining? (*Yes, No*)
548	549

Reverend Jesse Jackson stresses education, maintaining it is the key to success.	*Mrs. Kern held on to the purse-snatcher.* **She shouted for help.**
	(Don't lose *Mrs. Kern* in your revision.)
	_____
818	_____ 819

	For the sake of variety, move the adverb clause to the beginning of the sentence and set it off with a comma:
a	**Dad would bring me a pennant whenever he returned from a trip.**
	_____
1088	_____ 1089

	Then as you continue thinking, you decide to qualify your statement by adding an adverb clause.
period	**Charles Sifford plays golf.** *Whenever he has time.*
	Because you have already closed your sentence with a period, the clause becomes a sentence _____.
1358	1359

pretending 1628	*To face your problems squarely* **is more healthful than** *to run away from them.* In spite of their difference, the italicized word groups are parallel because the infinitive *To face* is matched by the infinitive _____. 1629
No 1897	We add an *s* to a verb *in the present tense* whenever we talk about any singular noun (*a car, the lunch, my friend*) or about any singular pronoun in the third person (*he, she, it, one*). Underline the two singular subjects that would require a verb ending in *s*: **Planes The road They It** 1898
laid, laid 2166	Underline the correct words: **My pen has** (*lain, laid*) **on the desk ever since I** (*lay, laid*) **it there.** 2167
coat 2435	**The popcorn smelled so** *good* **that we couldn't resist it.** We use the adjective *good* because the word **smelled** is used as (*an action, a linking*) verb in this sentence. 2436
	In this and the following frames, underline the correct pronoun. Do not go "by ear," but think of a reason for each choice you make. **Between you and** (*I, me*), **Mrs. Colby doesn't like the gift.** 2705
house: *or* house— 2973	**Our cat likes only the most expensive foods for example, liver, salmon, and tuna fish.** 2974

dog 9	The old black dog **wagged its shaggy tail.** The *telling part* of a sentence is called the **complete predicate.** The **complete predicate** of this sentence consists of _____ words. (How many?) 10
a 279	a. **Ralph fell** *down* **the stairs.** b. **Ralph fell** *down.* In sentence *a, down* is a preposition because it is followed by the object **stairs.** In sentence *b, down* is an adverb that modifies the verb _____. 280
Yes 549	**A boy who had never fished before caught the most fish.** In this sentence the adjective clause starts with the relative pronoun _____ and ends with the word _____. 550
Holding on to the purse-snatcher, Mrs. Kern shouted for help. 819	Eliminate the **and** by changing the italicized statement to a participial phrase: *The company expected a strike* **and bought a large amount of steel.** 820
Whenever he returned from a trip, Dad would bring me a pennant. 1089	For the sake of variety, move the adverb clause to the beginning of the sentence and set it off with a comma: **Sandy makes new friends wherever he goes.** _____ _____ 1090
fragment 1359	**Charles Sifford plays golf** *whenever he has time.* Although the sentence could have ended after **golf,** does it end at this point? (*Yes, No*) 1360

to run

1629

Miss Ross gets acquainted with her students by *talking to them* **and** *discovering what their interests are.*

Although the italicized word groups are quite different, they are parallel because the gerund *talking* is matched by the gerund _____.

1630

The road, It

1898

---

a. { A factory . . .
    The boat . . .
    She . . . }

b. { Factories . . .
    The boats . . .
    They . . . }

Suppose that each of these items were the subject of a sentence in the present tense.

With which group would you use verbs that end in *s*? _____

1899

---

lain, laid

2167

To sit means "to take a sitting position" or "to be in place."
To set means "to place something."

You always set *something*. You *set* a pan on the stove, a glass on the table, a box on the floor.

I *set* **the pie on the windowsill to cool.**

What was *set* on the windowsill? _____

2168

---

a linking

2436

Underline the correct word in each sentence:

   a. **Cheap perfume doesn't smell** (*good, well*).
   b. **A person with a cold can't smell** (*good, well*).

2437

---

me

2705

Unless someone actually asks for your advice, don't offer (*him or her, them*) **any.**

2706

---

foods;
or
foods—

2974

Lesson **83** How to Use Quotation Marks

[Frames 2976–3014]

four 10	The complete predicate is built around the simple predicate, which we shall hereafter refer to as the **verb**. A **verb** makes—or helps to make—a statement about the subject. **The old black dog wagged its shaggy tail.** The **simple predicate**, or **verb**, around which the complete predicate is built is the one word _____. 11
fell 280	a. **The farmers stood** *around* **and chatted.** b. **The farmers stood** *around* **the courthouse.** In which sentence is *around* a preposition? _____ 281
who . . . before 550	**A boy who had never fished before caught the most fish.** **A boy** **caught the most fish.** When we omit the adjective clause, do we have a complete sentence remaining? (*Yes, No*) 551
Expecting a strike, the company bought a large amount of steel. 820	Eliminate the **and** by changing the italicized statement to a participial phrase: **We walked along the shore and** *looked for a place to swim.* _____ _____ 821
Wherever he goes, Sandy makes new friends. 1090	For the sake of variety, move the adverb clause to the beginning of the sentence and set it off with a comma: **A host should not eat until every guest has been served.** _____ _____ 1091
No 1360	**Charles Sifford plays golf** *whenever he has time.* This sentence does not end after **golf** because the adverb clause modifies the verb _____ in the main statement. 1361

discovering 1630	To avoid monotony, you may omit repeated words without destroying the parallelism. **Fractions** *can be changed to decimals,* **and** *decimals can be changed to fractions.* The three words that can be omitted from the word group after **and** are _____. 1631
a 1899	PREP ph. The ability (of gymnasts) astonishes everyone. The verb **astonishes** agrees with the subject, which is (*ability, gymnasts*). 1900
pie 2168	After you *set* something, it *sits* there until you *set* it somewhere else. Fill in the missing words: I _____ **a chair on the porch so that Dad could** _____ **in the sun.** 2169
a. good b. well 2437	In this and the following frames, underline the correct modifier after you have decided whether the verb is used as an *action* or a *linking* verb: **Mr. Sutin felt quite** (*angry, angrily*) **about the bill.** 2438
him or her 2706	(*We, Us*) **fellows can finish the job in a few hours.** 2707

	A **direct quotation** repeats a person's remark directly in his own words. An **indirect quotation** reports a person's remarks indirectly in someone else's words.
	
	    a. **Pia said, "I'll be home by ten."**
	    b. **Pia said that she would be home by ten.**
	
	The direct quotation is in sentence (*a, b*).
	
	2976

wagged 11	The *subject* and the *verb* are the most important words in any sentence because they carry most of the meaning. **Two small boys | rang our doorbell.** The *subject* of this sentence is the noun _____. The *verb* is the word _____. 12
b 281	a. **The bus went *by* without stopping.** b. **The bus went *by* the corner without stopping.** STO P 1-3 1 In which sentence is *by* a preposition? _____ 282
Yes 551	If a complete sentence does not remain after we omit the adjective clause, we have not selected the clause correctly. a. **The rope (which controls the curtain broke).** b. **The rope (which controls the curtain) broke.** The clause is correctly selected in sentence (*a, b*). 552
We walked along the shore, looking for a place to swim. 821	*Lita worked until midnight* **and finally completed her theme.** _____ _____ 822
Until every guest has been served, a host should not eat. 1091	In this and the following frames, emphasize the italicized words by moving them from their normal position to another position in the sentence: **He never could understand *geometry*.** _____ 1092
plays 1361	Does the fact that a sentence could end at a certain point mean that it does end at this point? (*Yes, No*) 1362

can be changed 1631	**I feared** *that he would change his mind* **or** *that he would raise the price.* The three words that can be omitted from the word group after **or** are _____. 1632
ability 1900	**The ability of gymnasts astonishes everyone.** The noun **gymnasts** is not the subject of the sentence but the object of the preposition _____. 1901
set, sit 2169	PRESENT PAST PAST PARTICIPLE **sit** **sat** **(have) sat** **set** (to place) **set** **(have) set** The verb whose three forms are all alike is_____. 2170
angry 2438	**Your voice sounds** (*differently, different*) **on the tape.** 2439
We 2707	**Students should be encouraged to think for** (*themselves, theirselves*). 2708

a
 	
2976
	The word **that** is frequently used in changing a direct to an indirect quotation.
	Rewrite the following sentence to make the quotation indirect (and use no quotation marks).
	    Mother said, "I am ready."
	    Mother said _____.
	
	2977

(subject) boys (verb) rang 12	Throughout this book, we shall underscore the subject with one line and the verb with two lines. **Two small <u>boys</u> | <u><u>rang</u></u> our doorbell.** Indicate the *subject* and *verb* in the following sentence by underscoring: **A handsome blue car | stopped in front of our house.** 13
b 282	**UNIT 2: THE PROCESS OF COMPOUNDING** Lesson **8** Compound Parts and Compound Sentences [Frames 284–324]
b 552	a. **The blood (which flows from a wound) washes away the germs.** b. **The blood (which flows from) a wound washes away the germs.** The clause is correctly selected in sentence (*a, b*). 553
Working until midnight, Lita finally completed her theme. 822	**A milk truck overturned and** *caused a traffic jam for several miles.* _____ _____ 823
Geometry he never could understand. 1092	**I have never eaten** *such food.* _____ 1093
No 1362	**We built a cottage | on a hill | overlooking a lake | which was surrounded by pine trees.** At how many points could this sentence have been ended before the final period? _____ 1363

that he would 1632	Put parentheses ( ) around the three words that can be omitted without destroying the parallelism: **Ray Tall Chief, our bookkeeper, keeps track of how much is coming in and how much is going out.** 1633
of 1901	a. **The ability of gymnasts astonishes everyone.** b. **The ability of gymnasts astonish everyone.** In which sentence is the verb correct? _____ 1902
set 2170	PRESENT PAST PAST PARTICIPLE **sit** **sat** **(have) sat** **set** (to place) **set** **(have) set** Fill in the missing words: **Don't _____ the package where someone might _____ on it.** 2171
different 2439	**We looked through every drawer very** (*thorough, thoroughly*). 2440
themselves 2708	**Let's you and** (*me, I*) **try out for track.** 2709
(that) she was ready. 2977	Use quotation marks ("quotes" for short) to enclose only a *direct* quotation—one that repeats a person's exact words. a. **Dad said** **You can use the car, Jim.** b. **Dad said** **that Jim could use the car.** Which sentence requires quotes because it is a direct quotation? _____ 2978

A handsome blue car | stopped in front of our house.

The subject **car** and the verb **stopped** carry more of the meaning of this sentence than any other two words we could possibly choose. (*True, False*)

14

Mr. Kwan | owns a garage.

This sentence—like all complete sentences—can be divided into two major parts: the *complete subject* and the *complete*

_____.

284

---

a

553

The clause signal **where** can start either an adverb clause or an adjective clause.

If the clause modifies a verb, it is considered an adverb clause.

If the clause modifies a noun or pronoun, it is considered an

_____ clause.

554

A milk truck overturned, causing a traffic jam for several miles.

823

Several planes circled the airport **and waited their turn to land.**

_____

_____

824

Such food I have never eaten.

1093

I never expect to be *a millionaire.*

_____

1094

---

three

1363

We built a cottage | on a hill | overlooking a lake | which was surrounded by pine trees.

This sentence could have been ended at each point marked by a vertical line. It does not end, however, until the final period because each phrase or clause modifies a word in the (*preceding, following*) phrase or clause.

1364

(how much is)	Put parentheses ( ) around the two words that can be omitted without destroying the parallelism:
	I showed Jimmie how to set the camera and how to take pictures.
1633	1634

	a. **The abilities of a gymnast astonishes everyone.**
a	b. **The abilities of a gymnast astonish everyone.**
	In which sentence is the verb correct? _____
1902	1903

set, sit	Underline the correct words:
	Tommy (*set, sat*) **down where Mrs. Gibb had** (*set, sat*) **the biggest piece of cake.**
2171	2172

thoroughly	**Barbara feels** (*bad, badly*) **about losing her library card.**
	(Is this an action of Barbara's hands?)
2440	2441

me	**I don't like mine as well as** (*yours, your's*).
2709	2710

	Always capitalize the first word of a direct quotation because it is the beginning of someone's sentence.
a	a. **Dad said, "you can use the car, Jim."**
	b. **Dad said, "You can use the car, Jim."**
2978	Which sentence is correct? _____
	2979

True 14	Verbs have a special characteristic that helps us to identify them. Verbs are the only words that can show by a change in their spelling whether they mean *present* or *past* time; for example, **cook—cooked, see—saw, speak—spoke.** What is the *past* form of the verb **jump?** _____ 15
predicate 284	**Mr. Kwan and his <u>son</u> | <u>own</u> a garage.** The part of this sentence that now has two parts is the complete (*subject, predicate*). 285
adjective 554	a. **I eat at the store** *where I work.* b. **I eat** *where I work.* In one sentence the clause is an adverb clause because it modifies a verb; in the other, it is an adjective clause because it modifies a noun. The adjective clause is in sentence (*a, b*). 555
Circling the airport, several planes waited their turn to land. 824	A present participle always ends with the letters _____. 825
A millionaire I never expect to be. 1094	(Are you moving only the italicized word or words for emphasis?) **He would** *go* **in spite of everyone's advice.** _____ _____ 1095
preceding 1364	A sentence is something like a train. A train might have only five cars. However, we cannot point to the fifth car and say, "There's the end of the train" until we look to make sure no more cars are coming. Similarly, a sentence ends only when the (*first, last*) *grammatically connected* idea has been expressed. 1365

(how to)

1634

Put parentheses ( ) around the two words that can be omitted without destroying the parallelism:

A tree can stand a strong wind because it is flexible and because it has deep roots.

1635

---

b

1903

a. **Flowers** *decorate* **each table.**
b. **A vase of flowers** *decorates* **each table.**

Why are the verbs different? Their subjects are different.
In *a*, the plural noun **Flowers** is the subject.
In *b*, **flowers** has become the object of the preposition **of,**

and the subject is now the singular noun _____.

1904

---

sat, set

2172

Underline the correct words:

Why would anyone want to (*sit, set*) **where George** (*set, sat*)?

2173

---

bad

2441

Rayna looked (*beautiful, beautifully*) **in her new spring outfit.**

2442

---

yours

2710

Ray Charles showed (*we, us*) **fans his collection of gold records.**

2711

---

b

2979

Underline the correct word:

Eleanor said to Sandy, "(*that, That***) is your third piece of pie."**

2980

page 30

jumped

15

PRESENT: **I never eat oysters.**
PAST: **I never ate oysters.**

In the changing of this sentence from *present* to *past* time,
the only word that changed was the verb _____.

16

---

subject

285

Mr. Kwan │ owns and operates a garage.

The part of this sentence that now has two parts is the
complete (*subject, predicate*).

286

---

a

555

I eat at the store *where I work.*

The clause *where I work* is an adjective clause because it
modifies the noun _____.

556

---

ing

825

A participle is considered a verbal because it has the characteristics of both a verb and an _____.

826

Go he would,
in spite of
everyone's
advice.

1095

Fran's *original and imaginative* **paintings won the interest
of a famous artist.**

_____

_____

1096

---

last

1365

If you close a sentence with a period before you have included
a *grammatically connected* word group, you produce a
sentence _____.

1366

page 31

(because it) 1635	In this and the following frames, rewrite the word group in parentheses, making it parallel with the italicized phrase: *An old book* **is not necessarily better than** _____ _____. (one that is new) 1636
vase 1904	**A vase of flowers . . . each table.** Since the plural noun **flowers** comes right before the verb, it will try to grab the verb, which belongs to the singular subject **vase.** If you are not on your guard, this can easily happen. **A vase of flowers** (*decorates, decorate*) **each table.** 1905
sit, sat 2173	Underline the correct words: **The box was still** (*sitting, setting*) **where I had** (*set, sat*) **it.** 2174
beautiful 2442	**You can hear very** (*good, well*) **in the balcony.** 2443
us 2711	**I repeated the directions until I was sure that he understood** (*it, them*). 2712
That 2980	**Pam said, "You can use the car, Jim."** What punctuation mark separates the direct quotation from the words that introduce it? _____ 2981

eat 16	PRESENT: **Some of the boys ride to school.** PAST: **Some of the boys rode to school.** Because **ride** is the only word that changed, we can be sure that it is a _____. 17
predicate 286	*Compound* means "having more than one part." When a structural part of a sentence consists of two or more parts, that part is said to be **compound.** <u>Mr. Kwan</u> and his <u>son</u> │ <u>own</u> and <u>operate</u> a garage. Both parts of this sentence are _____. 287
store 556	a. **We camped** *where there were few trees.* b. **We camped on a field** *where there were few trees.* The adjective clause is in sentence (*a, b*). 557
adjective 826	A participial phrase can come either before or after the noun it modifies. (*True, False*) 827
Fran's paintings, original and imaginative, won . . . *or* Original and imaginative, Fran's . . . 1096	You can give a word or word group its greatest emphasis by leaving it in its normal position. (*True, False*) 1097
fragment 1366	Remember, too, that the length of a word group has nothing to do with its being a sentence or not. Two words may form a sentence provided they are a subject and verb and make sense by themselves. a. **Neighbors objected.** b. **The neighbors.** Which is a complete sentence? _____ 1367

a new one. 1636	**The doctor advised Uncle John** *to get a pole* **and** _____ _____. (that he should go fishing) 1637
decorates 1905	**The operation (of this machine) requires much skill.** The singular verb **requires** agrees with the singular subject of this sentence, which is (*operation, machine*). 1906
sitting, set 2174	**To rise** means "to go up" or "to get up." **To raise** means "to make something rise" or "to lift something." We always raise *something*—a cover, a window, or a cloud of dust. As a result of our action, the cover, the window, or the cloud of dust (*raises, rises*). 2175
well 2443	**I didn't sleep** (*good, well*) **because of the noise.** 2444
them 2712	(*Those, Them*) **are the finest cattle in the state.** 2713
a comma 2981	**Pam said, "You can use the car, Jim."** Both the comma and the period come (*before, after*) the quotation marks with which they are used. 2982

verb
 	
17
	A small number of verbs have the same form for both present and past time; for example, *hit, cut, let, put, hurt, cost.*
	
	    a. **We** *hit* **the ball back and forth.**
	    b. **We** *bat* **the ball back and forth.**
	
	In which sentence could the verb mean either present or past time? _____ 18

compound 287	**Mr. Kwan and his son │ own and operate a garage.** Although both the subject and the predicate of this sentence are compound, the sentence can still be divided into two major parts. These two major parts are the *complete subject* and the *complete* _____. 288

b
 	
557
	Although the clause signal **when** generally starts adverb clauses, it can also start an adjective clause.
	
	    a. **My friend telephoned** *when I was very busy.*
	    b. **My friend telephoned on a day** *when I was very busy.*
	
	The clause that is used as an adjective clause because it modifies a noun is in sentence (*a, b*). 558

True 827	Lesson **22** Subordination by Past Participles [Frames 829–868]
False 1097	Putting an adverb or an adverbial word group ahead of the subject should not be done too often because it is the exception rather than the rule. (*True, False*) 1098
a 1367	**The neighbors** These two words do not form a sentence because there is no _____ to make a statement about the subject **neighbors.** 1368

(to) go fishing. 1637	**Peggy had the habit** *of turning on the radio* **and** _____ _____. (to forget to turn it off) 1638
operation 1906	(Remember always to keep your eye on the subject when choosing your verb.) **The operation of this machine requires much skill.** If we changed **this machine** to **these machines,** would you need to change the verb? (*Yes, No*) 1907
rises 2175	PRESENT PAST PAST PARTICIPLE **rise** (to get up) **rose** **(have) risen** **raise** (to lift) **raised** **(have) raised** Fill in the correct words: **Be sure to** _____ **when I** _____ **my hand.** 2176
well 2444	**Taste the soup** (*well, good*) **before you add more salt.** 2445
Those 2713	**Are you going to ride with** (*they, them*) **or** (*we, us*)? 2714
before 2982	Now let's turn our sentence around: **"You can use the car, Jim," said Pam.** A comma still separates the quotation from the rest of the sentence. Does this comma still come before the quotes? (*Yes, No*) 2983

a 18	Underscore the subject with one line and the verb with two lines: **Players from both teams scrambled over the field.** 19
predicate 288	Any sentence that can be divided into two parts—a subject and a predicate—is a simple sentence. It doesn't matter if either part or both parts are compound. **Mr. Kwan and his** <u>son</u> | <u>own</u> **and** <u>operate</u> **a garage.** Although this sentence has a compound subject and a compound predicate, is it still considered a simple sentence? (*Yes, No*) 289
b 558	**A man (that looked like a reporter) asked me several questions.** The adjective clause starts with the word _____ and ends with the word _____ _____. 559
	the *cracking* **ice** **a** *falling* **rock** **a** *steaming* **potato** All the italicized words are used like adjectives because they modify _____. (What class of words?) 829
True 1098	Lesson **29** Some Useful Adverb Clause Devices [Frames 1100–1138]
verb (*or* predicate) 1368	**The neighbors,** *who were annoyed by Joanne's practicing her trombone at all hours of the day and night,* Now the subject **neighbors** is followed by a long adjective clause that modifies it. As yet, does the subject **neighbors** have a verb to tell what the annoyed neighbors *did?* (*Yes, No*) 1369

(of) forgetting to turn it off.	Ruth's friends and relatives like her *because she is generous and* _____. (her unselfishness) (*Note:* Do not repeat words unnecessarily.)
1638	1639

No	The opportunity for advancement seems very good. If we changed **opportunity** to **opportunities,** would you need to change the verb? (*Yes, No*)
1907	1908

rise, raise	PRESENT **rise** (to go up) **raise** (to lift) PAST **rose** **raised** PAST PARTICIPLE **(have) risen** **(have) raised** Underline the correct word: **Food prices had** (*risen, rose*) **because of the severe drought.**
2176	2177

well	**This engine won't run** (*good, well*) **on ordinary gasoline.**
2445	2446

them, us	(*Ours, Our's*) **steers more easily than** (*theirs, their's*).
2714	2715

Yes	**Pam said, "You can use the car, Jim."** **"You can use the car, Jim," said Pam.** When a comma and quotes or a period and quotes come together, always put the comma or period first. Punctuate this sentence completely: **This is going to be hard to explain sighed Jerry**
2983	2984

Players <u>scrambled</u> 19	Underscore the subject with one line and the verb with two lines: **A huge, spreading maple stands in front of the church.** 20
Yes 289	**The <u>wind</u> | <u>was blowing</u>.** **The <u>water</u> | <u>was</u> rough.** Each of these sentences can be divided into a subject and a predicate. Therefore each of these sentences is a (*simple, compound*) sentence. 290
that . . . reporter 559	**A man that looked like a reporter asked me several questions.** Write the sentence that remains after you remove the clause. _____ _____ 560
nouns 829	**the** *cracking* **ice** **a** *falling* **rock** **a** *steaming* **potato** The italicized words, which resemble both adjectives and verbs, are participles. They are *present* participles because they end in _____. 830
	You are familiar with adverb clauses that begin with **if** and answer the question, "On what condition?" *If I had taken more time,* **I could have done better.** The verb in the clause consists of the two words _____ _____. 1100
No 1369	**The neighbors,** *who were annoyed by Joanne's practicing her trombone at all hours of the day and night,* In spite of its eighteen words, this word group is still *not* a sentence but only a subject modified by a clause. It cannot become a sentence until we supply a verb to make a statement about the subject _____. 1370

unselfish.

1639

Watching the game on television **was almost as good as**

_____. (if you were there)

1640

Yes

1908

Don't let the object of a preposition steal your verb. It's the subject that counts.

    a. **The purpose of these laws . .** ⟩ STEALS
    b. **The purposes of this law . .** ⟩ STEAL

Which subject would require a singular verb—*a* or *b?* _____

1909

---

risen

2177

Underline the correct word:

    As the water flows into the lock, the ship (*raises, rises*).

2178

---

well

2446

Lesson 68 Review: Adjective and Adverb Problems

[Frames 2448–2466]

Ours, theirs

2715

People should try to see (*theirselves, themselves*) **as others see them.**

2716

"This is going to be hard to explain," sighed Jerry.

2984

---

    a. **"I have a dream", said Martin Luther King, Jr.**
    b. **"I have a dream," said Martin Luther King, Jr.**

Which sentence is correct? _____

2985

---

maple stands 20	Underscore the subject with one line and the verb with two lines: **A large white cat with yellow patches emerged from the bushes.** 21
simple 290	Now let's combine our two simple sentences into one sentence by using the conjunction **and.** **The <u>wind</u> <u><u>was blowing</u></u>, and the <u>water</u> <u><u>was</u></u> rough.** Can we split this sentence into two parts so that we will have just a subject on one side and just a predicate on the other? (*Yes, No*) 291
A man asked me several questions. 560	**The world owes its scientific progress to men and women who are driven by an insatiable curiosity.** The adjective clause starts with the word _____ and ends with the word _____. 561
ing 830	a. **the** *cracking* **ice** **a** *falling* **rock** **a** *steaming* **potato** b. **the** *cracked* **ice** **a** *fallen* **rock** **a** *steamed* **potato** The italicized words after letter *b* are also used as adjectives. Were they also formed from verbs? (*Yes, No*) 831
had taken 1100	The "if" idea can also be expressed without using the clause signal **if** at all. *<u>Had</u> <u>I</u> <u><u>taken</u></u> more time,* **I could have done better.** We recognize this as a clause only because of its unusual word order. The subject *I*, instead of coming first, comes between the two parts of the _____. 1101
neighbors 1370	**The neighbors,** *who were annoyed by Joanne's practicing her trombone at all hours of the day and night,* **complained.** Now we have a completed sentence because we have added the verb _____, which makes a statement about the subject **neighbors.** 1371

being there.	**Frank had the choice** *of making up his back payments* **or** _____. (he would lose the car)
1640	1641
a	**One of you** (*is, are*) **always teasing the other.** Suppose that the prepositional phrase **of you** were omitted. Which verb would you choose to agree with the subject **One?** _____
1909	1910
rises	Underline the correct words: **This** (*raised, rose*) **a problem that never had** (*arose, arisen*) **before.**
2178	2179
	In this and the following frames, underline the correct modifier or, in some cases, the word appropriate for formal usage: **You will** (*sure, surely*) **sleep** (*soundly, sound*) **after so much strenuous exercise.**
	2448
themselves	(*He, Him*) **and** (*I, me*) **were the only ones who knew.**
2716	2717
b	For variety, we sometimes split a quoted sentence and put the *he said,* or a similar expression, between its two parts. **"A blowout at high speed,"** *he said,* **"may prove fatal."** We must use two sets of quotes in order to exclude the words _____ from the quotation.
2985	2986

cat emerged

21

Continue to follow the directions for the previous frame:

An expensive silver pin disappeared from the counter.

22

No

291

The wind was blowing, *and* the water was rough.

When we divide this sentence at the conjunction, we have a complete sentence—not just a subject or a predicate—on each side of the conjunction.

This is not a simple sentence because we cannot divide it into two parts: a *subject* and a _____

292

---

who . . . curiosity

561

The statistics which the speaker quoted were out-of-date.

The adjective clause starts with the word _____

and ends with the word _____ .

562

Yes

831

a. **the *cracking* ice**   **a *falling* rock**   **a *steaming* potato**
b. **the *cracked* ice**   **a *fallen* rock**   **a *steamed* potato**

The italicized words after *b* are also participles because they were formed from verbs and are used as adjectives. However, they are not *present* participles because they do not end in _____ .

832

---

verb

1101

a. *I had taken more time*
b. *Had I taken more time*

Do both word groups contain exactly the same words? (*Yes, No*)

1102

---

complained

1371

Could a word group consist of fifty or sixty words and still not be a sentence? (*Yes, No*)

1372

page 43

(of) losing the car. 1641	**Our biggest problem is** *to plan programs* **and** _____ _____. (keeping up the members' interest) 1642
is 1910	a. **One of you is always teasing the other.** b. **One of you are always teasing the other.** In which sentence is the verb correct? _____ 1911
raised, arisen 2179	Underline the correct words: **Although prices** (*rose, raised*), **my salary didn't** (*raise, rise*). 2180
surely, soundly 2448	**He can't do the work** (*satisfactory, satisfactorily*) **in such a short time.** 2449
He, I 2717	**The amount of the bill surprised Dad more than** (*I, me*). 2718
he said 2986	**"A blowout at high speed,"** *he said,* **"may prove fatal."** If we omit the words *he said* from the above sentence, we have (*one sentence, two sentences*) remaining. 2987

<u>pin</u> <u>disappeared</u> 22	**The pond across the road seldom freezes before December.** <div align="right">23</div>

predicate
 	
292
	A sentence made by joining two (or more) simple sentences with the conjunction **and, but,** or **or** is called a **compound sentence.**
	
	    a. **The <u>wind</u> <u>was blowing</u>, and the <u>water</u> <u>was</u> rough.**
	    b. **<u>Mr. Kwan</u> and his <u>son</u> <u>own</u> and <u>operate</u> a garage.**
	
	Which can be split into two separate sentences? _____ <div align="right">293</div>

which . . . quoted 562	**This soap is for people whose skin is sensitive to ordinary soap.** The adjective clause starts with the word _____ and ends with the word _____. <div align="right">563</div>
ing 832	a. **the** *cracking* **ice** a *falling* **rock** a *steaming* **potato** b. **the** *cracked* **ice** a *fallen* **rock** a *steamed* **potato** The participles after *b* are **past participles.** The participles that do not end in *-ing* are the (*present, past*) participles. <div align="right">833</div>
Yes 1102	a. <u>*I had taken* </u> *more time* b. <u>*Had I taken*</u> *more time* Which word group by its unusual word order tells you that it is not a sentence but a clause? _____ <div align="right">1103</div>
Yes 1372	Each of the following news items consists of several word groups. Where necessary, insert a period and a capital letter to show where one sentence ends and the next begins. **Roy dropped his penny into the slot and picked up the card which was supposed to tell his fortune his friends laughed because the card was blank.** <div align="right">1373</div>

(to) keep up the members' interest.

1642

The Riveras were *the first to arrive* **and** _____

_____. (they left last)

1643

---

a

1911

Here is another rule of subject-verb agreement:

A verb should agree in number with its subject, not with a subject complement that may follow it.

    a. **My favorite fruit is apples.**
    b. **Apples are my favorite fruit.**

Which sentence contains a plural subject? _____

1912

---

rose, rise

2180

Two forms of **lie-lay, sit-set,** or **rise-raise** (of which only the first letters are printed) are needed in each sentence. Complete each word, remembering not to use any form of **lay, set,** or **raise** unless the sentence tells to *what* the action is done.

L_____ down and I'll l_____ a cold cloth on your forehead.

2181

---

satisfactorily

2449

Don's excuse seemed very (*reasonable, reasonably*) **to his employer.**

2450

---

me

2718

Dad was more surprised about the bill than (*I, me*).

2719

---

one sentence

2987

"A blowout at high speed," *he said,* **"may prove fatal."**

Because the second part of the quotation is a continuation of the same sentence that was interrupted by *he said,* it begins with a (*small, capital*) letter.

2988

<u>pond</u> <u>freezes</u> 23	**My only key to the house fell through a crack in the steps.** 24
a 293	One of these sentences is a compound sentence; the other is a simple sentence with a compound subject and predicate. a. **The <u>wind</u> <u>was blowing</u>, and the <u>water</u> <u>was rough</u>.** b. **<u>Mr. Kwan</u> and his <u>son</u> <u>own</u> and <u>operate</u> a garage.** Which sentence is compound because it can be split into two separate sentences? _____ 294
whose . . . soap 563	**The car which won the first automobile race traveled at five miles per hour.** The adjective clause starts with the word _____ and ends with the word _____. 564
past 833	Most past participles end in *-ed* (entertai*ned*), *-d* (tol*d*), *-en* (brok*en*), *-n* (tor*n*), and *-t* (ben*t*). The past participle of a verb is the form you would use after *have;* for example, *have* **opened,** *have* **broken,** *have* **torn.** The past participle of **see** is _____. 834
b 1103	a. *If I had taken more time,* **I could have done better.** b. *Had I taken more time,* **I could have done better.** The word order of the clause in sentence *b*—just like the clause signal _____ in sentence *a*—tells us that the word group is an adverb clause. 1104
fortune. His 1373	Continue to follow the directions for the previous frame. Be careful not to produce any sentence fragments. **To attract a deer a hunter attached a pair of antlers to his head mistaking him for a deer another hunter shot him he was not injured seriously.** 1374

the last to leave. 1643	**Carlota Espinoza showed her artistry** *by looking at a subject* **and** _____ _____. (she would draw it accurately) 1644
b 1912	**Tires . . . my biggest expense.** The missing verb should agree in number with the subject (*Tires, expense*). 1913
Lie, lay 2181	Continue to follow the directions for the previous frame: **Christie I_____ her beach towel on the sand and I_____ down for a nap.** 2182
reasonable 2450	**You can** (*sure, surely*) **get a job** (*easily, easy*) **right before Christmas.** 2451
I 2719	(*It's, Its*) **all** (*your's, yours*) **for the asking.** 2720
small 2988	Underline the correct word: **"Everything here,"** complained Mrs. Rizzo, **"(*seems, Seems*) to be out of order."** 2989

A big green milk truck

This group of words is only a subject. There is no predicate to tell what the truck did or what happened to it.

key fell

A big green milk truck a. **ahead of our car**
                                    b. **stopped suddenly**

24

Which group of words is a predicate—*a* or *b*? ____

25

---

a

a. **The fall and winter are cold.**
b. **The winters are cold, and the summers are hot.**

Which is a simple sentence with a compound subject? ____

294

295

---

which . . . race

Lesson **15** Variations of the Adjective Clause

[Frames 566–594]

564

---

seen

Remember that the past participle of a verb is the same form you would use after *have*.

The past participle of **teach** is _____.

834

835

If

a. *If I had taken more time,* **I could have done better.**
b. *Had I taken more time,* **I could have done better.**

The adverb clause in sentence *b* is not better or worse than the adverb clause in sentence *a*. It enables you, however, to add greater (*clearness, variety*) to your sentences.

1104

1105

---

head. Mistaking
. . . him. He

Mr. McGeorge put up a scarecrow   to keep the robins away   from his strawberry patch   later he saw a robin perching right on the scarecrow's head.

1374

1375

(by) drawing it accurately. 1644	*Being a good listener* **is just as important as** _____ _____ . (to talk well) 1645
Tires 1913	a. **Tires . . . my biggest expense.** b. **My biggest expense . . . tires.** In which sentence would you use the singular verb **was**— *a* or *b*? _____ 1914
laid, lay 2182	**Judy's coat has I_____ on that chair ever since she** **I_____ it there.** 2183
surely, easily 2451	**The fan will run more** (*quiet, quietly*) **if you oil it** (*good, well*). 2452
It's, yours 2720	**Two women, Irene and** (*she, her*), **did most of the artwork.** 2721
seems 2989	**"Everything here,"** complained Mrs. Rizzo, **"seems to be out of order."** We set off **complained Mrs. Rizzo** with commas because it interrupts the quoted sentence. Both commas, as well as the period, come (*before, after*) the quotes. 2990

b

25

Do not mistake words or phrases that merely describe the subject for a predicate. A predicate must have a verb to help make a statement about the subject.

A large crowd
a. **of curious and noisy youngsters**
b. **surrounded the TV truck**

Which group of words is a predicate—*a* or *b*? _____

26

---

a

295

a. **The fall and winter are cold.**
b. **The winters are cold, and the summers are hot.**

Which is a compound sentence? _____

296

RELATIVE PRONOUNS: **who (whose, whom), which, that**

These are the relative pronouns that serve as clause signals

for _____ clauses.

566

---

taught

835

The past participle of **wear** is _____.

836

---

variety

1105

If you should hear of a job, **let me know.**

Eliminate the *If* in this clause by putting the subject between the two parts of the verb *should hear*.

_____, **let me know.**

1106

---

patch. Later

1375

A father advised his young son   who was interested in collecting moths   to go to the library   and get a book on moths   the boy came back with a book   entitled *A Handbook for Young Mothers.*

1376

being a
good talker.

1645

Our purpose should be *to discover the truth* **rather than**

_____.

(proving ourselves right)

1646

---

b

1914

Careless drivers are our main traffic problem.

Now let's turn this sentence around and supply the correct verb:

Our main traffic problem _____ careless drivers.

1915

---

lain, laid

2183

Why would anyone I_____ a glass where Allen has I_____ it?

2184

---

quietly, well

2452

The company is usually quite (*prompt, promptly*) in giving service.

2453

---

she

2721

I like to play chess because it makes (*you, me*) think.

2722

---

before

2990

Punctuate this sentence:

The only thing we have to fear   said President Franklin D. Roosevelt   is fear itself

2991

b 26	In this and the following frames, write *S* if the word group is just a subject; *P* if it is just a predicate; *SP* if it has both a subject and predicate that form a complete sentence. (Capitals and periods are omitted so as not to reveal the answer.) **most large European cities** _____ 27
b 296	Only one of these sentences is a compound sentence because it can be split into two parts—each with its own subject and predicate. a. **I paid my check and waited for my change.** b. **I paid my check, and the waiter brought me my change.** Which is the compound sentence? _____ 297
adjective 566	We sometimes use a preposition before the relative pronoun; for example, **with which, for which, to whom.** In such cases the preposition belongs to the adjective clause. **The pen** *with which he wrote* **was scratchy.** The first word of the adjective clause is (*with, which*). 567
worn 836	Past participles—like present participles—also form useful phrases that modify nouns and pronouns. **The woman,** *annoyed by the smoke,* **changed her seat.** The past participial phrase in this sentence modifies the noun _____. 837
Should you hear of a job, 1106	*If I were in your place,* **I should do the same thing.** The verb in the adverb clause is _____. 1107
moths. The (boy) 1376	**Annoyed by crows a New Brunswick farmer set a box trap for them going to his trap the next day he saw an unusual sight a silver fox and a litter of five little ones.** 1377

(to) prove ourselves right. 1646	The teacher can't tell whether an error is caused *by ignorance* **or** _____. (whether you were careless) 1647
is 1915	**The main attraction of the town is the fine shops.** Now let's turn this sentence around and supply the correct verb: **The fine shops _____ the main attraction of the town.** 1916
lay, laid 2184	**Mother I_____ awake, wondering where she had I_____ her diamond ring.** 2185
prompt 2453	**If you can think** (*clearly, clear*), **you should be able to write** (*good, well*). 2454
me 2722	**Let's you and** (*I, me*) **circulate a petition.** 2723
"The only . . . fear," said President . . . Roosevelt, "is fear itself." 2991	Punctuate this sentence: **Whenever I play said Louis Armstrong I give it all I've got** 2992

S

27

S, P, or SP?

complained about the very slow service _____

28

---

b

297

Pelé's teammates shook his hand and patted him on the back.

There are a subject and a verb *before* the conjunction **and.** Are there also a subject and a verb *after* the conjunction **and?** (*Yes, No*)

298

---

with

567

The pen with (which he wrote) was scratchy.
The pen (with which he wrote) was scratchy.

Read each sentence, omitting the words in parentheses. If the remaining words are a sentence, the clause was correctly selected.

The preposition **with** (*is, is not*) part of the clause.

568

---

woman

837

A past participial phrase can often be shifted about.

Annoyed by the smoke, **the woman changed her seat.**
The woman, *annoyed by the smoke,* **changed her seat.**
The woman changed her seat, *annoyed by the smoke.*

Can a past participial phrase be some distance away from the noun it modifies? (*Yes, No*)

838

---

were

1107

a. *If I were in your place,* . . .
b. *Were I in your place,* . . .

The verb in clause *a* consists of one word—*were.*

To eliminate the *If* in clause *a*, put the verb (*before, after*) the subject *I.*

1108

---

them. Going

1377

Motorists near Albany   suddenly turned up their car windows   and shifted into reverse gear   when they saw   three hundred skunks parading across the state highway.

1378

Lesson 46 Avoiding *Is When* and *Is Where* Constructions

are

1916

In this and the following frames, underline the verb that agrees in number with its subject. Don't be fooled by the object of a preposition that might come between the subject and the verb or by a subject complement that might follow the verb.

The decision (of the judges) (*is, are*) final.

1917

lay, laid

2185

Aunt Lou s_____ the biggest piece of pie at the place where Ronnie would s_____.

2186

clearly, well

2454

The legislature was (*kind of, rather*) indifferent to the passage of this bill.

2455

me

2723

In this and the following frames, underline the pronoun that is appropriate for careful speech and formal writing:

(*Who, Whom*) **will the American people elect to the Presidency next November?**

2724

"Whenever I play," said Louis Armstrong, "I give it all I've got."

Another way to obtain variety is to put the *he said* (or whatever expression you use) between two separate sentences.

"I can't believe it," *said Tom.* **"You must be joking."**

If we omit the words *said Tom* from the above sentence, we have (*one sentence, two sentences*) remaining.

2993

S, P, or SP?

the music stopped _____

No

Pelé's teammates shook his hand and patted him on the back.

Is this a compound sentence? (*Yes, No*)

298

299

is

The man for whom Matthew Henson worked urged him to get an education.

The first word of the adjective clause is (*whom, for*).

568

569

Yes

Hayes threw himself down, *exhausted from the race.*

The participial phrase is separated by several words from

the word it modifies, the noun _____ .

838

839

a. *If I were in your place,* **I should do the same thing.**
b. *Were I in your place,* **I should do the same thing.**

The unusual word order of the clause in sentence *b* serves

before

the same purpose as the clause signal _____ in sentence

a in telling us that the word group is an adverb clause.

1108

1109

This is all
one sentence.

A farmer examined his cow's foot   to see why she had been limping   for the past five weeks   in her hoof he found his wife's diamond ring   which had disappeared   exactly five weeks ago.

1378

1379

It is not reasonable to define something as a *time* or *place* when it clearly is *not* a time or a place.

WRONG: **A tragedy** *is when* **a play has an unhappy ending.**
WRONG: **A tragedy** *is where* **a play has an unhappy ending.**

Is a **tragedy** either a *time* or a *place*? (*Yes, No*)

1649

---

is

1917

His only source of income (*was, were*) **odd jobs.**

1918

---

set, sit

2186

Our guest s_____ **down before we had even s**_____ **the table.**

2187

---

rather

2455

The jury was (*somewhat, sort of*) **surprised that the judge's sentence was not more** (*severe, severely*).

2456

Whom

2724

It should have been (*they, them*) **who were penalized.**

2725

---

two sentences

2993

"I can't believe it," *said Tom.* **"You must be joking."**

To show that the second part of the quotation is a new sentence, we put a period after *Tom* and follow it with a (*small, capital*) letter.

2994

S, P, or *SP?*

supplies electric power to several states _____

30

No

299

Pelé's teammates shook his hand and patted him on the back.

Although this is not a compound sentence, one of its parts is compound.

This sentence has a compound (*subject, predicate*).

300

---

for

569

The man for whom Matthew Henson worked urged him to get an education.

The adjective clause begins with the preposition **for** and ends with the word _____.

570

Hayes

839

PRESENT PARTICIPLE: *Neglecting his friends,* **Carl read the newspaper.**

PAST PARTICIPLE: *Neglected by his friends,* **Carl read the newspaper.**

The phrase with the (*present, past*) participle represents Carl as *doing something.*

840

If

1109

In this and the following frames, eliminate the *if* in each italicized adverb clause by changing the word order of the clause:

I should have written Alva *if I had known her address.*

I should have written Alva _____

_____.

1110

---

weeks. In

1379

Alvin Phalen   a Canadian trapper   caught a wolf by its tail   he dragged it over the snow   and killed it with one of the skis   which he was wearing.

1380

No
 	
1649
	To define a **tragedy** as a *time* or a *place* seems as far off the track as to define an elephant as a kind of vegetable.
	
	    a. **A tragedy** *is when* **a play has an unhappy ending.**
	    b. **A tragedy** *is where* **a play has an unhappy ending.**
	    c. **A tragedy is a** *play* **with an unhappy ending.**
	
	Which definition makes the best sense? _____
	
	                                           1650

was 1918	**Conditions in this hospital** (*require, requires*) **investigation.** 1919
sat, set 2187	**I s**____ **my chair under a tree to avoid s**_____ **in the hot sun.** 2188
somewhat, severe 2456	**Mrs. Rosen treats the kindergarteners** (*lovely, in a lovely manner*). 2457
they 2725	**I cannot see how anybody in** (*their, his or her*) **right mind can believe such nonsense.** 2726

capital
 	
2994
	Punctuation and capitals are omitted from the following sentences to avoid revealing the answers.
	
	    a. **If Seaver pitches** *said Foster* **we will surely win**
	    b. **Seaver is pitching** *said Foster* **we will surely win**
	In which line does *said Foster* stand between two separate sentences? _____
	
	2995

S, P, or *SP?*

my dad has a good sense of humor _____

31

---

predicate

300

The most common conjunctions that connect the two parts of a compound sentence are **and, but,** and **or.**

   a. **The movie bored the adults but pleased the children.**
   b. **The movie bored the adults, but the children liked it.**

In which sentence does the conjunction **but** connect the two parts of a compound sentence? _____

301

---

worked

570

The bottle *in* **which the lotion comes costs more than the lotion.**

Is the preposition *in* part of the adjective clause? (*Yes, No*)

571

---

present

840

PRESENT PARTICIPLE: *Neglecting his friends,* **Carl read the newspaper.**

PAST PARTICIPLE: *Neglected by his friends,* **Carl read the newspaper.**

The phrase with the (*present, past*) participle represents Carl as *having had something done to* him.

841

---

had I known
her address.

1110

If Stover were willing to run, **he would win hands down.**

_____**, he would win hands down.**

1111

---

tail. He

1380

Because his truck wouldn't start   on a cold day   a man built a fire under the engine   a barrel of oil exploded   blowing the roof off his garage   and burning his house down   a friend was also injured.

1381

c 1650	The temptation to use *is when* or *is where* arises whenever you are asked to explain a technical term used in school studies, science, business, sports, fashions, and so on. The first step in defining something is to ask yourself what general type of thing it is. **A tariff is a** (*game, tax, fine*) . . . 1651
require 1919	**One of your sleeves** (*look, looks*) **shorter than the other.** 1920
set, sitting 2188	**Although our costs have r_____ considerably, we have not r_____ our prices.** 2189
in a lovely manner 2457	**The vase of pink and white peonies looked** (*nice, nicely*) **on the desk.** 2458
his or her 2726	**The Martins always insist on** (*our, us*) **staying for dinner.** 2727
b 2995	Note the difference in the punctuation and capitalization in these sentences: a. "If Seaver pitches," said Foster, "we will surely win." b. "Seaver is pitching," said Foster. "We will surely win." Quotation *b* is handled differently from quotation *a* because it consists of (*one sentence, two sentences*). 2996

S, P, or SP?

a bottle of red ink _____

32

---

b

301

a. **The movie bored the adults but pleased the children.**
b. **The movie bored the adults, but the children liked it.**

In which sentence is a comma used before the conjunction

but? _____

302

Yes

571

The bottle in which the lotion comes costs more than the lotion.

The adjective clause begins with the preposition **in** and ends

with the word _____ .

572

---

past

841

To show that something _has been done to_ a person or a
thing, we use a (_present, past_) participle.

842

Were Stover
willing to run,

1111

I'll let you know _if I should change my mind._

I'll let you know _____

_____ .

1112

---

engine. A (barrel)
down. A (friend)

1381

**A police officer gave a man a traffic ticket   for walking
slowly   in front of an automobile   and forcing the driver to
jam on his brakes   the man was Eddie Tolan   the former
champion runner.**

1382

tax 1651	**A tariff is a _tax_ . . .** After you give the general classification, add a word, phrase, or clause to differentiate the thing you are defining from other things of the same class. **A tariff is a tax charged on** (_income, imports_). 1652
looks 1920	**One important cause of traffic congestion** (_is, are_) **the huge office buildings.** 1921
risen, raised 2189	**Gloria r_____ the cover to see if the dough had** **r_____.** 2190
nice 2458	Should we choose the adverb _badly_ to describe the action of the team's hands, or the adjective _bad_ to describe the team's emotions? **The team felt** (_badly, bad_) **about the poor attendance at the game.** 2459
our 2727	**Just suppose that it was** (_we, us_) **who were starving.** 2728
two sentences 2996	**"Seaver is pitching," said Foster. "We will surely win."** **"We will surely win"** is a separate sentence. Before starting our new sentence with a capital, we must close the first sentence by putting a _____ after **Foster.** 2997

S	*S, P, or SP?* **the linoleum on our kitchen floor** _____
32	33

b	a. **I can call for you or meet you at school.** b. **I can call for you, or we can meet at school.** In which sentence does the conjunction **or** connect the two parts of a compound sentence? _____
302	303

comes	**The bottle in which the lotion comes costs more than the lotion.** **The bottle** **costs more than the lotion.** When we omit the adjective clause, do we have a complete sentence remaining? (*Yes, No*)
572	573

past	To emphasize that the action of a participle has been entirely completed before another action, use *having* before the past participle (*having finished, having seen*). a. *Glancing through the paper,* **I laid it aside.** b. *Having glanced through the paper,* **I laid it aside.** Which sentence is correct? _____
842	843

should I change my mind.	*If it were not for the mosquitoes,* **camping would be fun.** _____ , **camping would be fun.**
1112	1113

brakes. The (man)	**Disturbed by yowling cats a woman in Maine fired her husband's revolver into the dark to frighten them away she found a dead wildcat the next morning and collected fifteen dollars the state bounty for a wildcat.**
1382	1383

imports

1652

---

a. **A tariff is when a tax is charged on imports.**
b. **A tariff is where a tax is charged on imports.**
c. **A tariff is a tax charged on imports.**

Sentence *c* is correct because a **tariff** is not defined as a *when* or a *where*, but as a _____.

1653

---

is

1921

Movies (*was, were*) **her main topic of conversation.**

1922

---

raised, risen

2190

Just as they r_____ to leave, Carmen r_____ another problem.

2191

---

bad

2459

Because it was April Fool's Day, Dick tasted the candy (*suspicious, suspiciously*).

2460

---

we

2728

To (*who, whom*) **did Washington turn for advice?**

2729

---

period

2997

---

a. **"I love conducting," said Sarah Caldwell. "It's my life."**
b. **"I love conducting," said Sarah Caldwell, "it's my life."**

Which quotation is correct? _____

2998

S 33	*S, P,* or *SP?* **some parts of the world get mail only once or twice a year** _____ 34
b 303	a. **I can call for you or meet you at school.** b. **I can call for you, or we can meet at school.** In which sentence is a comma used before the conjunction **or?** _____ 304
Yes 573	a. **The things (at which the audience laughed) were very silly.** b. **The things at (which the audience laughed) were very silly.** In which sentence is the clause correctly identified? _____ 574
b 843	a. *Having finished his homework,* **Fred went to bed.** b. *Finishing his homework,* **Fred went to bed.** Which sentence is correct? _____ 844
Were it not for the mosquitoes, 1113	**We should have started earlier** *if we had known the distance.* **We should have started earlier** _____ _____. 1114
away. She 1383	**Benjamin Morris of Kansas City couldn't sleep because the scratching of a branch against his house disturbed him after sawing off the limb he found himself back in bed but this time in a hospital he had sat on the wrong end of the limb while he sawed.** 1384

tax	a. **Astronomy is the science of the heavenly bodies.** b. **Astronomy is when you study the heavenly bodies.** Sentence _a_ is correct because **astronomy** is not defined as a _when_, but as a _____.
1653	**1654**

were	_SUBJECT_ **Kellie's years of experience** (_qualify, qualifies_) **her for the job.**
1922	**1923**

rose, raised	Lesson **61** Keeping Your Tenses Consistent [Frames 2193–2230]
2191	

suspiciously	**Burning leaves smell very** (_pleasant, pleasantly_) **in the autumn.**
2460	**2461**

whom	**Nobody likes to feel that** (_he or she is, they are_) **being pushed around.**
2729	**2730**

a	Supply all necessary punctuation. (_Note:_ Since **Cats** starts a new sentence, watch your punctuation after **Sally.**) **You are wrong said Sally Cats do show affection**
2998	**2999**

S, P, or *SP?*

moves through the water by a kind of jet propulsion _____

35

We put a comma before the conjunction **and, but,** or **or** when it connects the two parts of a compound (*sentence, predicate*).

305

---

a. **We were eager to try the dishes which have made this inn famous.**
b. **We were eager to try the dishes for which this inn is famous.**

In which sentence does a preposition precede the relative pronoun which signals the clause? _____

575

It is very simple to change a sentence to a past participial phrase when its verb consists of two words—some form of *be* followed by a past participle; for example, *is* **built,** *was* **invited,** *were* **surprised.**

It was taken from a plane.

Does the above sentence contain such a verb? (*Yes, No*)

845

The adverb **once** can sometimes be used as an adverb clause signal in place of *if, when, after,* or *as soon as.*

a. **If** *you break the seal,* **you can't return the film.**
b. **Once** *you break the seal,* **you can't return the film.**

In which sentence does the condition expressed by the clause seem more emphatic and final? _____

1115

As he saw a man   running from his delivery truck   with a crate of eggs   a milkman hurled a bottle of milk   at the thief   and knocked him unconscious   the milkman identified himself to the police as Art Wells   star pitcher for the Bowman Dairy baseball team.

138?

science

1654

Astronomy is the science of the heavenly bodies.

In defining **astronomy,** first we classify it as a **science.** Then to distinguish it from many other sciences, we add the modifying phrase _____.

1655

---

qualify

1923

?

This article claims that high wages (*is, are*) the best way of preventing a business depression.

1924

Tense means *time*. The tense of a verb shows the time of its action—present, past, or future.

        a. I *feel* good today.
        b. I *felt* good yesterday.

The verb is in the past tense in sentence _____.

2193

---

pleasant

2461

The scheme sounded rather (*dishonest, dishonestly*) to me.

2462

---

he or she is

2730

Pasadena and (*we, ourselves*) are tied for first place.

2731

"You are wrong," said Sally. "Cats do show affection."

2999

Supply all necessary punctuation:

This snapshot isn't good   said Dick   There wasn't enough sun

3000

P	*S, P,* or *SP?*
	the kindly old doctor in this small Iowa town _____
35	36

sentence	**The man fumbled in his pocket and pulled out a letter.**
	Should a comma be inserted after the word **pocket?** (*Yes, No*)
305	306

	The conditions . . . *which we played* **were difficult.**
b	The adjective clause in this sentence requires a preposition.
	Underline the preposition that would make the best sense:
	by under at with
575	576

	(It was) taken from a plane.
Yes	To change the above sentence to a past participial phrase, start your phrase with the "ready-made" past participle
	_____, dropping all the words that precede it.
845	846

	Underline the clause signal that makes the clause more emphatic:
b	
	(*Once, If*) *you feed a stray cat,* **you can't get rid of it.**
1115	1116

unconscious. The (milkman)	**To celebrate the opening of his theater the owner decided to give a television set to the person holding the lucky ticket when the number was called seventy-two people flocked to the box office each having the lucky number the printer had made a slight mistake.**
1385	1386

of the heavenly bodies 1655	a. **A polygon is where a figure has more than four sides.** b. **A polygon is a figure having more than four sides.** Which definition is correct? _____ 1656
are 1924	**One in every eight persons in the United States** (*own, owns*) **a dog.** 1925
b 2193	a. **I** *feel* **good today.** b. **I** *felt* **good yesterday.** c. **I** *shall feel* **better tomorrow.** The verb is in the future tense in sentence _____ 2194
dishonest 2462	**Many people felt** (*badly, bad*) **about the results of the election.** 2463
we 2731	**The first ones to arrive were Olga and** (*her, she*). 2732
"This . . . good," said Dick. "There wasn't enough sun." 3000	Use only one set of quotes ("—") to cover any number of sentences provided that the quotation is not interrupted. Supposing that each line represents a separate sentence, supply the necessary quotation marks: **The announcer said,** _____. _____. _____. 3001

S, P, or SP?

S

a giant explosion with the force of a billion atom bombs sometimes occurs on the sun _____

36   37

The man fumbled in his pocket and ↓ **pulled out a letter.**

No

Suppose that we added the pronoun **he** at the point indicated by the arrow. Would it then be correct to insert a comma after **pocket?** (*Yes, No*)

306   307

The conditions under which we played were difficult.

under

The adjective clause begins with the preposition **under** and ends with the word _____.

576   577

This is a picture of our town. (*It was*) *taken from a plane.*
This is a picture of our town *taken from a plane.*

taken

The participial phrase modifies the noun _____.

846   847

Make this sentence more emphatic by using a "once" clause:

Once

After my tests are over, **I shall have more time.**

_____, **I shall have more time.**

1116   1117

---

ticket. When . . .
number. The
(printer)

A sparrow picked up a lighted cigarette butt   and carried the butt to its nest   on the Henrys' house   a two-story frame structure   which caught on fire   the nest was a total loss   although firefighters put out the blaze   before much damage was done to the house.

1386   1387

b

1656

---

a. **Amnesia is when one loses his memory.**
b. **Amnesia is loss of memory.**

Which definition is correct? _____

1657

---

owns

1925

(Think this one over carefully before you select your verb.)

A few drops of oil (*do, does*) **the trick.**

1926

---

c

2194

---

a. **I** *feel* **good today.**
b. **I** *felt* **good yesterday.**
c. **I** *shall feel* **better tomorrow.**

In which sentence is a change in time shown by a change in the spelling of the verb? _____

2195

---

bad

2463

A cold shower feels (*good, well*) **on a hot day.**

2464

---

she

2732

We are unable to take a step without (*them, their*) **complaining of the noise.**

2733

The announcer said, "_____.
_____. _____."

3001

Supply the necessary quotation marks. (Note that a colon is generally used to introduce a long or formal quotation.)

As Professor Brown remarked: A people that is ignorant of its history is like an individual without a memory. It can learn nothing from its past experience. It will make the identical mistakes again and again.

3002

S, P, or SP?

several families in our neighborhood _____

38

Yes

307

The three conjunctions commonly used to connect the two parts of a compound sentence are **and, but,** and **or.**

In a compound sentence, we generally put a comma before the _____ **and, but,** or **or.**

308

---

played

577

Although relative pronouns are usually a signal that an adjective clause is starting, the relative pronoun is sometimes omitted.

Most of the things (_that_) _we fear_ **never happen.**

Can the clause signal be omitted in the above sentence? (_Yes, No_)

578

---

picture

847

The roads were covered with ice.

What is the two-word verb in this sentence? _____

_____.

848

Once my tests are over,

1117

Subordinate the italicized statement by changing it to a "once" clause:

You sign the contract, **and you can't change your mind.**

_____, **you can't change your mind.**

1118

---

fire. The (nest)

1387

Lesson **38** Pronouns as a Cause of Run-on Sentences

[Frames 1389–1430]

b
 	
1657
	Of course, when we are really speaking about *time* or *place*, it is permissible to use *is when* or *is where*.
	
	    a. **Saturday** *is when* **the contest closes.**
	    b. **A yearling** *is when* **an animal is one year old.**
	
	In which sentence is the use of *is when* permissible? _____
	
	                                        1658

do 1926	*Sn Sub Prep phrase* **The construction of houses, churches, and schools** (*continue, continues*) **at a high rate.** *Phrase* 1927

b
 	
2195
	a. I *feel* **good today.**
	    b. I *felt* **good yesterday.**
	    c. I *shall feel* **better tomorrow.**
	
	In which sentence is a change in time shown by the addition of a helping verb? _____
	
	                                        2196

good 2464	**These scissors don't cut as** (*well, good*) **as they once did.** 2465
their 2733	(*Who, Whom*) **can a child trust more than his or her own parents?** (*Note:* The subject of the verb **can trust** is the noun **child.**) 2734
remarked: "A people . . . again." 3002	Whenever the speaker changes, begin a new paragraph and use another set of quotes. **It's a burglar said Ron. It's a dog said Ann. It's your imagination said Dad.** How many paragraphs and sets of quotes would this material require? _____ 3003

S

38

The *predicate* of a sentence makes a statement about the

_____.

39

---

conjunction

308

The man fumbled in his pocket and pulled out a letter.
The movie bored the adults but pleased the children.
I can call for you or meet you at school.

Not one of these sentences is a compound sentence.

Each one is a sentence with a compound (*subject, predicate*).

309

Yes

578

We can learn to recognize these "no signal" clauses if we watch for a *subject-verb* combination right after a noun.

Most of the things *we fear* never happen.

Here we have a *subject-verb* combination right after the

noun _____.

579

---

were covered

848

The roads *were covered* with ice.

Is one of the words in the two-word verb a past participle? (*Yes, No*)

849

Once you sign
the contract,

1118

Subordinate the italicized statement by changing it to a "once" clause:

A false idea gets into circulation, **and it is difficult to up-root it.**

_____

_____, **it is difficult to uproot it.**

1119

Running one sentence into another without a period (or other end mark) and a capital letter to separate them produces a **run-on** sentence. A run-on sentence is the opposite error of a sentence fragment.

A fragment is less than a sentence; a run-on sentence is

_____ than a sentence.

1389

1658

a

1659

a. **A pinch hitter** *is where* **one player bats for another.**
b. **The city hall** *is where* **you register to vote.**

In which sentence is the use of *is where* permissible? _____

1927

continues

Lesson 54 Recognizing Singular and Plural Subjects

[Frames 1929–1969]

2196

c

2197

Do not shift from one tense to another unless there is an actual shift in the time of the action.

Phil *accepted* **the job and then** *changes* **his mind.**

Are both italicized verbs in the same tense? (*Yes, No*)

2465

well

2466

Our new radio doesn't sound as (*well, good*) **as the old one.**

(*Note:* The test for this Unit is combined with the test for Unit 11.)

2734

Whom

2735

Everybody held (*his or her, their*) **breath as the car skidded into the intersection.**

3003

three

3004

In this and the following frames, circle the letter of the sentence that is correctly punctuated and capitalized:

a. **The doctor said, "That I needed more sleep."**
b. **The doctor said, "You need more sleep, Clyde."**

subject 39	Every word in a sentence belongs to either the *complete subject* or the *complete* _____. 40
predicate 309	**The man fumbled in his pocket and pulled out a letter.** **The movie bored the adults but pleased the children.** **I can call for you or meet you at school.** Does any one of these sentences have a comma before the conjunction **and, but,** or **or?** (*Yes, No*) 310
things 579	**Most of the things we fear never happen.** The subject of the adjective clause is _____, and the verb is _____. 580
Yes 849	(*The roads were*) *covered with ice.* **They were treacherous.** We can change the italicized sentence to a participial phrase by starting the phrase with the past participle _____. 850

Once a false idea gets into circulation,
 	
1119
	Another more unusual type of adverb clause begins with **now that.** These words, similar in meaning to **because,** are useful in sentences stating *cause and effect.*
	
	    a. **Because** *you are eighteen,* **you can vote.**
	    b. **Now that** *you are eighteen,* **you can vote.**
	
	Which sentence suggests that the cause is recent? _____
	
	1120

more 1389	The writer of a run-on sentence doesn't know where a sentence ends. He is like an absent-minded person who reaches the end of a dock and keeps right on walking. WRONG: **The lights were dimmed the concert began.** Here one sentence runs into the next. The first sentence should end with the word 1390

b 1659	Be on guard against the *is when* and *is where* mistake whenever you are asked to point out the climax, turning point, surprise, or most interesting incident in a book or story. a. **The turning point was where Rita decided to become a nun.** b. **The turning point was Rita's decision to become a nun.** Which sentence is correct? _____ 1660
  1929	The following words are singular because they refer to only one person or thing at a time. They require singular verbs. each either neither any one each one either one neither one every one Underline the correct verb: **Each** (*is, are*) **right.**
No 2197	a. **Phil** *accepted* **the job and then** *changes* **his mind.** b. **Phil** *accepted* **the job and then** *changed* **his mind.** Which sentence is correct because both verbs are in the same tense? _____ 2198
good 2466	UNIT 11: SOLVING YOUR PRONOUN PROBLEMS Lesson **69** The Nominative and the Objective Case [Frames 2468–2501]
his or her 2735	**Paul and** (*myself, I*) **wrote all the invitations.** 2736
b 3004	a. **Will Rogers, the cowboy philosopher, once said, "So live that you wouldn't be afraid to sell the family parrot to the village gossip."** b. **Will Rogers, the cowboy philosopher, once said, "so live that you wouldn't be afraid to sell the family parrot to the village gossip."** 3005

predicate 40	The heart of the *complete subject* is the *subject*. The heart of the *complete predicate* is the *simple predicate*, commonly called the _____. 41
No 310	We do not ordinarily use a comma before the conjunction that connects the two parts of a compound (*predicate, sentence*). 311
(subject) we (verb) fear 580	A good test for a "no signal" adjective clause is to see whether we can insert a relative pronoun before it. **Sue described the kind of boat she expects to build.** Can we insert *which* or *that* before the word **she?** (*Yes, No*) 581
covered 850	(*The roads were*) *covered with ice.* **They were treacherous.** <div align="right">*Covered with ice,* **they were treacherous.**</div>In changing the italicized sentence to a participial phrase, we lost the subject _____. 851
b 1120	a. *Because Dale has a job,* **he takes more interest in his appearance.** b. *Now that Dale has a job,* **he takes more interest in his appearance.** Which sentence suggests that Dale's job is something recent? _____ 1121

dimmed
 	
1390
	In most run-on sentences, we find a comma between the two run-together sentences.
	
	  a. **After the lights were dimmed, the concert began.**
	  b. **The lights were dimmed, the concert began.**
	
	Which is a run-on sentence? _____
	
	1391

Since words such as *climax, turning point, surprise,* and *incident* are nouns, they are best explained by other nouns or gerunds (verbal nouns ending in *-ing*).

a. **The climax** *was when* **Velvet won the National Derby.**
b. **The climax was Velvet's** *victory* **in the National Derby.**

In which sentence is **climax** explained by a noun? _____

b

1660
1661

The words **each, either,** and **neither** can be used as either pronouns or adjectives.

a. *Each* **is right.** *Either* **is right.** *Neither* **is right.**
b. *Each* **one is right.** *Either* **answer is right.** *Neither* **answer is right.**

The italicized words are used as adjectives in group (*a, b*).

is

1929
1930

It is perfectly correct to shift tense when we really mean to indicate a change in the time of the action.

I *admire* (*present*) **the courage that Sue** *showed* (*past*).

Because you *admire* at the present time the courage that Sue *showed* at a past time, the shift in tenses is (*correct, incorrect*).

b

2198
2199

---

a. *Children* **love** *dogs.*   b. *Dogs* **love** *children.*

In sentence *a, Children* is the subject and *dogs* is the direct object.

In sentence *b, Dogs* is the subject and _____ is the direct object.

2468

UNIT 12: SKILL WITH GRAPHICS

Lesson **76** Commas in Compound Sentences

[Frames 2738–2766]

l

2736

---

a. **"We should have won this game," sighed Coach Higgins.**
b. **"We should have won this game", sighed Coach Higgins.**

a

3005
3006

verb 41	When we change a sentence from *present* to *past* or from *past* to *present,* the only word that would ordinarily change is the _____. 42
predicate 311	a. **We can't give everybody everything he wants and reduce taxes at the same time.** b. **The strike was finally settled and the men went back to work.** Which sentence requires a comma before the conjunction because it is a compound sentence? _____ 312
Yes 581	**Sue described the kind of boat she expects to build.** The adjective clause begins with the word _____ and ends with the word _____. 582
roads 851	(*The roads were*) *covered with ice.* **They were treacherous.** **the roads** *Covered with ice,* ~~they~~ **were treacherous.** To let the reader know what the sentence is about, we must substitute **the roads** for the pronoun _____ in the main statement. 852
b 1121	In this and the following frames, subordinate the italicized statement by changing it to a "now that" clause: *Christmas is over,* **and life can return to normal.** _____, **life** **can return to normal.** 1122
b 1391	**The lights were dimmed, and the concert began.** This is *not* a run-on sentence. It is a correct compound sentence formed by combining two simple sentences with the conjunction _____. 1392

b

1661

a. **The climax was Velvet's** *winning* **of the National Derby.**
b. **The climax** *was when* **Velvet won the National Derby.**

In which sentence is **climax** explained by a gerund (a verbal noun ending in *-ing*)? _____

1662

---

b

1930

a. **Each is right.**
b. **Each one is right.**

The subject of sentence *a* is the pronoun **Each.**

The subject of sentence *b* is the pronoun _____.

1931

---

correct

2199

Mrs. Clark *moved* (*past*) **to Omaha, where she now** *manages* (*present*) **a large drugstore.**

Because Mrs. Clark *moved* to Omaha in the past but *manages* the drugstore at the present time, the shift in tenses is (*correct, incorrect*).

2200

---

children

2468

Children **love** *dogs.* (*Dogs* **love** *children.*)

When we turn this sentence around, do we change the form or spelling of the nouns *children* and *dogs*? (*Yes, No*)

2469

The word **graphics** is one of many English words derived from the Greek word *graphein,* meaning *to write.* We have, for example, *telegraph* (distance writing), *phonograph* (sound writing), and *graphite* (the "lead" in pencils).

The word **graphics,** therefore, applies to (*speaking, writing*).

2738

---

a

3006

a. **"Nothing great,"** wrote Emerson, **"Was ever achieved without enthusiasm."**
b. **"Nothing great,"** wrote Emerson, **"was ever achieved without enthusiasm."**

3007

Lesson 2 A Closer Look at Subjects and Verbs

[Frames 44–82]

---

a. **A worker must stop for rest but a machine can work continuously.**

b. **I looked into the microscope but saw only a confusing blur.**

Which sentence requires a comma before the conjunction because it is a compound sentence? _____

b

312

313.

---

she . . . build

People are known by the company they keep.

We could insert the clause signal *which* or *that* before the word _____ .

582

583

---

they

If you lose a noun in making a participial phrase, put this noun back at the *beginning* of your main statement.

The book was autographed by Nin. **It brought a high price.**

Fill in the blank space:

Autographed by Nin, _____ **brought a high price.**

852

Now that Christmas is over,

Summer is here, **and people are planning their vacations.**

_____, **people are planning their vacations.**

1122

1123

---

and

There is another correct way of combining two simple sentences into a compound sentence.

The lights were dimmed; the concert began.

Instead of using the conjunction *and* to combine two simple sentences, we may use a _____ .

1392

1393

a. **The climax was where the tea was dumped into Boston Harbor.**
b. **The climax was the dumping of the tea into Boston Harbor.**

Which sentence is correct? _____

---

each	either	neither	any one
each one	either one	neither one	every one

Watch your verb closely when an "of" phrase follows any of these words. A plural verb often tries to slip itself in.

Each one of the answers is right.

The subject of this sentence is (*one, answers*).

---

a. **The story is about a man who** *achieved* **great wealth but** *loses* **his happiness.**
b. **The story is about a man who** *achieved* **great wealth but** *lost* **his happiness.**

Which sentence is correct? _____

I recognized him. (*He* **recognized** *me.*)

When we turn this sentence around, do we use the same forms of the pronouns *I* and *him*? (*Yes, No*)

In the field of language, *graphics* means the devices that are used only in writing, not in speech.

When we speak, is it possible to make an error in punctuation, capitalization, or spelling? (*Yes, No*)

---

a. **"We've had no rain," said the farmer. "Crops are drying up."**
b. **"We've had no rain," said the farmer, "crops are drying up."**

One or more helping verbs (sometimes called *auxiliary verbs*) are often used with the main verb to express our meaning more exactly.

The rope will break.

The helping verb used with **break** to make its meaning more exact is _____.

44

---

a

313

a. **I just returned from my vacation, and found your letter waiting for me.**
b. **Good judgment comes from experience, and experience comes from bad judgment.**

From which sentence should the comma be removed because it is not a compound sentence? _____

314

---

they

583

People are known by the company they keep.

The "no signal" clause in this sentence consists of two words:

_____ _____.

584

---

the book

853

Put a comma after any participial phrase that comes at the beginning of a sentence.

a. *Located near a factory* **the store does a big business.**
b. **We visited an old church** *built before the American Revolution.*

Which sentence requires a comma? _____

854

Now that
summer
is here,

1123

We have spent all our money, **and we might as well go home.**

_____

_____, **we might as well go home.**

1124

---

semicolon

1393

WRONG: **The lights were dimmed, the concert began.**

This sentence is wrong because there is neither a conjunction nor a semicolon to connect the two sentences.

Does a comma by itself have the power to connect two simple sentences? (*Yes, No*)

1394

The coincidence *was when* the brothers met in the Paris airport.

Correct the above sentence by writing a gerund in the blank space:

The coincidence was the _____ of the brothers in the Paris airport.

b

1663   1664

Each one of the answers . . . right.

We pay no attention to the plural noun **answers** when we select the missing verb.

The noun **answers** is not the subject of the sentence but

one

the object of the preposition _____.

1932   1933

---

a. **Smith then invested in an oil well in which he lost all his savings.**
b. **Smith then invested in an oil well in which he loses all his savings.**

b

Which sentence is correct? _____

2201   2202

NOUNS: *Children* **love** *dogs.* (*Dogs* **love** *children.*)
PRONOUNS: *I* **recognized** *him.* (*He* **recognized** *me.*)

No

The words that change in form when their use in the sentence changes are (*nouns, pronouns*).

2470   2471

---

a. **Omission of a capital**
b. **Wrong form of verb**

No

Which would be an error in graphics because it could occur only in writing? _____

2739   2740

---

a. **My Uncle Dan remarked, "I much prefer living in a small town." "Everyone knows everyone else." "People have more time to be courteous and friendly."**
b. **My Uncle Dan remarked, "I much prefer living in a small town. Everyone knows everyone else. People have more time to be courteous and friendly."**

a

3008   3009

The rope will break.
The rope might break.

will

The meaning of the first sentence changes when we change the helping verb from **will** to _____.

44

45

---

a

Ambassador Young remained calm and cool and he didn't raise his voice.

This sentence contains two **and**'s.

A comma should be placed before the (*first, second*) **and.**

314

315

---

they keep

The drawer was full of things nobody would ever want.

We could insert the clause signal *which* or *that* before the word _____.

584

585

---

a

Put a comma before a participial phrase at the end of a sentence only if it modifies the subject at the beginning of the sentence.

a. **We stayed at a delightful inn** *operated by the state.*
b. **The audience grew restless** *bored by the long speech.*

Which sentence requires a comma? _____

854

855

Now that we have spent all our money,

Mrs. Bilby has explained the problem, **and it seems very simple.**

_____

_____, **it seems very simple.**

1124

1125

No

When we incorrectly combine two simple sentences by means of a comma, we produce a _____ sentence, which is considered just as serious an error as a fragment.

1394

1395

meeting 1664	A simple way to avoid the *is when* or *is where* error is to use such a verb as *occurred, happened,* or *took place,* thus supplying an action verb that your "when" clause can modify. a. **The climax occurred when the submarine was grounded.** b. **The climax was when the submarine was grounded.** Which sentence is correct? _____ 1665
of 1933	**Either one of these recipes** (*make, makes*) **a good cake.** We select the verb _____ to agree with the subject _____. 1934
a 2202	When you tell a story, it is very easy to make the mistake of shifting back and forth between the past and the present tense. If you start to tell a story in the past tense, you should continue to use the _____ tense consistently throughout the entire story. 2203
pronouns 2471	The change in form of pronouns to show their relationship to other words in the sentence is called **case.** <div align="center">**he****his****him**</div>All three pronouns can be used to refer to the same person. Their difference in form is due to their difference in _____. 2472
a 2740	In this first lesson on graphics, we review the use of the comma in compound sentences. A compound sentence consists of two (or more) main clauses joined by the conjunction **and, but,** or **or.** In a compound sentence there are a subject and a predicate both before and after the _____ 2741
b 3009	In the remaining frames, punctuate each sentence and supply capitals where necessary. Remember that commas and periods always come *before,* not *after,* quotation marks. **A sign along the highway said remember, telephone poles hit people only in self-defense.** 3010

might

45

Mary <u>can rescue</u> the child.
Mary <u>should rescue</u> the child.

The meaning of the first sentence changes when we change the helping verb from **can** to _____.

46

---

second

315

Food became cheap and plentiful and the automobile came into common use.

A comma should be placed before the (*first, second*) **and.**

316

---

nobody

585

The drawer was full of things nobody would ever want.

The "no signal" adjective clause begins with the word _____ and ends with the word _____.

586

---

b

855

Combine each pair of sentences by changing the italicized sentence to a past participial phrase. Insert a comma wherever needed.

The trainer entered the cage. *He was armed only with a whip.* _____

_____

856

Now that Mrs. Bilby has explained the problem,

1125

We have moved to the city, **and we miss our farm very much.**

_____,

we miss our farm very much.

1126

---

run-on

1395

Let us look into a common cause of the sentence collisions that we call run-on sentences.

The <u>motor</u> <u>was</u> wet. The <u>motor</u> <u>refused</u> to start.

Here we have two separate sentences, each with its own _____ and verb.

1396

a 1665	**The turning point** *was when* **Josephine Baker met Bessie Smith.** This sentence can be corrected by substituting the verb _____ for the verb **was.** <div align="right">1666</div>

(verb) makes
(subject) one
 	
1934
	Supply the correct verb in sentence *b,* paying no attention to the object of the preposition.
	
	    a. **Neither fits me.**
	    b. **Neither of the coats** _____ **me.**
	
	<div align="right">1935</div>

past (*or* same) 2203	The following student's summary of "The Necklace," a famous story by the French author Guy de Maupassant, is written mainly—but not entirely—in the past tense. Cross out each verb in the present tense and write the past form of the verb above it. If the sentence contains no error in tense, write *Correct.* (*Turn to the next frame.*) <div align="right">2204</div>
case 2472	a. *I* **recognized** *him.* b. *He* **recognized** *me.* The pronoun *I* in sentence *a* and the pronoun *me* in sentence *b* mean the same person. Are the pronouns *I* and *me* in the same case? (*Yes, No*) <div align="right">2473</div>
conjunction 2741	In the following diagrams, a single line represents the subject and a double line the predicate. a. _____ _____, and _____ _____. b. _____ _____ and _____. Which diagram represents a compound sentence? _____ <div align="right">2742</div>
said, "Remember . . . self-defense." 3010	**Education is much more than studying books** **began the speaker.** <div align="right">3011</div>

a. Mary <u>settled</u> the argument.
b. Mary <u>could have settled</u> the argument.

In sentence *a*, the main verb is used by itself.

In sentence *b*, two helping verbs have been added to change its meaning—_____ and _____.

should

46

47

This paint doesn't show brush or roller marks and it dries quickly.

A comma should be placed before (*or, and*).

second

316

317

Now let's review some of the things we have learned about adjective clauses in this and the previous lesson.
a. An adjective clause is one that does the work of a single adjective.
b. An adjective clause is one that begins with an adjective.
Which definition of an adjective clause is correct? _____

nobody . . . want

586

587

Continue to follow the directions for the previous frame:

Little Women *was written by Louisa May Alcott in 1868.* **It soon became a favorite story.**

_____

_____

The trainer
entered the
cage, armed
only with a whip.

856

857

Another unusual type of adverb clause can sometimes be used very effectively in place of an "although" clause.

Cheap as it is, **the car is no bargain.**

This adverb clause is unusual because instead of beginning with a clause signal, it begins with (*a verb, an adjective*).

Now that we
have moved to
the city,

1126

1127

It
The motor was wet. ~~The motor~~ refused to start.

Since we are still talking about the motor, we do not need to repeat the noun **motor** in the second sentence.

We therefore put the pronoun _____ in place of the noun **motor** as the subject of the second sentence.

subject

1396

1397

Any one of the following verbs: occurred, took place, came (about)	**The climax** *was when* **Banquo's ghost appeared at the banquet.** Fill in the blank so as to avoid the *was when* construction: **The climax** _____ **when Banquo's ghost appeared at the banquet.**
1666	1667
fits	Supply the correct verb in sentence *b*, paying no attention to the object of the preposition. a. **Every one needs washing.** b. **Every one of the windows** _____ **washing.**
1935	1936
	Continue to follow the directions for the previous frame: **Mathilde was a pretty French girl who was married to a poor but pleasant clerk in the government service.**
2204	2205
No	*I* **recognized** *him. He* **recognized** *me.* The pronoun *him* in sentence *a* and the pronoun *He* in sentence *b* mean the same person. Are the pronouns *him* and *He* in the same case? (*Yes, No*)
2473	2474
a	a. **Lupe gets high grades and plans to attend college.** b. **Lupe gets high grades, and her teachers urge her to attend college.** Which sentence is compound because there are a subject and a predicate both before and after the conjunction? _____
2742	2743
"Education . . . books," began the speaker.	**I find that most people know what a story is said Flannery O'Connor until they sit down to write one**
3011	3012

could, have 47	Learn to recognize these important helping verbs: HELPING VERBS: **shall, will** **may, can** **could, would, should** **must, might** Vera _____ **study.** Could each of these helping verbs be used with the main verb **study?** (*Yes, No*) 48
and 317	**Mr. Sims had accumulated much money and property but he wasn't happy or contented.** A comma should be placed before (*and, but, or*). 318
a 587	An adjective clause, like an adjective, modifies a _____ or a pronoun. 588
Written by Louisa May Alcott in 1868, *Little Women* soon became a favorite story. 857	**Tatum intercepted the pass.** *It was intended for Warfield.* _____ _____ 858
an adjective 1127	a. *although it is cheap* b. *cheap as it is* In which clause is the subject complement *cheap* not in its normal position? _____ 1128
It 1397	a. **The motor refused to start.** b. **It refused to start.** Both *a* and *b* are complete sentences. If you were writing only one sentence in isolation, which sentence would you write? _____ 1398

<table>
<tr>
<td>Any one of the following verbs: occurred, took place, came (about)

1667</td>
<td>The climax was when Banquo's ghost appeared at the banquet.

Fill in the blank so as to avoid the was when construction:

The climax was the _____ of Banquo's ghost at the banquet.

1668</td>
</tr>
<tr>
<td>needs

1936</td>
<td>Singular subjects joined by and are plural and require a plural verb.

Underline the correct verb:

The air and the water (was, were) perfect for swimming.

1937</td>
</tr>
<tr>
<td>Correct

2205</td>
<td>Because of his small income, her husband is not able to give her the life of luxury and romance for which she had always yearned.

2206</td>
</tr>
<tr>
<td>No

2474</td>
<td>A pronoun is in the nominative case when it fits before an action verb as its subject—he laughed; she fell; we won; they lost.

Underline the nominative pronoun:

They blamed us.

2475</td>
</tr>
<tr>
<td>b

2743</td>
<td>Use a comma generally before the conjunction and, but, or or in a compound sentence. The comma gives each part greater distinctness and makes the sentence easier to read.

Insert the necessary comma:

We had only five minutes to play and every second counted.

2744</td>
</tr>
<tr>
<td>"I find that most people know what a story is," said Flannery O'Connor, "until they sit down to write one."

3012</td>
<td>The coffee wasn't too strong   commented Uncle Pete   the people were just too weak.

3013</td>
</tr>
</table>

Yes	The three verbs below may serve as either *main verbs* or *helping verbs*.
	be (is, am, are—was, were, been) **have (has, had)** **do (does, did)**
	Which verb has the largest number of forms? _____
48	49

but	A sentence that can be separated into two parts—a subject and a predicate—is a (*simple, compound*) sentence.
318	319

noun	An adjective clause always comes (*before, after*) the word it modifies.
588	589

Tatum intercepted the pass intended for Warfield.	*The candidate was questioned about his policies.* **He gave only vague answers.** _____ _____
858	859

b	a. *cheap as it is* b. *although it is cheap* In which clause does the adjective *cheap* occupy a more prominent position? _____
1128	1129

a	a. **The motor refused to start.** b. **It refused to start.** If the sentence were to follow another sentence that had already mentioned the **motor,** which sentence would you write? _____
1398	1399

appearance *or* appearing 1668	**The turning point** *is when* **Coach Perry takes charge of the team.** Eliminate the *is when* construction: _____ **when** **Coach Perry takes charge of the team.** 1669
were 1937	Underline the correct verb. (Keep in mind that a verb that ends in *s* is always singular.) **Her face** *and* **her way of talking** (*remind, reminds*) **me of you.** 1938
was ~~is~~ 2206	**One day he joyously brings home an invitation to a fancy ball.** 2207
They 2475	**. . . invited Rosa.** Underline three pronouns that are in the nominative case because they could serve as the subject in the sentence above: **I him she we them her** 2476
play, and 2744	Insert the necessary comma: **His eyes were closed but he wasn't sleeping.** 2745
"The . . . strong," commented Uncle Pete. "The . . . weak." 3013	**Miss Morris said, Never offer too many excuses. Too many excuses make people suspicious. People are more likely to believe a single excuse.** 3014

be 49	a. **The <u>weather</u> <u>is</u> bad.** b. **The <u>weather</u> <u>is</u> improving.** In one sentence **is** serves as the main verb; in the other, as a helping verb. Does **is** serve as a helping verb in sentence *a* or *b*? _____ 50
simple 319	A compound sentence can be formed by combining two simple sentences with a _____. 320
after 589	If a clause can be shifted from one position to another in a sentence, it is an (*adjective, adverb*) clause. 590
Questioned about his policies, the candidate gave only vague answers. 859	*The bandit was surrounded by police.* **He gave himself up.** _____ _____ 860
a 1129	a. *Although it is cheap,* **the car is no bargain.** b. *Cheap as it is,* **the car is no bargain.** In which sentence does the clause give more emphasis to the *cheapness* of the price? _____ 1130
b 1399	**The motor was wet. It refused to start.** **It refused to start** is a complete sentence because the reader knows from the previous sentence that the word **It** means _____. 1400

The turning point occurs (takes place, comes, comes about) 1669	**The turning point** *is where* **Coach Perry takes charge of the team.** Eliminate the *is where* construction: **The turning point is Coach Perry's** _____ **charge of the team.** <div align="right">1670</div>
remind 1938	When the two singular subjects joined by **and** mean the same person or thing, a singular verb is proper. a. **The owner** *and* **manager is Mr. Harris.** b. **The owner** *and* **the manager is pleased with each other.** In which sentence is the singular verb **is** correct? _____ <div align="right">1939</div>
brought <s>brings</s> 2207	**His wife, however, was not happy because she lacks suitable clothes for such an affair.** <div align="right">2208</div>
I, she, we 2476	A pronoun is in the **objective case** when it fits *after* an action verb as its direct object—pushed *me*; stopped *him*; asked *her*; beat *us*; called *them*. Underline the objective pronoun: <div align="center">*They* **blamed** *us*.</div> <div align="right">2477</div>
closed, but 2745	Insert the necessary comma: **The clothes must be slightly damp or the wrinkles will not iron out.** <div align="right">2746</div>
Miss Morris said, "Never . . . a single excuse." 3014	Lesson **84** **When Quotations Are Questions** [Frames 3016–3049]

b	a. **I have brought my camera along.** b. **I have my camera with me.** Is **have** used as a helping verb in sentence *a* or *b?* _____
50	51

conjunction	The three most common conjunctions are *and,* _____, and *or.*
320	321

adverb	The adjective clause signals **who (whose, whom), which,** and **that** are called *relative* (*adjectives, pronouns*).
590	591

Surrounded by police, the bandit gave himself up.	Eliminate the **and** by changing the italicized statement to a past participial phrase. Insert a comma wherever needed. *The car was forced off the road* **and went into a ditch.** _____ _____
860	861

b	a. *Large as the house is,* **we find it too small for our family.** b. *Although the house is large,* **we find it too small for our** **family.** In which sentence does the clause give more emphasis to the *largeness* of the house? _____
1130	1131

motor	You need have no hesitation in starting a new sentence with
	the pronoun **It.** Don't let this pronoun trick you into making
	a run-on sentence error.
	
	    a. **The motor was wet, it wouldn't start.**
	    b. **The motor was wet. It wouldn't start.**
	
	Which is correct? _____

1400	1401

taking 1670	In this and the following frames, fill in the blank space so as to eliminate the *is when* or *is where* construction: **A pinch hitter is where one player bats for another.** **A pinch hitter _____ who bats for another.** 1671

a
 	
1939
	If the two singular subjects joined by **and** are thought of as a single unit, use a singular verb.
	
	    a. **Tea** *and* **coffee is served with every meal.**
	    b. **Bread** *and* **butter is served with every meal.**
	
	In which sentence is the singular verb **is** correct? _____
	
	1940

lacked <s>lacks</s> 2208	**Although her husband gave up buying a gun in order to finance a new dress, she was still unhappy because she had no jewels to wear.** 2209
us 2477	**Rosa invited . . .** Underline three pronouns that are in the objective case because they could serve as the direct object in the sentence above: **I him we she them her** 2478
damp, or 2746	**The pilot received a storm warning, and** *she* **moved up to a higher altitude.** If you omitted the italicized pronoun *she* from this compound sentence, would you still retain the comma? (*Yes, No*) 2747
	When a quotation asks a question, you first decide whether you are repeating the actual words of the question or merely reporting in your own words what was asked. When you repeat the actual words of the question, your quotation is (*direct, indirect*). 3016

a

a. **We did the dishes.**
b. **Yes, we did wash the dishes.**

Is **did** used as a helping verb in sentence *a* or *b?* _____

51

52

---

but

Should a comma be placed before the conjunction that connects the two parts of a compound predicate? (*Yes, No*)

321

322

---

pronouns

When we omit an adjective clause from a sentence, a grammatically (*complete, incomplete*) sentence remains.

591

592

Forced off the
road, the car
went into a
ditch.

Follow the directions given in the previous frame:

A crowd gathered around the excavation, and *they were fascinated by the steam shovel.*

_____

_____

861

862

---

a

Sometimes this type of clause begins with an adverb shifted from its usual position at the end of the sentence.

a. *Although we came early,* **we got poor seats.**
b. *Early as we came,* **we got poor seats.**

In which sentence does the clause give more emphasis to

the adverb *early?* _____

1131

1132

---

b

Sentences may begin with other pronouns, too.

He will watch the baby.

Since you would know from some previous sentence whom the pronoun **He** stands for, this is a (*fragment, sentence*).

1401

1402

is a player 1671	Arson is when someone commits the crime of willfully setting fire to property. Arson _____ of willfully setting fire to property. 1672

b
 	
1940
	A phrase introduced by **with, along with, together with,** or **as well as** often follows the subject. Do not mistake the noun in such a phrase for part of the subject.
	
	    a. **Mr. Davis and his son are in Alaska.**
	    b. **Mr. Davis, with his son, are in Alaska.**
	
	In which sentence is the plural verb **are** correct? _____ 1941

Correct 2209	**She solves her problem by borrowing a diamond necklace from a friend in better circumstances.** 2210
him, them, her 2478	a. **I** **he** **she** **we** **they** b. **me** **him** **her** **us** **them** Which group consists of objective pronouns? _____ 2479
No 2747	**Coach Blair moved some of his boys around and ‸ put several new players into the game.** If you added *he* at the point indicated, would you insert a comma after the word **around?** (*Yes, No*) 2748
direct 3016	a. **Leroy asked, "Where's my ticket?"** b. **Leroy asked where his ticket was.** In which sentence is the question a direct quotation? _____ 3017

b 52	a. <u>I have studied</u> my lesson. b. <u>I should have studied</u> my lesson. c. <u>I should have been studying</u> my lesson. In which sentence does the verb have the largest number of helping verbs? _____ 53
No 322	In a compound sentence, there are a subject and verb both before and after the conjunction. (*True, False*) 323
complete 592	Is a relative pronoun such as **who, which,** or **that** always the first word in an adjective clause? (*Yes, No*) 593
A crowd gathered around the excavation, fascinated by the steam shovel. 862	*The article was written hastily* **and contained many inaccuracies.** _____ _____ 863
b 1132	In this and the following frames, make each "although" clause more emphatic by beginning it with an adjective or an adverb, always followed by the word *as*. *Although I replied courteously,* **Don took offense.** _____, **Don took offense.** 1133
sentence 1402	a. **Jorge is staying home today. He will watch the baby.** b. **Jorge is staying home today, he will watch the baby.** Which is correct? _____ 1403

is the crime

1672

Osmosis is where plants absorb moisture from the soil.

Osmosis is the process by which _____

_____.

1673

---

a

1941

By shifting the prepositional phrase to the end of this sentence, we see that the noun **son** is not part of the subject.

Mr. Davis, *with his son,* **is in Alaska.**
Mr. Davis is in Alaska *with his son.*

This sentence has only one subject, which is _____.

1942

---

solved
~~solves~~

2210

After making a great hit at the ball because of her clothes and her beauty, she found, when she arrives home, that the necklace is gone.

2211

---

b

2479

You **saw** *it.* (*It* **saw** *you.*)

Do the pronouns *You* and *it* change in form when we turn this sentence around? (*Yes, No*)

2480

Yes

2748

---

a. **Our dog often runs away, but it always comes back.**
b. **Our dog often runs away, but always comes back.**

From which sentence should the comma be dropped? _____

2749

---

a

3017

Leroy asked *where his ticket was.*

Are the italicized words the actual words of the original question? (*Yes, No*)

3018

The driver should have been watching the road.

c

The three helping verbs in this frame are _____,

_____, and _____.

53 | 54

True

In a compound sentence, the comma should be placed (*before, after*) the conjunction.

323 | 324

We called a doctor whom a neighbor had recommended.

We called a doctor a neighbor had recommended.

No

Does an adjective clause always contain a relative pronoun? (*Yes, No*)

593 | 594

Written hastily, the article contained many inaccuracies.

Mrs. Li owns a sports car, and *it was imported from Italy.*

_____

_____

863 | 864

Courteously as I replied,

I had to finish my theme, *although it was late.*

I had to finish my theme, _____.

1133 | 1134

---

a

Suppose that you had just written this sentence:

Carew hit a single.

Then you wished to explain what followed. Circle the letter indicating the way in which you would continue your thought:

a. **Carew hit a single, this won the game.**

1403 | b. **Carew hit a single. This won the game.** | 1404

plants absorb
moisture from
the soil.

1673

The climax is when Tina reveals family secrets on a children's television program.

The climax _____ when Tina reveals family secrets on a children's television program.

1674

Mr. Davis

1942

---

a. The camera, together with the case, sell for $39.
b. The camera and the case sell for $39.

In which sentence is the plural verb **sell** incorrect? _____

1943

---

arrived
~~arrives~~
was
~~is~~

2211

By going hopelessly into debt, they buy another necklace to replace the one they had lost.

2212

No

2480

You **saw** *it. It* **saw** *you.*

Do *you* and *it*—like the other pronouns—have different forms for the nominative and objective case? (*Yes, No*)

2481

---

b

2749

---

a. New words may become part of our language or they may soon disappear.
b. New words may become part of our language or may soon disappear.

In which sentence should a comma be inserted after the word **language?** _____

2750

No

3018

When you do not repeat the actual words of the question but report it in your own words, your quotation is (*direct, indirect*).

3019

should,
have,
been

54

The *complete* verb in any sentence includes the main verb plus whatever helping verbs it may have.

The driver should have been watching the road.

The *complete* verb in this sentence consists of _____ words. (How many?)

55

before

324

Lesson **9** The Proper Use of the Compound Sentence

[Frames 326–359]

No

594

Lesson **16** Choosing Your Relatives

[Frames 596–636]

Mrs. Li owns a sports car imported from Italy.

864

Small boats were warned by the Coast Guard **and headed for shore.**

_____

_____

865

late as it was.

1134

Although we tried hard, **we couldn't make a touchdown.**

_____, **we couldn't make a touchdown.**

1135

b

1404

a. **Many advertisements do not state the total price, they merely state the monthly payments.**
b. **Many advertisements do not state the total price. They merely state the monthly payments.**

Which is correct? _____

1405

occurs (takes place, comes, comes about) 1674	To baste is when you sew with long, loose, temporary stitches. To baste is _____ with long, loose, temporary stitches. (*Note:* Don't forget the principle of parallel construction.) 1675
a 1943	Underline the correct verb: A tennis court, as well as a swimming pool, (*is, are*) available to guests. 1944
bought ~~buy~~ 2212	For ten years they lived in attics and scrimped and struggled to pay off their enormous debt. 2213
No 2481	Use the nominative case of a pronoun when it is used as the subject of a verb. Underline the correct pronoun: You and (*I, me*) can study together. (*Note:* The use of the nominative case after forms of the verb **be** will be studied in the following lesson.) 2482
a 2750	A compound sentence without a comma might sometimes be misread. We found it too expensive to stay at hotels and motels were hard to find. We can prevent the misreading of this compound sentence by inserting a comma after _____. 2751
indirect 3019	Leroy asked *where his ticket was.* Since the italicized words are not the actual words of a question, do we need to use either a question mark or quotes? (*Yes, No*) 3020

We shall now, for a moment, need to turn our attention to **adverbs,** which most commonly modify verbs.

This has happened frequently.

Because **frequently** modifies the verb **has happened,** it is an

_____.

56

A compound sentence is very easy to make. We merely need to combine two simple sentences by using one of these conjunctions: *and,* _____, or _____.

326

Here again are the **relative pronouns** that are used as clause signals to start adjective clauses.

RELATIVE PRONOUNS: **who (whose, whom), which, that**

Are these the same clause signals that start adverb clauses? (*Yes, No*)

596

a. **hearing, intending, thinking, falling**
b. **filled, sold, spoken, worn, spent, followed**

Which group of words could be used as past participles?

_____

866

In the remaining frames, subordinate each italicized statement by changing it to an adverb clause beginning with an adjective or an adverb.

Webb is able, **but he Is not able enough for this job.**

_____, **he is not able enough for this job.**

1136

a. **Jerry was smiling in a peculiar way. He had apparently been up to some mischief.**
b. **Jerry was smiling in a peculiar way, he had apparently been up to some mischief.**

Which is correct? _____

1406

to sew

1675

The turning point was where Columbus went to Queen Isabella for help.

The turning point _____ Columbus went to Queen Isabella for help.

1676

---

is

1944

Singular subjects joined by **or** or **nor** are singular and require a singular verb.

      a. **A doctor** *and* **a nurse** ...
      b. **A doctor** *or* **a nurse** ...

Which subject is singular because it means only one person

—*a* or *b*? _____

1945

Correct

2213

In the meantime, she loses her beauty and becomes so plain and worn that no one could have recognized her for the beautiful girl she once had been.

2214

I

2482

Use the objective case of a pronoun when it is used as the object of a verb or a preposition.

Underline the correct pronouns:

      Several friends save (*them, they*) **for** (*me, I*).

2483

---

hotels

2751

Commas are generally omitted in short compound sentences. The reader can find his way without their help.

a. **British humor depends on understatement** *but* **American humor is based largely on exaggeration.**
b. **I knocked** *but* **no one answered.**

Which compound sentence does not require a comma? _____

2752

No

3020

(*Note:* Punctuation is omitted from the following sentences to avoid revealing the answer.)

      a. **The child asked   whether our dog bites**
      b. **The child asked   Does your dog bite**

Which sentence contains an indirect question, which requires neither a question mark nor quotes? _____

3021

adverb 56	a. **This has happened** frequently. b. **This has** frequently **happened.** In which sentence does the adverb **frequently** break into or interrupt the verb? _____ 57
but, or 326	Because compound sentences are so easy to make, we must avoid overusing them. Use a compound sentence to combine only *similar* or *related* ideas that are of equal importance. **Natachee studies Spanish, and our school has a gym.** Should these two ideas have been combined? (*Yes, No*) 327
No 596	Use **who, whose,** and **whom** to refer only to *people.* Underline the correct relative pronoun: **The clerk** (*who, which*) **took my order made a mistake in the bill.** 597
b 865	A phrase built on either a present or a past participle is used as an _____ to modify a noun or pronoun. 867
Able as Webb is, 1136	*Mr. Gross was angry,* **but he didn't show his temper.** _____, **he didn't show his temper.** 1137
a 1406	A sentence may begin with a pronoun such as *it, he, she,* or *they* even though the noun that the pronoun stands for is in another sentence. (*True, False*) 1407

occurred (took place, came, came about) when 1676	A straw vote is when an unofficial vote is taken to find out public opinion. A straw vote _____ taken to find out public opinion. <div align="right">1677</div>
b 1945	Underline the correct verb: **A doctor or a nurse** (*is, are*) **always on hand.** <div align="right">1946</div>
lost ~~loses~~ became ~~becomes~~ 2214	**One day she happens to meet the friend who had lent her the unlucky necklace that had brought them so much misfortune.** <div align="right">2215</div>

them, me
 	
 2483
	Pronoun errors occur most often when pronouns are used in pairs or when a noun and a pronoun are coupled together.
	
	     a. *He* **refereed the game.**
	     b. **Frank and** (*he, him*) **refereed the game.**
	
	 In sentence *b*, which pronoun is correct? _____
	
	<div align="right">2484</div>

b 2752	A short compound sentence does not need to be broken into shorter units for the convenience of the reader. a. **Several parents complained about overcrowding in the schools** *and* **the mayor agreed to take immediate action.** b. **They rode** *and* **we walked.** In which sentence would you use a comma before *and*? _____ <div align="right">2753</div>
a 3021	Now let's look at a question that is quoted directly: **Leroy asked, "Where's my ticket?"** To show that the quotation is a question, we put the question mark (*inside, outside*) the quotes. <div align="right">3022</div>

a. **This engine will immediately start in the coldest weather.**
b. **This engine will start immediately in the coldest weather.**

In which sentence does an adverb come between the main verb and its helper? _____

58

---

a. **Natachee studies Spanish, and our school has a gym.**
b. **Natachee studies Spanish, and Carol studies French.**

Which compound sentence is better because the ideas are similar? _____

328

Use **which** to refer only to *things* and *animals*.

Underline the correct relative pronoun:

The store (*who, which*) sells these games is making a fortune.

598

---

a. **Frank was raised on a farm.**   b. **He knew the problems of the farmer.**

Which sentence could be changed to a past participial phrase? _____

868

The material cost of war is great, **but the human cost is infinitely greater.**

_____,

the human cost is infinitely greater.

1138

There are several methods of correcting a run-on sentence.
    WRONG: **I approached the squirrel, it ran away.**
    RIGHT: **I approached the squirrel. It ran away.**
1. Separate the run-together sentences by using a period and a _____ letter.

1408

The surprise is where the father demands that the kidnappers pay him to take back his rowdy son.

The surprise is the father's _____ that the kidnappers pay him to take back his rowdy son.

1678

---

is

1946

Father _and_ Elsie do the dishes.

Suppose that you changed _and_ to _or_. Would you need also to change the plural verb **do** to the singular verb **does**? (_Yes, No_)

1947

---

happened
~~happens~~

2215

Now that they had finally got out of debt, she decides to tell her friend how she had lost the borrowed necklace and had supplied a substitute for which she had paid such a great price.

2216

---

he

2484

You would never say, "_Him_ pushed the car" or "_Me_ pushed the car"; so don't make the same mistake by saying, "_Him_ and _me_ pushed the car."

Underline the correct pronouns:

(_He, Him_) **and** (_I, me_) **counted the votes.**

2485

---

a

2753

Do not mistake a sentence with a compound predicate for a compound sentence.

Flo Kennedy <u>was pleased</u> _and_ <u>praised the program.</u>

The above sentence is not compound because there is no (_subject, predicate_) after the conjunction _and_.

2754

---

inside

3022

a. **Roberta asked, "Is this poison ivy"?**
b. **Roberta asked, "Is this poison ivy?"**

In which sentence is the question mark properly placed to show that the question, not the entire sentence, is a quotation? _____

3023

a 58	**One should immediately try artificial respiration.** What adverb comes between the main verb and its helper? _____ 59
b 328	a. **The road was muddy, and we bought eggs at a farm.** b. **The road was muddy, and we got stuck several times.** Which compound sentence is better because the ideas are related? _____ 329
which 598	Use **which** to refer to *things* and *animals*. **It was the Rosses' dog** (*which, who*) **tore up our flower bed.** 599
a 868	Lesson **23** Making Use of Gerunds [Frames 870–907]
Great as the material cost of war is, 1138	Lesson **30** Two Useful Adjective Clause Devices [Frames 1140–1166]
capital 1408	WRONG: **I approached the squirrel, it ran away.** RIGHT: **I approached the squirrel, and it ran away.** 2. Correct the run-on sentence by adding the conjunction _____. 1409

demand (demanding) 1678	A boondoggler is where a person is hired to do a needless job. A boondoggler _____ hired to do a needless job. 1679
Yes 1947	a. Father and Elsie do the dishes. b. Father or Elsie do the dishes. In which sentence is the plural verb **do** incorrect? _____ 1948
decided <s>decides</s> 2216	"Oh, my poor Mathilde!" her friend gasps with amazement. "Why, that necklace I lent you was only paste!" (*End of story*) 2217
He, I 2485	When you use pronouns in pairs or when you couple a pronoun with a noun, use the same case that you would use if the pronouns were used singly. These flowers are from *Pete*. These flowers are from *me*. Underline the correct pronoun: These flowers are from *Pete* and (*I, me*). 2486
subject 2754	Do not ordinarily use a comma before the conjunction that connects the two parts of a compound predicate. a. Gary left his salad, but ate his dessert. b. Gary left his salad, but he ate his dessert. From which sentence should the comma be omitted? _____ 2755
b 3023	Now we shall put the same question at the beginning of the sentence: "Is this poison ivy?" asked Roberta. When the quotation is a question, is a comma used between the question and the rest of the sentence? (*Yes, No*) 3024

There is something else besides adverbs that can separate a main verb from its helper.

STATEMENT:	**Judy can drive.**
QUESTION:	**Can Judy drive?**

The verb **can drive** is interrupted in the (*statement, question*).

_____

immediately

59   60

Our tree is small. It gives very little shade.

Because there is a relationship between the size of a tree and the amount of shade, these sentences would make a (*good, poor*) compound sentence.

b

329   330

Use **that** to refer to anything—*people, things,* or *animals.*

Underline the correct relative pronoun:

Marian wrote a theme about the teacher (*which, that*) **had helped her most.**

which

WRONG - USE "WHO" FOR PEOPLE

599   600

Present and past participles, as we have seen, are forms of verbs that serve as adjectives. Now we look at verbs that have crossed over into noun territory.

Tennis **is good exercise.**

Tennis is an ordinary noun. It is the subject of the verb

_____.

870

A special type of adjective clause is useful when you wish to state a fact about only a *part* or a *number* of a larger group.

Gloria has three sisters, *one of whom is a nurse.*

The adjective clause states a fact about (*all, one*) of the sisters.

1140

WRONG:	**I approached the squirrel, it ran away.**
RIGHT:	**I approached the squirrel; it ran away.**

and

3. The third way to correct a run-on sentence is to insert a

_____.

1409   1410

is a person

1679

The climax of the story was when Jeff announced that he would not study law.

The climax of the story was _____

_____ that he would not study law.

1680

---

b

1948

Oil, lotion, *or* cold cream relieves sunburn.

Suppose that you changed *or* to *and*. Would you need to change the singular verb **relieves** to the plural verb **relieve?** (*Yes, No*)

1949

---

gasped

~~gasps~~

2217

Use the present tense to state facts that are permanently true—for example, the facts of science, mathematics, geography, etc.

    a. There *are* eight quarts in a peck.
    b. There *are* eight people in the car.

Which sentence states a permanent truth? _____

2218

---

me

2486

You can't blame the *Kirks* for objecting.
You can't blame *them* for objecting.

Underline the correct pronoun:

You can't blame the *Kirks* or (*them, they*) for objecting.

2487

---

a

2755

---

a. Shall we buy a new car or shall we repair the old one?
b. Shall we buy a new car or repair the old one?

Which sentence requires a comma? _____

2756

No

3024

"Is this poison ivy?" asked Roberta.

The question mark is placed at the end of the (*question, sentence*).

3025

question	STATEMENT: **Dad will want the car tonight.** QUESTION: **Will Dad want the car tonight?** The verb **will want** is interrupted in the (*statement, question*). _____
60	61

good	**Our tree is small. We bought it at a nursery.** Although both these sentences are about a tree, they have little relationship to each other. Therefore, they would make a (*good, poor*) compound sentence.
330	331

that	The main point to remember is never to use **which** to refer to *people.* Underline the correct relative pronoun: **citizens** (*who, which*)
600	601

is	*Tennis* **is good exercise.** *Walking* **is good exercise.** Both *Tennis* and *Walking* are nouns used as subjects of the verb **is.** Which one of these two italicized nouns was formed from a verb? _____
870	871

one	**Along the coast are many small islands,** *some of which are uninhabited.* The clause states a fact about (*some, all*) of the islands.
1140	1141

semicolon	There is sometimes a fourth way to correct a run-on sentence. The best solution may be to subordinate one of the sentences. WRONG: **I approached the squirrel, it ran away.** RIGHT· *As I approached the squirrel,* **it ran away.** 4. Change one of the sentences to a phrase or clause. In this case, we used a _____.
1410	1411

Lesson 47 Do Your Pronouns Have Antecedents?

[Frames 1682–1719]

Yes

1949

Underline the correct verb:

A thick hedge or a high wall (*give, gives*) **a feeling of privacy.**

1950

---

a

2218

a. **There** *are* **eight quarts in a peck.**
b. **There** *were* **eight quarts in a peck.**

In which sentence is the tense of the verb wrong? _____

2219

---

them

2487

The *Smiths* **will call for you.**
We **will call for you.**

Underline the correct pronoun:

The *Smiths* **or** (*us, we*) **will call for you.**

2488

---

a

2756

In this and the following frames, insert any necessary commas. If no comma is required, write *None*.

Kim's arm was around the collie's neck and the dog was licking her face affectionately.

2757

---

question

3025

When the question comes first, be sure to put the question mark at the end of the question, not at the end of the sentence.

a. **"What are we having for dinner?" questioned Don.**
b. **"What are we having for dinner," questioned Don?**

The question mark is properly placed in sentence (*a, b*).

3026

question	**Will Dad want the car tonight?**
	The main verb **want** is separated from its helper **will** by the subject _____.
61	62

poor	a. **Our tree is small, and it gives very little shade.**
	b. **Our tree is small, and we bought it at a nursery.**
	Which compound sentence is better? _____
331	332

who	Underline the correct relative pronoun:
	the horse (_who, which_)
601	602

Walking	_Walking_ **is good exercise.**
	The noun _Walking_ was formed by adding _____ to the verb _walk_.
871	872

some	These adjective clauses begin with such words as **one of whom, several of whom, two of which, most of which.**
	The room has three windows, _one of which is always locked._
	The word in the clause that specifies the number to which the statement applies is the (_first, last_) word.
1141	1142

clause	WRONG: **I approached the squirrel, it ran away.**
	RIGHT: _On my approaching the squirrel,_ **it ran away.**
	Here we used a (_phrase, clause_).
1411	1412

Pronouns are generally used in place of nouns to avoid repeating the nouns.

Marian Anderson said she practiced her singing daily.

The two pronouns in this sentence are _____ and

_____.

1682

---

gives

1950

Neither Gary's mother *nor* his father was at home.
(Neither his mother *was* at home nor his father *was* at home.)

Because we are thinking of Gary's parents one at a time, we use a (*singular, plural*) verb.

1951

---

b

2219

When a fact permanently true follows an expression in the past tense such as "I didn't know that . . ." or "I forgot that . . . ," you might feel a strong pull to state this fact in the past, instead of the present, tense.

I forgot that there *were* eight quarts in a peck.

Is the verb *were* in the proper tense? (*Yes, No*)

2220

---

we

2488

The reporter snapped a picture of *her*.
The reporter snapped a picture of *me*.

Underline the correct pronouns:

The reporter snapped a picture of (*her, she*) and (*I, me*).

2489

---

neck, and

2757

The waves pound the rocks and gradually break them up into sand.

2758

---

a

3026

Here is another type of problem:

"Don't feed the animals."

Is this quotation a question? (*Yes, No*)

3027

Dad 62	Most of the questions we ask begin with a *helping verb*. a. **Will this pen write?** c. **Who borrowed my book?** b. **Is the water boiling?** d. **Does Tom like spinach?** Which is the only one of the above questions that does not begin with a helping verb? _____ 63
a 332	The two parts of a compound sentence should be *equal in importance*. **The Ortegas have a dog, and it is brown.** The fact that the dog is brown is much less important than the fact that the Ortegas have a dog. Is this a good compound sentence? (*Yes, No*) 333
which 602	Underline the correct relative pronoun: **any doctor** (*which, that*) 603
ing 872	A noun that is formed by adding *-ing* to a verb is called a **gerund** (pronounced *jare-und*). We can turn any verb into a gerund by adding *-ing* to it (sometimes making minor changes in the spelling). The gerund form of the verb *cook* is _____. 873
first 1142	The number of the group that these clauses single out may vary from **none of whom** to **all of whom**. Fill in the missing words to show that *none* of the coins are rare. (*None* may take either a singular or plural verb.) **I have many old coins,** _____ *are rare.* 1143
phrase 1412	a. **I approached the squirrel; it ran away.** b. **On my approaching the squirrel, it ran away.** c. **I approached the squirrel. It ran away.** d. **I approached the squirrel, it ran away.** e. **As I approached the squirrel, it ran away.** Which is a run-on sentence? _____ 1413

she, her 1682	**Marian Anderson said** *she* **practiced** *her* **singing daily.** The pronouns **she** and **her** refer to the noun _____. 1683
singular 1951	Underline the correct verb: **Neither Jack nor his sister** (*drive, drives*) **the car.** 1952
No 2220	**I** *forgot* **that there** *were* **eight quarts in a peck.** It is the verb *forgot* in the past tense that influenced the writer of this sentence to use the past tense *were* to express the permanent truth, instead of the present tense _____. 2221
her, me 2489	**The** *Whittens* **and** *we* **were the first to arrive.** This sentence is correct because if we used each subject separately, we would say: **The** *Whittens* **were the first to arrive.** (*Us, We*) **were the first to arrive.** 2490
None 2758	**An intriguing book title may get your attention but it takes a strong plot and interesting characters to hold it.** 2759
No 3027	**Did you hear the keeper say, "Don't feed the animals"?** The question is (*quotation, entire sentence*). 3028

c	A helping verb at the beginning of a sentence is the signal that a question is coming.
	a. **Will this pen write?**
	b. **Does Tom like spinach?**
	In each of these questions, we find the subject between the two parts of the _____.
63	64

	a. **The Ortegas have a brown dog.**
	b. **The Ortegas have a dog, and it is brown.**
No	Sentence *a* is a *simple* sentence; sentence *b* is a *compound* sentence. The sentence which is better because it doesn't give too much importance to the color of the dog is the (*simple, compound*) sentence.
333	334

that	Underline the correct relative pronoun:
	the school (*which, who*)
603	604

cooking	The gerund form of the verb *lie* is _____.
873	874

none of which	Fill in the missing words to show that *all* the coins are rare:
	I have many old coins, _____ *are rare.*
1143	1144

d	Before you correct a run-on sentence, consider the possibility of subordination.
	WRONG: **Illinois has a quarterback, nobody can stop him.**
	a. **Illinois has a quarterback, and nobody can stop him.**
	b. **Illinois has a quarterback whom nobody can stop.**
	Which sentence is a better repair—*a* or *b*? _____
1413	1414

Marian Anderson

1683

Marian Anderson said *she* **practiced** *her* **singing daily.**

The noun to which a pronoun refers is called its **antecedent.** It is the antecedent that gives a pronoun definite meaning.

The antecedent of the pronouns *she* and *her* is the noun

_____.

1684

---

drives

1952

If one of the subjects joined by **or** or **nor** is singular and the other plural, the verb should agree with the closer word.

Neither the words nor the music . . . very original.

The noun **words** is plural, and the noun **music** is singular. The missing verb should agree with (*words, music*) and should be (*is, are*).

1953

---

are

2221

I forgot that there were eight quarts in a peck.

Although this sentence is acceptable in colloquial (conversational) English, it does not meet the more rigid standards of formal speech or writing, which require that a fact that is permanently true should be stated in the (*present, past*) tense.

2222

We

2490

There will be plenty of room for *you* **and** *me.*

This sentence is correct because if we used each pronoun separately, we would say:

There will be plenty of room for *you.*
There will be plenty of room for (*me, I*).

2491

---

attention, but

2759

Most of us think of taxes as a necessary evil and we seldom think of what we get in return for them.

2760

---

entire sentence

3028

Did you hear the keeper say, "Don't feed the animals"?

Since the entire sentence and not the quotation is a question, we put the question mark (*inside, outside*) the quotes.

3029

verb 64	**Does this key fit?** The verb in this sentence consists of the two words _____ _____ . 65
simple 334	**We have an old apple tree, and it is in our back yard.** The important fact is that we have an apple tree. Whether it is located in the back yard or the front yard is a mere detail. The two ideas are (*equal, unequal*) in importance. 335
which 604	Underline the correct relative pronoun: **a bumblebee** (*who, which*) 605
lying 874	We often wish to talk about actions. We can't talk about *walked, stole,* or *studied,* but we can talk about *walking, stealing,* or _____ . 875
all of which 1144	Fill in the missing words to show that *a few* of the coins are rare: **I have many old coins,** _____ *are rare.* 1145
b 1414	One of the following sentences is a run-on sentence. Correct this sentence by supplying a period and a capital. Write only the word before and after the period. a. **I don't believe this rumor, it can't be true.** b. **If the fan is oiled, it will run more quietly.** _____ 1415

Marian Anderson	**The break was so small that I could hardly see** *it*.
	The antecedent of the pronoun *it* is the noun _____.
1684	1685

music	**Neither the words nor the music** *seems* **very original.**
is	If we reversed the order of **words** and **music,** would we need to change the verb *seems*? (*Yes, No*)
1953	1954

present	In this and the following frames, the first verb in each sentence is in the past tense. Underline the second verb which is in the proper tense. Remember that standard usage requires that a fact permanently true should be expressed in the present tense.
	The article *stated* **that potatoes** (*are, were*) **fattening.**
2222	2223

me	In this and the following frames, underline the correct pronouns. In each case, choose the form of the pronoun that you would use if the pronoun were used by itself.
	The remark made Roxanne and (*me, I*) **angry.**
2491	2492

evil, and	**Nations rise and nations fall.**
2760	2761

outside	a. **Would any good American want to admit to a child, "I didn't vote because the weather was bad"?**
	b. **Would any good American want to admit to a child, "I didn't vote because the weather was bad?"**
	The question mark is properly placed in sentence (*a, b*).
3029	3030

Does fit	**Must the tire be changed?** The verb in this sentence consists of the three words _____ _____ _____.
65	66
unequal	a. **We have an old apple tree in our back yard.** b. **We have an old apple tree, and it is in our back yard.** Sentence *a* is *simple;* sentence *b* is *compound.* The sentence which is better because it doesn't give too much importance to the location of the tree is the (*simple, compound*) sentence.
335	336
which	Underline the correct relative pronoun: **the nurse** (*who, which*)
605	606
studying	To talk about actions, we must give them names. We give actions names by adding *-ing* to verbs, thus changing the verbs into nouns which we call by the special name of _____.
875	876
a few of which	In using this type of clause, be careful to use **whom,** and not **which,** to refer to people. **The Adamos have three sons,** *two of (which, whom) are now attending college.*
1145	1146
rumor. It	Continue to follow the directions for the previous frame: a. **Whenever we buy a used car, we have a mechanic check it thoroughly.** b. **The Smiths didn't come, we waited until 9 o'clock.**
1415	1416

break

1685

Bananas are harvested while *they* **are still green.**

The antecedent of the pronoun *they* is _____.

1686

Yes

1954

a. **A few flowers or a plant is a good gift.**
b. **A plant or a few flowers is a good gift.**

Which sentence is correct? _____

1955

---

are

2223

The teacher *reminded* **us that "all right"** (*was, is*) **two separate words.**

2224

---

me

2492

Roger and (*her, she*) **disturbed everyone with their talking.**

2493

None

2761

The customer upset everything on the counter but finally bought nothing.

2762

---

a

3030

a. "_____?"   "_____!"
b. "_____"?   "_____"!

In diagrams *a*, the question mark and exclamation point are inside the final quotes; in diagrams *b*, outside the quotes.

Which diagrams show that the entire sentence, not the quotation, is a question or an exclamation? _____

3031

Must be changed
 	
66
	Sometimes, for emphasis, we put the verb ahead of its subject.
	
	    a. **The <u>rain</u> <u>came</u> down.**
	    b. **Down <u>came</u> the <u>rain</u>.**
	
	In which sentence does the verb precede the subject? _____
	
	                                                67

simple 336	a. **She bought an old lamp at a rummage sale, and it was brass.** b. **She bought an old lamp at a rummage sale, and it turned out to be a valuable antique.** Which compound sentence is better because the two ideas are more nearly equal in importance? _____ 337

who
 	
606
	How do we choose between **who** and **whom?** Which form we use depends on its use *within* the clause itself.
	Use **who** when the pronoun is the subject of the verb.
	Use **whom** when it is the object of a verb or preposition.
	    Any player <u>*who can beat Evert*</u> must be very good.
	
	The pronoun *who* is the subject of the verb _____.
	                                   607

gerunds 876	A gerund is a noun that is formed from a _____. 877
whom 1146	**Customs officials,** *many of (whom, which) speak English,* **examine your luggage.** 1147
come. We 1416	a. **This song is not original, it was adapted from a popular piece.** b. **Although Cambridge was a small town, it produced several of our most famous authors.** 1417

Bananas 1686	**Bananas are harvested while** *they* **are still green.** The noun **Bananas** is the _____ of the pro-noun *they*. 1687
a 1955	**The teacher or the students** (*select, selects*) **the topic.** The singular subject **teacher** requires a singular verb, but the plural subject **students** requires a plural verb. Because the plural subject **students** is closer to the verb, we choose the plural verb _____. 1956
is 2224	**The family** *moved* **to Hollywood, where Verna** (*gets, got*) **a job as an extra.** 2225
she 2493	**Neither the Mannings nor** (*us, we*) **would sell our land.** 2494
None 2762	**It took Columbus seventy days to cross the Atlantic but a modern jet makes the trip in less than six hours.** 2763
b 3031	First decide whether just the quotation or the entire sentence is a question. Then complete the punctuation at the end of this sentence: **When you get the wrong number, do you say, "I'm sorry** 3032

b 67	You are more likely to select the right subject if you look for the verb first. **Out jumped the rabbit.** After you find the verb **jumped,** ask yourself, "*Who* or *what* **jumped?**" The answer will always tell you the subject. The subject of this sentence is _____. 68
b 337	a. **The house was attractive. The neighborhood appealed to us.** b. **The house was attractive. Rents are high in our city.** Which pair of sentences would make a better compound sentence because their ideas are similar? _____ 338
can beat 607	The relative pronoun that starts an adjective clause is not always the subject. **Any player** *whom* <u>Ross</u> <u>can beat</u> **must be very poor.** The subject of the verb *can beat* is not the pronoun *whom,* but the noun _____. 608
verb 877	Do you remember that we also formed present participles by adding *-ing* to verbs? Could the word *swinging* be either a present participle or a gerund? (*Yes, No*) 878
whom 1147	In this and the following frames, subordinate the italicized statement by changing it to an adjective clause built on the "one of which" or "some of whom" pattern: **We have three clocks,** *and none of them keeps good time.* **We have three clocks,** _____ *keeps good time.* 1148
original. It 1417	a. **If you will sometimes agree with other people, they will be more likely to agree with you.** b. **Whales do not actually spout water, they merely blow out their moist breath.** _____ 1418

antecedent 1687	The pronouns *I* and *you* require no antecedents because there can be no doubt about to whom they refer. *I* always means the speaker and *you* the person(s) spoken to. If someone should say to you, "I know him" or "You know him," the only pronoun about which there can be any doubt is the pronoun (*I, you, him*). 1688

select
 	
1956
	Though a sentence with a singular and a plural subject joined by **or** or **nor** is correct when the verb agrees with the closer word, careful writers try to avoid such sentences.
	
	    a. **The teacher or the students select the topic.**
	    b. **The teacher selects the topic, or the students do.**
	
	A careful writer would prefer sentence (*a, b*).
	
	1957

got 2225	**Copernicus** *believed* **that the earth** (*revolves, revolved*) **around the sun.** 2226
we 2494	**I understand that Rick told** (*them, they*) **and** (*us, we*) **entirely different stories.** 2495
Atlantic, but 2763	**Are we solving this problem or merely postponing it?** 2764

. . . sorry"?
 	
3032
	When *both* the sentence and the quotation are questions, we use only one question mark, not two. This question mark goes inside the quotation.
	
	    Did the referee ask, "Are you ready?"
	
	Complete the punctuation at the end of this sentence:
	
	    Will Elena ask, "Have you seen Ralph
	
	3033

rabbit	**This story the class really enjoyed.** First find the verb—**enjoyed.** Then ask yourself, "*Who* or *what* **enjoyed?**" The subject of this sentence is _____.
68	69

a	a. **Brad apologized to Cathy. She was with her sister.** b. **Brad apologized to Cathy. She accepted his apology.** Which pair of sentences would make a better compound sentence because their ideas are related? _____
338	339

Ross	**Any player** *whom Ross can beat* **must be very poor.** Look at the arrow in the above sentence. The relative pronoun *whom* stands for the noun _____.
608	609

Yes	To decide whether an *-ing* word is a present participle or a gerund, we must see how it is used in the sentence. If the *-ing* word is used as an adjective, it is a _____ _____.
878	879

none of which	**Rita baby-sits with two children,** *and one of them is very mischievous.* **Rita baby-sits with two children,** _____ *is very mischievous.*
1148	1149

water. They	In this and the following frames, correct each run-on sentence by adding a conjunction (*and, but, or*), with a comma at the end of the first statement. Write only the word before and after the conjunction. **It wasn't what he said, it was the way he said it.**
1418	_____ 1419

Pronouns require antecedents whenever there can be any doubt about *whom* or *what* they refer to.

  a. **As soon as the boys got paid, they spent** *it.*
  b. **As soon as the boys got their pay, they spent** *it.*

In which sentence does the pronoun *it* have an antecedent?

_____

1689

---

a. **The kitchen wasn't large enough, and neither were the bedrooms.**
b. **Neither the kitchen nor the bedrooms were large enough.**

Although each subject has its proper verb, a careful writer would prefer sentence (*a, b*).

1958

Ethel Waters *met* **an editor who** (*urged, urges*) **her to write her life story.**

2227

We have decided that Ken and (*I, me*) **will play against Iris and** (*him, he*).

2496

The producers must give the program more variety or it will not survive.

2765

Exclamation points are handled in exactly the same way as question marks.

        "Which tooth hurts?" asked the dentist.
        "It's another home run!" shouted Lisa.

Is a comma used in addition to either a question mark or an exclamation point in these sentences? (*Yes, No*)

3034

class 69	In this and the following frames, underscore the verb with two lines; then underscore the subject with one line: **To this old inn came a strange visitor.** 70
b 339	a. **Cars were a luxury in those days, and they did not have self-starters.** b. **Cars were a luxury in those days, and few people could afford them.** Which is a better compound sentence? _____ 340

player
 	
609
	Keeping in mind that the pronoun *whom* stands for the noun *player*, let us straighten out the clause.
	
	    (player) (player)
	  whom Ross can beat = Ross can beat whom
	In this clause, the subject of the verb *can beat* is *Ross,* and its direct object is the relative pronoun _____.
	
	610

present participle 879	If the *-ing* word is used as a noun, it is a _____. 880
one of whom 1149	**The air is full of bacteria,** *but most of them are harmless.* **The air is full of bacteria,** _____ *are harmless.* 1150
said, but it 1419	**There will be a thorough inquiry, the truth will come out.** _____ 1420

b

1689

a. **Collecting stamps is an interesting hobby if one can afford to buy** *them.*
b. **Stamp collecting is an interesting hobby if one can afford to buy** *them.*

In which sentence does the pronoun *them* have an antecedent? _____

1690

---

a

1958

A few flowers or a plant is a good gift.

Although this sentence is correct, rewrite it so that each of the two subjects will have its own verb that agrees with it in number.

_____

_____

1959

---

urged

2227

Dorothea Dix's work *proved* **that the nurse** (*was, is*) **an indispensible aid in any war.**

2228

I, him

2496

Unfortunately, neither (*him, he*) **nor Connie remembered to feed the dog.**

2497

---

variety, or

2765

Andy eats like a horse but gains no weight.

2766

No

3034

a. **"Just look at that sunset!" exclaimed Mother.**
b. **"Just look at that sunset," exclaimed Mother!**

The exclamation point is properly placed in sentence (*a, b*).

3035

<u>came</u> <u>visitor</u>

70

Underline the verb and its subject:

Away sped the blue car.

71

---

b

a. **My birthday was approaching, and I was beginning to think about gifts.**
b. **My birthday was approaching, and I had always wanted to go deer hunting.**

Which is a better compound sentence? _____

340

341

---

whom

610

Here is a quick way to decide whether the clause signal is a subject or an object: When you see no other word before the verb that could possibly serve as its subject, then the relative pronoun is its subject, and **who** is correct.

who <u>escaped</u>   who <u>were</u> absent   who <u>bought</u> our car

The only word that could be the subject here is _____.

611

---

gerund

880

---

a. *Swinging* **makes me dizzy.**
b. **She went through the** *swinging* **door.**

In which sentence is *swinging* a present participle because it is used as an adjective to modify a noun? _____

881

---

most of which

1150

The college has eight hundred students, *and many of them come from foreign countries.*

The college has eight hundred students, _____

_____ *come from foreign countries.*

1151

---

inquiry, and the

1420

You had better take your time, you might make many mistakes.

_____

1421

a 1690	a. **It is advisable to have farming experience before buying** *one*. b. **It is advisable to have experience on a farm before buying** *one*. In which sentence does the pronoun *one* have an antecedent? ____ 1691
A few flowers are a good gift, and so is a plant. (*or* a similar sentence) 1959	If you were to add the words printed in parentheses at the point marked by the caret ($_\wedge$), would you need to change the italicized verb? If a change would be necessary, write only the form of the verb that would be required. If the verb would remain the same, write *Correct*. **Neither** $_\wedge$ *has* **a fur collar. (of my coats)** _____ 1960
is 2228	**The bus driver** *informed* **us that Philadelphia** (*is, was*) **very close to New York.** 2229
he 2497	**The "Devil's Ride" made Kathy and** (*she, her*) **sick.** 2498
None 2766	Lesson **77** Commas After Introductory Expressions [Frames 2768–2801]
a 3035	a. **Mr. Lutz exclaimed, "What a silly thing to buy!"** b. **Mr. Lutz exclaimed, "What a silly thing to buy"!** The exclamation point is properly placed in sentence (*a, b*). 3036

sped car 71	Underline the verb and its subject: **Here stands the monument to Frederick Douglass.** 72
a 341	**You can always add salt to your food, but you cannot remove it once it is in.** The first part of this sentence concerns adding salt to food; the second part concerns removing it. This compound sentence, therefore, is (*good, poor*). 342
who 611	If, on the other hand, the verb already has a subject, then the relative pronoun must be its object, and **whom** is correct. *whom I admire* *whom we invited* *whom the dog bit* The verbs in the above clauses already have subjects; therefore *whom* must be the (*subject, object*) in each clause. 612
b 881	a. *Swinging* **makes me dizzy.** b. **She went through the** *swinging* **door.** In which sentence is *swinging* a gerund because it is used as a noun to name an action? _____ 882
many of whom 1151	**The school has twelve rooms,** *and three of them are not used.* **The school has twelve rooms,** _____ *are not used.* 1152
time, or you 1421	**The election was close at hand, everyone was discussing politics.** _____ 1422

b 1691	Jo became a *scientist* because *science* interested her. Vi became a *musician* because *music* interested her. Jan became a *lawyer* because _____ interested her. 1692
Correct 1960	∧ These buses *go* to the stadium. (Either of) _____ 1961
is 2229	The author *went* back to Italy, where she (*visits, visited*) her birthplace. 2230
her 2498	The Chandlers and (*they, them*) attend the same church. 2499

	For variety or emphasis, we often begin a sentence with an adverbial modifier—a word, a phrase, or a clause.
	
	    a. **Our team has been winning recently.**
	    b. **Recently our team has been winning.**
	
	Which sentence begins with an introductory adverb? _____
	
	2768

a
 	
3036
	In this and the following frames, circle the letter of the sentence that is properly punctuated and capitalized:
	
	    a. **Our neighbor asked, "If he could borrow our lawnmower?"**
	    b. **Our neighbor asked, "May I borrow your lawnmower?"**
	
	3037

stands monument 72	Underline the verb and its subject. Don't overlook the helping verb. **Never has our team played any better.** 73
good 342	**Arthur drove most of the way, and we had two flat tires.** This compound sentence is (*good, poor*). 343
object 612	*whom I admire* *whom we invited* *whom the dog bit* When the relative pronoun that stands for a person is the direct object of the verb within the clause, we use the object form (*who, whom*). 613
a 882	Although gerunds serve as nouns, they still bear some resemblance to verbs. Like verbs, gerunds may take direct objects or subject complements, as no ordinary noun can do. *Observing ants* **is fascinating.** Because the noun *ants* receives the action of the gerund *observing*, it is its (*direct object, subject complement*). 883
three of which 1152	**Ralph brought his parents,** *and I had met neither of them before.* **Ralph brought his parents,** _____ *I had met before.* 1153
hand, and everyone 1422	In this and the following frames, correct the run-on sentence by inserting a semicolon. Write only the word before and after the semicolon. It isn't the car that kills, it's the driver behind the wheel. _____ 1423

law 1692	**Jan wants to be a lawyer because** *it* **interests her.** The person who made this sentence had *law* in mind when he used the pronoun *it*. As the sentence turned out, is the noun *law* present to serve as the antecedent for the pronoun *it*? (*Yes, No*) 1693
goes 1961	**Unseasonable weather** ⋀ *forces* **us to cut our prices. (and a heavy stock)** _____ 1962
visited 2230	Lesson **62** Using the Present Perfect Tense [Frames 2232–2261]
they 2499	**Gloria, not (***me, I***), thought up this slogan.** 2500
b 2768	To decide whether to use a comma after an introductory adverb such as *Recently* or *Finally* requires judgment. Using a comma sets the adverb apart and gives it more emphasis. a. *Finally,* **Ted arrived with the refreshments.** b. *Finally* **Ted arrived with the refreshments.** In which sentence is *Finally* given more emphasis? _____ 2769
b 3037	a. "How does the story end?" asked Miss Nolan. b. "How does the story end," asked Miss Nolan? 3038

has <u>team</u> <u>played</u>

73

Underline the verb and its subject:

Neither did Pam receive an invitation.

74

---

poor

343

We cannot prevent tornadoes, but we can minimize their destructiveness.

This compound sentence is (*good, poor*).

344

---

whom

613

Mr. Dolby is a person . . . <u>*worries*</u> *about nothing.*

Since the clause has no other subject, the relative pronoun would have to be the subject.

We would therefore choose the subject form (*who, whom*).

614

---

direct object

883

Being selfish **is a good way to lose friends.**

(Do you recall that *be,* with all its forms, is a linking verb?)

Because the adjective *selfish* completes the meaning of the gerund *Being,* it is its (*direct object, subject complement*).

884

---

neither of whom

1153

In a similar type of adjective clause, a noun precedes the words **of which**; for example, **the price of which, the result of which, the purpose of which.**

There are many words *the meanings of which have changed.*

What noun precedes *of which?* _____

1154

---

kills; it's

1423

Male mosquitoes do not bite people, they live on the juice of plants.

_____

1424

WRONG: **Jan wants to be a lawyer because** *it* **interests her.**
RIGHT: **Jan wants to be a lawyer because** *law* **interests her.**

This sentence was corrected by (*changing the pronoun to a noun, supplying an antecedent*).

1694

The sprayer ∧ *sells* **for two dollars. (with the chemical)**

_____

1963

A tense formed by combining a past participle with a form of **have** is called a **perfect tense.**

a. **decided**   b. **have decided**

Which verb is an example of a perfect tense? _____

2232

This is something for you and (*me, I*) **to think about**

2501

The pause at the comma gives the meaning of the introductory adverb more time to "sink in."

a. *Fortunately,* **the water was shallow.**
b. *Fortunately* **the water was shallow.**

The adverb *Fortunately* gets more attention in sentence *a* because it is set off with a _____.

2770

---

a. **"Just what I wanted!" exclaimed Ellen as she opened the box.**
b. **"Just what I wanted!", exclaimed Ellen as she opened the box.**

3039

<table>
<tr>
<td>

did Pam receive
(underlined)

74

</td>
<td>

Underline the verb and its subject:

Must each member participate in the discussion?

75

</td>
</tr>
<tr>
<td>

good

344

</td>
<td>

The car had no lights, and the accident occurred on our corner.

This compound sentence is (*good, poor*).

345

</td>
</tr>
<tr>
<td>

who

614

</td>
<td>

Mr. Dolby is a person . . . *nothing worries.*

Since the clause already has the subject *nothing,* the relative pronoun would have to be the object.

We would therefore choose the object form (*who, whom*).

615

</td>
</tr>
<tr>
<td>

subject
complement

884

</td>
<td>

The phrases formed by gerunds with their related words are called **gerund phrases.** These phrases can be used in any way that nouns are used.

Reading this book **changed her entire life.**

In this sentence the gerund phrase *Reading this book* is used as the _____ of the verb **changed.**   885

</td>
</tr>
<tr>
<td>

meanings

1154

</td>
<td>

Mr. Kerr bought several stocks *the value of which is very doubtful.*

What noun precedes *of which?* _____

1155

</td>
</tr>
<tr>
<td>

people; they

1424

</td>
<td>

It is not enough merely to feel appreciation, one should also express it.

_____

1425

</td>
</tr>
</table>

changing the pronoun to a noun	WRONG: Jan wants to be a lawyer because *it* interests her. RIGHT: Jan wants to study *law* because *it* interests her. This sentence was corrected by (*changing the pronoun to a noun, supplying an antecedent*).
1694	1695

Correct	ʌ **These questions** *are* **answered in this chapter. (Every one of)** _____
1963	1964

b	Just as we have three simple tenses—the present, past, and future—we also have three corresponding pertect tenses— the present perfect, the past perfect, and the _____ perfect.
2232	2233

me	Lesson **70** Informal and Formal Pronoun Usage [Frames 2503–2546]
2501	

comma	An introductory phrase gets more attention, too, when it is set off with a comma.
	     a. *For a child* he was remarkably strong.
	     b. *For a child,* he was remarkably strong.
	 Which sentence gives more emphasis to the prepositional phrase? ____

2770	2771

a	a. Lucinda screamed, "Look out for that child"! b. Lucinda screamed, "Look out for that child!"
3039	3040

Must member participate	Underline the verb and its subject: **Where does Mother keep the tools?**
75	76
poor	Use a compound sentence when you want your reader to think of two ideas in connection with each other. a. **The engine runs smoothly. It uses too much gas.** b. **The engine runs smoothly, but it uses too much gas.** Which arrangement brings the two ideas into closer relationship—*a* or *b?* _____
345	346
whom	Underline the correct relative pronoun after deciding whether it is used as the subject or the object of the verb: **People** (*who, whom*) <u>are</u> *honest themselves* **usually trust others.**
615	616
subject	**Your mistake was** *enclosing money in a letter.* The gerund phrase completes the meaning of the linking verb **was** and explains the subject **mistake.** The gerund phrase is therefore a (*direct object, subject complement*).
885	886
value	Ordinarily, the relative pronoun **whose** provides a smoother sentence than **of which** and requires fewer words. a. **I read a novel** *the ending of which is disappointing.* b. **I read a novel** *whose ending is disappointing.* Sentence *b* is _____ words shorter than sentence *a*. (How many?)
1155	1156
appreciation; one	One of the following sentences is a run-on sentence. In the other, the error was avoided by subordination. a. **After the children left, the cozy home seemed empty and cheerless.** b. **The children left, the cozy home seemed empty and cheerless.** Which sentence is correct?
1425	1426

supplying an antecedent	When a pronoun lacks an antecedent, we can correct the sentence in either of two ways: (1) Eliminate the pronoun; (2) supply an _____ to give the pronoun meaning.
1695	1696

is	The janitor ∧ *helps* the younger children cross the street. (or an older pupil)
	_____
1964	1965

future	Whether a verb is in the present perfect, past perfect, or future perfect tense depends on whether the participle is combined with a present, past, or future form of **have**.
	Underline the two present forms of **have**:
	has had have will have
2233	2234

	Now we consider a rule that holds more rigidly for writing than it does for speaking:
	Use the nominative case for a pronoun that follows any form of the verb **be** (*is, am, are—was, were, been*).
	Underline the correct pronoun:
	It must be (*they, them*) **who called.**
	2503

b	*In desperation* **the mayor threatened to resign.**
	To give more emphasis to the introductory phrase, would you put a comma after *desperation*? (*Yes, No*)
2771	2772

b	a. I get tired of being asked, "Is it hot enough for you"?
	b. I get tired of being asked, "Is it hot enough for you?"
3040	3041

<u>does</u> <u>Mother</u> <u>keep</u> 76	Underline the verb (three words) and its subject: **Can this dress be washed in soap and water?** 77
b 346	a. **You must shut the gate, or the dog will get out.** b. **You must shut the gate. The dog will get out.** Which arrangement brings out the relationship between the two ideas more clearly? _____ 347
who 616	Underline the correct relative pronoun: **The speaker** (*who, whom*) **he introduced was embarrassed by so much praise.** 617
subject complement 886	a. **We paid thirty dollars for** *repairs.* b. **We paid thirty dollars for** *repairing the motor.* In which sentence is a gerund phrase the object of the preposition **for?** _____ 887
two 1156	The relative pronoun **whose,** unlike **who** and **whom,** can be used for things as well as for persons. a. **I ordered a French soup** *the name of which I can't pronounce.* b. **I ordered a French soup** *whose name I can't pronounce.* Are both sentences correct? (*Yes, No*) 1157
a 1426	a. **We hiked through a dense woods, the sunlight hardly penetrated the thick foliage.** b. **We hiked through a dense woods, where the sunlight hardly penetrated the thick foliage.** Which sentence is correct? _____ 1427

page 153

It is sometimes used not as a pronoun, but as an introductory word to get a sentence started—especially in remarks about *time* or the *weather*. This usage is perfectly correct.

    a. *It* **was ten o'clock, and** *it* **was starting to rain.**
    b. **I guess I'm not musical because I've never enjoyed** *it*.

In which sentence is *it* correctly used? _____

1697

Correct

1965

A few cookies ∧ *satisfy* **my hunger after school. (or a sandwich)**

_____

1966

---

has, have

2234

Using a present form of **have** (*have* or *has*) with a participle gives us the **present perfect** tense.

Using the past form of **have** (*had*) with a participle gives us the **past perfect** tense.

        a. **have decided**   b. **had decided**

Which verb is in the present perfect tense? _____

2235

---

they

2503

Why is it that after every other verb in the English language we use an objective pronoun but that after any form of the verb **be** we use a nominative pronoun?

        The *chairman* **was** *he*. (*He* **was the** *chairman*.)

Can this sentence be turned around without changing the meaning? (*Yes, No*)

2504

Yes

2772

A comma is more frequently used after a long introductory phrase than after a short one.

a. **After several weeks of hard and persistent practice the team perfected this play.**
b. **For weeks the team practiced this play.**

In which sentence would you use a comma? _____

2773

---

b

3041

a. **Can't you just hear Aunt Inés saying, "I told you so"?**
b. **Can't you just hear Aunt Inés saying, "I told you so?"**

3042

<u>Can dress</u> <u>be washed</u> 77	Can a verb consist of more than one word? (*Yes, No*) 78
a 347	a. **I liked the dog. It was a collie.** b. **I liked the dog. The dog liked me.** Which pair of sentences would you connect with *and* to bring the two ideas into closer relationship? _____ 348
whom 617	Underline the correct relative pronoun: **Lucille Clifton is the poet** (*who, whom*) **I selected for my report.** 618

b
 	
887
	In this and the following frames, underline each gerund phrase and indicate its use by writing one of the following abbreviations in the parentheses:
	   S = Subject *SC = Subject Complement*
	   DO = Direct Object *OP = Object of Preposition*
	The sign forbids *fishing from this dock.* ( )
	
	888

Yes 1157	Even though **whose** may be used for things, there are times when you might prefer the **of which** construction. Change the **whose** to the **of which** construction (*see frame 1154*): **She makes chili** *whose preparation takes an entire day.* **She makes chili** _____ *takes an entire day.* 1158
b 1427	a. **The restaurant being crowded, we decided not to wait.** b. **The restaurant was crowded, we decided not to wait.** Which sentence is correct? _____ 1428

a	We often move a word group used as a subject to the end of the sentence and use an introductory *It* to fill the gap. (Such a subject, by the way, is called a *delayed subject*.) a. *To walk* **would be fun.** b. *It* **would be fun** *to walk.* In sentence *b*, the subject *to walk* has been moved to the end, and the gap is filled by the word _____.
1697	1698

satisfies	**A pedigreed cocker spaniel** ˄ *goes* **to the winner. (, as well as a year's supply of dog food,)** _____
1966	1967

a	Using a future form of **have** (*shall have* or *will have*) with a participle gives us the **future perfect** tense. a. **have decided** b. **shall have decided** c. **had decided** Which verb is in the future perfect tense? _____
2235	2236

Yes	**The** *chairman* **was** *he.* (*He* **was the** *chairman.*) This sentence can be turned around because any pronoun that follows a form of **be** means the same person or thing as the subject. In the above sentence, the pronoun *he* means the same person as the subject _____.
2504	2505

a	After short introductory phrases that state *time* or *place* (*In June, On Monday, At Buffalo*), commas are usually omitted. a. **On Friday, the Student Council meets.** b. **On the last Friday of each month, the Student Council meets.** The comma might well be omitted in sentence (*a, b*).
2773	2774

a	In the remaining frames, punctuate each sentence and supply capitals where necessary. Each sentence requires, among other things, a question mark or an exclamation point. **Are these flowers from your own garden asked Mrs. Chavez**
3042	3043

Yes

a. **shall, could, should, can, must, might**
b. **soon, never, now, always, not, surely**

Which group of words consists of helping verbs? _____

78   79

---

b

I liked the dog, and the dog liked me.

Because both parts of the sentence concern the relationship between the person and the dog, this is a (*good, poor*) compound sentence.

348   349

---

whom

When the relative pronoun is the object of a preposition, use the object form **whom**; for example, **to whom, for whom, from whom.**

Underline the correct relative pronoun:

Most of the candidates *for* (*who, whom*) *I voted* **were elected.**

618   619

---

fishing from
this dock (DO)

$S = Subject$ $SC = Subject\ Complement$
$DO = Direct\ Object$ $OP = Object\ of\ Preposition$

His violation was *driving through a red light.* (   )

888   889

---

the preparation
of which

Change the **whose** to the **of which** construction:

The minister told a story *whose point most people missed.*

The minister told a story _____

most people missed.

1158   1159

---

a

a. **Having no one to play with, the child turned to books for companionship.**
b. **The child had no one to play with, she turned to books for companionship.**

Which sentence is correct? _____

1428   1429

page 157

It 1698	Move the italicized subject to the end of the sentence and put the introductory word *It* in its place: *To take chances* **is foolish.** _____ 1699
Correct 1967	∧ **The boys** *are* **very willing to help. (Each of)** ——— 1968
b 2236	a. **Barbra Streisand** *sang* **for an hour.** b. **Barbra Streisand** *has sung* **for an hour.** In which sentence is the verb in the present perfect tense? ——— 2237
chairman 2505	**The** *chairman* **was** *he.* Since *he* could just as well be the subject of this sentence, we put it in the same case as if it were the subject of the sentence—that is, in the (*nominative, objective*) case. 2506
a 2774	Use a comma after an adverb clause that comes at the beginning of a sentence, ahead of the main clause. a. **You will change your mind** *when you hear all the facts.* b. *When you hear all the facts* **you will change your mind.** Which sentence requires a comma because the adverb clause comes first? ——— 2775
"Are . . . garden?" asked Mrs. Chavez. 3043	**The agent asked is the lady of the house at home** 3044

a	A main verb is sometimes separated from its helper by other words. (*True, False*)
79	80

good	a. **I was born in Utah. Our family soon moved to Oregon.** b. **I was born in Utah. This state has magnificent scenery.** Which pair of sentences could better be combined into a compound sentence? _____
349	350

whom	**Most of the candidates** *for whom I voted* **were elected.** We use the object form *whom* because the relative pronoun is the object of the preposition _____ .
619	620

driving through a red light (SC)	(Beginning with this frame, gerund phrases are not italicized.)
	
	    $S = Subject$ $SC = Subject\ Complement$
	  $DO = Direct\ Object$ $OP = Object\ of\ Preposition$
	
	Saving the precious topsoil is one of the aims of conservation. ( )

889	890

the point of which	Change the **whose** to the **of which** construction: **The doctor recommended a cough medicine** *whose name I can't recall.* **The doctor recommended a cough medicine** _____ _____ *I can't recall.*
1159	1160

a	a. **Ruth looked admiringly at Bob, she was impressed with his quick thinking.** b. **Ruth looked admiringly at Bob, impressed with his quick thinking.** Which sentence is correct? _____
1429	1430

It is foolish to
take chances.

1699

Move the italicized subject to the end of the sentence and
put the introductory word *It* in its place:

That he forgot his own birthday **seems strange.**

_____

_____

1700

---

is

1968

The superb acting ∧ *makes* **this an outstanding movie. (and
the fine directing)**

_____

1969

---

b

2237

Use the present perfect tense for an action that began in
the past but that continues, or whose effect continues, into
the present.

a. **Pat** *lived* **in Chicago for ten years.**
b. **Pat** *has lived* **in Chicago for ten years.**

In which sentence is Pat still living in Chicago? _____

2238

---

nominative

2506

WRONG: **The** *chairman* **was** *him.*

If we used the objective pronoun *him* after the verb **was,**
could we turn this sentence around without changing the
pronoun? (*Yes, No*)

2507

---

b

2775

Shorthand is difficult *unless you are a good speller.*
Unless you are a good speller, **shorthand is difficult.**

Only one of the above sentences contains a comma.

The comma is used when the adverb clause comes (*first,
last*).

2776

The agent asked,
"Is . . .
home?"

3044

Stop   shouted the bandleader

3045

True	The subject always comes ahead of the verb in every sentence. (*True, False*)
80	81

a	**I was born in Utah, but our family soon moved to Oregon.** This is a good compound sentence because both parts concern (*location, growth*).
350	351

for	Underline the correct relative pronoun: **My grandfather was a man to** (*whom, who*) **everyone came for advice.**
620	621

Saving the precious topsoil (S)	*S = Subject* *SC = Subject Complement* *DO = Direct Object* *OP = Object of Preposition* **The clerk made an error in adding the figures. ( )**
890	891

the name of which	In this and the following frames, subordinate each italicized statement to an **of which** construction, preceded by a noun ("the cause of which," "the price of which"): **Our school had an assembly,** *and the purpose was to improve sportsmanship.* **Our school had an assembly** _____
1160	_____ *was to improve sportsmanship.* 1161

b	Lesson **39** Adverbs as a Cause of Run-on Sentences
	[Frames 1432–1465]
1430	

It seems strange
that he forgot
his own birthday.

1700

Although such expressions as **"It says"** are commonly used, they are rather roundabout and clumsy.

It says **in the Bible that all men are brothers.**

Is there any noun in this sentence that tells you *who* or *what* the mysterious *It* is? (*Yes, No*)

1701

---

make

1969

---

b

2238

If a past action or its effect continues into the present time, use the (*present perfect, present*) tense.

2239

No

2507

Underline the correct pronoun—the one that you could use if you turned the sentence around:

The culprits were (*they, them*).

2508

---

first

2776

a. **Most voters have made up their minds before the campaign starts.**
b. **Before the campaign starts most voters have made up their minds.**

Which sentence requires a comma? _____

2777

"Stop!"
shouted the
bandleader.

3045

Will all these new inventions   asked the speaker   make people any happier

3046

False	You are less likely to make a mistake in selecting the sub- ject and the verb if you select the _____ first.
81	82
location	Use the conjunction **and** merely to add one idea to another. Use the conjunction **but** to point out a contrast or contra- diction between the two ideas. **I didn't want a reward, . . . Mr. Lopez made me take it.** Would **and** or **but** make better sense in this sentence?
351	_____ 352
whom	a. **Everyone values a friend . . . is dependable.** b. **Everyone values a friend upon . . . he can depend.** In which sentence would **whom** be correct? _____
621	622
adding the figures (OP)	$S = Subject$ $SC = Subject\ Complement$ $DO = Direct\ Object$ $OP = Object\ of\ Preposition$ **Being a road hog increases the likelihood of automobile accidents. ( )**
891	892
the purpose of which	**My tropical fish contracted a disease,** *and the cause of it is not known.* **My tropical fish contracted a disease** _____ _____ *is not known.*
1161	1162
	There is a special group of *adverbs* that we use to lead the reader smoothly from one sentence to the next: **then besides furthermore otherwise therefore however consequently nevertheless** Would you be likely to start a new piece of writing with one of these adverbs as your very first word? (*Yes, No*)
	1432

No

1701

---

a. **It says in the Bible that all men are brothers.**
b. **The Bible says that all men are brothers.**

Which sentence is more direct and to the point? _____

1702

In an adjective clause, a verb should agree with its subject—often the relative pronoun **who, which,** or **that.**

Whether these pronouns are singular or plural depends on whether their antecedents are singular or plural.

I like a dog *that is friendly.*

The antecedent of the pronoun *that* is the noun _____.

1971

---

present perfect

2239

Mr. Carter *spoke* **for an hour.**

This could mean that Mr. Carter spoke yesterday, last year, or ten years ago. The action belongs entirely to the past. To show that Mr. Carter is still speaking, we must replace *spoke* with the present perfect verb _____ *spoken.*

2240

---

they

2508

Underline the correct pronoun:

The only other girl in the class was (*her, she*).

2509

---

b

2777

---

a. **As the number of cars increases, many highways become inadequate.**
b. **Many highways become inadequate, as the number of cars increases.**

From which sentence should the comma be omitted? _____

2778

"Will . . .
inventions,"
. . . speaker,
"make . . . happier?"

3046

In punctuating this sentence, place the exclamation point just as you would place a question mark if the quotation were a question.

The people behind him were shouting   sit down

3047

Lesson 3 Two Sentence Patterns Built on Action Verbs

[Frames 84–128]

Use the conjunction **or** to express a choice between two ideas.

a. **I steered for the shore, . . . the wind kept turning the boat.**

b. **The course is getting harder, . . . I am getting lazier.**

In which sentence would **or** make good sense? _____

353

When a phrase such as **I think, I suppose, we hope** follows the relative pronoun, choose the same form of the pronoun you would choose if the phrase were not there.

> **It is John** *who* I think *should apologize.*

Disregarding the phrase *I think,* we choose *who* because it

is the subject of the verb _____ _____.

623

Railroads are still one of the cheapest means of hauling heavy loads. (   )

893

Our television set has a knob, *and I have never discovered its purpose.*

Our television set has a knob _____

_____ *I have never discovered.*

1163

| then | besides | furthermore | otherwise |
| therefore | however | consequently | nevertheless |

These words usually refer to something previously said. Besides pointing back to something previously said, do these adverbs lead on to the next idea? (*Yes, No*)

1433

b	a. **The sign said that hunting was not allowed.** b. **It said on the sign that hunting was not allowed.** Which sentence is more direct and to the point? _____
1702	1703

dog	**I like a dog** *that is friendly.* Because the pronoun *that* stands for the singular noun **dog,** it requires the singular verb _____.
1971	1972

has (spoken)	a. **Lynn** *built* **a fire.** b. **Lynn** *has built* **a fire.** One sentence means that the fire is past history. The other means that, although the fire was built in the past, the effect of the action continues into the present moment. Which sentence means that the fire is still burning? _____
2240	2241

she	Why is this rule so frequently disregarded in informal English? It is because after every verb except **be,** we are accustomed to hearing and seeing the *objective* form of pronouns. **Tom knows** *me.* **The police stopped** *him.* **Colby beat** *us.* The verb in each of the above sentences is followed by (*a nominative, an objective*) pronoun.
2509	2510

b	If an introductory adverb clause is shifted to the end of a sentence, a comma is usually (*necessary, unnecessary*).
2778	2779

shouting, "Sit down!"	**It was Cain who asked am I my brother's keeper**
3047	3048

Nearly every simple sentence that we make falls into one of three basic patterns. Two of these patterns involve *action verbs*.

Underline the one verb which indicates an *action:*

was   pushed   seemed

84

---

b

353

Our school is small, . . . we have good teams.

Which conjunction would bring out the meaning more clearly—**and** or **but?** _____

354

---

should apologize

623

I think   **I suppose**   **we hope**   **we guess**

When a clause like one of these follows the relative pronoun, pay no attention to it when choosing between **who** and **whom.**

Briggs is the candidate (*who, whom*) *will win.*
Briggs is the candidate (*who, whom*) I suppose *will win.*

In both sentences, the correct pronoun is (*who, whom*). 624

---

hauling heavy
loads (OP)

893

The next step is removing the tire from the rim. (**)**

894

---

the purpose
of which

1163

The county constructed a road, *and the need for it was very great.*

The county constructed a road _____

_____ *was very great.*

1164

Yes

1433

then   besides   furthermore   otherwise
therefore   however   consequently   nevertheless

Because these special adverbs point both backward and forward, they are useful steppingstones between sentences. Which of these adverbs would fit in best below?

I enjoy movies. _____**, I seldom go.**

1434

a 1703	**It shows in the diagram how to adjust the carburetor.** Rewrite the above sentence, eliminating the introductory **It**. _____ _____ 1704
is 1972	a. **I like a dog** _that is friendly._ b. **I like dogs** _that are friendly._ In which sentence does the relative pronoun _that_ have a plural antecedent? _____ 1973
b 2241	The present perfect tense always ties up the action in some way with the present. If the action is not still continuing, it at least has some effect upon a present situation. Underline the correct verb: **If Dad** (_took, has taken_) **the car, we shall have to walk.** 2242
an objective 2510	People find it difficult to make a single exception to the general pattern of our language and often say, "It was _us_" or "It was _them_"—just as they say, "It followed _us_" or "It followed _them._" Underline the pronouns that are _formally_ correct: **It was** (_we, us_). **It was** (_they, them_). 2511
unnecessary 2779	An adverb clause that comes at the end of a sentence does not usually require a comma. However, when the end clause begins with **for** (meaning **because**), a comma is needed to prevent misreading. **She had to wait** _for_ **the doctor was out.** Without a comma, might this sentence be puzzling? (_Yes, No_) 2780
asked, "Am . . . keeper?" 3048	**Wasn't it P. T. Barnum who said there's a sucker born every minute** 3049

pushed	Some action verbs indicate actions of the *body;* others indicate actions of the *mind.* a. **worked, drove, washed, wrote, lifted** b. **thought, hoped, believed, decided, understood** Which group of verbs indicates actions of the mind—*a* or *b?*
84	_____ 85
but	**Hockey originated in Canada, . . . many of the best players are Canadians.** Which conjunction would bring out the meaning more clearly—**and** or **but?** _____
354	355
who	**There are some customers . . . *you can never please.*** Because *you* is the subject of the verb *can please* in the adjective clause, the missing relative pronoun would be its direct object. We would therefore choose the relative pronoun (*who, whom*).
624	625
removing the tire from the rim (SC)	**Norman dreaded going to the dentist. ( )**
894	895
the need for which	**We studied a poem by Alice Walker, *and its meaning was very difficult.*** **We studied a poem by Alice Walker** _____ _____ *was very difficult.*
1164	1165
However, (*or* Nevertheless,)	then besides furthermore otherwise therefore however consequently nevertheless These adverbs modify the entire word group to which they are attached rather than a single word. **I enjoy movies.** *However,* **I seldom go.** The adverb *However* modifies (*go, I seldom go*).
1434	1435

The diagram shows how to adjust the carburetor.

1704

In this movie it shows how flour is manufactured.

Rewrite the above sentence, eliminating the introductory **It**.

_____

_____

1705

---

b

1973

I like dogs _that are friendly._

Because the pronoun _that_ stands for the plural noun **dogs**, it requires the plural verb _____.

1974

---

has taken

2242

---

a. **Mrs. Perkins** _was_ **our mayor for twelve years.**
b. **Mrs. Perkins** _has been_ **our mayor for twelve years.**

Which sentence would mean that Mrs. Perkins is still your mayor? _____

2243

---

we, they

2511

The use of objective pronouns after **be** has been gaining ground in informal usage. "It's _me_" is now generally accepted as correct speech. "It's _us_" is trailing close behind.

Although "It's _me_" violates the formal rule, it is acceptable in free-and-easy conversation. (_True, False_)

2512

Yes

2780

---

a. **I did not apply for the job was in another town.**
b. **I did not apply because the job was in another town.**

In which sentence is a comma needed to prevent misreading? _____

2781

---

said, "There's . . . minute"?

3049

Lesson **85** Pinning Down the Apostrophe

[Frames 3051–3093]

b

85

Action verbs can sometimes make complete statements about their subjects without the need of any other words.

 a. **Harvey** <u>stumbled</u>.
 b. **Harvey** <u>sharpened</u> . . .

Does the action verb make a complete statement about its subject in *a* or *b*? _____

86

---

and

355

Machinery is supposed to make life easier, . . . people seem to be busier than ever.

Which conjunction would bring out the meaning more clearly—**and** or **but?** _____

356

---

whom

625

There are some customers *whom you can never please.*

Now insert the phrase *I suppose* after the clause signal *whom.*

Underline the correct relative pronoun:

There are some customers (*who, whom*) I suppose *you can never please.*

626

---

going to the
dentist (DO)

895

We can sometimes improve a weak compound sentence by changing one of its statements to a gerund phrase used as the object of a preposition.

Nan watched the men work, **and she learned about motors.**
By *watching the men work,* **she learned about motors.**

We change the verb *watch* to the gerund _____.

896

---

the meaning
of which

1165

We camped at the foot of Silver Mountain, *and its top is snow-capped.*

We camped at the foot of Silver Mountain _____

_____ *is snow-capped.*

1166

I seldom go

1435

| then | besides | furthermore | otherwise |
| therefore | however | consequently | nevertheless |

Because these special adverbs are useful in leading smoothly from one idea to the next, they are called **conjunctive adverbs.** They are, however, adverbs. Do adverbs have the power of conjunctions to form compound sentences? (*Yes, No*)

1436

This movie
shows how flour
is manufactured.

1705

We often use the pronoun *you* to mean people in general. It is best to avoid this usage when it leads to absurdity.

You should remove all lipstick for a photograph.

This sentence becomes absurd when it is addressed to (*a girl, your father*).

1706

---

are

1974

Duke Ellington wrote the piece *which was played.*

If you changed the noun **piece** to **pieces,** would you also need to change the verb that follows it? (*Yes, No*)

1975

---

b

2243

a. **From that day on, I always** *feared* **the water.**
b. **From that day on, I always** *have feared* **the water.**

Which sentence is correct because the fear continues to exist at the present time? _____

2244

True

2512

Many people who accept "It's *me*" and perhaps "It's *us*" draw the line at "It's *him*," "It's *her*," and "It's *them*."

You are less likely to be criticized for saying "It's *me*" than for saying "It's *them*." (*True, False*)

2513

---

a

2781

Use a comma before **for** whenever you can put **because** in its place.

    a. **They sold us two** *for* **the price of one.**
    b. **We didn't stop** *for* **the light had turned green.**

Which sentence requires a comma before *for*? _____

2782

Fred Sims misplaces and loses keys and other things and then blames his brothers.

How many words in this sentence end with **s**? _____

3051

a	a. **Our guest brought**
	b. **Our guest arrived**
	Does the action verb make a complete statement about its subject in *a* or *b*? _____
86	87

but	It is not a good idea to begin a sentence with a conjunction. Let the conjunction stand between the two parts of the sentence where it can do its job of connecting.
	a. **It was a hot day. And all the windows were open.**
	b. **It was a hot day, and all the windows were open.**
	The conjunction **and** is properly used in (*a, b*).
356	357

whom	Underline the correct relative pronoun in this and the following frames. (Pay no attention to the added phrase **I believe.**)
	It is the parents (*who, whom*) **I believe are responsible.**
626	627

watching	*Nan watched the men work,* **and she learned about motors.**
	By *watching the men work,* **she learned about motors.**
	After changing the verb *watch* to the gerund *watching,* we put an appropriate preposition before it—in this case, the preposition _____.
896	897

the top of which	Lesson **31** Noun Clause Devices
	[Frames 1168–1196]
1166	

No	Many run-on sentences result from mistaking conjunctive adverbs for conjunctions. It is easy to prove that these words are not conjunctions.
	The line broke, *and* **the fish got away.**
	Can the conjunction *and* be shifted to any other position in this sentence? (*Yes, No*)
1436	1437

your father

1706

You should remove all lipstick for a photograph.
One should remove all lipstick for a photograph.
Girls should remove all lipstick for a photograph.

Because **You** does not apply to the person spoken to, we can substitute the pronoun _____ or the noun _____.

1707

Yes

1975

---

a. **Banks will not hire people** *who gamble.*
b. **Banks will not hire a person** *who gambles.*

In which sentence would you consider *who* a plural pronoun?

_____

1976

---

b

2244

---

a. **Archie** *has lost* **his voice.**
b. **Archie** *lost* **his voice.**

Which sentence would you use to indicate that Archie's voice is still gone? _____

2245

True

2513

Is there general agreement about the informal usage of all pronouns after forms of the verb **be?** (*Yes, No*)

2514

---

b

2782

When an introductory adverb clause is short, you may omit the comma, as you do in short compound sentences.

a. **When I saw the price, I changed my mind.**
b. **When I saw that the price was unreasonably high, I changed my mind.**

From which sentence might the comma be omitted? _____

2783

---

eight

3051

Fred Sims misplaces and loses keys and other things and then blames his brothers.

Every word in this sentence is correctly spelled.

Is there an apostrophe before any one of the eight final **s's?** (*Yes, No*)

3052

b	The action verb that makes a complete statement about its subject gives us our first sentence pattern:
	
	PATTERN I: *Subject—Action Verb*
	
	    a. **Our guest brought . . .**
	    b. **Our guest arrived.**
	
	Which word group represents **Pattern I?** _____

87	88

b	a. **I dropped the light bulb, but it didn't break.** b. **I dropped the light bulb. But it didn't break.** The conjunction **but** is properly used in (*a, b*).
357	358

who	**Most of the women** (*who, whom*) **take our business course get excellent jobs.**
627	628

By	*Nan watched the men work,* **and she learned about motors.** <div align="center">**Nan**</div>**By** *watching the men work,* ~~she~~ **learned about motors.** Since we lost the subject *Nan,* we put it back at the beginning of the main statement in place of the pronoun _____.
897	898

	A noun clause is one that is used as a _____.
	1168

No	WRONG: **The line broke,** *therefore* **the fish got away.** WRONG: **The line broke, the fish** *therefore* **got away.** Can the adverb *therefore* be shifted from its position between the two statements? (*Yes, No*)
1437	1438

Mother, you can't play professional football without getting a few scratches.

Substitute another word for **you:**

Mother, _____ can't play professional football without getting a few scratches.

1708

---

a

1976

Ordinarily we have no trouble in making the subject and verb of an adjective clause agree.

When the relative pronoun stands for a singular noun, we use a singular verb. When the relative pronoun stands for a plural noun, we use a _____ verb.

1977

---

a

2245

Underline the correct verb:

When I was a small child, I (*disliked, have disliked*) **spinach.**

2246

No

2514

What are we to do while we wait for time to settle this problem of pronoun usage? One solution might be to use whatever pronoun seems natural and comfortable to us in our everyday speech (as many people do).

If you adopted this policy, would you be entirely free from criticism? (*Yes, No*)

2515

---

a

2783

Use a comma wherever it is needed to prevent misreading—regardless of the length of the introductory phrase or clause.

Insert a comma to prevent misreading of this sentence. (Try pausing after each word until you find the point where the pause makes sense.)

If you can get some information about campus life.

2784

No

3052

Should you put an apostrophe before the final **s** in every word that ends in **s?** (*Yes, No*)

3053

88

b

Any sentence is **Pattern I** if the action verb *by itself* makes a complete statement about its subject—no matter how many other words and phrases may be present.

a. **Our guest arrived.**

b. **Our guest from Ohio arrived by plane this morning.**

Both *a* and *b* are **Pattern I** sentences. (*True, False*)

89

---

a

a. **You must follow the recipe precisely. Or the fudge will be a failure.**

b. **You must follow the recipe precisely, or the fudge will be a failure.**

The conjunction **or** is properly used in (*a, b*).

358

359

---

who

Most of the women (*who, whom*) **we train get excellent jobs.**

628

629

---

she

He sent a check, and *he didn't sign his name.*

He sent a check _____ *signing his name.*

After you've changed the verb *sign* to the gerund *signing*, what preposition would make good sense in the blank space?

_____

898

899

---

noun

Many noun clauses begin with the clause signal **that.**

That I had saved the receipt **was fortunate.**

The noun clause is the _____ of the verb **was.**

1168

1169

Yes

WRONG: **The line broke,** *therefore* **the fish got away.**

WRONG: **The line broke, the fish** *therefore* **got away.**

If *therefore* had the power of the conjunction *and* to bind these two sentences together, could it be shifted from its position between the two statements? (*Yes, No*)

1438

1439

one, a person, a player (*or a similar word*) 1708	In this and the following frames, if the italicized pronoun needs an antecedent, cross out the pronoun and write in the parentheses the word or words it is supposed to mean. Where the pronoun is correctly used, write *Correct*. **I seldom cook because I don't enjoy it.** (_____) 1709
plural 1977	However, in sentences that contain expressions like "one of those fellows who . . . ," people are sometimes confused as to which of two words the relative pronoun stands for. **Roy was one of those fellows** *who . . . always in debt.* If *who* stands for **one,** we would say *who is;* if *who* stands for **fellows,** we would say *who* _____. 1978
disliked 2246	Underline the correct verb: **Ever since I was a small child, I** (*disliked, have disliked*) **spinach.** 2247
No 2515	Another solution might be to use the nominative case on "dress-up" occasions or when we are with people who observe the traditional rule. a. **It must have been** *them.* b. **It must have been** *they.* Which sentence would be preferred by people who strictly follow the traditional rules of English? _____ 2516
can, get 2784	Insert a comma to prevent misreading: **To help the government started an extensive relief program.** 2785
No 3053	An apostrophe is not an ornament for decorating a final **s.** One of its main uses is to show ownership. To own something means to possess it. We say, therefore, that a word that shows ownership is in the **possessive case.** Underline two nouns that are in the possessive case: **Another boy's name was in Paul's book.** 3054

True 89	**Our guest** from Ohio **arrived by plane this morning.** This is a **Pattern I** sentence because **Our guest arrived** is (*complete, incomplete*) in its meaning. 90
b 359	**Lesson 10 The Compound Predicate as a Word-saver** [Frames 361–393]
whom 629	**It was the principal** (*who, whom*) **issued the order.** 630
without 899	Eliminate the **and** by changing each italicized statement to a gerund phrase used as the object of a preposition. (Prepositions: *by, for, of, on, in, before, after, without*) **Jerry has an annoying habit, and** *it is slamming doors.* _____ _____ 900

subject
 	
1169
	Using a "that" noun clause at the beginning of a sentence sounds rather stiff and formal for ordinary conversation.
	
	    a. *That I had saved the receipt* **was fortunate.**
	    b. **It was fortunate** *that I had saved the receipt.*
	
	Which sentence sounds more informal? _____
	
	1170

No 1439	WRONG: **The line broke,** *therefore* **the fish got away.** The above sentence is a run-on sentence because there is no (*adverb, conjunction*) to hold the two statements together. 1440

cooking 1709	Continue to follow the directions for the previous frame: **Typing would make your paper look neater if you can borrow** *one*. (_____) <div align="right">1710</div>
are 1978	<div align="center">**Roy was one of those fellows** *who . . . always in debt.*</div> Does *who* stand for **one** or **fellows?** Let's reason it out: Roy is just one of many fellows. What kind of fellows? Fellows *who are* always in debt. Since *who* refers to the plural noun **fellows,** we use the plural verb (*is, are*) in our problem sentence. <div align="right">1979</div>
have disliked 2247	Underline the correct verb: **We don't want to move because we** (*lived, have lived*) **in our present house for many years.** <div align="right">2248</div>

b
 	
2516
	Or you can play safe by putting your sentence in a way that avoids the problem altogether (and offends no one).
	    a. **It was** *we* **who made the suggestion.**
	    b. **We were the** *ones* **who made the suggestion.**
	Which sentence sidesteps the problem of whether to use the nominative or the objective case after a form of **be?** _____
	<div align="right">2517</div>

help, the 2785	Insert a comma to prevent misreading: <div align="center">**With John Sonia formed a business partnership.**</div> <div align="right">2786</div>

boy's, Paul's
 	
3054
	To form the possessive case of a singular noun, add an apostrophe *s* (**'s**) without making any change in the spelling.
	
	    a boy's haircut **the boss's desk**
	    a lady's dress **Miss Jones's room**
	
	Look at the word that precedes each apostrophe.
	
	Each of these words is (*singular, plural*). <div align="right">3055</div>

a. **The coaches agreed with each other.**
b. **The coaches compared the two teams.**

Read just the *subject* and *verb* in each sentence, omitting the words that follow them.

Which sentence is **Pattern I** because the verb by itself can make a statement about its subject that is *complete* in meaning? _____

complete	
90	91

In a compound sentence, the conjunction **and, but,** or **or** stands between two word groups, each with a subject and a predicate.

Hank swung at the ball, but he missed it by a foot.

What is the subject of the part of the sentence that follows the conjunction **but?** _____

361

---

who	**The major under** (*who, whom*) **he served was a strict disciplinarian.**
630	631

(Prepositions: *by, for, of, on, in, before, after, without*)

We used the old lumber **and saved a lot of money.**

Jerry has an annoying habit of slamming doors.	_____
	_____
900	901

That I had saved the receipt **was fortunate.**
. . . was fortunate *that I had saved the receipt.*

b	Moving the noun clause to the end of the sentence leaves a gap that must be filled before the verb _____.
1170	1171

---

a. **The line broke,** *therefore* **the fish got away.**
b. **The line broke, and** *therefore* **the fish got away.**

conjunction	Which sentence is correct because a conjunction connects the two statements? _____
1440	1441

a typewriter (a machine)	The straight and narrow path would not be so narrow if more people traveled *it*. (_____)
1710	1711
are	Underline the correct verb: **Roy was one of those fellows** *who* (*is, are*) *always in debt.*
1979	1980
have lived	Underline the correct verb: **Before entering law school, my brother** (*spent, has spent*) **three years in the Navy.**
2248	2249
b	a. **It was Irene who answered the phone.** b. **It was she who answered the phone.** c. **She was the one who answered the phone.** The two sentences that are so worded as to avoid the problem of case after the verb **be** are _____ and _____.
2517	2518
John, Sonia	This and the following frames review the main points of this lesson. *In England* **motor traffic keeps to the left-hand side of the road.** Would inserting a comma after the italicized phrase make this phrase more emphatic? (*Yes, No*)
2786	2787

singular	To form the possessive case of a plural noun that ends in **s** (as most plural nouns do), add only an apostrophe.
	
	    the boys' voices **the players' uniforms**
	    the ladies' coats **the Joneses' cottage**
	
	Look at the word that precedes each apostrophe.
	
	Each of these words is (*singular, plural*).

3055	3056

a

91

a. **The coaches agreed**
b. **The coaches compared**

Which group of words requires the addition of other words to complete its meaning? _____

92

---

he

361

Hank <u>swung</u> **at the ball, but (he)** <u>missed it by a foot.</u>

Would this sentence still make good sense if we omitted the subject **he** that follows the conjunction? (*Yes, No*)

362

---

whom

631

All the young people (*who, whom*) **the company hires must have high school diplomas.**

632

By using the old lumber, we saved a lot of money.

901

(Prepositions: *by, for, of, on, in, before, after, without*)

The customer left the store, and *he didn't wait for his change.*

_____

_____

902

---

was

1171

It **was fortunate** *that I had saved the receipt.*

We fill the gap left as a result of moving the noun clause with

the *introductory* word _____.

1172

---

b

1441

| then | besides | furthermore | otherwise |
| therefore | however | consequently | nevertheless |

If you mistake these conjunctive adverbs for conjunctions, you are likely to write many run-on sentences.

Al shut off the alarm, *then* **he went back to sleep.**

This sentence is a (*run-on, correct*) sentence.

1442

Correct 1711	If you park there, *they* (_____) will tow away your car. 1712
are 1980	On the other hand, our meaning might be different so that the pronoun refers to the singular word **one**, and not to the plural noun that follows it. **Fred was the** *only one* **of those fellows** *who was hired.* Several fellows applied for the job, but only _____ was hired. 1981
spent 2249	Now we shall consider a problem that sometimes arises when we use infinitives. Infinitives, too, have a present perfect form in which they are combined with the verb **have**. a. **to write** b. **to have written** Which infinitive is in the present perfect tense? _____ 2250
a, c 2518	In all formal speech or writing, remember to use a nominative pronoun after any form of the verb **be** (*is, am, are—was, were, been*). a. **I** **he** **she** **we** **they** b. **me** **him** **her** **us** **them** The pronouns to be used after forms of **be** are in group (*a, b*). 2519
Yes 2787	*Recently* **complaints about rising taxes have been increasing.** Inserting a comma after *Recently* would give this adverb (*more, less*) emphasis. 2788
plural 3056	a. **boy's** **lady's** **teacher's** **player's** b. **boys'** **ladies'** **teachers'** **players'** The plural possessive pronouns are those that end with an (*apostrophe, apostrophe s*). 3057

The coaches compared . . . (What?)

What did the coaches compare—the fans, the stadiums, or the teams? We don't know.

Until we answer this question, the meaning of the sentence is (*complete, incomplete*).

93

Yes

362

Hank swung at the ball but missed it by a foot.

This is no longer a compound sentence because, after the conjunction **but,** we now have only a (*subject, predicate*).

363

---

whom

632

This water color was painted by a girl (*who, whom*) **I think has unusual talent.** (Pay no attention to the explanatory words **I think.**)

633

The customer left the store without waiting for his change.

902

(Prepositions: *by, for, of, on, in, before, after, without*)

I consulted a number of people **and decided to become a chemist.**

_____

_____

903

It

1172

That anyone should believe this story **seems absurd.**
It **seems absurd** *that anyone should believe this story.*

After moving the noun clause to the end of the sentence, we put the *introductory* word *It* in the (*subject, object*) position, which has become vacant.

1173

---

run-on

1442

A true conjunction would have to stand between the two word groups that it holds together.

WRONG: **Al shut off the alarm,** *then* **he went back to sleep.**
WRONG: **Al shut off the alarm, he** *then* **went back to sleep.**

We know that *then* is not a conjunction because it (*can, cannot*) be shifted to another position.

1443

the police (*or whoever it might be*) 1712	Although Mr. Neville was very wealthy, he made poor use of *it*. (_____) 1713
one 1981	Fred was the *only one* of those fellows *who was hired.* If we said ". . . fellows *who were hired*," we should be stating something that isn't true. Because only *one* of the fellows was hired, the pronoun *who* stands for the noun (*one, fellows*). 1982
b 2250	Verbs such as **hope, plan, expect,** and **intend** all look ahead to some future action or event. Can you hope, plan, expect, or intend to do something in time that is already past? (*Yes, No*) 2251
a 2519	In this and the following frames, underline the *two* pronouns —nominative or objective—that would be correct in each sentence. Where pronouns follow any form of the verb **be,** select only nominative pronouns, according to the standard of formal usage. **If I were** (*he, her, them, she, him*), **I should accept the offer.** 2520
more 2788	**Plants grew on our earth** *long before people appeared on the scene.* If you shifted the italicized clause to the beginning of the sentence, would you insert a comma after the word *scene*? (*Yes, No*) 2789
apostrophe 3057	a. **the boy's room** b. **the boys' room** Which means the room of *one* boy because the word that precedes the apostrophe is the singular noun **boy?** _____ 3058

incomplete 93	**The coaches compared the two teams.** Now we know what the coaches compared, and the meaning of our sentence is complete. Which word follows the verb **compared** to complete the meaning of the sentence? _____ <div align="right">94</div>
predicate 363	**Hank <u>swung at the ball</u> but <u>missed it by a foot</u>.** This sentence has two predicates. Each predicate makes a statement about the same subject, _____. <div align="right">364</div>
who 633	**The magician called up a boy** (*who, whom*) **I suppose he had planted in the audience.** <div align="right">634</div>
After consulting a number of people, I decided to become a chemist. 903	Continue to follow the directions for the previous frames: **Leslie has a handy gadget, and** *it slices vegetables.* _____ _____ <div align="right">904</div>
subject 1173	*That the weather affects people's moods* **has been proved.** Supply the missing words, using the introductory word *It*: _____ *that the weather affects people's moods.* <div align="right">1174</div>
can 1443	a. **Al shut off the alarm. Then he went back to sleep.** b. **Al shut off the alarm; then he went back to sleep.** c. **Al shut off the alarm, then he went back to sleep.** Which is a run-on sentence? _____ <div align="right">1444</div>

his wealth (his money)	Here is a remark about the weather:
	It (_____) **is always cool in the evening.**
1713	1714

one	Underline the correct verb:
	Fred was the *only one* **of those fellows** *who* (*was, were*) **hired.**
1982	1983

	After verbs that point to the future, such as **hope, plan, expect,** and **intend,** use a present infinitive (*to go, to see*), not a present perfect infinitive (*to have gone, to have seen*).
No	Underline the correct infinitive:
	I intended (*to write, to have written*) **you about my operation.**
2251	2252

	Judy drove Phil and (*I, us, she, they, her*) **to the game.**
	Note: When a pronoun is coupled with a noun—or another pronoun—remember the device of using each pronoun singly:
he, she	**Judy drove Phil to the game.**
	Judy drove __?__ to the game.
2520	2521

	On Tuesday **the new semester begins.**
	In Europe **gasoline is more expensive.**
Yes	Is a comma necessary after a short introductory phrase that states *time* or *place*? (*Yes, No*)
2789	2790

	a. **the boy's room**
	b. **the boys' room**
a	Which means the room of *more than one* boy because the word that precedes the apostrophe is the plural noun **boys?**
3058	3059

teams 94	A word that follows a verb and completes the meaning of a sentence is known as a **complement,** which is the grammar name for a *completer.* A complement, or completer, is sometimes needed after a verb to _____ the meaning of a sentence. 95
Hank 364	a. **Hank swung at the ball, but he missed it by a foot.** b. **Hank swung at the ball but missed it by a foot.** Sentence *a* is a compound sentence because the conjunction **but** connects two sentences. Sentence *b* is a simple sentence with a compound predicate because the conjunction **but** connects two _____. 365
whom 634	In free-and-easy conversation, **who** has largely driven out **whom.** In formal speech and writing, however, **whom** should be used for all objects. a. INFORMAL: **I just met a woman . . . you know.** b. FORMAL: **Our director is a woman . . . citizens respect.** The pronoun **who** would be considered an error in (*a, b*). 635
Leslie has a handy gadget for slicing vegetables. 904	*Sue got out of the car* **and turned her ankle.** (It happened as Sue was getting out.) _____ _____ 905
It has been proved 1174	Make the following sentence more informal by moving the noun clause to the end: *That Norma won both prizes* **seems unfair.** _____ _____ 1175
c 1444	**His parents needed his help, or** *otherwise* **Ken would have gone to college.** If you omitted the conjunction **or,** the above sentence would then be a (*compound, run-on*) sentence. 1445

Correct 1714	**We found a delightful souvenir shop where** *they* (_____ _____) **spoke English and Zuñi.** 1715
was 1983	To make a statement about the *only one* among a larger number, always use a singular verb in the adjective clause. Otherwise, your clause will apply to the entire group. **We bought the** *only one* **of the TV sets** *that was on sale.* How many TV sets were on sale? (*Only one, More than one*) 1984
to write 2252	Underline the correct infinitive: **I had hoped** (*to have baked, to bake*) **a cake for your birthday.** 2253
us, her 2521	**Bob and** (*me, him, her, I, he*) **secured most of the advertisements.** 2522
No 2790	*Whenever you are in doubt about manners,* **do what seems reasonable to you.** If you shifted the italicized clause to the end of the sentence, would this sentence still require a comma? (*Yes, No*) 2791
b 3059	There are a small number of plural nouns that do not end in **s,** as nearly all plural nouns do. a. **boy**　　**doctor**　　**student**　　**engineer** b. **men**　　**women**　　**children**　　**people** In neither group do the nouns end in **s.** Which group consists of plural nouns? _____ 3060

	The police blocked the road.
complete	Because the noun **road** is needed to complete the meaning of this sentence, it is a _____.
95	96

	A careful writer streamlines his writing by eliminating all useless words. Words that add nothing to the meaning, clearness, or interest of a sentence should be dropped.
predicates (*or* verbs)	a. **Hank swung at the ball, but he missed it by a foot.** b. **Hank swung at the ball but missed it by a foot.**
	Which sentence says the same thing in fewer words? _____
365	366

	a. **It is the original thinker . . . the world needs today.** b. **Is Dick the boy . . . you invited?**
b	In which sentence would *who* be acceptable as informal usage? _____
635	636

In (on, *etc.*) getting out of the car, Sue turned her ankle.	**Paul parked the car on a hill, and** *he didn't pull the brake.* _____ _____
905	906

	Make the following sentence more informal by moving the noun clause to the end:
It seems unfair that Norma won both prizes.	*That snakes have the power to hypnotize* **is a false idea.** _____ _____
1175	1176

	WRONG: **His parents needed his help,** *otherwise* **Ken would have gone to college.**
run-on	You can repair this run-on sentence either by inserting a period after the word *help* and then using a capital letter or by inserting a _____. (What punctuation mark?)
1445	1446

the clerks, the owners (*or whoever it might have been*) 1715	**Our friends fished all morning but didn't catch a single** *one.* (_____) 1716
Only one 1984	Now we shall change the meaning by making the verb in the adjective clause plural: **We bought** *one* **of the TV sets** *that were on sale.* How many TV sets were on sale? (*One, More than one*) 1985
to bake 2253	Underline the correct infinitive: **I meant** (*to pay, to have paid*) **this bill on time.** 2254
I, he 2522	Be on the alert for pronouns that follow forms of the verb **be** (*is, am, was—are, were, been*). **How can you be sure that it was** (*we, us, me, they, her*)? 2523
No 2791	**We had to cut our speed** *because* **the road suddenly became very rough.** If you changed *because* to *for,* would you insert a comma after the word **speed?** (*Yes, No*) 2792
b 3060	Of the nouns having irregular plurals that do not end in **s,** the most frequently used are— **men women children people** These plural nouns look like singular nouns. We make them possessive in the same way that we make singular nouns possessive: by adding an (*apostrophe, apostrophe s*). 3061

The kind of complement that *receives the action* of the verb or *shows the result* of this action is called a **direct object.**

The teacher will correct the tests.

Which word is a direct object because it *receives the action* of the verb **will correct?** _____

97

---

b

366

Bobby frightened the bird, and it flew up into a tree.

What is the subject of the part of the sentence which follows the conjunction **and?** _____

367

---

b

636

Lesson **17** Subordination by Adjective Clauses

[Frames 638–676]

Paul parked the car on a hill without pulling the brake.

906

Beth had not yet completed her commercial course, **and she was offered a good job.** (Try *before.*)

_____

_____

907

It is a false idea that snakes have the power to hypnotize.

1176

Combine each pair of sentences into a single sentence by changing the italicized sentence to a noun clause. Begin your sentence with *It* and put the noun clause at the end.

I took along a flashlight. **This was very lucky.**

_____

_____

1177

---

semicolon

1446

It was his own fault. *Nevertheless,* **I felt sorry for him.**
It was his own fault; *nevertheless,* **I felt sorry for him.**

Are both arrangements correct? (*Yes, No*)

1447

fish 1716	*It* (_____) **is very strange that Briggs refused the promotion.** 1717
More than one 1985	When you use the words *the only one,* always use a singular verb in the adjective clause. Otherwise the clause will apply to the entire group, which you don't want it to do. Underline the correct word: **This is** *the only one* **of our clocks which** (*keeps, keep*) **accurate time.** 1986

to pay
 	
2254
	On the other hand, you can be happy or unhappy about an action that has already been completed.
	
	    a. **I intended** *to have seen* **this game.**
	    b. **I am happy** *to have seen* **this game.**
	
	In which sentence does the present perfect infinitive make good sense because it refers to a completed action? _____
	
	2255

we, they 2523	**My brother divided his stamp collection between Cliff and** (*she, me, him, he, I*). 2524
Yes 2792	**When I read** *long and tiresome descriptions of nature,* **I get drowsy.** If you omitted the italicized words, would it be all right to omit the comma? (*Yes, No*) 2793

apostrophe s
 	
3061
	To form the possessive of the few plural nouns that do not end in **s,** add **'s**—just as you do with any singular noun.
	
	    the men's lounge **the children's program**
	    women's fashions **the people's choice**
	
	We know that each of these possessive nouns is plural because the word that precedes each apostrophe is (*singular, plural*).
	
	3062

tests	**The cashier made a slight mistake.** Which word is a direct object because it *shows the result* of the action of the verb **made?** _____
97	98

it	**Bobby** <u>frightened</u> **the bird, and (it)** <u>flew</u> **up into a tree.** Would this sentence still make good sense if we omitted the subject **it,** which follows the conjunction? (*Yes, No*)
367	368

	The adjective clause is useful in combining sentences when one sentence states an explanatory fact about a noun or pronoun in the previous sentence. **Our yearbook comes out in June.** *It sells for one dollar.* The italicized sentence states an explanatory fact about the noun _____ in the first sentence.
	638

Before completing her commercial course, Beth was offered a good job. 907	Lesson **24** Making Use of Infinitives [Frames 909–943]

It was very lucky that I took along a flashlight. 1177	Continue to follow the directions for the previous frame: *Emily Dickinson rarely went out.* **This seemed strange to the neighbors.** _____ _____ 1178

Yes 1447	a. **If you don't care about your appearance,** *then* **nobody else will.** b. **The salesman neglected his appearance,** *then* **he began to lose business.** Which sentence is a run-on sentence? _____ 1448

Correct	**In British traffic** *they* (_____) **keep to the left.**
1717	1718

keeps	Suppose that you have *several* library books that *are* overdue. *The Yearling* is just one of them.
	Underline the verb which shows that *The Yearling* is among these overdue books.
	The Yearling **is one of my library books that** (*is, are*) **overdue.**
1986	1987

b	a. **Roberta was disappointed** *to have sold* **so few tickets.**
	b. **Roberta hoped** *to have sold* **many more tickets than she did.**
	In which sentence is the perfect infinitive correctly used because it refers to a completed action? _____
2255	2256

me, him	**Marge and** (*me, ~~I, her,~~ him, we*) **were in charge of the decorations.**
2524	2525

Yes	**While we tour we eat lightly.**
	Is a comma necessary after the word **tour?** (*Yes, No*)
2793	2794

plural	a. **all singular nouns**
	b. **the few plural nouns not ending in s**
	c. **plural nouns ending in s**
	To form the possessive case, add an **'s** to all nouns except those in group _____.
3062	3063

mistake

98

a. **The company manufactures trucks.**
b. **The company repairs trucks.**

In one sentence, the **trucks** already exist and receive the action of the verb; in the other, the **trucks** are the result of the action.

The direct object *receives the action* in sentence (*a, b*). _____

99

No

368

Bobby frightened the bird, and (it) flew up into a tree.

Our word-saving device does not work here because each predicate makes a statement about (*a different, the same*) subject.

369

---

yearbook

638

Our yearbook comes out in June. *It sells for one dollar.*

Which word in the italicized sentence means the same thing as the noun **yearbook** in the first sentence? _____

639

Infinitives are the forms of verbs most commonly listed in the dictionary. If you should look up the words *grew* and *broken,* the dictionary would refer you to the words *grow* and _____.

909

It seemed strange
to the neighbors
that Emily
Dickinson
rarely went out.
1178

Children pick up a foreign language very fast. **This is a well-known fact.**

_____

_____

1179

---

b

1448

a. **All our bills were paid,** *consequently* **we had little to worry about.**
b. **Because all our bills were paid, we** *consequently* **had little to worry about.**

Which sentence is a run-on sentence? _____

1449

cars, automobiles, drivers, people (*or similar* *words*) 1718	Telly Savalas is bald, but his brother is well supplied with *it*. (———————) 1719
are 1987	Now, on the other hand, suppose that you have several library books but that *only one* of them *is* overdue. Underline the correct verb: *The Yearling* is the *only one* of my library books that (*is, are*) overdue. 1988
a 2256	Underline the correct infinitive: We are happy (*to be, to have been*) of service to you in the recent sale of your home. 2257
I, we 2525	The evidence indicates that it was (*he, them, her, they, me*) who divulged this secret information. 2526
No 2794	If Jim doesn't tell the truth will never be known. Is a comma necessary in this sentence? (*Yes, No*) 2795
c 3063	A simple way to apply these rules is to look at the word you have written and ask yourself, "Who is the owner?" Then put the apostrophe right after the word that answers this question. this boys jacket (Who is the owner? boy) Now go back and put the apostrophe after boy. 3064

The sentence that contains a direct object gives us our second sentence pattern.

PATTERN II: *Subject—Action Verb → Direct Object*

A sentence in Pattern II has three basic parts.

The third basic part is the _____ object.

b

99 | 100

---

a different

Hank **swung at the ball**, but (he) **missed it by a foot.**

We can change this compound sentence to a sentence with a *compound predicate* because both predicates make statements about the same person, _____.

369 | 370

It

which
Our yearbook comes out in June. ~~It~~ *sells for one dollar.*

To change the italicized sentence to an adjective clause, we put the relative pronoun _____ in place of *It*.

639 | 640

---

break

An **infinitive** is the basic form of a verb from which all other forms are derived. The infinitive is usually combined with the preposition *to;* for example, *to walk, to drive, to sleep.*

The infinitive from which the verbs *flew, flying,* and *flown* are derived is _____.

909 | 910

It is a well-known fact that children pick up a foreign language very fast.

A noun clause is often used as an appositive after the words **the fact.**

The fact *that the door was open* **made me suspicious.**

The clause *that the door was open* is an appositive because it explains the noun _____ ___.

1179 | 1180

---

a

a. **We printed our own programs,** *thus* **saving considerable expense.**
b. **We printed our own programs,** *thus* **we saved considerable expense.**

Which sentence is a run-on sentence? _____

1449 | 1450

---

is

1988

There are many factors that cause war. Greed is one of them.

Underline the correct verb:

Greed is one of the many factors that (*cause, causes*) **war.**

1989

---

to have been

2257

Underline the correct infinitive:

Jim had hoped (*to receive, to have received*) **a college recommendation.**

2258

---

he, they

2526

The car missed Donna and (*him, we, he, me, she*) **by only a hair's breadth.**

2527

Yes

2795

In this and the following frames, insert any necessary commas. If no comma is required, write *None*.

In the writings of Maxine Hong Kingston a past time is brought to life.

2796

---

this boy's
jacket

3064

these boys grades (Who is the owner? **boys**)

Now go back and put the apostrophe after **boys.**

3065

direct 100	PATTERN II: **The speaker showed a movie of his travels.** Notice that the action begins with the subject and ends with the direct object. The direct object of an action verb is the goal of its action. Which word is the *direct object* in the example above? _____ 101
Hank 370	**Bobby frightened the bird, and (it) flew up into a tree.** We *cannot* change this compound sentence to a sentence with a *compound predicate* because the first predicate makes a statement about **Bobby,** and the second predicate makes a statement about _____. 371
which 640	*which* **Our yearbook comes out in June.** ~~It~~ *sells for one dollar.* The clause *which sells for one dollar* should be inserted in the sentence right after the noun (*yearbook, June*), which it modifies. 641

to fly
 	
910
	An infinitive—like a gerund—is often used to name an action. It is often interchangeable with a gerund.
	        GERUND: *Walking* **is good exercise.**
	        INFINITIVE: *To walk* **is good exercise.**
	Both the gerund and the infinitive are used as nouns. Each is the _____ of the verb **is.**
	911

fact 1180	The "the fact that . . ." construction sometimes proves useful in tightening up a loose compound sentence. *I ate the stew,* **but that doesn't mean that I liked it.** Supply the "the fact that" construction: _____ *I ate the stew* **doesn't mean that I liked it.** 1181
b 1450	If the second word group begins with a conjunctive adverb, supply a period and a capital. If it begins with a conjunction, merely add a comma. Write only the word before and after your punctuation mark. **The play was dull besides, the acting was mediocre.** _____ 1451

The meaning of a pronoun usually depends upon its antecedent, the word to which it refers. This referring to another word is known as the **reference** of a pronoun.

When a pronoun has no antecedent to give it meaning, we say the pronoun lacks _____.

1721

---

cause

1989

Your friend has had many pictures taken, but you think that only one of them looks at all like him.

Underline the correct verb:

This is the only one of the pictures that (*look, looks*) **at all like you.**

1990

---

to receive

2258

Underline the correct infinitive:

Alison intended (*to apply, to have applied*) **for this job.**

2259

---

him, me

2527

It was (*us, they, him, me, she*) **who objected to the new policy.**

2528

Kingston, a

2796

If dogs and cats have such a remarkable sense of direction why do so many get lost only a block or two away from their homes?

2797

---

these boys'
grades

3065

man's	children's	women's	child's	woman's	men's
1	2	3	4	5	6

These mixed-up singular and plural possessive nouns all end in **'s.** However, we can tell which are which by looking at the word that precedes the apostrophe and names the owner(s).

The numbers of the plural possessive nouns are _____
_____ _____.

3066

movie 101	Don't mistake another word that may follow an action verb for a direct object. To be a **direct object,** a word must either receive the action of the verb or show the result of this _____. 102
it *or* bird 371	We can change a compound sentence to a sentence with a compound predicate only when both predicates make statements about the _____ subject. 372
yearbook 641	a. **Our yearbook,** *which sells for one dollar,* **comes out in June.** b. **Our yearbook comes out in June,** *which sells for one dollar.* In which sentence is the adjective clause properly placed? —— 642
subject 911	Fill the blank with the infinitive form of *traveling:* GERUND: *Traveling* **broadens the mind.** INFINITIVE: _____ **broadens the mind.** 912
The fact that 1181	In this and the following frames, improve each compound sentence by changing the italicized statement to the "the fact that" construction: *Fred's mom is a dentist,* **and that influenced him to study dentistry.** _____ _____ 1182
dull. Besides, 1451	Continue to follow the directions for the previous frame: **We play one game for several weeks then we tire of it and take up another.** _____ 1452

reference 1721	When we say that a pronoun lacks reference, we mean that there is no word that serves as its _____. 1722
looks 1990	Another situation that invites trouble is the sentence in which we use an expression like "one of the best games that..." or "one of the worst floods that...." We solve this problem in the same way: If the relative pronoun refers to **one,** we choose a singular verb; if it refers to a plural noun, we choose a _____ verb. 1991
to apply 2259	Underline the correct infinitive: **Our town seems** (*to change, to have changed*) **a lot during the past five years.** 2260
they, she 2528	**The entire incident was no surprise to the Sampsons or** (*us, we, them, I, they*)**.** 2529
direction, why 2797	**When he tries he succeeds.** 2798
2, 3, 6 3066	In this and the following frames, ask yourself, "Who is the owner?" or "Who are the owners?" Underline the part of the possessive noun that answers this question and insert an apostrophe at this point; for example, **one man's car, both men's cars.** **these girls voices** 3067

102

action

a. **Mr. Price returned** *recently*.
b. **Mr. Price returned the** *money*.

Does the word *recently* or *money* receive the action of the verb **returned?** _____

103

---

same

The students went to England by boat. They returned by plane.

In combining these two sentences, which word would you omit? _____

372
373

---

a

a. **Our yearbook comes out in June, and it sells for one dollar.**
b. **Our yearbook, which comes out in June, sells for one dollar.**

One sentence is *compound;* the other is *complex*.

The sentence that is complex because it contains a subordinate clause is (*a, b*).

642
643

To travel

Fill the blank with the infinitive form of *swimming:*

GERUND: **Her favorite sport is** *swimming*.

INFINITIVE: **Her favorite sport is** _____ .

912
913

The fact that Fred's mom is a dentist influenced him to study dentistry.

Smith knew Madden. **That doesn't make him a party to the crime.**

_____

_____

1182
1183

---

weeks. Then

It had rained all night   and consequently the field was muddy.

_____

1452
1453

antecedent 1722	In the previous lesson we repaired sentences in which the pronouns had no antecedents to make their meaning clear. a. **Odetta sang and everyone enjoyed** *it.* b. **Odetta sang a song, and everyone enjoyed** *it.* Which sentence is faulty because the pronoun *it* lacks reference? _____ 1723
plural 1991	**The wheel was one of the greatest inventions** *that* . . . **ever made.** The antecedent of *that* is **inventions,** not **one,** for we surely do not mean to say that only *one* great invention was ever made. Since the relative pronoun *that* stands for **inventions,** it requires a (*singular, plural*) verb. 1992
to have changed 2260	Underline the correct infinitive: **I meant** (*to mail, to have mailed*) **this card on my way home from school.** 2261
us, them 2529	**It could not have been** (*us, them, we, I, him*) **who broke the window.** 2530
None 2798	**To unite the Colonies needed to forget their local interests and rivalries.** 2799
<u>girls'</u> 3067	Be sure to underline the part of the possessive noun that identifies the owner or owners before inserting the apostrophe at this point: **my doctors opinion** 3068

money

103

a. **Mr. Price returned** *recently*.
b. **Mr. Price returned the** *money*.

Which sentence contains a direct object? _____

104

They

373

a. **The coach went to the blackboard, and he drew a diagram of the play.**
b. **The curtain went up, and the show began.**

Which compound sentence can be changed to a sentence with a compound predicate because both predicates make statements about the same subject? _____

374

---

b

643

a. **Our yearbook comes out in June, and it sells for one dollar.**
b. **Our yearbook, which comes out in June, sells for one dollar.**

The two facts are brought into closer relationship by the (*compound, complex*) sentence.

644

---

to swim

913

Like participles and gerunds, infinitives can take direct objects and subject complements, as no ordinary noun can do.

To waste food **is sinful.**

Because the noun *food* receives the action of the infinitive *To waste*, it is its (*direct object, subject complement*).

914

The fact that Smith knew Madden doesn't make him a party to the crime.

1183

The lights were on, **and that made me think that the Lins were at home.**

_____

_____

1184

---

night, and

1453

People once considered the night air poisonous   therefore they kept their windows tightly closed.

_____

1454

a 1723	Sentences are even more confusing when it is not clear to which of two words a pronoun refers. Suppose that while staying at a summer cottage, you received the following message. **Take the motor off the boat and sell** *it*. Could *it* refer to either the **motor** or the **boat**? (*Yes, No*) 1724
plural 1992	Underline the correct verb: **The wheel was one of the greatest inventions that** (*was, were*) **ever made.** 1993
to mail 2261	Lesson **63** Using the Past Perfect and the Future Perfect Tenses [Frames 2263–2298]
we, I 2530	In this and the following frames, the italicized pronouns are correct. If a person should find them awkward to say, how could he change the wording to eliminate the pronoun after the form of the verb **be**? "May I speak to Pedro?" "This is *he* speaking." "May I speak to Pedro?" "This is _____ speaking." 2531
unite, the 2799	**The messenger kept feeling his pocket for the papers were very valuable.** 2800
doctor's 3068	**the childrens department** 3069

a. **The rain stopped the** game.
b. **The rain stopped** suddenly.

Which sentence contains a direct object? _____

The coach went to the blackboard, and he drew a diagram of the play.

The coach went to the blackboard and drew a diagram of the play.

When we change a compound sentence to a sentence with a compound predicate, we (*keep, drop*) the comma.

Our yearbook comes out in June, and it sells for one dollar.

By using a compound sentence we give (*equal, unequal*) emphasis to the two facts that the conjunction **and** connects.

To be healthy **is a great advantage.**

The adjective *healthy* completes the meaning of the infinitive *To be.*

The adjective *healthy*, therefore, is the (*direct object, subject complement*) of the infinitive.

The fact that
the lights were
on made me
think that the
Lins were at
home.
1184

We shall now learn to avoid a common error that is sometimes made when using noun clauses.

I knew *that the cement would harden.*

This sentence contains a _____ clause.

The plane took off an hour late   or otherwise we should have missed it.

_____

Yes 1724	**Take the motor off the boat and sell** *it.* Because this sentence has two possible meanings, we say that it is **ambiguous,** which means "having more than one possible meaning." The word that makes this sentence ambiguous is the pronoun ————.　　　　　　　　　　　　　　　　　　1725
were 1993	Suppose that someone made a list of the most unusual stories that *were* ever written. It is likely that Stevenson's "The Bottle Imp" would be one of these. Underline the correct word: **Stevenson's "The Bottle Imp" is one of the most unusual stories that** (*was, were*) **ever written.**　　　　1994
	The past perfect tense is formed by combining **had** (the past tense of **have**) with the past participle of a verb (*seen, walked, taken*). 　　　　　　a. **had decided**　　　b. **has decided** Which verb is in the past perfect tense? ———— 　　　　　　　　　　　　　　　　　　　　　　2263
Pedro 2531	**It might have been** *we* **who were hurt.** **We might have been the** ————————————. 　　　　　　　　　　　　　　　　　　　　　　2532
pocket, for 2800	**I know that Juan can keep a secret because he has never told me anything confidential about anyone else.** 　　　　　　　　　　　　　　　　　　　　　　2801
children's 3069	**both parents consent** 　　　　　　　　　　　　　　　　　　　　　　3070

a 105	*Pattern I* is built around a two-part framework: a *subject* and an *action verb*. *Pattern II* is built around a three-part framework: a *subject,* an *action verb,* and a _____ _____. 106
drop 375	a. **We won our first game, but we lost the second.** b. **We won our first game but lost the second.** No comma is used before a conjunction that connects the two parts of a compound (*sentence, predicate*). 376
equal 645	You have learned that to *subordinate* a fact or an idea means to put it into a word group that is (*more, less*) than a sentence. 646
subject complement 915	Since an infinitive is a mixture of both a verb and a noun, it may be modified by an adverb. **Test pilots like** *to live dangerously.* The adverb *dangerously* modifies the infinitive _____. 916
noun 1185	**I knew** *that the cement would harden* *if I didn't hurry.* Besides a noun clause, this sentence now has a second clause, which is an (*adverb, adjective*) clause. 1186
late, or 1455	Continue to follow the directions for the previous frame, with only one change: Use a semicolon where you have previously been using a period and a capital. Both are equally correct. **I had paid my bill** **however, I could not find my receipt.** 1456

Take the motor off the boat and sell *it.*

it

This sentence is ambiguous because there are *two* nouns before the pronoun *it* that could serve as its antecedent.

These nouns are _____ and _____.

1725

1726

Many large catfish were caught in Mud Lake. Dad caught one of these many large fish.

were

Underline the correct verb:

Dad caught one of the largest catfish that (*was, were*) **ever caught in Mud Lake.**

1994

1995

Ellen *bought* **a flute but later** *returned* **it.**

a

There are two verbs in this sentence.

Does the order of the verbs represent the order in which the actions occurred? (*Yes, No*)

2263

2264

---

ones who were hurt.

I'm sure that it was *she* **in the front seat.**

I'm sure that _____.

2532

2533

None

Lesson 78   Commas to Separate Items in a Series

[Frames 2803–2839]

2801

---

parents'

Be careful with this one! Who are the owners of the property?

some peoples property

3070

3071

direct object 106	a. **All good citizens vote on Election Day.** b. **All good citizens cast their vote on Election Day.** Which sentence is **Pattern II** because the verb is followed by a direct object? _____ 107
predicate 376	a. **We heard a voice, but we couldn't recognize it.** b. **We heard a voice, but couldn't recognize it.** In which sentence should the comma before the conjunction be dropped because it is not a compound sentence? _____ 377
less 646	a. **It sells for one dollar.** b. **which sells for one dollar** Both word groups state a fact about *price*. The word group that *subordinates* the fact about *price* is the (*clause, sentence*). 647
to live 916	The phrases formed by infinitives with their related words are called **infinitive phrases.** These phrases can be used in most of the ways that nouns are used. *To teach a dog tricks* **requires endless patience.** The infinitive phrase is used as the _____ of the verb **requires.** 917
adverb 1186	a. **I knew** *that the cement would harden if I didn't hurry.* b. **I knew** *that if I didn't hurry the cement would harden.* In which sentence is the adverb clause inserted between parts of the noun clause? _____ 1187
bill; however, 1456	**I wrote down my answer and then I changed my mind.** _____ 1457

motor, boat 1726	a. **Take the** *motor* **off the** *boat* **and sell** *it*. b. **Sell the** *motor* **after you take** *it* **off the** *boat*. Which sentence is clear because there is only *one* noun before the pronoun *it* that could serve as its antecedent? ——— 1727
were 1995	In this and the following frames, think over each sentence to decide whether the adjective clause applies to **only one** or to the plural noun that follows it. Then underline the verb that expresses the intended meaning. **Mr. Slocum is one of those speakers who never** (*seem, seems*) **to come to the point.** 1996
Yes 2264	a. **Ellen** *bought* **a flute but later** *returned* **it.** b. **Ellen** *returned* **the flute that she** *had bought*. In which sentence is the last action mentioned first and the first action mentioned last? _____ 2265
she was (the one) in the front seat. 2533	WHO AND WHOM AS INTERROGATIVE PRONOUNS **Who** is nominative; **whom** is objective. *Who* **was the inventor of wireless telegraphy?** The nominative pronoun *Who* is correct because it is the subject of the verb _____. 2534
	A series is a number of similar things that follow one after another. We speak of a series of games, accidents, or coincidences. In a sentence, a series is *three or more* words, phrases, or clauses all used in the same way. **There was sand** *on the floor, in our beds,* **and** *in our food.* This sentence contains a series of (*words, phrases, clauses*). 2803
people's 3071	**the boys locker room** 3072

b

107

a. **Each student keeps a list of every misspelled word.**
b. **The wheezing motor finally stopped completely.**

Which sentence is **Pattern II** because the verb is followed by a direct object? _____

108

---

b

377

a. **A large tree had fallen and was blocking traffic.**
b. **A large tree had fallen and traffic was slowed down.**

In which sentence should a comma be inserted before the conjunction? _____

378

---

clause

647

a. **Our yearbook,** *which sells for one dollar,* **comes out in June.**
b. **Our yearbook comes out in June, and it sells for one dollar.**

In which sentence is the *price* of the yearbook subordinated?

_____

648

---

subject

917

Shirley Bluewind's plan is *to save money for law school.*

The infinitive phrase completes the meaning of the linking verb **is** and identifies the subject **plan.**

The infinitive phrase, therefore, is a (*direct object, subject complement*).

918

---

b

1187

We often interrupt a noun clause after the clause signal *that* to insert an adverb phrase or clause.

Put parentheses around the adverb clause that now interrupts the noun clause:

I knew *that if I didn't hurry the cement would harden.*

1188

---

answer, and

1457

The two essays were judged equally good   therefore the prize was divided between us.

_____

1458

b

1727

---

the motor
Take the motor off the boat and sell ~~it~~.

Another very simple way to clear up the meaning of this sentence is to eliminate the pronoun *it* by repeating the noun _____.

1728

---

seem

1996

Hawley's is the only one of the gas stations that (*stay, stays*) **open all night.**

1997

---

b

2265

---

a. **Ellen** *bought* **a flute but later** *returned* **it.**
b. **Ellen** *returned* **the flute that she** *had bought*.

In which sentence do you find a verb in the past perfect tense? _____

2266

---

was

2534

Whom **did the Yankees defeat for the pennant?**
(The Yankees did defeat *whom* **for the pennant?)**

The objective pronoun *Whom* is correct because it is the direct object of the verb _____ _____.

2535

---

phrases

2803

It takes at least _____ items to form a series.
(How many?)

2804

---

boys'

3072

SINGULAR: **lady**   PLURAL: **ladies**

When you write a possessive noun, be sure that you have the correct spelling of the owner(s) before the apostrophe.

a. **a ladie's coat**   b. **a lady's coat**

Which is correct because the word before the apostrophe is correctly spelled? _____

3073

The pitcher threw Reggie a fast curve.

After the verb **threw,** we have two nouns—**Reggie** and **curve.**

To decide which is the **direct object,** ask yourself, "What did the pitcher throw?"

The direct object is the noun _____.

a

108

109

The teacher liked the movie. She urged her classes to see it.

If you were to combine these two sentences, it would be better to use a compound (*sentence, predicate*).

b

378

379

To subordinate a fact or an idea is like taking an article from the front of a showcase and putting it in the back, where it is less conspicuous.

A fact or an idea gets less emphasis when we put it in a (*sentence, clause*).

a

648

649

A good citizen does not refuse *to be a witness.*

The infinitive phrase is used as a (*direct object, subject complement*).

subject
complement

918

919

When we interrupt a noun clause in this way, we must guard against a common error.

WRONG: **I knew** *that (if I didn't hurry) that the cement would harden.*

The sentence above is incorrect because the clause signal _____ is repeated.

(if I didn't hurry)

1188

1189

The doctor was exhausted **but nevertheless she kept on working.**

good; therefore

1458

1459.

motor

1728

After Mother left Eve at camp, *she* **felt lonesome.**

This sentence is ambiguous because *she* might refer to either _____ or _____.

1729

---

stays

1997

The Netherlands was one of the many neutral countries that (*was, were*) **invaded by the Nazis.**

1998

---

b

2266

Use the past perfect tense of a verb for an earlier action that is mentioned after a later action.

Suppose that John *picked* an apple and then *ate* it.

You would put the verb *picked* in the past perfect tense if you mentioned it (*first, last*).

2267

---

did defeat

2535

To *whom* **will the President entrust this responsibility?**

The objective form *whom* is correct because it is the object of the preposition _____.

2536

---

three

2804

a. **Many friends and relatives were invited.**
b. **Many friends, relatives, and neighbors were invited.**

Which sentence contains a series of nouns? _____

2805

---

b

3073

SINGULAR: **baby**   PLURAL: **babies**

a. **the babies' mothers**   b. **the babys' mothers**

Which is correct because the word before the apostrophe is correctly spelled? _____

3074

curve 109	**The pitcher threw Reggie a fast curve.** What does the noun **Reggie** do? It shows *to whom* the pitcher threw the **curve**. We call such a noun (or pronoun) an **indirect object**. Curve is the *direct object;* **Reggie** is the _____ *object.* 110
predicate 379	**The teacher liked the movie and urged her classes to see it.** Should a comma be inserted before the conjunction **and?** (*Yes, No*) 380
clause 649	**Our yearbook,** *which comes out in June,* **sells for one dollar.** This complex sentence states two facts: one about *price* and another about *time of issue.* This sentence gives greater emphasis to the fact about (*price, time of issue*). 650

direct object
 	
919
	In addition to being used as nouns, infinitives are also used as modifiers—both as adjectives and as adverbs.
	
	   I want a chance *to work.* **I want a chance** *to play.*
	   I want a chance *to rest.* **I want a chance** *to travel.*
	
	Each sentence means a different kind of **chance** because
	
	the _____ is different in each sentence.
	                                                                   920

that 1189	It is easy to forget that you have already written the word *that* and repeat it when you continue the clause. a. **I decided that after I graduated I would go to college.** b. **I decided that after I graduated that I would go to college.** Which sentence is correct? _____ 1190
exhausted, but 1459	**The job provided me with spending money furthermore, it built up my self-confidence.** _____ 1460

Mother, Eve 1729	You can often get rid of ambiguity by shifting the "false" antecedent to a position *after* the pronoun, where it can't confuse the reader. **Mother felt lonesome after** *she* **left Eve at camp.** Now we know that *she* means **Mother** and not **Eve** because the noun _____ has been put after the pronoun *she*. 1730
were 1998	**His boss was one of those employers who** (*don't, doesn't*) **welcome suggestions from their employees.** 1999
last 2267	**John** *ate* **the apple that he** *had picked.* Are the actions mentioned in the order in which they occurred? (*Yes, No*) 2268
To 2536	a. . . . **was Bess Myerson's Consul General?** b. . . . **did Bess Myerson appoint as her Consul General?** In which sentence would **Whom** be correct because it is the direct object of the verb? _____ 2537
b 2805	Use commas *between* the items in a series but not before or after the series (unless a comma is required for another reason). Punctuate the following sentence: **Many of the world's greatest books paintings and inventions were produced by people past sixty.** 2806
a 3074	Here is another problem that concerns apostrophes: WRONG: **the dentist who pulled my tooth's office** This sentence is wrong because the apostrophe is not in the right word. The owner of the office is not **tooth** but _____. 3075

The pitcher threw Reggie a fast curve.

indirect

The indirect object **Reggie** comes (*before, after*) the direct object **curve.** _____

110

111

No

We have good traffic laws. They are strictly enforced.

If you were to combine these two sentences, you would need to use a compound (*sentence, predicate*).

380

381

---

price

a. **Our yearbook,** *which comes out in June,* **sells for one dollar.**

b. **Our yearbook,** *which sells for one dollar,* **comes out in June.**

One sentence emphasizes the *price;* the other, the *time of issue.* Which emphasizes the *time of issue?* _____

650

651

---

infinitive

I want a chance *to work.*   **I want a chance** *to play.*
I want a chance *to rest.*   **I want a chance** *to travel.*

Each infinitive in the above sentences modifies the noun

_____.

920

921

---

a

a. **We knew that if we appeared too eager that the price would be raised.**

b. **We knew that if we appeared too eager the price would be raised.**

Which sentence is correct? _____

1190

1191

---

money;
furthermore,

Copy each pair of sentences, inserting the word in parentheses between them. Show by your punctuation whether they form one sentence or two.

The trip takes all day. The scenery is interesting. (*but*)

_____

_____

1460

1461

Eve	**Lola backed the car out of the garage and cleaned** *it*.
	This sentence is ambiguous because we don't know whether
	it refers to the **car** or to the _____.
1730	1731

don't	**Are you one of those newspaper readers who** (*read, reads*) **only the headlines?**
1999	2000

No	Use the past perfect tense when the first action is mentioned (*first, last*).
2268	2269

b	In ordinary conversation, the nominative form **who** is generally used even though it may be the object of a verb or a preposition.
	INFORMAL: *Who* **did you see at church today?**
	This violates the rule for formal usage because *Who* is the direct object of the verb _____ _____.
2537	2538

books, paintings,	Make a count to see how, in a series, the number of commas compares with the number of items:
	_____, _____, **and** _____
	_____, _____, _____, **and** _____
	The number of commas is always one (*more, less*) than the number of items in a series.
2806	2807

dentist	The apostrophe belongs in the word that shows the owner, not in a word that is part of a modifying phrase or clause.
	WRONG: **The dentist who pulled my tooth's office**
	Now switch the **'s** to the noun **dentist,** and read the sentence with this change.
	Does moving the **'s** to **dentist** solve the problem? (*Yes, No*)
3075	3076

before 111	a. **The pitcher threw Reggie a fast curve.** b. **The pitcher threw him a fast curve.** In which sentence is the indirect object not a noun but a pronoun? _____ 112
sentence 381	**We have good traffic laws and they are strictly enforced.** Should a comma be inserted before the conjunction **and**? (*Yes, No*) 382
b 651	The type of sentence we use depends on the emphasis we wish to give various facts or ideas. If we wish to give two facts equal emphasis, we would use a (*compound, complex*) sentence. 652
chance 921	**I want a chance** *to work.* **I want a chance** *to play.* **I want a chance** *to rest.* **I want a chance** *to travel.* Because each infinitive modifies the noun **chance**, it is used as an _____. 922
b 1191	a. **I am sure that if we don't buy the car someone else will.** b. **I am sure that if we don't buy the car that someone else will.** Which sentence is correct? _____ 1192
The trip takes all day, but the scenery is interesting. 1461	**The trip takes all day. The scenery is interesting.** (*however*) _____ _____ 1462

garage

1731

We can always reconstruct a faulty sentence to make the reference of a pronoun perfectly clear.

Lola cleaned the car after backing *it* **out of the garage.**
Lola cleaned the garage after backing out the car.

Does either sentence leave any doubt as to what was cleaned? (*Yes, No*)

1732

---

read

2000

This was one of the worst floods that (*has, have*) **ever occurred in the South.**

2001

---

last

2269

a. **Howard . . . off the alarm and went back to sleep.**
b. **Howard went back to sleep after he . . . off the alarm.**

In which sentence should the past perfect verb **had shut** be used? _____

2270

---

did see

2538

The widespread use of **who** instead of **whom** is due to the fact that it comes in the subject position at the head of the sentence, and position is an important factor in our language.

Whom **did Rosie Casals beat in a tennis match?**

Can a word occupy the subject position and still not be the subject of the sentence? (*Yes, No*)

2539

---

less

2807

In a series of *three* items, we would use *two* commas.

In a series of *four* items, we would use _____ commas.

2808

No

3076

WRONG: **the dentist who pulled my tooth's office**

To avoid this error, it is necessary to show the ownership of the office by using an **of** phrase.

RIGHT: **the office of the dentist who pulled my tooth**

Instead of using an **'s** to show ownership, we use the prepositional phrase _____.

3077

An indirect object can show **to what**, as well as **to whom**, something was done.

These shoes give your feet more support.

The noun **support** is the _____ *object*.

The noun **feet** is the _____ *object*.

112

113

Yes

The crowded bus stopped. It took on still more people.

If you were to combine these two sentences, it would be better to use a compound (*sentence, predicate*).

382

383

---

compound

If we wish to subordinate one idea to another, we would use a (*compound, complex*) sentence.

652

653

---

adjective

I learned a new way *to play checkers.*

The infinitive phrase *to play checkers* modifies the noun

_____.

922

923

---

a

Copy each sentence, inserting the word group in parentheses after the clause signal **that**. Do not repeat *that* when you continue the interrupted clause.

I was afraid that I would not be ready. (*when my turn came*)

_____

_____

1192

1193

---

day. However,
or
day; however,

The dogs growled at each other. They began to fight. (*then*)

_____

_____

1462

1463

No

1732

a. **Stan was out of practice when Jack beat** *him.*
b. **Stan beat Jack when** *he* **was out of practice.**
c. **Jack was out of practice when Stan beat** *him.*

In which sentence is the reference of the italicized pronoun confusing because we can't tell to whom the pronoun refers?

_____

1733

---

have

2001

This is just one more of those stupid prejudices that (*is, are*) **passed on from one generation to another.**

2002

---

b

2270

a. **The police captured the prisoner who . . . .**
b. **The prisoner . . . but the police captured him.**

In which sentence should the past perfect verb **had escaped** be used? _____

2271

Yes

2539

In formal writing or speaking, use **whom** if the interrogative pronoun is the object of a verb or a preposition.

a. *Who* **did Jimmy take to the prom?**
b. *Who* **will the new party select for its first candidate?**

Your use of *Who* instead of *Whom* would be more subject to criticism in sentence _____.

2540

---

three

2808

a. **We export, food, cotton, and machinery to many countries.**
b. **We export food, cotton, and machinery to many countries.**
c. **We export food, cotton, and machinery, to many countries.**

Which sentence is correctly punctuated? _____

2809

---

of the dentist

3077

a. **the wife of the man in the other car**
b. **the man in the other car's wife**

Which is correct? _____

3078

(support) direct (feet) indirect 113	Besides showing *to whom* (or *to what*) something was done, an **indirect object** can also show *for whom* (or *for what*) something was done. **Cindy Yazzie sang us a song.** *For whom* did Cindy Yazzie sing? For _____. 114
predicate 383	In this and the following frames, combine each pair of sentences, using a compound predicate whenever possible. Indicate your answer by writing the conjunction and the two words surrounding it. Insert any necessary comma. **Garvey made a two-base hit. The ball game was over.** _____ 384
complex 653	Now let's look more closely into the process of subordinating an idea by changing it to an adjective clause. **Tony read some notices.** *Few students heard them.* The italicized sentence provides information about the noun _____ in the first sentence. 654
way 923	**I learned a new way** *to play checkers.* Because the infinitive phrase modifies the noun **way,** it is used as an _____. 924
I was afraid that when my turn came I would not be ready. 1193	Continue to follow the directions for the previous frame: **Many believe that they could write a song hit.** *(if they took the time)* _____ _____ 1194
other. Then *or* other; then 1463	**The college is small. Its school spirit is excellent.** *(nevertheless)* _____ _____ 1464

b 1733	In this and the following frames, one of each pair of sentences is clear. The other is ambiguous because the pronoun has two possible antecedents. Circle the letter of the correct sentence. a. **When our bus reached the station, it was almost empty.** b. **Our bus was almost empty when it reached the station.** 1734
are 2002	**Milner was the only one of our players who** (*was, were*) **selected for the all-state team.** 2003
a 2271	After you decide which action came first, underline the preferred verb: **The witness made this statement but later** (*denied, had denied*) **it.** 2272
b 2540	In this and the following frames, underline the pronoun that is proper for formal usage: (*Who, Whom*) **will be in favor of this new tax?** 2541
b 2809	Punctuate the following sentence: **Immediate pursuit quick arrest and certain conviction reduce crime.** 2810
a 3078	Rewrite the following sentence correctly, using a prepositional phrase, instead of a possessive noun, to show the owner of the name: **The girl in the front seat's name is Linda.** _____ _____ 3079

us	**Cindy Yazzie sang us a song.** The direct object is _____. The indirect object is _____.
114	115

---

hit, and the	It is important that you read the directions in the previous frame once again. Then be sure to select a conjunction that expresses the meaning most clearly. Supply a comma *only* when you form a compound sentence. **Paul wanted a date. He was too timid to ask.** _____
384	385

---

notices	**Tony read some notices.** *Few students heard them.* Which word in the italicized sentence means the same thing as **notices** in the first sentence? _____
654	655

---

adjective	**I learned a new way** *to play checkers.* We have seen that the infinitive *to play,* like an ordinary adjective, modifies the noun **way.** The fact that the infinitive *to play* can at the same time take the direct object *checkers* shows that an infinitive can also do the job of a _____.
924	925

Many believe that if they took the time they could write a song hit.	**The study shows that school grades drop sharply.** (*when students get their own cars*) _____ _____
1194	1195

---

small. Nevertheless, *or* small; nevertheless,	**The college is small. Its school spirit is excellent.** (*but*) _____ _____
1464	1465

b

1734

Continue to circle the letter of the correct sentence:

a. **As soon as Larry gets a kennel, he is going to keep the dog in it.**
b. **Larry is going to keep the dog in a kennel as soon as he gets one.**

1735

---

was

2003

Lesson **56** A Few Remaining Problems

[Frames 2005–2044]

---

denied

2272

Underline the preferred verb:

The witness later denied the statement that he (*made, had made*).

2273

Who

2541

By (*who, whom*) **will thls new tax be favored?**

2542

---

pursuit,
arrest,

2810

Punctuate the following sentence:

The bellhop stopped me asked me my name and handed me a telegram.

2811

The name of
the girl in
the front seat
is Linda.

3079

Rewrite the following sentence correctly:

The family next door's dog tears up our lawn.

_____

_____

3080

(direct object) song (indirect object) us 115	**Cindy Yazzie sang us a song.** As it always does when it is present, the indirect object comes (*before, after*) the direct object. 116
date but was 385	**It was getting late. The children were growing restless.** _____ 386
them 655	*which* **Tony read some notices.** *Few students heard* ~~them.~~ To change the italicized sentence to an adjective clause, we put the relative pronoun _____ in place of *them.* 656
verb 925	a. **I learned a new way** *to play checkers.* b. **I learned a new way of** *playing checkers.* One sentence contains a gerund phrase; the other an infinitive phrase. Which sentence contains an infinitive phrase? _____ 926
The study shows that when students get their own cars school grades drop sharply. 1195	**Employers find that production increases.** (*when rest periods are allowed*) _____ _____ 1196
small, but its 1465	Lesson **40** Review: The Sentence Unit [Frames 1467–1486] *page 231*

a

1735

---

a. **The Red Sox will play the Yankees. They have a great team.**
b. **The Red Sox will play the Yankees, who have a great team.**

1736

To make sentences more forceful, we often start them with the words **There is, There are,** or **Here is, Here are.**

      a. **A <u>spot</u> <u>is</u> on your coat.**
      b. **There <u>is</u> a <u>spot</u> on your coat.**

In which sentence is the usual order of the subject and verb turned around? _____

2005

---

had made

2273

Underline the preferred verb:

I read the article and (*made, had made*) **a summary of it.**

2274

---

whom

2542

(*Who, Whom*) **will the President appoint to this new post?**

2543

---

me, name,

2811

Three or more short and closely related sentences may be written in series as a single sentence without being considered a run-on sentence error.

Punctuate the following sentence:

The toast burned the coffee boiled over and Bobby spilled his orange juice.

2812

The dog of the family next door tears up our lawn.

3080

Be sure to recognize possessive nouns when the thing that is owned is understood but not expressed.

    Your voice sounds just like Mary's (voice).

We put an apostrophe in the word **Mary's** because the noun

_____ is understood.

3081

The club bought the church a new organ.

The indirect object is the noun _____.

(Are you sure that you recall all points in the directions given in frames 384 and 385?)

Most Americans want their children to attend college. They will make great sacrifices to send them.

_____

---

which
Tony read some notices. *Few students heard ~~them~~.*
Tony read some notices, *which few students heard.*

Since a relative pronoun usually starts an adjective clause, we move **which** to the front of the clause, before the word

_____.

Lyle ran *to catch the bus.*

The infinitive phrase *to catch the bus* explains **why** about the verb _____.

Lesson **32** Three Effective Sentence Devices

[Frames 1198–1229]

In this and the following frames, one of each pair of items is a sentence; the other is a fragment. Circle the letter of the complete sentence.

a. **A good citizen helps with the work of his community.**
b. **A good citizen who helps with the work of his community.**

b	a. **If you find any worms in the cabbages, destroy them.**
	b. **Destroy any worms that you find in the cabbages.**
1736	1737

	In sentences that begin with **There is, There are,** or **Here is, Here are,** the verb precedes the subject.
b	**There is a spot on your coat.**
	We use the singular verb **is** because its subject _____
2005	is singular. 2006

made	Underline the preferred verb:
	I remembered what the coach (*said, had said*) **about forward passes.**
2274	2275

Whom	(*Who, Whom*) **was the patriot who said, "Give me liberty or give me death"?**
2543	2544

	a. **I looked at the dog, the dog looked at me, and we immediately became friends.**
	b. **I looked at the dog, the dog looked at me.**
burned, over,	Which is a correct series of sentences and not a run-on
	sentence? _____
2812	2813

voice	Supply the missing apostrophe:
	A porpoise's brain is as large as a persons.
3081	3082

church

117

An **indirect object** shows *to whom* or *what* or _____ *whom* or *what* something is done.

118

---

college and will

387

You must be completely satisfied. We will return your money.

_____

388

---

few

657

Tony read some notices, *which few students heard.*
The adjective clause is in its proper position right after the word _____, which it modifies.

658

---

ran

927

Lyle ran *to catch the bus.*
Because the infinitive phrase modifies the verb **ran**, it is used as an _____.

928

---

1. The "no sooner . . . than" device:
a. **When we sat down to eat, company arrived.**
b. *No sooner* **had we sat down to eat** *than* **company arrived.**
Which sentence shows more effectively that one event followed the other almost immediately? _____

1198

---

a

1467

Circle the letter of the complete sentence:
a. **Posted in the most conspicuous place on the bulletin board.**
b. **The notice was posted on the bulletin board.**

1468

b	a. **Father said to Bobby, "Your hands are always dirty."**
	b. **Father told Bobby that his hands were always dirty.**
1737	1738

	There are spots on your coat.
spot	We use the plural verb **are** because its subject _____ is plural.
2006	2007

	Even though the actions are mentioned in the order of their occurrence, we sometimes use the past perfect tense to emphasize that the first action was completed before the second action began.
had said	**After we** *had washed* **the car, it** *rained* **very hard.**
2275	Was the washing completed when it began to rain? (*Yes, No*)
	2276

Who	(*Who, Whom*) **does the law hold responsible in such cases?**
2544	2545

	If there is a comma *before* a series, it is not used because of the series but for another reason.
a	**When I arrived home from school, Louis, Ron, and Carlos were waiting for me.**
	The comma after the word **school** is correct because it follows (*an introductory, a main*) clause.
2813	2814

	In this and the following frames, supply the necessary apostrophes. Remember that possessive pronouns are never written with apostrophes—*yours, hers, its, ours, theirs*. If no apostrophes are required, write *None*.
person's	**Eleanors theme was more original than either Pats or hers.**
3082	3083

for
 	
118
	An **indirect object**—if one is present—always comes *before* the **direct object,** and the word *to* or *for* is understood but never used.
	
	     a. **I offered** *Frank* **my ticket.**
	     b. **I offered my ticket to** *Frank.*
	
	Is *Frank* an indirect object in sentence *a* or *b?* _____
	
	119

satisfied, or we 388	**My sister can play several instruments. Her favorite is the violin.** _____ 389
notices 658	**Several of Don's friends play college football.** *He went to high school with them.* The pronoun *them* is the object of the preposition *with.* Underline the clause signal you would put in place of *them* in changing the italicized sentence to an adjective clause: **which** **whose** **whom** **who** 659
adverb 928	We can sometimes combine two sentences by changing one sentence to an infinitive phrase. **Larry gave a cough.** (*This was*) *to prove that he was sick.* **Larry gave a cough** *to prove that he was sick.* To change the italicized sentence to an infinitive phrase, we drop the words before the _____. 929
b 1198	*No sooner* **had we sat down to eat** *than* **company arrived.** The words *no sooner* must be followed later in the sentence by the word _____. 1199
b 1468	Continue to circle the letter of the complete sentence: a. **Which was Mr. Egan's way of getting us to read a book.** b. **This was Mr. Egan's way of getting us to read a book.** 1469

a	a. **At the time of Clem's birth, his father was a bandleader.** b. **Clem's father was a bandleader at the time of his birth.**
1738	1739

spots	**There is no stamp on this letter.** If you changed the noun **stamp** to **stamps,** you would need to change the verb **is** to _____.
2007	2008

Yes	PAST: I *finished* **my work when Jim arrived.** PAST PERFECT: I *had finished* **my work when Jim arrived.** Do both sentences have the same meaning? (*Yes, No*)
2276	2277

Whom	**To** (*who, whom*) **can small nations appeal for protection?**
2545	2546

an introductory	If there is a comma *after* a series, it is not used because of the series but for another reason. **For better schools, better roads, and clean government, cast your vote for Mrs. Henshaw.** The comma after **government** is used because it follows an introductory (*phrase, clause*) which includes a series.
2814	2815

Eleanor's, Pat's	**Both suspects fingerprints were in the police departments files.** (*Note:* The fingerprints belong to two **suspects;** the files belong to one police **department.** Place your apostrophes to show this.)
3083	3084

An indirect object tells *to whom* or *for whom* by its position alone—by coming *before* the direct object. A noun or pronoun used with *to* or *for* is never an indirect object.

a

a. **Jan found a better job for her** *friend.*
b. **Jan found her** *friend* **a better job.**

119

Is *friend* an indirect object in sentence *a* or *b*? _____ 120

Shall I write a new theme? Shall I revise the old one?

instruments,
but her

_____

(*Note:* Because these sentences are questions, this problem is slightly different. Besides omitting the second subject, you will also need to omit the helping verb **shall.**)

389

390

Several of Don's friends play college football. *He went to*

whom

high school with ~~them.~~

whom

We choose *whom* rather than *who* because it is the object of the preposition _____.

659

660

Change the italicized sentence to an infinitive phrase:

Wendy touched the flowers. *She wanted to see if they were real.*

infinitive

_____

_____

929

930

---

a. **When I last saw Ben, he was looking for a job.**
b. **When the picnic table was set, it began to rain.**

than

Which of the above sentences could best be put into the "no sooner . . . than" arrangement because the two events occurred at about the same time? _____

1199

1200

---

a. **Virginia Woolf was a fine writer.**
b. **Virginia Woolf, one of the finest writers of English literature.**

b

1469

1470

a 1739	a. **Whenever Dad discusses politics with Mr. Hart, he gets very excited.** b. **Dad gets very excited whenever he discusses politics with Mr. Hart.** <div align="right">1740</div>
are 2008	In sentences that begin with **There is, There are,** or **Here is, Here are,** don't choose your verb until you look ahead to see whether a singular or a plural subject is coming. <div align="center">**There . . . several ways of making frosting.**</div> Before we supply **is** or **are** in this sentence, we must look ahead to the subject _____. <div align="right">2009</div>
No 2277	<div align="center">a. I *finished* **my work when Jim arrived.** b. I *had finished* **my work when Jim arrived.**</div> In which sentence was your work already completed at the time of Jim's arrival? ____ <div align="right">2278</div>
whom 2546	Lesson **71** A Number of Pronoun Problems <div align="right">[Frames 2548–2586]</div>
phrase 2815	Although it's not wrong to omit the comma between the last two items of a series, many writers prefer to use this comma —especially in formal writing. <div align="center">a. **Gas, electricity, and water are included in the rent.** b. **Gas, electricity and water are included in the rent.**</div> Are both sentences punctuated correctly? (*Yes, No*) <div align="right">2816</div>
suspects' department's 3084	<div align="center">**The girls study hall is right next to the boys.**</div> <div align="right">3085</div>

b 120	a. **This machine will save much time.** b. **This machine will save the company much time.** The noun **time** is the direct object in both sentences. Which sentence also contains an indirect object? _____ 121
theme or revise 390	Sometimes we want the balanced effect of a compound sentence even though a compound predicate would express our meaning in fewer words. a. **Fashions come and fashions go.** b. **Fashions come and go.** Which sentence gives a more balanced effect? _____ 391
with 660	**Several of Don's friends play college football.** *He went to high school with* ~~*them.*~~ *whom* After we move *with whom* to the front of the clause, we should insert it in the sentence after the word (*friends, football*), which it modifies. 661
Wendy touched the flowers to see if they were real. 930	Change the italicized sentence to an infinitive phrase: **Vic's dad set the clock ahead.** *This was to prevent Vic from being late.* _____ _____ 931
b 1200	a. **When the picnic table was set, it began to rain.** b. *No sooner* **was the picnic table set** *than* **it began to rain.** Which sentence is more novel and forceful? _____ 120?
a 1470	a. **We consider spinach good for our health.** b. **Because we consider spinach good for our health.** 1471

b

1740

Sentences that report someone's remark often leave the reader guessing as to which person the pronoun *he* or *she* means.

The doctor told Dad that *he* needed a vacation.

This sentence is ambiguous because *he* could mean either the _____ or _____.

1741

---

ways

2009

Underline the correct verb:

There (*is, are*) several ways of making frosting.

2010

---

b

2278

a. **We *had* just *finished* scrubbing the floor when Larry came in with his muddy shoes.**
b. **We just *finished* scrubbing the floor when Larry came in with his muddy shoes.**

Which sentence emphasizes the fact that the first action had been completed when the second action occurred? _____

2279

PRONOUNS IN COMPARISONS

When we use the word **than** or **as** to make a comparison, we generally shorten our sentence by omitting one or more unnecessary words.

The Smiths have a larger house than we (have).

The omitted word in this sentence is _____.

2548

Yes

2816

Do not omit the comma between the last two items of a series if there is any chance of misunderstanding.

We served *coffee, salad, cheese* and *egg* sandwiches.

Can you be sure whether one or two kinds of sandwiches were served? (*Yes, No*)

2817

---

girls'
boys'

3085

His mother buys and sells all kinds of stamps and coins.

3086

b

Father made the boys some sandwiches.

The direct object is _____.

The indirect object is _____.

122

---

a

391

a. **He couldn't eat and couldn't sleep.**
b. **He couldn't eat, and he couldn't sleep.**

Which sentence is more effective because of the repetition

of the subject? _____

392

---

friends

661

a. **Several of Don's friends play college football** *with whom he went to high school.*
b. **Several of Don's friends** *with whom he went to high school* **play college football.**

In which sentence is the clause properly placed? _____

662

Vic's dad set
the clock ahead
to prevent Vic
from being late.

931

After changing the italicized sentence to an infinitive phrase, insert it in the sentence next to the noun it modifies:

Johnny's ambition was typical of a child. *It was to become a firefighter.* _____

_____

932

---

b

1201

a. *No sooner* **was** *the picnic* **table** **set** *than* **it began to rain.**
b. **The picnic** **table** **was** *no sooner* **set** *than* **it began to rain.**

In which arrangement does the subject **table** come between

the two parts of the verb? _____

1202

---

a

1471

a. **In time to save the firefighter from being crushed by the toppling wall.**
b. **She shouted her warning in time to save the firefighter.**

1472

doctor, Dad 1741	**The doctor told Dad that** *he* **needed a vacation.** Usually the only way to eliminate the ambiguity in a sentence like this is to use a direct quotation. **The doctor told Dad, "You need a vacation."** This means that (*the doctor, Dad*) needs a vacation. 1742
are 2010	a. **Here . . . the key to the car.** b. **Here . . . the keys to the car.** Which sentence requires the plural verb **are?** _____ 2011
a 2279	Here is a sentence with an "if" clause that states a condition under which something could have or would have happened: **If I** *had seen* **the light, I** *would have stopped.* The past perfect verb is used in the part of the sentence that states the (*condition, result*). 2280
have 2548	**Mr. Metz gave Fred just as good a grade as (he gave) me.** The omitted words in this sentence are _____. 2549
No 2817	**These sports shoes are available in** *green, red, brown* **and** *white.* If four different kinds of shoes are available, would you insert a comma after *brown?* (*Yes, No*) 2818
None 3086	**These childrens good manners reflect their parents training at home.** (*Note:* This is a high-error frame because **children** is one of those few plural nouns that do not end in **s.** Be sure to place the apostrophe after the part of the noun that names the owners.) 3087

(direct object) sandwiches (indirect object) boys 122	A sentence in **Pattern II** always contains an action verb and its direct object. Does it always contain an indirect object? (*Yes, No*) 123
b 392	Except where we wish to produce a special effect, we should try to save words by using a compound (*sentence, predicate*). 393
b 662	**A local firm got the order.** *Its bid was the lowest.* Underline the clause signal you would put in place of the possessive pronoun *Its* in changing the italicized sentence to an adjective clause: who whose that which 663
Johnny's ambition to become a firefighter was typical of a child. 932	**Jerry pounded the table once again.** *This showed that he was his own boss.* **Jerry pounded the table once again** *to show that he was his own boss.* We changed the italicized sentence to an infinitive phrase by changing the verb *showed* to the infinitive _____. 933
a 1202	In a "no sooner . . . than" sentence, we usually need a helping verb such as **was, did,** or **had** with the main verb. a. **The two <u>boys</u> <u>met</u>, and they began to argue.** b. **No sooner <u>had</u> the two <u>boys</u> <u>met</u> than they began to argue.** The verb **met** in sentence *a* becomes _____ in *b*. 1203
b 1472	a. **This fact surprised even our closest friends.** b. **A fact that surprised even our closest friends.** 1473

Dad	**The doctor told Dad, "You need a vacation."** If it were the doctor who needed the vacation, we would change **You** to _____.
1742	1743

b	Since **There's** and **Here's** are contractions of **There is** and **Here is,** they should be used only before singular subjects.
	
	    a. . . . **no battery in this flashlight.**
	    b. . . . **no batteries in this flashlight.**
	
	In which sentence would **There's** be correct? _____

2011	2012

condition	**If I** _had seen_ **the light, I** _would have_ **stopped.** Notice that _would have_ is used in only one part of the sentence—the part that shows what _would have_ happened if an earlier action (past perfect) _had_ occurred. Are the words _would have_ used in the "if" clause? (_Yes, No_)
2280	2281

he gave	When a pronoun follows the word **than** or **as** in a comparison, think of the missing words and you will have no trouble in deciding which case of the pronoun to use. **Don can print much better than** _I_ **(can print).** We use the nominative pronoun _I_ because it is the subject of the omitted verb _____ _____.
2549	2550

Yes	Do not use commas when all the items in a series are connected by _and, or,_ or _nor._ **The heat** _and_ **the noise** _and_ **the confusion were too much for my mother.** Does this sentence require any commas? (_Yes, No_)
2818	2819

children's parents'	**Mr. Barrys daughter knows all the players batting averages.**
3087	3088

No

123

In this and the following frames, $S = Subject$, $V = Verb$, $IO = Indirect\ Object$, $DO = Direct\ Object$.

Fill in the missing word:

This bakery makes the best doughnuts in town.

    S V DO

bakery   **makes**   _____

124

predicate

393

Lesson 11 The Semicolon as a Connector

[Frames 395–437]

whose

663

                                        whose

A local firm got the order. ~~Its~~ *bid was the lowest.*

a. **A local firm** *whose bid was the lowest* **got the order.**
b. **A local firm got the order** *whose bid was the lowest.*

In which sentence is the clause properly placed? _____

664

to show

933

Change the italicized sentence to an infinitive phrase:

We boiled our drinking water. *This killed all the bacteria.*

_____

_____

934

had met

1203

a. **When I sit down to study, someone usually disturbs me.**
b. **No sooner do I sit down to study than someone usually disturbs me.**

The verb **sit** in sentence *a* becomes _____ in sentence *b*.

1204

a

1473

a. **We stood at the door and waited for the store to open.**
b. **Standing at the door and waiting for the store to open.**

1474

Paula told Doris that *her* friend was waiting.

Complete this sentence with a direct quotation to show that *Doris's* friend was waiting:

Paula told Doris, "_____

_____**."**

1743

1744

I

a. . . . **some scraps for your dog.**
b. . . . **a bone for your dog.**

In which sentence would **Here's** be correct? _____

2012

a

2013

No

Be sure not to use the words *would have* in the "if" clause.

a. **If I *would have* seen the light, I *would have* stopped.**
b. **If I *had seen* the light, I *would have* stopped.**

Which sentence is correct? _____

2281

2282

---

can print

The noise didn't bother Dad as much as (it bothered) *her*.

We use the objective pronoun *her* because it is the direct object of the omitted verb _____.

2550

2551

No

Books about space exploration, sports, *or* animals interest many readers.

If you inserted another *or* before **sports**, would this sentence require any commas? (*Yes, No*)

2819

2820

Mr. Barry's
players'

Peoples ages are nobodys business but their own.

(Do you recall that a few irregular plural nouns do not end in **s**?)

3088

3089

Anyone can show you the way to the bridge.

Fill in the missing words:

S	V	IO	DO
Anyone	_____ _____	_____	**way.**

125

---

a

664

We have seen that two *similar* or *related* sentences that are *equal in importance* can be combined into a compound sentence by using the _____ **and,** **but,** or **or.**

395

A local firm *whose bid was the lowest* **got the order.**

The adjective clause is properly placed because it comes after the noun _____, which it modifies.

665

We boiled our drinking water to kill all the bacteria.

934

Change the italicized sentence to an infinitive phrase:

Always keep receipts. *They will prove that you have paid your bills.*

_____

_____

935

---

do sit

1204

Put this sentence into the "no sooner . . . than" arrangement. Count your sentence right whether the *no sooner* comes at the beginning of your sentence or later.

When I saw him, I recognized him.

_____

_____

1205

---

a

1474

a. **Each family taking a favorite dish to the church supper.**
b. **Each family took a favorite dish to the church supper.**

1475

Paula told Doris that _her_ friend was waiting.

Complete this sentence with a direct quotation to show that _Paula's_ friend was waiting:

Paula told Doris, "_____

_____.**"**

1745

The problem of subject-verb agreement is the same when a sentence begins with **There was, There were, There has been, There have been.**

Underline the correct verb:

There (_was, were_) **sixteen lighted candles on the cake.**

2014

---

a. **If it had rained another ten minutes, the game would have been called off.**
b. **If it would have rained another ten minutes, the game would have been called off.**

Which sentence is correct? _____

2283

Sometimes the meaning of a sentence depends on whether we use the nominative or objective case of a pronoun.

Hank owes Roy more money than _I_ (owe him).
Hank owes Roy more money than (he owes) _me_.

Do the sentence with _I_ and the sentence with _me_ have the same meaning? (_Yes, No_)

2552

---

a. **Jerry couldn't decide whether to add, or subtract, or multiply the numbers.**
b. **Jerry couldn't decide whether to add or subtract or multiply the numbers.**

Which sentence is correct? _____

2821

Sudden starts and stops wear out tires and brakes very rapidly.

3090

V can show IO you 125	**Franklin's experiments with electricity brought him international fame.** Fill in the missing words: *S* *V* *IO* *DO* **experiments** **brought** _____ _____ 126
conjunction 395	Another useful device for holding two sentences together is the semicolon (;). In many compound sentences, we can use a semicolon in place of the conjunction. **The ceiling was low,** *and* **all planes were grounded.** **The ceiling was low; all planes were grounded.** The semicolon replaces the conjunction _____. 396
firm 665	We can often strengthen a weak compound sentence by changing one of the statements to an adjective clause. **We have a neighbor, and she has her own private plane.** **We have a neighbor** *who has her own private plane.* The two facts are brought into closer relationship by the (*compound, complex*) sentence. 666
Always keep receipts to prove that you have paid your bills. 935	*Don't nag a child to practice.* **It does no good.** *To nag a child to practice* **does no good.** Here we have replaced the words *Don't nag* with the infinitive _____. 936
No sooner had I seen him than I recognized him. *or* I no sooner saw him than I recognized him. 1205	Continue to follow the directions for the previous frame. (*Note:* Be sure to follow the "no sooner" construction with "than," not "when.") **When the concert started, the lights went out.** _____ _____ 1206
b 1475	In this and the following frames, label each item according to the following key: *S = Correct Sentence; F = Fragment;* *R-S = Run on Sentence* **Although cotton is still an important crop in the South.** _____ 1476

"My friend is waiting."

1745

The cashier told the clerk that *she* **had made a mistake.**

Rewrite this sentence with a direct quotation to show that the *clerk* had made a mistake:

_____

_____

1746

---

were

2014

Underline the correct verb:

There (*has, have*) **been too many accidents lately.**

2015

---

a

2283

Sometimes the "if" clause comes at the end of the sentence.

Underline the correct verb:

It is very likely that they would have struck oil if only they (*had drilled, would have drilled*) **twenty feet more.**

2284

No

2552

a. **Sue wrote Bob more often than** *I.*
b. **Sue wrote Bob more often than** *me.*

Each of the above sentences has a different meaning.

Which sentence means that Sue wrote to Bob more often than she wrote to you? _____

2553

---

b

2821

Use a comma between two adjectives—even though they are not a series—when they modify the same noun and are not connected by a conjunction.

Sanding rust off a car is a *messy* **and** *tiresome* **job.**

If you omitted the conjunction **and,** would you insert a comma after the adjective *messy*? (*Yes, No*)

2822

None

3090

Their guests cars were blocking the Donaldsons driveway.

(*Note:* The cars belong to the **guests;** the driveway belongs to all the **Donaldsons.**)

3091

IO
him
DO
fame

126

The editor gave a better title to my article.

Fill in the missing words:

S   V   DO

editor   gave   _____

127

---

and

396

The ceiling was low; all planes were grounded.

After the semicolon, the compound sentence continues with a (*small, capital*) letter.

397

---

complex

666

In this and the following frames, convert each *compound* sentence into a *complex* sentence by changing the italicized sentence to an adjective clause:

We parked next to a fireplug, and *nobody had noticed it.*

_____

_____

667

To nag

936

Change the italicized sentence to an infinitive phrase:

Don't start eating before your host. **It is bad manners.**

_____

_____

937

The concert
had no sooner
started (No sooner
had the concert
started) than the
lights went out.

1206

We got to the corner, and the engine stopped.

_____

_____

1207

F

1476

S = *Correct Sentence*; F = *Fragment*;
R-S = *Run-on Sentence*

You can't run away from a problem, it has a way of trailing you. _____

1477

The cashier told the clerk (*or* said to the clerk), "You have made a mistake." 1746	Clear up the meaning of this sentence by substituting a noun for the ambiguous pronoun: **If the lids won't fit the jars, throw** *them* **out.** **If the lids won't fit the jars,** _____ _____. 1747
have 2015	In interrogative sentences, too, the verb (or part of the verb) usually precedes the subject, and we must look ahead to see whether a singular or a plural subject is coming. a. **Where . . . your father? How . . . your father?** b. **Where . . . your parents? How . . . your parents?** Which sentences require the plural verb **are?** _____ 2016
had drilled 2284	Underline the correct verb: **I'm certain Frank would not have bought the car if he** (*would have known, had known*) **the reputation of the dealer.** 2285
b 2553	**Sue wrote Bob more often than (she wrote)** *me.* The objective pronoun *me* is the direct object of the omitted verb _____. 2554
Yes 2822	Insert the necessary comma: **There are long dreary stretches of desert in the West.** 2823
guests' Donaldsons' 3091	**Todays paper tells about these girls experience in Sundays blizzard.** (*Note:* Look for three possessive nouns.) 3092

DO title 127	**The editor gave my article a better title.** Fill in the missing words: *S*　　*V*　　　　*IO*　　　　　*DO* editor　gave　_____　_____ 128
small 397	**The committee discussed the problem,** *but* **they reached no conclusions.** **The committee discussed the problem; they reached no conclusions.** The semicolon replaces the conjunction _____. 398
We parked next to a fireplug, which (that) nobody had noticed. 667	**Bill Cosby planned the puppet show, and** *he is very fond of children.* (Be sure to put the clause after the word it modifies.) _____ _____ 668
To start eating before your host is bad manners. 937	A sentence with an infinitive phrase as subject may sound stiff and formal. We can move the phrase to the end of the sentence, putting an introductory *It* in its place. 　　a. *To change one's mind* **is no crime.** 　　b. **It is no crime** *to change one's mind.* Which sentence sounds more informal? _____　　938
No sooner had we got to the corner than the engine stopped. 1207	**When I reached the dentist's office, my tooth stopped aching.** _____ _____ 1208
R-S 1477	*S = Correct Sentence; F = Fragment;* *R-S = Run-on Sentence* **We hunted for night crawlers, using our pocket flashlights.** _____ 1478

throw the lids
(the jars) out

1747

Clear up the meaning of this sentence by substituting a noun for the ambiguous pronoun:

When Fred saw Bruce, *he* was in uniform. _____

1748

---

b

2016

Underline the correct verb:

How much (*is, are*) the tickets?

2017

---

had known

2285

Supply the proper tense of the verb **see:**

You too would have bought the dress if you _____
_____ **it.**

2286

---

wrote

2554

---

a. **Sue wrote Bob more often than *I*.**
b. **Sue wrote Bob more often than *me*.**

Which sentence means that Sue wrote Bob more often than you wrote Bob? _____

2555

---

long, dreary

2823

Insert the necessary comma:

Their smiling friendly faces gave me confidence.

2824

Today's
girls'
Sunday's

3092

Ladies fashions change more frequently than mens.

3093

Lesson 4 The Sentence Pattern Built on Linking Verbs

[Frames 130–170]

---

but

398

The deadline was rapidly approaching; we worked furiously to meet it.

In this sentence, the semicolon replaces the conjunction

_____.

399

Bill Cosby, who
is very fond
of children,
planned the
puppet show.
668

Mrs. Won owned a beagle, and *she was very much attached to it.* (Try *to which.*)

_____

_____

669

---

b

938

To beat a dead horse **does no good.**

Rewrite this sentence, moving the infinitive phrase to the end of the sentence and putting an introductory *It* in its place.

_____

_____

939

No sooner had
I reached the
dentist's office
than my tooth
stopped aching.
1208

We raised the price, and our sales dropped.

_____

_____

1209

S

1478

S, F, or *R-S?*

Never paying the least attention to how he dressed or what people thought of him. ____

1479

Bruce (*or* Fred) 1748	Clear up the meaning of this sentence by substituting a noun for the ambiguous pronoun: **If there are any misspelled words in your themes, copy** *them* **correctly.** **If there are any misspelled words in your themes, _____** _____. <div align="right">1749</div>
are 2017	Underline the correct verb: (*Has, Have*) **there been any complaints about the service?** <div align="right">2018</div>
had seen 2286	The future perfect tense is formed by combining **will have** or **shall have** with the past participle of a verb. a. **will save** b. **had saved** c. **will have saved** Which verb is in the future perfect tense? _____ <div align="right">2287</div>
a 2555	**Sue wrote Bob more often than** *I* **(wrote Bob).** The nominative pronoun *I* is the subject of the omitted verb _____. <div align="right">2556</div>
smiling, friendly 2824	Do not put a comma after the last adjective in a series of adjectives. Put commas only *between* the adjectives, just as you do in any other series. **Irish terriers are friendly, intelligent, and obedient dogs.** Should a comma be inserted after the adjective **obedient**? (*Yes, No*) <div align="right">2825</div>
Ladies' men's 3093	Lesson **86** **Apostrophes for Contractions and Special Plurals** <div align="right">[Frames 3095–3129]</div>

Suppose that you wish to point out that your friend Henry is happy. You would not be likely to say—

Happy Henry
Henry happy

Is either of these pairs of words a sentence? (*Yes, No*)

130

---

and

399

I could see them; they couldn't see me.

In this sentence, the semicolon replaces the conjunction

_____.

400

Mrs. Won owned a beagle to which she was very much attached.

669

I have a friend, and *her mother is a judge.*

_____

_____

670

It does no good to beat a dead horse.

939

In this and the following frames, eliminate the **and** by changing the italicized statement to an infinitive phrase:

I have a job, and *I must finish it before dinner.*

_____

_____

940

No sooner had we raised the price than our sales dropped.

1209

2. The "not only . . . but also" device:

a. **Jimmy cooked the dinner and washed the dishes.**
b. *Not only* **did Jimmy cook the dinner,** *but* **he** *also* **washed the dishes.**

Which sentence is more forceful in emphasizing how much work Jimmy did? _____

1210

F

1479

S, F, or *R-S?*

The only one in our family who plays a musical instrument.

_____

1480

copy the words (*or* themes) correctly. 1749	Rewrite each sentence so that the italicized pronoun can mean only the underlined word. Do not merely substitute nouns for pronouns. (Count any answer correct if the antecedent of the pronoun is entirely clear.) **If the <u>blouse</u> doesn't match the skirt, you can return *it*.** 1750
Have 2018	The nouns **kind, sort,** and **type** are singular and require singular verbs. **The other kind of cookies *is* easier to make.** We use the singular verb *is* because the subject in the above sentence is (*kind, cookies*). 2019
c (will have saved) 2287	Use the future perfect tense for an action that *will have been completed* at a specified future time. **By tomorrow night, this car *will have traveled* one hundred thousand miles.** What is the specified future time at which the action will have been completed? _____ 2288
wrote 2556	Underline the correct pronoun: **Mick is jealous because Dad praises Boyd more than** (*he, him*). 2557
No 2825	Insert the necessary commas: **The company needs an honest reliable and experienced salesman with a thorough understanding of cars and people.** 2826
	As a short cut, we frequently run two separate words together by omitting one or more letters; for example, **we've** (*we have*), **doesn't** (*does not*). These two-in-one words are called **contractions.** **Let's** is a contraction of the two words _____ _____. 3095

No

130

---

a. **Happy Henry**
b. **Henry happy**
c. **Henry is happy.**

Which one of these groups of words is a sentence? _____

131

---

but

400

The bottle should be tightly closed; the perfume will evaporate.

In this sentence, the semicolon replaces the conjunction

_____.

401

I have a friend
whose mother is
a judge.

670

Some friends arrived suddenly, and *we were not expecting them.* (Be sure to put the clause after the word it modifies.)

_____

_____

671

I have a job
to finish
before dinner.

940

We sent out cards, and *these reminded members of the meeting.*

_____

_____

941

---

b

1210

---

a. *Not only* **did Jimmy cook the dinner,** *but* **he** *also* **washed the dishes.**
b. **Jimmy** *not only* **cooked the dinner,** *but* **he** *also* **washed the dishes.**

In which sentence is the subject **Jimmy** put between two parts of the verb? _____

1211

F

1480

S, F, or *R-S?*
I cleaned and adjusted all the spark plugs, then I replaced them in the motor.

_____

1481

You can return the blouse (the skirt) if it doesn't match the skirt (the blouse). 1750	Whenever Miss Ross talks to Sally, *she* seems embarrassed. _____ _____ (*Note: She* will become *her* in your revised sentence.) 1751
kind 2019	Underline the correct verb: **The newer type of automatic machines** (*washes, wash*) **the clothes faster.** 2020
(By) tomorrow night 2288	a. **When Mother unwraps the gift, she** *will have discovered* **who sent it.** b. **After I buy gas, I** *shall have spent* **my last cent.** In which sentence is the future perfect tense correctly used because the action will have been completed at a specified future time? _____ 2289
him 2557	Underline the correct pronoun: **Since Jack always feeds the dog, it obeys him better than** (*me, I*). 2558
honest, reliable(,) 2826	Sometimes an adjective is used so commonly with a noun that we think of it as part of the noun—for example, *old man, little boy, gold watch, fresh air, wild animal.* a. **gold watch** **fur coat** **brick house** b. **expensive watch** **worn-out coat** **comfortable house** We think of the adjectives as part of the nouns after (*a, b*). 2827
Let us 3095	Put an apostrophe in place of the omitted letter or letters in a contraction. a. **it /s = it's** d. **we w/ll = we'll** b. **who /s = who's** e. **I h/ve = I've** c. **I w/o/u/ld = I'd** f. **you /re = you're** In which of the above contractions does the apostrophe take the place of the largest number of letters? _____ 3096

a. **Henry happy**
b. **Henry is happy.**

c

The adjective **happy** by itself cannot make a statement about **Henry.**

We change *a* to a sentence by adding the verb _____.

131   132

A semicolon can also take the place of **because,** which is not a regular conjunction such as **and, but,** or **or.**

or

a. **Doris had made up her mind; nothing could change it.**
b. **Virginia didn't vote; she couldn't make up her mind.**

In which sentence does the semicolon take the place of

because? _____

401   402

Some friends whom (that) we were not expecting arrived suddenly.

The teacher asked a question, and *nobody could answer it.*

_____

_____

671   672

We sent out cards to remind members of the meeting.

The city issued a request, and *it was to refrain from wasting water.*

_____

_____

941   942

---

a

The food was expensive and poor.

Supply the missing words to complete the "not only . . . but also" device:

Not only _____,

but _____.

(Some variation in the wording is allowable.)

1211   1212

R-S

S, F, or *R-S?*

While he was looking for his lost nickel, Harvey found a quarter. _____

1481   1482

Sally seems embarrassed whenever Miss Ross talks to her. 1751	**When Fred saw <u>Bruce</u>, *he* was in uniform.** _____ (*Note: He* will become *him* in your revised sentence.) 1752

washes
 	
2020
	Because the nouns **kind, sort,** and **type** are singular, use the singular adjectives **this** and **that** (not the plural adjectives **these** and **those**) to point them out.
	    a. **This kind of berries is better for shipping.**
	    b. **These kind of berries are better for shipping.**
	Which sentence is correct—*a* or *b?* _____
	
	2021

b 2289	Underline the correct verb: **By next week, I** (*shall save, shall have saved*) **enough money for a vacation.** 2290
me 2558	PRONOUNS AS APPOSITIVES Pronouns are frequently used as appositives; that is, they are set after nouns to explain more precisely to whom the nouns refer. Underline the pronoun used as an appositive: **Both players, Greg and he, were penalized.** 2559
a 2827	Do not use a comma between two adjectives when you think of the second adjective as part of the noun it modifies. **The tiger is a ferocious *wild animal*.** We do not use a comma between the adjectives *ferocious* and *wild* because we think of the adjective *wild* as part of the noun _____. 2828

c *or* I'd
 	
3096
	The adverb **not**, shortened to **n't**, is part of many contractions.
	
	    isn't don't hasn't couldn't
	    aren't doesn't wasn't shouldn't
	
	The apostrophe always comes between the **n** and the **t** because it takes the place of the missing letter _____.
	
	3097

is

132

Henry happy
Henry is happy.

The verb **is** helps to turn the adjective **happy** into a statement about the subject _____.

133

---

b

402

---

a. **The child fell asleep; she was tired out from playing.**
b. **We listened very carefully; we could hear nothing.**

In which sentence does the semicolon take the place of

because? _____

403

The teacher asked a question that (which) nobody could answer.

672

Someone made a rude remark, and _there was no excuse for it._
(Try _for which._)

_____

_____

673

The city issued a request to refrain from wasting water.

942

We are planning a pageant, and _it will dramatize the history of our town._

_____

_____

943

(Not only) was the food expensive, (but) it was also poor.

1212

The food was expensive and poor.

This sentence can be changed to the "not only . . . but also" arrangement in still another way. Supply the missing words:

The food _____

but _____ **poor.**

1213

S

1482

_S, F,_ or _R-S?_

The dodo, a large, clumsy bird that was unable to fly. _____

1483

Bruce was in uniform when Fred saw him. 1752	**My aunt heard <u>Vikki Carr</u> sing when *she* was a child.** _____ _____ 1753
a 2021	Underline the correct words: (*This, These*) **sort** (*is, are*) **much harder to grow.** 2022
shall have saved 2290	In this and the following frames, underline the verb whose tense expresses the time relationship in the sentence more accurately: **Lincoln felt that his speech at Gettysburg** (*had been, was*) **a failure.** 2291
he 2559	When you use a pair of pronouns (or a noun and a pronoun) as appositives after a noun, use the same pronouns that you would use if you omitted the noun they explain. Underline the correct pronoun: ~~Two girls,~~ **Diane and** (*she, her*)**, made all the posters.** 2560
animal 2828	a. **All of us respected this dignified old man.** b. **All of us respected this dignified elderly man.** In which sentence would you insert a comma after the adjective **dignified?** _____ 2829
o 3097	a. **is'nt does'nt was'nt should'nt** b. **isn't doesn't wasn't shouldn't** The apostrophes are correctly placed in group (*a, b*). 3098

Henry 133	a. **Henry <u>washed</u> the car.** b. **Henry <u>is</u> happy.** Which sentence does *not* contain an *action* verb? _____ 134
a 403	a. **Few people attended the game because of the bad weather.** b. **Paula didn't worry because she was well-prepared for the test.** In which sentence could a semicolon take the place of **because?** _____ 404
Someone made a rude remark for which there was no excuse. 673	**My sister works for Dr. Mack, and** *his office is downtown.* _____ _____ 674
We are planning a pageant to dramatize the history of our town. 943	## Lesson **25** Subordination by Appositives [Frames 945–984]
(The food) was not only expensive (but) also poor. 1213	a. **The food was** *not only* **expensive** *but also* **poor.** b. **The food was** *not only* **expensive** *but* **poor.** Both sentences are correct. In which sentence do we omit the word *also* from our device? _____ 1214
F 1483	*S, F,* or *R-S?* **We had been eating sweets, therefore we had no appetite for dinner.** _____ 1484

When Vikki Carr
was a child,
my aunt heard
her sing.

1753

If you use high-grade oil in your <u>motor</u>, *it* will last longer.

_____

_____

1754

This, is

2022

Underline the correct words:

     (*That, Those*) **type** (*seems, seem*) **sturdier to me.**

2023

---

had been

2291

The fire inspector eventually found the short circuit that (*had caused, caused*) **the fire.**

2292

---

she

2560

Underline the correct pronoun:

All the posters were made by ~~two girls,~~ Diane and (*she, her*).

2561

---

b

2829

In this and the following frames, insert the necessary commas. If no commas are required, write *None*.

The child's shiny hair large eyes and wide smile make her an artist's dream.

2830

---

b

3098

Insert the needed apostrophes:

     It wouldnt burn because it wasnt dry enough.

3099

Henry is happy.

The verb **is** does not show action—like *washed* or *fixed*. What does it do?

The verb **is** ties up or *links* the adjective **happy** with the subject _____, which it *describes*.

b

134

135

We can combine two simple sentences into a compound sentence by using either a conjunction or a _____.

b

404

405

My sister works for Dr. Mack, whose office is downtown.

a. **The woman** *who owns the lot* **lives across the street.**
b. **The woman** *who lives across the street* **owns the lot.**

Which of the above sentences emphasizes where the woman lives—*a* or *b?* _____

674

675

Joseph Priestley discovered oxygen.

Because most people might not know who **Joseph Priestley** was, it would be well to add an explanation.

Joseph Priestley, *an English minister,* **discovered oxygen.**

The noun *minister* explains the noun _____

_____.

945

Put each sentence into the "not only . . . but also" arrangement, omitting the *also* if you wish. Count your answer right so long as the words *not only* and *but* are present.

Linda is a good student and a good athlete.

b

_____

_____

1214

1215

S, F, or *R-S?*

Many settlers headed back to the East, discouraged by all the hardships of pioneer life. _____

R-S

1484

1485

Your motor will last longer if you use high-grade oil in it. 1754	**Mom** doesn't like Diane to practice when *she* is tired. _____ _____ 1755

That, seems
 	
2023
	A noun that means a group or collection of persons or animals is called a **collective noun**.
	
	    a. **member, child, student, chairman, goat**
	    b. **team, family, class, audience, flock**
	
	Which group of words consists of collective nouns? _____
	
	2024

had caused 2292	**Mr. Dawson wrote an angry letter and then** (*tore, had torn*) **it up.** 2293
her 2561	Underline the correct pronouns: **The article mentioned only two players,** (*he, him*) **and** (*I, me*). 2562
hair, eyes(,) 2830	**Bob and Leslie came to the test without paper or pens or pencils.** 2831
wouldn't wasn't 3099	When you write contractions, don't change any letters in the original words. (The contractions *won't* for *will not* and *can't* for *cannot* are the exceptions.) Merely substitute an apostrophe for the letter or letters you omit. The contraction for **does not** is (*doesn't, dosen't*). 3100

	⌒ Henry <u>was</u> the chairman.
Henry	In this sentence, the verb **was** ties up or *links* the noun _____ with the subject **Henry,** which it *identifies*.
135	136

	When might we use a semicolon in preference to a conjunction? If there are too many *and*'s in a sentence, we may get rid of one by substituting a semicolon.
semicolon	**The patient asked for steak and potatoes, and the doctors and nurses were astonished.**
	How many **and**'s are there in this sentence? _____
405	406

	Ron's mother, *who bandaged my arm,* **is a doctor.**
	Rewrite this sentence so as to emphasize the fact that Ron's mother *bandaged my arm* and to subordinate the fact that she is a *doctor*.
a	_____
	_____
675	676

	A noun or pronoun—often with modifiers—that is set after another noun or pronoun to explain it is called an **appositive.**
Joseph Priestley	**Joseph Priestley,** *an English* <u>*minister,*</u> **discovered oxygen.**
	The appositive is the noun _____.
945	946

Linda is not only a good student but (also) a good athlete. *or* Not only is Linda . . . but (also) . . .	Continue to follow the directions for the previous frame:
	The article misspelled my name and gave a wrong age.
	_____
	_____
1215	1216

	One of the following items is *not* correct:
	a. **Some drugs quicken the heartbeat, others slow it down.**
S	b. **Some drugs quicken the heartbeat; others slow it down.**
	c. **Some drugs quicken the heartbeat, and others slow it down.**
	The run-on sentence is _____.
1485	1486

When Mom is tired, she doesn't like Diane to practice. 1755	**Vern couldn't notify <u>Earl</u> because *he* has no telephone.** _____ _____ (*Note:* Use an adjective clause beginning with *who*.) 1756

b
 	
2024
	A collective noun takes a singular verb when the group acts together *as a single unit*; a plural verb when the members of the group act *individually*.
	
	  a. **The class *is* now in the library.**
	  b. **The class *are* giving their talks on famous inventors.**
	
	We think of the class *as a single unit* in sentence (*a, b*).
	
	2025

tore 2293	**Fortunately, Mr. Dawson tore up the angry letter that he** (*wrote, had written*). 2294
him, me 2562	To decide between **we** and **us** in expressions like "*we* (or *us*) fellows" or "*we* (or *us*) girls," omit the appositive *fellows* or *girls,* and you will see instantly which pronoun is right. Underline the correct pronoun: (*We, Us*) ~~boys~~ **can get our own lunch.** 2563
None 2831	**Tom Black Bull sat down on the sofa opened a book and began reading.** 2832
doesn't 3100	The contraction for **are not** is (*aren't, arn't*). 3101

chairman 136	Henry is happy. Henry was the chairman. A verb like **is** or **was** is called a **linking verb** because it *links* a noun, pronoun, or adjective that follows it with the _____ of the sentence. 137
three 406	The patient asked for steak and potatoes, and the doctors and nurses were astonished. To get rid of one of the three **and**'s, we can substitute a semicolon for the **and** which follows the word _____. 407
Ron's mother, who is a doctor, bandaged my arm. 676	Lesson **18** A Final Attack on *And* [Frames 678–702]
minister 946	Anna won the first prize, *a trip to Washington.* The noun *trip* explains the noun _____. 947
The article not only misspelled my name but (also) gave a wrong age. 1216	Insulation saves fuel and keeps a house more comfortable. _____ _____ 1217
a 1486	UNIT 7: THE SMOOTH-RUNNING SENTENCE Lesson **41** Placing Modifiers Sensibly [Frames 1488–1526]

Vern couldn't notify Earl, who has no telephone. 1756	**Mr. Brock said to <u>Dad</u> that *he* needed more insurance.** _____ _____ 1757
a 2025	a. **The class *is* now in the library.** b. **The class *are* giving their talks on famous inventors.** We think of the members of the class as acting *individually* in sentence (*a, b*). 2026
had written 2294	**Loren would probably have driven more carefully if Peggy (*would have, had*) suggested it.** 2295
We 2563	Underline the correct pronoun: **The man asked (*we, us*) fellows to push his car.** 2564
sofa, book(,) 2832	**It was a gray cold cheerless morning in February.** 2833
aren't 3101	The contraction for **were not** is (*weren't, were'nt*). 3102

subject

137

Be is by far the most common *linking verb*. Be sure that you can recognize its various forms.

FORMS OF *BE:* is, am, are—was, were, been

The crops . . . good.

Which two forms of *be* could be used to link **good** with **crops** in the above sentence? _____, _____

138

---

potatoes

407

The weather was hot and sticky, and the boys and girls were listless.

To get rid of one of the three **and**'s, we can substitute a semicolon for the **and** which follows the word _____.

408

And is a good word to use when you wish merely to *add* one idea to another equal idea.

    a. **I recognized Jo, and she recognized me.**
    b. **I recognized Jo, and I hadn't seen her for years.**

In which sentence is **and** more appropriate—*a* or *b?* _____

678

---

prize

947

Anna won the first prize, *a trip to Washington.*

The appositive is the noun _____.

948

Insulation not only saves fuel but (also) keeps a house more comfortable.
1217

Franklin was a great statesman and a distinguished scientist.

_____

_____

1218

The meaning of a sentence often depends on where we place adverbs such as *only, just, merely, almost, nearly,* and *even.*

    a. **Steve** *only* **glanced at the advertisements.**
    b. **Steve glanced** *only* **at the advertisements.**

Which sentence means that Steve did not read the advertisements thoroughly? _____

1488

Lesson 49 Incorrect Omission of Words

[Frames 1759–1797]

---

b

Underline the correct verb in each sentence:

a. **The class** (*is, are*) **now in the library.**
b. **The class** (*is, are*) **giving their talks on famous inventors.**

2026

2027

---

had

If we (*had urged, would have urged*) **him a little more, Rafael would have sung for us.**

2295

2296

---

us

Underline the correct pronouns:

The lifeguard had warned (*we, us*) **boys, but** (*we, us*) **boys wouldn't listen.**

2564

2565

---

gray, cold,

Grange went dodging and twisting and bucking through the Buckeye tackles.

2833

2834

---

weren't

Write in the contractions for the italicized words:

It *does not* (_____) **taste good when it** *is not*
(_____) **ripe.**

3102

3103

FORMS OF *BE*: **is, am, are—was, were, been**

I . . . the first speaker.

Which two forms of *be* could be used to link **speaker** with **I**
in the above sentence? _____ , _____

(any two)
are, were,
have been,
had been

138

139

**The gold and the silver finally gave out, and many miners
settled down and became farmers.**

To get rid of one of the three **and**'s, we can substitute a

semicolon for the **and** which follows the word _____.

---

sticky

408

409

---

a. **I recognized Jo,** *and* **I hadn't seen her for years.**
b. **I recognized Jo** *although* **I hadn't seen her for years.**

Which word brings the two facts into closer relationship—

and or *although*? _____

---

a

678

679

**Both parties, the Republicans and the Democrats, favored
the bill.**

This sentence contains _____ appositives. (How many?)

---

trip

948

949

Joan Baez wrote the words and composed the music.

_____

_____

Franklin was
not only a great
statesman but
(also) a
distinguished
scientist.
1218

1219

---

a. **Steve** *only* **glanced at the advertisements.**
b. **Steve glanced** *only* **at the advertisements.**

Which sentence means that Steve paid no attention to the

news articles or editorials? _____

---

a

1488

1489

When the same form of a word fits in two places in a sentence, we may avoid repetition by using it only once and taking it for granted in the other position.

You *have* **four and I** *have* **three.**

May we omit the second *have*? (*Yes, No*)

1759

---

a. is
b. are

2027

Underline the correct verb in each sentence:

a. **The team** (*has, have*) **not yet worn their new uniforms.**
b. **The team** (*has, have*) **won every game this season.**

2028

---

had urged

2296

By the time my sister Dorothy is ready for college, she (*will save, will have saved*) **a thousand dollars.**

2297

---

us, we

2565

a. **. . . girls can meet at my house.**
b. **All of . . . girls can meet at my house.**

In which sentence would the objective pronoun **us** be correct? _____

2566

None

2834

Heavy drapes rugs and overstuffed furniture are giving way to simpler streamlined furnishings.

(*Note:* This sentence requires two commas with a third comma optional.)

2835

---

doesn't, isn't

3103

Write in the contractions for the italicized words:

Edward *did not* (_____) **come because he** *was not* (_____) **invited.**

3104

(any two)
am, was,
had been

139

We have seen that some *action verbs* make complete statements about their subjects and that others do not.

a. **The engine started.**
b. **The engine uses . . .**

In which sentence does the action verb make a complete statement? _____

140

---

out

409

If you have a good ear for the sound of sentences, you have noticed that a semicolon produces a quicker, brisker rhythm than a conjunction.

a. **You need your school, and your school needs you.**
b. **You need your school; your school needs you.**

Which sentence is more brisk and forceful? _____

410

---

although

679

a. **His mother wasn't home. Luis started the dinner.**
b. **Luis started the dinner. His mother finished it.**

Which pair of sentences would it be better to combine by **and** to form a compound sentence—*a* or *b?* _____

680

---

two

949

Both parties, the Republicans and the Democrats, favored the bill.

The two appositives are the words _____

and _____.

950

Joan Baez not only
wrote the words
but (also)
composed the
music.
1219

3. The "the more . . . the more" or "the more . . . the less" device:

The more **you eat,** *the more* **you want.**

Does this sentence have any connecting word between the two word groups? (*Yes, No*)

1220

---

b

1489

a. **Eng's Shop** *just* **repairs radios.**
b. **Eng's Shop repairs** *just* **radios.**

Which sentence means that the shop repairs radios but not other appliances? _____

1490

Yes

a. **You** *have* **four and I . . . three.**
b. **You** *have* **four and he . . . three.**

In which sentence would the verb *have* not fit in the blank space? _____

1760

---

a. have
b. has

2028

It is sometimes difficult to decide whether a group is acting as a single unit or as individuals. Whatever you decide, be sure to keep your pronoun consistent with the verb.

a. **The class** <u>was</u> (*singular*) **ready for** <u>their</u> (*plural*) **test.**
b. **The class** <u>was</u> (*singular*) **ready for** <u>its</u> (*singular*) **test.**

The pronoun is consistent with the verb in sentence (*a, b*).

2029

---

will have saved

2297

After I sell two more tickets, I (*shall sell, shall have sold*) **my quota for the game.**

2298

---

b

2566

A very common error is the expression "Let's you and I . . . ," which should be "Let's you and *me*. . . ."

Let's is a contraction of *Let us.* Since *us* is the object of the verb *Let,* the pronouns that explain whom we mean by the objective pronoun *us* should also be in the (*nominative, objective*) case.

2567

---

drapes, rugs(,)
simpler,

2835

After we planted the corn potatoes and cabbages we had little room for anything else.

2836

---

didn't, wasn't

3104

Write in the contractions for the italicized words:

Let us (_____) **see if** *they will* (_____) **help us.**

3105

However, a linking verb cannot by itself make a complete statement about its subject.

Since the purpose of a *link* is to connect two things, a *linking verb* must be followed by a complement that it can link with the _____ of the sentence.

141

---

a. **You can sell your home; you can't sell rent receipts.**
b. **You can sell your home, but you can't sell rent receipts.**

Which sentence is more brisk and forceful? _____

411

Luis started the dinner, and his mother finished it.

This is a good compound sentence because the **and** connects two *similar* ideas of (*equal, unequal*) importance.

681

An appositive generally comes (*before, after*) the noun or pronoun it explains.

951

This sentence device is useful to show that as one thing increases or decreases, something else increases or decreases.

The more **you eat,** *the more* **you want.**

As your eating increases, your wanting (*increases, decreases*).

1221

---

a. **Eng's Shop** *just* **repairs radios.**
b. **Eng's Shop repairs** *just* **radios.**

Which sentence means that the shop repairs radios but does not sell them? _____

1491

WRONG: **You** *have* **four and he three.**

This sentence is wrong because with **You** we use *have,* but with **he** we need (*have, has*).

b

1760   1761

---

b

Underline the correct words:

The audience (*was, were*) **rattling their programs.**

(Does the audience as a single unit rattle a single program?)

2029   2030

---

shall have sold

Lesson 64 Using Active Verbs for Directness

[Frames 2300–2334]

2298

---

objective

For the same reason that we say "Let *me,*" we should also say, "Let's you and (*I, me*)."

2567   2568

---

corn, potatoes(,) cabbages,

Mr. Stein has an anecdote to prove or disprove almost any political economic or educational theory.

(*Note:* This sentence requires one comma with a second comma optional.)

2836   2837

Let's, they'll

Do not confuse contractions with possessive pronouns which are pronounced the same.

CONTRACTIONS: **it's   you're   they're   who's**
POSSESSIVE PRONOUNS: **its   your   their   whose**

To show ownership you would choose one of the above words (*with, without*) an apostrophe.

3105   3106

subject 141	**The paint was . . . (What?)** Was the paint wet, dry, or sticky? Until we add a word that the linking verb **was** can connect with the subject, the meaning of the sentence is (*complete, incomplete*). 142
a 411	a. **Clyde sat right in front of me, and we soon became close friends.** b. **The brakes failed, and the car crashed into the truck.** In which sentence is the action more exciting? _____ 412
equal 681	**His mother wasn't home. Luis started the dinner.** Here the first sentence explains *why* about the second sentence. Which word would bring out this relationship more clearly— *and* (before **Luis**) or *because* (before **His**)? _____ 682
after 951	**The soprano, Camilla Williams, sang at the White House. Camilla Williams, the soprano, sang at the White House.** Is the appositive the same in both sentences? (*Yes, No*) 952
increases 1221	*The more* **one learns,** *the less* **positive one becomes.** This means that as one's learning increases, one's positiveness (*increases, decreases*). 1222
a 1491	Wherever misunderstanding might occur, place the adverb *only, just, merely, almost, nearly,* or *even* as near as possible to the word it modifies and generally before it. **We __(a)__ wash __(b)__ the towels.** To mean that you wash the towels, but not the sheets or pillowcases, put the word *only* in space (*a, b*). 1492

has

1761

---

a. **You** *have* **four and he three.**
b. **You** *have* **four and I three.**

Which sentence is correct? ____

1762

---

were

2030

Weights, measurements, periods of time, and amounts of money generally take singular verbs because they are thought of as single quantities rather than separate units. **Fifty feet of hose** *is* **enough. Ten dollars** *seems* **a fair price.** Although the subjects of these sentences are plural in form, they take (*singular, plural*) verbs.

2031

---

a. **The catcher dropped the ball.**
b. **The ball was dropped by the catcher.**

In one sentence, the subject of the verb performs an action; in the other, the subject is acted upon.

The subject performs an action in sentence (*a, b*).

2300

---

me

2568

Underline the correct pronoun:

Let's you and (*me, I***) exchange letters.**

2569

---

political,
economic(,)

2837

A neat little girl with curly red hair was bouncing a big rubber ball on the sidewalk.

2838

---

without

3106

a. **it's**   **you're**   **they're**   **who's**
b. **its**   **your**   **their**   **whose**

From which group would you choose your word if you could put two words in its place? ____

3107

The paint **was** *sticky*.

We have now completed our sentence by adding the complement *sticky*.

The complement *sticky* describes the subject _____.

---

incomplete

142

143

---

b

412

a. **Clyde sat right in front of me, and we soon became close friends.**
b. **The brakes failed, and the car crashed into the truck.**

Which sentence, because of its more exciting action, would benefit more from the brisk effect of a semicolon? _____

413

---

because

682

a. **His mother wasn't home, *and* Luis started the dinner.**
b. *Because* **his mother wasn't home, Luis started the dinner.**

Which sentence is better because it makes clear the relationship between the two facts—*a* or *b?* _____

683

No

952

The modifiers of an appositive may consist of words, phrases, and clauses.

Alfred Nobel, *the inventor* of dynamite, **established the Nobel prizes.**

The appositive *inventor* is modified by a (*phrase, clause*).

953

---

decreases

1222

a. *The more* **one learns,** *the less* **positive one becomes.**
b. **As one learns more, one becomes less positive.**

Which sentence makes the relationship between the two facts more striking? _____

1223

---

b

1492

We ___(a)___ wash ___(b)___ the towels.

To mean that you wash the towels but do not iron them, put the word *only* in space (*a, b*).

1493

b

1762

---

a. **Sue** *goes* **to high school, and he . . . to college.**
b. **Sue** *goes* **to high school, and I . . . to college.**

In which sentence do we not need to repeat the verb *goes*

because the same form would fit in the blank space? _____

1763

---

singular

2031

---

a. **Five minutes is enough time for my announcement.**
b. **Four yards of material are enough for a dress.**

In which sentence is the verb correct? _____

2032

---

a

2300

A verb is said to be **active** when its subject performs an action.

a. **The catcher** *dropped* **the ball.**
b. **The ball** *was dropped* **by the catcher.**

In which sentence is the verb *active* because its subject performs an action? _____

2301

---

me

2569

POSSESSIVE PRONOUNS BEFORE GERUNDS

A gerund, as you have learned, is a special kind of noun that is formed by adding *-ing* to a verb.

I enjoy all *sports,* **but I like** *skiing* **best.**

Which of the two italicized words is a gerund? _____

2570

None

2838

Because it was the day before Thanksgiving planes trains and buses were filled to capacity.

2839

---

a

3107

---

a. **. . . lunch is ready.**
b. **. . . making a mistake.**

The contraction **You're** would be correct in sentence (*a, b*).

3108

---

page 286

paint

143

Now instead of using an adjective to complete our sentence, we shall use a noun as our complement.

> Angela was . . . (What?)
> Angela was **the driver.**

The complement **driver** completes the meaning of the sentence and identifies the subject _____.

144

---

b

413

a. **The strike was called, and five thousand workers laid down their tools.**
b. **The game was very slow, and many fans left the stadium.**

In which sentence would the use of a semicolon reinforce the excitement of the action? _____

414

---

b

683

And is objectionable only when it steals the job of words such as **who, which, as, when, because,** and **although,** which show exactly _how_ two ideas are related to each other.

> a. **The water boils** _and_ **the kettle whistles.**
> b. _As soon as_ **the water boils, the kettle whistles.**

Which of the above sentences gives more specific information—_a_ or _b?_ _____

684

---

phrase

953

Alfred Nobel, _the chemist who invented dynamite,_ **established the Nobel prizes.**

The appositive _chemist_ is modified by a (_phrase, clause_).

954

---

a

1223

In this and the following frames, put each sentence into "the more . . . the more" or "the more . . . the less" arrangement:

> **As he earns more, he spends more.**

_____

_____

1224

---

a

1493

> **Vi can __(a)__ play __(b)__ any instrument.**

To mean that Vi can play many instruments, put _almost_ in space (_a, b_).

1494

a

1763

WRONG: **Sue** *goes* **to high school, and I to college.**

This sentence is wrong because with **Sue** we use *goes,* but with **I** we need _____.

1764

---

a

2032

One dollar seems too much to pay for this cake.

If you changed **One dollar** to **Three dollars,** would you need to change the verb **seems?** (*Yes, No*)

2033

---

a

2301

a. **The catcher** *dropped* **the ball.**
b. **The ball** *was dropped* **by the catcher.**

In which sentence is the subject of the verb acted upon?

_____

2302

---

skiing

2570

a. **I was surprised at** *his* **behavior.**
b. **I was surprised at** *his* **offering a tip.**

In which sentence is the possessive pronoun *his* followed by a gerund? _____

2571

Thanksgiving, planes, trains(,)

2839

Lesson **79** Commas for Interrupting Expressions

[Frames 2841–2876]

---

b

3108

a. **I wonder if . . . ready.**
b. **Which is . . . house?**

The contraction **they're** would be correct in sentence (*a, b*).

3109

page 288

Angela

144

A complement that follows a linking verb and describes or identifies the subject is sometimes called a *predicate nominative, predicate adjective,* or *subject complement.* In this text, we shall use the term **subject complement**. It is called a **subject complement** because it *describes* or *identifies* the

_____.

145

---

a

414

Don't use a comma without a conjunction to connect sentences. Only a semicolon has the power to hold two sentences together without the help of **and, but,** or **or.**

a. **Bea shook the branches, the apples came tumbling down.**
b. **Bea shook the branches; the apples came tumbling down.**

Which sentence is correctly punctuated? _____

415

---

b

684

You will greatly improve your writing if you use **and** only when you are sure that no *more specific* relationship exists.

a. *After* **Juan visited the club, he decided to join.**
b. **Juan visited the club,** *and* **he decided to join.**

The relationship between the two facts is clearer in (*a, b*).

685

---

clause

954

An appositive with its modifiers forms an **appositive phrase.**

Pete, *their youngest son,* **has just started college.**
Pete   **has just started college.**

When we omit the appositive phrase, does a complete sentence remain? (*Yes, No*)

955

The more he earns, the more he spends.

1224

Sometimes a comparative form (*-er*) of an adjective or an adverb is used in these arrangements.

When you drive faster, you see less.

_____

_____

1225

---

b

1494

Vi can ___(a)___ play ___(b)___ any instrument.

To mean that Vi really can't quite play any one instrument, put *almost* in space (*a, b*).

1495

go

1764

I never have *eaten* **and never will** *eat* **an oyster.**

Does the same form of the verb *eat* follow both **have** and **will?** (*Yes, No*)

1765

No

2033

In this and the following frames, underline the correct verb. Remember that a verb ending in *s* in the present tense is always singular.

There (*is, are*) **about twenty-four electric light bulbs in the average car of today.**

2034

---

b

2302

A verb is said to be **passive** when its subject is acted upon.

    a. **The catcher** *dropped* **the ball.**
    b. **The ball** *was dropped* **by the catcher.**

In which sentence is the verb *passive* because its subject is acted upon? _____

2303

---

b

2571

    a. **I was surprised at** *his* **behavior.**
    b. **I was surprised at** *his* **offering a tip.**

In which sentence might you sometimes hear the objective pronoun *him* used instead of the possessive pronoun *his?*

_____

2572

We often interrupt a sentence to insert an expression that is aside from our main thought. In speech, we keep such expressions in the background by dropping our voice and pausing before and after; in writing, we use commas.

Punctuate the interrupting expression:

The stories *on the whole* **are lacking in originality.**

2841

---

a

3109

    a. **I think . . . boiling.**
    b. **I like . . . design.**

The contraction **it's** would be correct in sentence (*a, b*).

3110

subject

145

The **subject complement** brings us to our third sentence pattern:

PATTERN III: *Subject—Linking Verb ← Subject Complement*

    a. **A forest ranger guards our forests.**
    b. **A forest ranger's life is rather lonely.**

Which sentence is an example of **Pattern III?** _____

146

---

b

415

    a. **The weather was raw, and the field was muddy.**
    b. **The weather was raw, the field was muddy.**

In which sentence is the comma correctly used? _____

416

---

a

685

By using fewer **and's** and more clause signals such as **which, whose, since, whenever,** and **although,** you will show the relationship between your ideas (*more, less*) clearly.

686

Yes

955

An appositive is useful for avoiding an "I-forgot-to-tell-you" type of sentence that explains something you have just named in the previous sentence.

    Mrs. Cross is the editor. *She is a friend of my teacher's.*

The second sentence explains _____ in the first sentence.

956

The faster you drive, the less you see.

1225

If a car is heavier, it rides more smoothly.

_____

_____

(Some variation in the wording is allowable.)

1226

---

a

1495

Sue __(a)__ earned __(b)__ ten dollars.

To mean that Sue came close to earning this money but that she didn't get the job, put *nearly* in space (*a, b*).

1496

No

1765

WRONG: **I never have and never will** *eat* **an oyster.**

This sentence is wrong because with **will** we use *eat,* but with **have** we need _____.

1766

---

are

2034

(*Here's, Here are*) **the list of contributors.**

2035

---

b

2303

a. **The catcher** *dropped* **the ball.**
b. **The ball** *was dropped* **by the catcher.**

In sentence *a,* the performer of the action is shown by the subject.

In sentence *b,* the performer of the action is shown by the prepositional phrase _____.

2304

---

b

2572

a. **I was surprised at** *his* **behavior.**
b. **I was surprised at** *his* **offering a tip.**

Since you would never use the objective pronoun *him* before the noun **behavior,** it would likewise seem reasonable not to use *him* before the gerund _____.

2573

, on the whole,

2841

There are several types of interrupting expressions. Any of them can be omitted without damaging the meaning or completeness of your sentence.

Underline and put commas around three words that form an interrupting expression:

The refreshments by the way were excellent.

2842

---

a

3110

a. **. . . ringing the doorbell?**
b. **. . . ticket is this?**

The pronoun **Whose** would be correct in sentence (*a, b*).

3111

b	**Some cameras are very expensive.** The subject complement that follows the linking verb in this sentence is _____.
146	147
a	a. **The weather was raw, the field was muddy.** b. **The weather was raw; the field was muddy.** Which sentence is correctly punctuated? _____
416	417
more	a. **This part controls the shutter,** *and* **it is very delicate.** b. **This part,** *which* **controls the shutter, is very delicate.** Which sentence is tighter because it brings the two facts into closer relationship—*a* or *b?* _____
686	687
Mrs. Cross	**Mrs. Cross is the editor.** *She is a friend of my teacher's.* **Mrs. Cross,** *a friend of my teacher's,* **is the editor.** We changed the italicized sentence to an appositive and put it next to the noun _____, which it explains.
956	957
The heavier a car is, the more smoothly it rides.	**As you get older, you have more responsibilities.** _____ _____
1226	1227
a	**Sue ___(a)___ earned ___(b)___ ten dollars.** To mean that Sue earned slightly less than ten dollars, put *nearly* in space (*a, b*).
1496	1497

eaten 1766	a. **I never have** *eaten* **and never will** *eat* **an oyster.** b. **I never have and never will** *eat* **an oyster.** Which sentence is correct—*a* or *b?* _____ 1767
Here's 2035	**License statistics show that there** (*is, are*) **more fishers than hunters in the United States.** 2036
by the catcher 2304	a. **The band** *played* **a march.** b. **A march** *was played* **by the band.** Which sentence contains an active verb? _____ 2305
offering 2573	INFORMAL: **I was surprised at** *him* **offering a tip.** Although an objective pronoun before a gerund is frequently heard in conversation, a possessive pronoun is more appropriate for careful writing and speaking. Underline the preferred pronoun: **The likelihood of** (*them, their*) **winning the game is slight.** 2574
by the way, 2842	PARENTHETICAL EXPRESSIONS Turn to the following frame, in which you will find some common interrupters known as **parenthetical expressions.** We often add these words and phrases to sentences to make their meaning clearer or more emphatic or to tie them up with the preceding sentences. (*Turn to the next frame.*) 2843
b 3111	In this and the following frames, underline the correct word in each pair. Be sure to choose the contraction whenever you can substitute two words: (*It's, Its*) **trying to escape from** (*it's, its*) **cage.** 3112

expensive

147

Although a form of **be** can be used by itself as a linking verb, it is often used as a *helper* with the main verb.

a. **The leaves are green.**   b. **The leaves are falling.**

In which sentence is **are** used as a helper? _____

148

---

b

417

If you omit the conjunction from a compound sentence, put a (*comma, semicolon*) in its place.

418

---

b

687

Eliminate the **and** in each sentence by changing the italicized idea to either an adverb or adjective clause, as the meaning requires. Write the full sentence.

Grandmother has many friends, and *they visit her often.*

_____

_____

688

Mrs. Cross

957

a. **Mrs. Cross is the editor.** *She is a friend of my teacher's.*
b. **Mrs. Cross,** *a friend of my teacher's,* **is the editor.**

Which arrangement is better because it puts the explanation of **Mrs. Cross** where it belongs—directly after the noun it explains? _____

958

The older you get, the more responsibilities you have.

1227

You go out farther, and the water gets deeper.

_____

_____

1228

---

b

1497

The man paid the bill with a *worthless* **check.**
The man paid the bill with a check *that was worthless.*

The adjective *worthless* comes before the noun **check,** which it modifies.

The adjective clause *that was worthless* comes (*before, after*) the noun **check,** which it modifies.

1498

a	We always have *paid* and always will *pay* our bills on time.
	Can we omit the verb *paid*? (*Yes, No*)
1767	1768

are	How much (*are, is*) those pads of paper?
2036	2037

	ACTIVE: **The band** *played* **a march.**
	↓
	PASSIVE: **A march** *was played* **by the band.**
a	What happens to the direct object **march** when we change the verb from active to passive?
	It becomes the _____ of the passive verb *was*
2305	*played.* 2306

	Underline the preferred pronoun:
their	**Political experts now see many reasons for (*his, him*) winning the election.**
2574	2575

	however of course for example after all
	therefore by the way nevertheless if possible
	a. **The cake was a failure** *after all* **our efforts.**
	b. **Freddy** *after all* **is only ten years old.**
	In which sentence should *after all* be set off with commas
2843	because it is an interrupter? _____ 2844

It's, its	(*It's, Its*) lightness is (*it's, its*) greatest advantage.
3112	3113

b

148

a. **The leaves are green.**   b. **The leaves are falling.**

Which sentence contains a subject complement? _____

149

---

semicolon

418

There are a number of adverbs that are sometimes mistaken for conjunctions.

ADVERBS: **however   otherwise   nevertheless
            therefore   consequently   furthermore**

Since these words are adverbs, they do not have the power

of _____ to combine sentences.

419

Grandmother
has many
friends who
visit her often.

688

Follow the directions given in the previous frame. Count your sentence right if it makes good sense even if you did not use the same clause signal given in the answer.

I got a poor seat, and *I arrived very early.*

_____

_____

689

---

b

958

Watch your writing for a weak sentence explaining something you have just written. If it contains the verb **is, are, was,** or **were,** followed by a noun, change it to an appositive phrase and fit it into the previous sentence.

a. **Ms. Lee urged us to win.**   b. **She is our new coach.**

Which sentence can be changed to an appositive? _____

959

The farther out
you go, the
deeper the
water gets.

1228

Traveling has made me appreciate my own town more.

_____

_____

1229

---

after

1498

Unless an adjective clause is placed directly *after* the word it modifies, your reader is likely to connect it with the wrong thing.

The pill came from this bottle *that the baby swallowed.*

The adjective clause is meant to modify **pill,** but it appears

to modify the noun _____.

1499

No

1768

a. **Did you put** *a* **pear or** *a* **peach in my lunch?**
b. **Did you put** *a* **pear or** *an* **apple in my lunch?**

We use the article **a** before a consonant sound (**a** *fish*) and the article **an** before a vowel sound (**an** *eel*).

In which sentence could we omit the article *a* because the same form of the article fits in both places? _____

1769

---

are

2037

There (*hasn't, haven't*) **been any changes in the rules.**

2038

---

subject

2306

ACTIVE: **The band** *played* **a march.**

PASSIVE: **A march** *was played* **by the band.**

Follow the arrow to see what happens to the subject **band** when we change the verb from active to passive.

The subject **band** becomes the object of the preposition _____.

2307

---

his

2575

Underline the preferred pronoun:

The principal has no objection to (*us, our*) **using her name.**

2576

---

b

2844

Here are other parenthetical expressions:

perhaps	**you know**	**on the whole**	**on the other hand**
it seems	**I suppose**	**on the contrary**	**generally speaking**

a. **The coach** *I suppose* **was very pleased.**
b. *I suppose* **that the coach was very pleased.**

I suppose should be set off with commas in sentence (*a, b*).

2845

Its, its

3113

(*It's, Its*) **tongue hangs out when** (*it's, its*) **thirsty.**

3114

The fans were *cheering.*
The fans were *enthusiastic.*

One of the italicized words is part of an action verb; the other is a subject complement.

The subject complement is the word _____.

a

149
150

---

a. **The air is humid, therefore the paint dries slowly.**
b. **The air is humid, and therefore the paint dries slowly.**

Which sentence is incorrect because there is no conjunction

to connect its two parts? _____

conjunctions

419
420

Shirley Chisholm made a statement, and *most people agreed with it.* (Try *with which.*)

_____

_____

I got a poor
seat although
I arrived very
early.

689
690

---

a. **Ms. Lee urged us to win.**   b. *She is our new coach*

Why is it easy to change sentence *b* to an appositive phrase?
It is easy because sentence *b* contains the verb *is,* followed

by the noun _____, which will become the appositive to
explain **Ms. Lee** in sentence *a.*

b

959
960

The more I
travel, the more
I appreciate my
own town.

Lesson **33** The Useful Noun–Participle
Phrase

[Frames 1231–1260]

1229

---

a. **The pill came from this bottle** *that the baby swallowed.*
b. **The pill** *that the baby swallowed* **came from this bottle.**

Which sentence is better because the adjective clause comes

right after the noun it modifies? _____

bottle

1499
1500

a 1769	**Did you put** *a* **pear or** *an* **apple in my lunch?** We cannot omit the *an* before **apple** because with **pear** we use *a*, but with **apple** we need to use _____. 1770
haven't 2038	(*Those, That*) **type of scissors** (*are, is*) **made for cutting hair.** 2039
by 2307	A passive verb always consists of a past participle combined with one of the tense forms of the verb **be.** Underline two passive verbs: **took was taken will give will be given** 2308
our 2576	In this and the following frames, underline the correct pronouns or, in some cases, the pronouns appropriate for formal usage. (*We, Us*) **boys saw no good reason for** (*them, their*) **postponing the game.** 2577
a 2845	Insert the necessary commas: **She plays the radio for example after everyone has gone to bed.** 2846
Its, it's 3114	(*You're, Your*) **circulation slows down when** (*you're, your*) **asleep.** 3115

enthusiastic

150

Be is not the only linking verb. Among other verbs that can serve as linking verbs are **seem, become, appear, look, feel,** and **get** (when it means **become**).

The candidate appeared cheerful.

The linking verb in this sentence is _____.

151

---

a

420

The air is humid, and therefore the paint dries slowly.

The word **therefore** is not a conjunction and has no connecting power. For this reason, we need to use the conjunction _____ in this sentence.

421

Shirley Chisholm made a statement with which most people agreed.

690

Cars become more complicated, **and mechanics require more training.**

_____

_____

691

---

coach

960

Ms. Lee once played college tennis. (*She is*) *our new coach.*
Ms. Lee, *our new coach,* **once played college tennis.**

In changing the italicized sentence to an appositive phrase, we dropped everything except the noun _____ and its modifiers.

961

A **noun-participle** phrase consists of a noun followed by a present or past participle that modifies this noun.

Knees trembling, **Dick stepped up to the stage.**

In the italicized phrase, the noun *Knees* is modified by the (*present, past*) participle *trembling*.

1231

---

b

1500

We sold our car to a used-car dealer *that had a cracked cylinder head.*

This sentence is absurd because the adjective clause appears to modify the noun **dealer** when it is really meant to modify the noun _____.

1501

an 1770	a. **Shall I make** *an* **apple or apricot pie?** b. **Shall I make** *an* **apple or pumpkin pie?** Which sentence is correct? _____ 1771
That, is 2039	(*This, These*) **kind** (*wears, wear*) **much longer than the cheaper ones.** 2040
was taken, will be given 2308	Underline two passive verbs: **sees is seen has sent has been sent** 2309
We, their 2577	*Reminder:* In expressions like *we* (or *us*) *boys,* use the same pronoun you would use if the noun (*boys*) were omitted. **Most of** (*we, us*) **boys are just as busy as** (*him, he*). 2578

, for example,
 	
2846
	Sometimes there is so little interruption—if any—that commas would only tend to make the reading jerky.
	    Of course **I'm going.** *Perhaps* **you will find it.**
	    a. **We** *therefore* **sent a telegram.**
	    b. **We decided** *therefore* **to send a telegram.**
	In which sentence would you use commas? _____
	
	2847

Your, you're 3115	(*You're, Your*) **not in** (*you're, your*) **right seat.** 3116

appeared 151	**The animals . . . cold.** Underline the two words that can be used as *linking verbs* in the above sentence: (feel) like (look) avoid 152
and 421	**The air is humid; therefore the paint dries slowly.** This sentence is correct because a semicolon has the power of a _____ to connect the two parts of a compound sentence. 422
As cars become more complicated, mechanics require more training. 691	**A friend recommended this book, and** *I value her opinion highly.* (Try *whose.*) _____ _____ 692
coach 961	**Ms. Lee once played college tennis.** (*She is*) *our new coach.* **Ms. Lee,** *our new coach,* **once played college tennis.** Then we put the appositive phrase directly after the noun _____, which it explains. 962
present 1231	*The dinner prepared,* **we waited for our guests.** In the italicized phrase, the noun *dinner* is modified by the (*present, past*) participle *prepared.* 1232
car 1501	a. **We sold our car** *that had a cracked cylinder head* **to a used-car dealer.** b. **We sold our car to a used-car dealer** *that had a cracked cylinder head.* Which sentence is better because the adjective clause comes directly after the noun it modifies? _____ 1502

Repeat an article (*a, an, the*) or a possessive pronoun (*my, your, his,* etc.) if there is any chance of misunderstanding.

a

    a. **The McCanns have** *a* **black and white dog.**
    b. **The McCanns have** *a* **black and** *a* **white dog.**

Which sentence means two dogs? _____

1771   1772

This, wears

singular

The entire Apache tribe (*was, were*) **against the sale of its property.**

2040   2041

---

is seen,
has been sent

A sentence with an active verb is shorter, stronger, and more direct than one with a passive verb.

    ACTIVE: **Paul** *found* **a dollar.**
    PASSIVE: **A dollar** *was found* **by Paul.**

The sentence that gives a clumsy, roundabout effect is the one with the (*active, passive*) verb.

2309   2310

---

us, he

Let's you and (*me, I*) **insist on** (*his, him*) **paying his own way.**

2578   2579

---

b

When the word **well, why, yes,** or **no** is used as a sentence opener, it is generally followed by a comma.

Punctuate the following sentences:

        Well maybe you're right.
        Why this is a surprise!

2847   2848

You're, your

(*You're, Your*) **eyes show that** (*you're, your*) **tired.**

3116   3117

feel, look 152	The animals . . . cold. Underline the two words that can be used as *linking verbs* in the above sentence to make **cold** describe **animals**. fear become prefer get 153
conjunction 422	a. **It rained all day, nevertheless everyone had a good time.** b. **It rained all day, but everyone had a good time.** Which sentence is correct because its two parts are connected by a conjunction? _____ 423
A friend whose opinion I value highly recommended this book. 692	*The score was tied,* **and we had to play another game.** _____ _____ 693
Ms. Lee 962	a. **Ms. Lee once played college tennis.** *She is our new coach.* b. **Ms. Lee,** *our new coach,* **once played college tennis.** In which arrangement does the explanation of **Ms. Lee** sound less like an afterthought? _____ 963
past 1232	A noun-participle phrase has no grammatical connection with the rest of the sentence. *Knees trembling,* **Dick stepped up to the stage.** Is there any connecting word such as *when, because, who,* or *which* to connect the phrase with the main statement? *(Yes, No)* 1233
a 1502	a. **The book is very modern that we use in our literature class.** b. **The book that we use in our literature class is very modern.** Which sentence is better because the adjective clause comes directly after the noun it modifies? _____ 1503

b	a. **Harvey ordered** *a* **cheese and** *a* **ham sandwich.** b. **Harvey ordered** *a* **cheese and ham sandwich.** Which sentence means two sandwiches? _____
1772	1773

was	(*Note:* A verb and a pronoun used with a collective noun must be consistent with each other in number.) **The band** (*was, were*) **tuning up** (*its, their*) **instruments.**
2041	2042

passive	a. **The pitcher** *took* **a chance and** *threw* **the ball to first base.** b. **A chance** *was taken* **by the pitcher, and the ball** *was thrown* **to first base.** Which sentence is better because it is more direct? _____
2310	2311

me, his	(*Us, We*) **girls think that the leading role suits you better than** (*her, she*).
2579	2580

Well,
Why,
	Punctuate the following sentences:
	
	       Yes I agree with you.
	       No I didn't see Joan.

2848	2849

Your, you're	(*They're, Their*) **delicious when** (*they're, their*) **toasted.**
3117	3118

become, get
 	
153
	You can be sure that a verb is a linking verb if you can put some form of **be (is, am, are—was, were, been)** in its place.
	
	    a. **The customer** *feels* **the material.**
	    b. **The weather** *feels* **muggy.**
	
	In which sentence can you substitute **is** for **feels?** _____
	
	                                                                         154

b 423	a. **It rained all day, nevertheless everyone had a good time.** b. **It rained all day; nevertheless everyone had a good time.** Which sentence is correctly punctuated? _____ 424
Because the score was tied, we had to play another game. 693	*This was my first speech,* **and I wasn't nervous at all.** _____ _____ 694
b 963	Do not confuse an appositive phrase with an adjective clause. An appositive phrase consists only of a noun (or pronoun) with its modifiers. An adjective clause always has a subject and a _____. 964
No 1233	In the participial phrases we studied earlier, the participle modified a noun or pronoun in the main statement. *Trembling with excitement,* **Bert stepped up to the stage.** In the above sentence the present participle *Trembling* modifies the noun _____ in the main statement. 1234

b
 	
1503
	a. **No joke** *that hurts our feelings* **amuses us.**
	    b. **No joke amuses us** *if it hurts our feelings.*
	
	One sentence contains an adverb clause; the other, an adjective clause.
	
	Which sentence contains the adverb clause? _____
	                                                        1504

a 1773	a. *My* cousin and best friend will go with me. b. *My* cousin and *my* best friend will go with me. Which sentence means two persons? _____ 1774
were, their 2042	Five tons (*were, was*) too big a load for the truck. 2043
a 2311	a. This play was practiced by the team until it was perfect. b. The team practiced this play until it was perfect. Which sentence is better? _____ 2312
We, her 2580	I intend to ask both our neighbors, Mr. Doyle and (*he, him*), if they object to (*me, my*) using their names for references. 2581

Yes,
No,
 	
2849
	We often use a "not" phrase to show what we do *not* mean in contrast to what we do mean. Such phrases require commas because they are strong interrupters.
	
	      The company, *not the salesman,* is to blame.
	
	Punctuate the following sentence:
	
	      Graphite not oil should be used on locks.
	
	2850

They're, they're 3118	(*They're, Their*) bringing out (*they're, their*) new models in October. 3119

a. **The customer** *feels* **the material.**
b. **The weather** *feels* **muggy.**

b

In one sentence **feels** is used as an *action* verb; in the other it is used as a *linking* verb.

In which sentence is it used as a *linking* verb? _____

154   155

---

a. **Our team was overconfident; consequently we lost.**
b. **Our team was overconfident, and consequently we lost.**
c. **Our team was overconfident, consequently we lost.**

b

Which one of these three sentences is incorrectly punctuated? _____

424   425

Although this
was my first
speech, I wasn't
nervous at all.

My uncle had a tent, and *he had no further use for it.*

_____

_____

694   695

---

verb
(*or* predicate)

a. **Ms. Lee,** *our new coach from Denver,* **played college tennis.**
b. **Ms. Lee,** *who is our new coach from Denver,* **played college tennis.**

Which sentence contains an appositive phrase?

964   965

Bert

Knees trembling, **Bert stepped up to the stage.**

In the noun-participle phrase, however, the present participle *trembling* does not modify a word in the main statement. It modifies the noun _____ in the phrase itself.

1234   1235

---

b

a. **No joke** *that hurts our feelings* **amuses us.**
b. **No joke amuses us** *if it hurts our feelings.*

The clause that can be shifted to other positions in the sentence is the (*adjective, adverb*) clause.

1504   1505

b	a. **We invited** *our* **coach and** *our* **math teacher to the picnic.** b. **We invited** *our* **coach and math teacher to the picnic.** Which sentence means two persons? _____
1774	1775

was	₅ ₅ ₚ **Two hours** (*seems, seem*) **hardly enough time to see all the sights.**
2043	2044

b	Unless you have a good reason for not doing so, always use (*an active, a passive*) verb.
2312	2313

him, my	**I couldn't understand** (*him, his*) **wanting to pay for all** (*us, we*) **students.**
2581	2582

, not oil,	Punctuate the following sentence: **It is the motion of the cloth not the red color that excites the bull.**
2850	2851

They're, their	(*They're, Their*) **fenders prove that** (*they're, their*) **poor drivers.**
3119	3120

b

155

a. **The restaurant** *looked* **crowded.**
b. **The speaker** *looked* **at his watch.**

In which sentence can you substitute **was** for **looked?** _____

156

---

c

425

ADVERBS: **however**   **otherwise**   **nevertheless**
          therefore   **consequently**   **furthermore**

It is equally correct to start a new sentence with one of these adverbs. Many writers prefer to do so.

Our team was overconfident. Consequently we lost.

This sentence is (*correct, incorrect*).

426

My uncle had a tent for which he had no further use. (*Or* which he had no further use for.)

695

You switch the tires around, **and they will wear longer.**

_____

_____

696

---

a

965

a. **We visited Monticello,** *which was the home of Thomas Jefferson.*
b. **We visited Monticello,** *the home of Thomas Jefferson.*

Which sentence contains an appositive phrase? _____

966

Knees

1235

a. *Trembling with excitement,* **Bert stepped up to the stage.**
b. *Knees trembling,* **Bert stepped up to the stage.**

In which sentence does the participle *trembling* modify a word in the main statement, thus connecting it grammatically with that statement? _____

1236

---

adverb

1505

a. *If it hurts our feelings,* **no joke amuses us.**
b. **No joke,** *if it hurts our feelings,* **amuses us.**
c. **No joke amuses us** *if it hurts our feelings.*

Does an adverb clause, like an adjective clause, need to come directly after the word it modifies? (*Yes, No*)

1506

a	Do not omit a word required by the meaning or grammatical construction of a sentence or by customary usage.
	Bob made fun . . . my suggestion.
	Bob made fun . . . and ridiculed my suggestion.
1775	What preposition is missing from both sentences? _____
	1776

seems	**Lesson 57** Review: Agreement of Subject and Verb
2044	[Frames 2046–2072]

an active	**The nomination will be accepted by Nolan.**
	To change this sentence to one with an active verb, you would make _____ the subject of your revised sentence.
2313	2314

his, us	**The other boys, Louis and (*he, him*), were envious because Mr. Ringler didn't pay them as much as (*I, me*).**
2582	2583

, not the red color,	APPOSITIVES
	An appositive is a noun or pronoun—often with modifiers— that follows another noun or pronoun to explain it.
	Mary Lou Williams, *a composer,* **spoke to the teen-agers.**
	Can the italicized appositive be omitted without damaging the meaning or completeness of this sentence? (*Yes, No*)
2851	2852

Their, they're	**Let's decide (*who's, whose*) going in (*who's, whose*) car.**
3120	3121

a 156	a. **The restaurant** *looked* **crowded.** b. **The speaker** *looked* **at his watch.** In one sentence, *looked* is used as an action verb; in the other, as a linking verb for which we could substitute *was*. In which sentence is *looked* used as a linking verb and followed by a subject complement? _____ 157
correct 426	a. **I lost my car keys; otherwise I would have driven.** b. **I lost my car keys, otherwise I would have driven.** c. **I lost my car keys. Otherwise I would have driven.** Which one of these three sentences is incorrectly punctuated? _____ 427
If you switch the tires around, they will wear longer. 696	A sentence consisting of a main statement and an adverb or adjective clause is a (*compound, complex*) sentence. 697
b 966	An appositive phrase should be set off from the rest of the sentence by two commas (or a single comma if it ends the sentence) because it is an "extra" that could be omitted. Punctuate the following sentence: **Only one other team the New York Giants did as well.** 967
a 1236	Because a noun-participle phrase has no grammatical connection with the rest of the sentence, it is often called an **absolute** phrase, *absolute* meaning *independent*. An example of an absolute phrase is a (*participial, noun-participle*) phrase. 1237
No 1506	Modifiers—words, phrases, and clauses—sometimes get in one another's way and produce an awkward or absurd sentence. When this happens, you can often solve your problem by shifting the (*adverb, adjective*) clause to the beginning of the sentence. 1507

of

1776

The team had no respect . . . their coach.
The team had no respect . . . or confidence in their coach.

What preposition is missing from both sentences? _____

1777

One situation causes more errors in subject-verb agreement than any other:

The color . . . changes.

No matter what plural nouns in prepositional phrases might come between the subject and the verb, the verb must remain (*singular, plural*).

2046

Nolan

2314

---

a. **The nomination** *will be accepted* **by Nolan.**
b. **Nolan** *will accept* **the nomination.**

The verb in sentence *b* is active because its subject **Nolan** (*acts, is acted upon*).

2315

---

he, me

2583

(*Us, We*) **girls get out of school earlier than** (*her, she*).

2584

Yes

2852

Set off an appositive and its modifiers with commas because it is not an essential part of the sentence.

Punctuate the following sentence:

Our principal an enthusiastic football fan attends every game.

2853

---

who's, whose

3121

(Be especially careful with this sentence!)

(*Who's, Whose*) **the girl** (*who's, whose*) **taking the part of the grandmother?**

3122

a 157	We have now studied two kinds of complements: *direct objects* and *subject complements*. With a little reasoning, we can avoid confusing the two. A *direct object* can follow only an *action verb*. A *subject complement* always follows a _____ verb.　　　　　　　　　　　　　　　　　　158
b 427	a. **Education must include the whole person; otherwise it is not true education.** b. **Education must include the whole person. Otherwise it is not true education.** Both *a* and *b* are correct. (*True, False*)　　　　　428
complex 697	The exact relationship between two facts or ideas is more clearly brought out by a (*compound, complex*) sentence. 　　　　　　　　　　　　　　　　　　　　　　698
team, . . . Giants, 967	Punctuate the following sentence: **The car belongs to Virginia Wade the English tennis star.** 　　　　　　　　　　　　　　　　　　　　　　968
noun-participle 1237	Because a noun-participle phrase, unlike a participial phrase, is related to the rest of the sentence only by our thought, it is classified as an ab _____ phrase. 　　　　　　　　　　　　　　　　　　　　　1238
adverb 1507	**Grace couldn't say good-by to her uncle (who was leaving the country) because she had measles.** **Because she had measles, Grace couldn't say good-by to her uncle (who was leaving the country.)** We get rid of the absurdity by shifting the (*adjective, adverb*) clause to the beginning of the sentence.　　　　1508

for	The teacher referred . . . a book. The book . . . which the teacher referred was not in the library. What preposition is missing from both sentences? _____
1777	1778

singular	The color of the lights . . . The color of the sky and the water . . . The color of various fish, birds, and animals . . . The color of the leaves on most trees and shrubs . . . The singular verb **changes** would be correct in each of these sentences. (*True, False*)
2046	2047

acts	Change the following sentence to one with an active verb: **These souvenirs** *will be appreciated* **by the children.** _____ _____
2315	2316

We, she	**Let's you and** (*me, I*) **see if Miss Haines won't let** (*we, us*) **girls organize a softball team.**
2584	2585

, an enthusiastic football fan,	Punctuate the following sentence: **The antelope the fastest animal in existence has been known to achieve a speed of sixty-two miles per hour.**
2853	2854

Who's, who's	(*Who's, Whose*) **mother is the woman** (*who's, whose*) **taking them camping?**
3122	3123

linking 158	Usually the subject and direct object are two *different* things, and the action passes from one to the other. 1 ⟶ 2 **The heavy downpour flooded many basements.** The action passes from **downpour** to _____. 159
True 428	In this and the following frames, insert the proper punctuation between the two word groups. Copy the word *before* the punctuation and *after* the punctuation. If a conjunction is present, insert a comma. If a conjunction is missing, insert a semicolon. **The field was muddy it didn't stop the Rangers.** _____ 429
complex 698	In changing a compound sentence to a complex sentence, you (*drop, add*) the conjunction *and, but,* or *or.* 699
Virginia Wade, 968	Punctuate the following sentence: **The Icelanders immigrants from Norway colonized their island in the ninth century.** 969
absolute 1238	To change a sentence to a noun-participle phrase is very simple. SENTENCE: **The fuel** *was running* **low.** NOUN-PARTICIPLE PHRASE: **The fuel** *running* **low . . .** We change the verb *was running* to a present participle by dropping the helping verb _____. 1239
adverb 1508	**Grace couldn't say good-by to her uncle who was leaving the country because she had measles.** Did Grace's uncle leave the country because of her measles? This amusing sentence contains an adjective clause beginning with the word **who** and an adverb clause beginning with the word _____. 1509

a. **We** *did* **many things that were fun.**
b. **We swam, fished, and many other things that were fun.**

What word is missing from sentence *b?* _____

1779

If you were to add the words printed in parentheses at the point marked by the caret (∧), would you need to change the italicized verb? If a change would be necessary, write only the form of the verb that would be required. If the verb would remain the same, write *Correct.*

∧ **Those records** *belong* **to Maxine. (One of)** _____

2048

Although you should generally try to use active verbs, there are times when passive verbs are very useful; for example, when the doer of an action is not known.

    a. **Our dog** *was stolen* **last night.**
    b. **The game** *was won* **by the Mustangs.**

In which sentence is the doer of the action not known? _____

2317

My two friends, Walt and (*him, he***), were disappointed because Mr. Hill didn't give them as good parts in the play as (***me, I***).**

2586

DIRECT ADDRESS

Direct address is a noun or other identifying words with which we sometimes interrupt a sentence to show to whom we are speaking.

      You know, *Nancy,* **that you're always welcome.**

Is the noun *Nancy* essential to the sentence? (*Yes, No*)

2855

APOSTROPHES FOR SPECIAL PLURALS

You have learned not to use apostrophes with ordinary plural nouns that do not show ownership.

      Several *girls'* **took** *boys'* **parts.**

The ordinary plural noun in this sentence that should not be written with an apostrophe is (*girls, boys*).

3124

basements

159

A subject complement, however, always *means the same thing* as the subject or *describes* the subject. We are dealing with *one* thing—not *two*.

1 ――――→2   1←―――― 1
a. **Mrs. Ford hired a lawyer.**   b. **Mrs. Ford is a lawyer.**

The noun **lawyer** is a subject complement in sentence (*a, b*).

160

---

muddy; it

429

Follow the directions given in the previous frame:

The wise are so uncertain   the ignorant are so positive.

_____

430

---

drop

699

Every compound sentence can be improved by changing it to a complex sentence. (*True, False*)

700

Icelanders, . . .
Norway,

969

Punctuate the following sentence:

A fierce battle of World War II was fought on Iwo Jima a very small Pacific island.

970

---

was

1239

Sometimes we need to change a one-word verb to a present participle.

SENTENCE: **The fuel *ran* low.**
NOUN-PARTICIPLE PHRASE: **The fuel *running* low . . .**

Here we change the verb *ran* to the present participle

_____.   1240

---

because

1509

Adverb phrases as well as adverb clauses are generally movable.

Underline the adverb phrase that could be shifted to the beginning of the sentence to get rid of its absurdity:

Dad glued together the vase that Chuck had broken with remarkable skill.

1510

did 1779	a. **The author has lived** *among* **the Eskimos.** b. **The author has lived, as well as written about, the Eskimos.** What word is missing from sentence *b*? _____ 1780
belongs 2048	**A friendly note** ∧ *doesn't* **take much time. (or a telephone call)** _____ 2049
a 2317	a. **The test** *had been passed* **by the student.** b. **The kitten** *had been left* **at our door.** In which sentence is a passive verb preferable because the doer of the action is not known? _____ 2318
he, me 2586	**Lesson 72** **Reflexive, Intensive, Demonstrative, and Possessive Pronouns** [Frames 2588–2625]
No 2855	Use commas to set off direct address because it interrupts the sentence and is not essential to its meaning. Underline and set off the direct address with commas: **Our team my friends needs your full support.** 2856

girls
 	
3124
	However, there are a few special cases where there is a good reason for using apostrophes to form ordinary plurals.
	
	    a. **Your os look like as.**
	    b. **Your o's look like a's.**
	
	Which sentence is easier to figure out? _____
	
	3125

a. **The owner of the restaurant hired a new cook.**
b. **The owner of the restaurant is the cook.**

b

In which sentence is the noun **cook** a subject complement because it means the same person as the subject? _____

160   161

---

uncertain; the

There are thirteen dogs on our block   and all of them seemed to be barking at once.

_____

430   431

False

For combining two similar or related ideas of equal importance, a (*compound, complex*) sentence is better.

700   701

Iwo Jima,

Change each italicized sentence to an appositive phrase, and insert it in the first sentence right after the word it explains. Supply the necessary commas.

Edith Hamilton is a respected scholar. *She is an expert on Greek mythology.* _____

_____

970   971

---

running

A noun-participle phrase consists of a noun plus a present participle that modifies *this noun*—not a noun in the main statement.

The fuel *running* low . . .

This is a noun-participle phrase because the present participle *running* modifies the noun _____.

1240   1241

---

with remarkable
skill

a. **We almost know everyone in town.**
b. **We know almost everyone in town.**

In which sentence is the adverb **almost** placed more sensibly?

_____

1510   1511

Do not omit *that* from a noun clause used as a subject complement after any form of the linking verb *be*.

RIGHT: **His excuse was that he didn't see the stop sign.**
WRONG: **His excuse was he didn't see the stop sign.**

What word is missing from the sentence that is labeled WRONG? _____

1781

Correct

2049

The shortage of goods ∧ *makes* prices skyrocket. (and the abundance of money)

_____

2050

---

b

2318

Passive verbs are also useful when the doer of an action is obvious or unimportant.

a. **The package *will be delivered* tomorrow.**
b. **The deliveryman *will deliver* the package tomorrow.**

Which sentence is better because the doer of the action is unimportant and had better be omitted? _____

2319

REFLEXIVE AND INTENSIVE PRONOUNS

Pronouns that end with *-self* or *-selves* can be used as either *reflexive* or *intensive* pronouns. When they reflect or turn back the action of the verb to the doer of the action, they are called **reflexive** pronouns.

A reflexive pronoun always ends with *-self* or _____.

2588

---

my friends,

2856

Punctuate the following sentence:

Let me know you lucky girl how you manage to get such high grades.

2857

---

b

3125

Use apostrophes to form the ordinary plurals of letters, numbers, signs, and words referred to as words.

There are two 3's and two 5's in our number.
The +'s should be changed to —'s.

Insert the needed apostrophes:

The temperature is usually in the 70s or 80s.

3126

The owner of the restaurant is energetic.

b

Because the adjective **energetic** describes the subject **owner** and is not something apart from it, **energetic** is a (*subject complement, direct object*).

161

162

---

block, and

Much of the soil is poor   consequently the Japanese farmer depends greatly upon fertilizers.

_____

431

432

---

compound

As you develop greater writing skill and see the relationship between your ideas more clearly, you tend to use (*more, fewer*) compound sentences.

701

702

Edith Hamilton, an expert on Greek mythology, is a respected scholar.

Farewell to Manzanar **was written by Jeanne Wakatsuki Houston.** *She is an American writer.*

_____

_____

971

972

---

fuel

a. *Running low,* **the fuel was insufficient to carry the plane to its destination.**
b. *The fuel running low,* **the pilot made an emergency landing.**

Which sentence contains a noun-participle phrase? _____

1241

1242

---

b

a. **With trembling knees, Bill walked into the office where the principal was sitting.**
b. **Bill walked into the office where the principal was sitting with trembling knees.**

In which sentence are the modifiers placed more sensibly?

1511

——

1512

that	In this and the following frames, if the omission is incorrect, add the necessary word. If the omission is allowable, write *Correct*.
	I *was* on one side and my two friends _____ on the other.
1781	1782

make	His father ∧ *plays* the piano. (, as well as his mother,)
	_____
2050	2051

a	Use a passive verb when you wish to avoid naming the person who made a mistake or did something wrong.
	a. **My boss** *threw* **out this important letter.**
	b. **This important letter** *was thrown* **out by mistake.**
	Which sentence would you use to avoid embarrassing your boss? _____
2319	2320

-selves	a. **Frank blamed** *me* **for his failure.**
	b. **Frank blamed** *himself* **for his failure.**
	Which sentence contains a reflexive pronoun that turns the action back to the doer of the action? _____
2588	2589

, you lucky girl,	Punctuate the following sentence:
	I wonder Fred if you have heard about Nancy Lopez.
2857	2858

70's, 80's	Insert the needed apostrophes:
	Bookkeeping is the only English word having three double letters in a row—two os, two ks, and two es.
3126	3127

a. **Otters are animals.**
b. **Otters are** *playful* **animals.**

In both sentences, the noun **animals** is a subject complement that identifies the subject **Otters.** In sentence *b*, we added the adjective *playful* to describe the noun **animals.**

In sentence *b*, the subject complement is (*playful, animals*).

163

Mrs. Merrill may be old   however, she is not old-fashioned.

_____

433

Lesson **19** Recognizing Noun Clauses

[Frames 704–743]

---

*Farewell to
Manzanar* was
written by Jeanne
Wakatsuki Houston,
an American
writer.
972

A great patriot founded the American Red Cross. *She was
Clara Barton.*

_____

_____

973

The fuel running low, **the pilot made an emergency landing.**

This is a noun-participle phrase because the participle *running* modifies the noun *fuel,* which is (*inside, outside*) the phrase.

1243

---

a. **They moved the chairs on which they were sitting closer
to the fire.**
b. **They moved the chairs closer to the fire on which they
were sitting.**

Which sentence is better? _____

1513

were 1782	I *was* on one side and my friend ＿＿＿＿＿ on the other. 1783
Correct 2051	ʌ These stories *deal* with sports. (Every one of) ＿＿＿＿＿＿＿＿＿ 2052
b 2320	a. **The room** *had* **not** *been cleaned* **after the party.** b. **Virginia** *had* **not** *cleaned* **the room after the party.** Which sentence is more tactful because it would not embarrass Virginia? ＿＿＿ 2321
b 2589	When pronouns that end with *-self* or *-selves* are used after a noun or another pronoun to emphasize or intensify it, they are called **intensive** pronouns. a. **The manager** *himself* **waited on me.** b. **The manager blamed** *himself* **for the mistake.** Is *himself* used as an intensive pronoun in *a* or *b*? ＿＿＿ 2590
, Fred, 2858	DATES AND ADDRESSES The date in the following sentence consists of three parts: **On** *Sunday, July 9, 1961,* **the new church was dedicated.** After the first part of the date, is there a comma both before and after each additional part? (*Yes, No*) 2859
o's, k's, e's 3127	Apostrophes make reading easier when we write the plurals of words referred to as words. a. **Tony has spelled all his toos wrong.** b. **Tony has spelled all his too's wrong.** Which sentence is easier to read? ＿＿＿ 3128

animals

163

Do not mistake an adjective that describes the subject complement for the subject complement of the sentence.

Otters are *playful* **animals.**

The subject complement in this sentence is (*the noun* **animals,** *the adjective* **playful**).

164

---

old; however

433

Fruit trees must be sprayed at the right time   or the fruit will be wormy.

_____

434

We have now completed our study of adverb and adjective clauses. We turn next to the third (and last) type of clause—the **noun clause.**

As its name suggests, a noun clause is a clause that is used as a _____.

704

A great patriot, Clara Barton, founded the American Red Cross.

973

John's mother gave him his first lessons in reporting. *She was the editor of a country paper.*

_____

_____

974

---

inside

1243

Now let's change a sentence to a noun-participle phrase that contains a past participle:

SENTENCE: **Her test** *was completed.*
NOUN-PARTICIPLE PHRASE: **Her test** *completed . . .*

We change the verb *was completed* to the past participle *completed* by dropping the helping verb _____.

1244

---

a

1513

---

a. **The letter carrier has to walk all day without sitting down to rest in the slushy snow.**
b. **The letter carrier has to walk all day in the slushy snow without sitting down to rest.**

Which sentence is better? _____

1514

Correct

1783

Alva never has _____ and never will *join* a sorority.

1784

---

deals

2052

The vacuum cleaner ∧ *sells* for $69. (and all its attachments)

_____

2053

---

a

2321

When you have a good reason for not mentioning the doer of an action or when you wish to focus attention on the person(s) or thing(s) acted upon, use (*an active, a passive*) verb.

2322

---

a

2590

a. **The manager** *himself* **waited on me.**
b. **He** *himself* **waited on me.**

In which sentence does the intensive pronoun emphasize

another pronoun? _____

2591

Yes

2859

The address in the following sentence consists of three parts:

The Atlas Company of *240 Oak Street, Dayton, Ohio 45417,* **will send you a catalogue.**

After the first part of the address, is there a comma both before and after each additional part? (*Yes, No*)

2860

---

b

3128

Insert the needed apostrophes:

Too many ands and sos make writing sound childish.

3129

the noun
animals
 	
164
	$S = Subject, LV = Linking Verb, SC = Subject Complement$
	This shallow lake often gets extremely rough.
	Fill in the missing words:
	
	      S LV SC
	  lake _____ _____ 165

time, or 434	**Fruit trees must be sprayed at the right time otherwise the fruit will be wormy.** _____ 435
noun 704	We have seen that adverb and adjective clauses offer almost endless possibilities for showing the various kinds of rel_____ that exist among our ideas. 705
John's mother, the editor of a country paper, gave him his first lessons in reporting. 974	**Thursday is named after Thor.** *He is the god of thunder in Norse mythology.* 975
was 1244	**Her test** *completed . . .* This is a noun-participle phrase because the past participle *completed* modifies the noun _____ within the phrase. 1245
b 1514	a. **The car was taken for investigation to the factory where it had been made after the crash.** b. **After the crash, the car was taken for investigation to the factory where it had been made.** Which sentence is better? _____ 1515

joined 1784	I must find *a* book or _____ article about politics. 1785
sell 2053	The vacuum cleaner ∧ *sells* for $69. (, with all its attachments,) _____ 2054
a passive 2322	In this and the following frames, make each sentence more direct by changing the verb from passive to active. To do so, make the object of the preposition **by** the subject of your revised sentence. **Nothing** *had been said* **by the teacher about a test.** _____ _____ 2323
b 2591	Be sure that you know the correct forms of the various reflexive and intensive pronouns: SINGULAR: **myself himself itself** **yourself herself oneself** PLURAL: **ourselves, yourselves, themselves.** Is there such a word as **hisself?** (*Yes, No*) 2592
Yes 2860	After writing the first part of a date or an address, put a comma both before and after each additional part. Punctuate the following sentence: **On Monday August 7 we left Phoenix Arizona and headed for El Paso Texas.** 2861
and's, so's 3129	Lesson **87** Controlling Your Capitals [Frames 3131–3162]

LV gets SC rough 165	$S = Subject, LV = Linking\ Verb, SC = Subject\ Complement$ **Hera was the powerful queen of the old Greek gods.** Fill in the missing words: S LV SC **Hera** _____ _____ 166
time; otherwise 435	**Before reading** *Jaws* **I never thought about sharks** **after reading** *Jaws* **I worried about sharks every summer.** _____ 436
relationship 705	Noun clauses do not begin to have the usefulness of the other clauses for sentence improvement. We use noun clauses so naturally that we study them mainly to complete our picture of the three kinds of clauses that we find in (*compound, complex*) sentences. 706
Thursday is named after Thor, the god of thunder in Norse mythology. 975	Eliminate the **and** by changing the italicized sentence to an appositive phrase and inserting it in the first sentence right after the word it explains. **Bermuda consists of 360 small islands, and** *it is a British* *colony.* _____ _____ 976

test
 	
1245
	a. *Her test completed,* **Carol turned in her paper.**
	   b. *Completing her test,* **Carol turned in her paper.**
	
	Which sentence contains a noun-participle phrase? _____
	
	                                                   1246

b 1515	In this and the following frames, rewrite each sentence to improve the placement of the modifiers: **The branch suddenly broke that she was climbing on.** _____ _____ 1516

an 1785	Dr. Shorr is looking for *a* typist and _____ receptionist. (Two persons) 1786
Correct 2054	Greene's is ∧ one of the groceries that *deliver*. (the only) _____ 2055
The teacher had said nothing about a test. 2323	Continue to follow the directions for the previous frame: **All your worries** *will be forgotten* **by you at this comedy.** _____ _____ 2324
No 2592	Underline the correct intensive pronoun: **Charlie Pride gave me this album** (*himself, hisself*). 2593
Monday, August 7, Phoenix, Arizona, El Paso, 2861	Punctuate the following sentence: **In Hants County England Jane Austen was born on December 16 1775.** 2862
	The eleven rules for capitals presented in this and the next lesson are all based upon one general principle: Use a capital letter for a proper noun—a name that fits only *one particular* person, group of people, place, or thing. Use a small letter for a common noun—a name that fits *any one* of its kind. (*Turn to the next frame.*) 3131

LV was SC queen 166	$S = Subject, LV = Linking Verb, SC = Subject Complement$ **An officer should feel responsible for those in his unit.** Fill in the missing words: S LV SC _____ **should feel** _____ 167
sharks; after 436	**Athletics keep a person physically fit and furthermore they develop a sense of teamwork.** _____ 437
complex 706	Since noun clauses are used exactly as nouns, let us review the various ways in which nouns are used. **His** *remark* **puzzled us.** The noun *remark* is the *subject* of the verb _____. 707
Bermuda, a British colony, consists of 360 small islands. 976	Continue to follow the directions for the previous frame: **My friend made cream puffs, and** *they are my favorite dessert.* _____ _____ 977
a 1246	*Her test completed,* **Carol turned in her paper.** This is a noun-participle phrase because the past participle *completed* modifies the noun *test,* which is (*inside, outside*) the phrase. 1247
The branch that **she** was climbing on suddenly broke. 1516	Continue to follow the directions for the previous frame: **Every student passed to whom the test was given.** _____ _____ 1517

a 1786	Supply a second verb only if the first verb does not fit in this position: **Cliff** *is* **seventeen and his sister** _____ **sixteen.** 1787
delivers 2055	**The yield of corn** ∧ *has* **been increased. (and wheat)** _____ 2056
You will forget all your worries at this comedy. 2324	(*Note:* There is no need to move the introductory phrase from its present position.) **After a long voyage, Tahiti** *was reached* **by the mutineers.** _____ _____ 2325
himself 2593	SINGULAR: **myself** **himself** **itself** **yourself** **herself** **oneself** PLURAL: **ourselves, yourselves, themselves** Is there such a word as **theirselves?** (*Yes, No*) 2594

Hants County, England, December 16,
 	
2862
	A one-part address is set off with commas only when there is no preposition such as *of, at,* or *on* to connect it with the sentence.
	   a. **Andy Shaw** *of* **778 Montclair Avenue was the winner.**
	   b. **Andy Shaw 778 Montclair Avenue was the winner.**
	The one-part address requires commas in sentence (*a, b*).
	
	2863

	1. Capitalize geographical names that apply to *particular* countries, sections of countries, states, cities, oceans, rivers, lakes, etc. **Canada** **North Dakota** **Pacific Ocean** **Hudson River** Copy one italicized word that requires a capital: **He lives in a** *city* **not far from** *cleveland.* _____ 3132

S officer SC responsible 167	The drunken driver is the greatest danger on our highways today. Fill in the missing words: S LV SC **driver** _____ _____ 168

UNIT 3: THE COMPLEX SENTENCE TO SHOW RELATIONSHIP

fit, and 437	Lesson **12** Recognizing Adverb Clauses [Frames 439–480]

puzzled 707	a. **His** *remark* **puzzled us.** b. *What he said* **puzzled us.** The clause *What he said* does the same job in sentence *b* that the noun *remark* does in sentence *a*. It is therefore a _____ clause. 708

My friend made cream puffs, my favorite dessert. 977	**Kitty Hawk is in North Carolina, and** *it was the birthplace of aviation.* (*Note:* The first sustained airplane flight was made by Orville Wright at the village of Kitty Hawk in 1903.) _____ _____ 978

inside 1247	*Her eyes shining with joy,* **Judy showed me her new car.** **Judy,** *her eyes shining with joy,* **showed me her new car.** **Judy showed me her new car,** *her eyes shining with joy.* Can a noun-participle phrase be shifted from one position to another in a sentence? (*Yes, No*) 1248

Every student to whom the test was given passed. 1517	**Rita Moreno was given the part in** *West Side Story* **of Anita.** _____ _____ 1518

Correct	Our country must be strong *on* the sea and _____ the air.
1787	1788

Correct	The team *was* ∧ in the gym. (weighing themselves)
	_____
2056	2057

After a long voyage, the mutineers reached Tahiti.	The high cost of medical service *is pointed* out by this article.
	_____
	_____
2325	2326

No	Underline the correct reflexive pronoun:
	The Lamberts have bought (*theirselves, themselves*) a boat.
2594	2595

b	The Speedy Cleaners *at* 600 Main Street give three-hour service on request.
	If you omitted the preposition *at*, would you set off 600 Main Street with commas? (*Yes, No*)
2863	2864

Cleveland	Copy one italicized word that requires a capital:
	Are there more *lakes* in *wisconsin* or in our *state*?
	_____
3132	3133

168

LV
is

SC
danger

The young children in the back seat were becoming very restless.

Fill in the missing words:

S	LV	SC
_____	_____	_____

169

---

a. **The whistle blew.**
b. **When the whistle blew**

Although both word groups have a subject and a verb, only one word group makes sense by itself.

Which word group makes sense by itself? _____

439

---

noun

708

We have seen that when we omit an adverb or adjective clause, we still have a grammatically complete sentence remaining.

What he said **puzzled us.**

When we omit the noun clause in this sentence, does a complete sentence remain? (*Yes, No*)

709

Kitty Hawk, the birthplace of aviation, is in North Carolina.

978

The game drew a crowd of 1,500, and *it was the largest attendance of the year.*

_____

_____

979

Yes

1248

a. **The audience grew restless, their patience exhausted.**
b. **Their patience exhausted, the audience grew restless.**

In which sentence does the noun-participle phrase come at

the end of the sentence? _____

1249

Rita Moreno was given the part of Anita . . . *or* In *West Side Story* Rita Moreno . . .

1518

I saw people waiting for the bus that looked frozen.

_____

_____

1519

in	**The steak** *was* **tough and the potatoes** _____ **overcooked.**
1788	1789

were	∧ **These doors** *lead* **to the basement. (Either of)** _____
2057	2058

This article points out the high cost of medical service.	**This event** *will* **always** *be remembered* **by our family.** _____ _____
2326	2327

themselves	All the *-self* pronouns are solid words. Do not split them! a. **my self, your self, her self, our selves, them selves** b. **myself, yourself, herself, ourselves, themselves** The pronouns are printed correctly after (*a, b*).
2595	2596

Yes	In line with the modern tendency to eliminate unnecessary commas, many publications omit commas in dates when *only* the month and the year are stated. a. **In May 1961 construction of the bridge was started.** b. **On May 27 1961 construction of the bridge was started.** Which sentence can do without commas? _____
2864	2865

Wisconsin	Copy only the words to which capitals should be added: **The Mississippi river begins at lake Itasca in minnesota.** _____
3133	3134

S children LV were becoming SC restless 169	**The coach of the other team was looking worried.** Fill in the missing words: S $\qquad$ LV $\qquad$ SC $\qquad$ _____ _____ _____ 170
a 439	a. **The whistle blew.** b. **When the whistle blew** Which word group is a sentence because it makes sense by itself? _____ 440
No 709	(*What he said*) **puzzled us.** If we omitted the noun clause, the sentence would lack a (*subject, direct object*). 710
The game drew a crowd of 1,500, the largest attendance of the year. 979	Doug Williams made the touchdown, and *he is the quarter-back.* _____ _____ 980
a 1249	a. **His eyelids drooping with sleepiness, Bob struggled through the last chapter.** b. **Bob struggled through the last chapter, his eyelids drooping with sleep.** In which sentence does the noun-participle phrase come at the end of the sentence? _____ 1250
I saw people that looked frozen waiting for the bus. 1519	**You should not put a glass into hot water that is cold.** _____ _____ 1520

were

1789

In this and the following frames, insert any word that has been *incorrectly* omitted. If the omission of the word is allowable, write *Correct*.

My sister takes Latin and I Spanish.

1790

---

leads

2058

In many parts of the world, the opportunity for education ∧ *does* **not exist. (and personal development)**

_____

2059

Our family will always remember this event.

2327

The rushing life of big cities *was* **never** *enjoyed* **by my father.**

_____

_____

2328

---

b

2596

Underline the correct reflexive pronoun:

Try to put (*yourself, your self*) **in my place.**

2597

---

a

2865

In this and the following frames, insert the necessary commas. If no commas are required, write *None*.

It is doubtful however whether any good will result from the change.

2866

River, Lake, Minnesota

3134

Capitalize **north, east, south,** and **west** when they name geographical sections of a country or of the world. Use small letters when they indicate directions on the compass.

    a. **The road turns** *south.*
    b. **The** *south* **is quite industrial.**

Capitalize *south* in sentence (*a, b*).

3135

Lesson 5 Reviewing Basic Sentence Patterns

[Frames 172–194]

---

a

440

a. **The whistle blew.**
b. **When the whistle blew**

Word group *b* is not a sentence because the word _____ has been added.

441

---

subject

710

We raise *vegetables*.

In this sentence the noun *vegetables* is the direct object of the verb _____.

711

Doug Williams,
the quarterback,
made the
touchdown.

980

An appositive generally comes (*before, after*) the noun it explains.

981

---

b

1250

A noun-participle phrase is a rather mature construction used by experienced writers to combine ideas.
In this and the following frames, combine the sentences by changing each italicized sentence to a noun-participle phrase.
I stood in the icy water. *My teeth were chattering.*

I stood in the icy water, _____.

1251

You should not
put a glass
that is cold
into hot water.

1520

Write the numbers of the three word groups to show in which order you would combine them. Be careful to avoid giving your sentence a ridiculous meaning.

1. **the club will show a movie**
2. **on how to play football**
3. **in the public library**

_____ _____ _____

1521

I *take* Spanish 1790	The truck was turning left and our car right. 1791
Correct 2059	ʌ The sparrows *wake* me every morning. (The noisy chirping of) _____ 2060
My father (has) never enjoyed the rushing life of big cities. 2328	Change the verb from active to passive to eliminate the present subject, which is obvious, unimportant, or tactless. Start your sentence with the thing or things *acted upon* and omit the doer of the action. **Someone *took* the injured man to the hospital.** _____ _____ 2329
yourself 2597	Supply the proper reflexive pronoun: **The Marines hid _____ behind some large rocks.** 2598
, however, 2866	**Send me word Virginia when you are well enough to have visitors.** 2867
b 3135	a. **Our house is on the *West* side of the street.** b. **The movie industry is in the *West*.** The word *west* should not be capitalized in sentence (*a, b*). 3136

Some action verbs can make complete statements about their subjects. Other action verbs require another word to complete the meaning of the sentence.

An action verb is (*always, sometimes*) followed by a direct object.

172

When

441

A word group that has a subject and a verb but does not make sense by itself is a **clause.**

    a. **The road was rough.**
    b. **Because the road was rough**

Which word group is a clause? _____

442

---

raise

711

    a. **We raise** *vegetables.*
    b. **We raise** *whatever we need.*

The noun clause *whatever we need* in sentence *b* is used just like the direct object _____ in sentence *a.*

712

---

after

981

Does an appositive phrase, like a clause, contain a subject and a verb? (*Yes, No*)

982

---

my teeth
chattering.

1251

Continue to follow the directions for the previous frame:

The band was playing. **The team rushed onto the field.**

_____, **the team rushed onto the field.**

1252

Either of these
is correct:
3–1–2
1–3–2

1521

Continue to follow the directions for the previous frame:

    1. **we bought an ashtray**
    2. **at the souvenir stand**
    3. **made of shells**   ____ ____ ____

1522

Correct	**The branch of medicine which Dr. Gomez specializes is nerve disorders.**
1791	1792

wakes	If making the change indicated after each sentence would make it necessary to change the italicized verb, write only the form of the verb that would be required. If the verb would remain the same, write *Correct*.
	Where *is* your ticket? (Change ticket to tickets.)
2060	_____ 2061

The injured man was taken to the hospital.	Continue to follow the directions for the previous frame:
	People *should* not *keep* bananas in a refrigerator.
	_____
	_____
2329	2330

themselves	Supply the proper reflexive pronoun:
	We can set our stove to turn _____ off.
2598	2599

, Virginia,	**Mr. Higgins my counselor understood how I a new student felt on my first day in high school.**
	(*Note:* Look for two appositives.)
2867	2868

	2. Capitalize the names of nationalities, languages, races, religions, and the adjectives formed from these names.
a	American Black Catholic Protestant
	Italian Indian Methodist Jew (Jewish)
	Copy the words that require capitals:
	There is an ancient catholic church in this spanish town.
3136	_____ 3137

a. **The price of steel rose as a result of the strike.**
b. **The price rose.**

Although sentence *a* provides more detail than sentence *b*, the verb **rose** makes a (*complete, incomplete*) statement about the subject in both sentences.

sometimes

172

173

Because the road was rough

This word group would become a sentence if we dropped the word _____.

b

442

443

We raise *whatever we need.*

When we omit the noun clause in this sentence, does a complete sentence remain? (*Yes, No*)

vegetables

712

713

When an appositive phrase is omitted from a sentence, does a grammatically complete sentence remain? (*Yes, No*)

No

982

983

The dog was shivering on the doorstep. *Its rough coat was covered with snow.*

The dog was shivering on the doorstep, _____
_____.

The band
playing,

1252

1253

Either of these
is correct:

2–1–3
1 3 2

1522

1. **my aunt flew to Florida**
2. **after María went to college**
3. **to bask in the sunshine**   ____ ____ ____

1523

medicine *in* which
or
specializes *in*

1792

Tony would not take any advice except his father.

1793

---

are

2061

Selecting the right color *is* very important. (Change **color** to **colors.**)

_____

2062

Bananas should
not be kept in
a refrigerator.

2330

(*Note:* The passive form of *left* is *was left;* the passive form of *had left* is *had been left.*)

Jamie *had left* the iron on all night.

_____

_____

2331

---

itself

2599

Supply an intensive pronoun to emphasize the subject **students:**

The students _____ **patrol the corridors.**

2600

, my counselor,
, a new student,

2868

The famous Dionne quintuplets were born on May 28 1934 in Callander Ontario.

2869

Catholic, Spanish

3137

Copy the words that require capitals:

The author described several french trading posts in the north.

_____

3138

complete	**The price of steel <u>rose</u> as a result of the strike.**
	Does the verb **rose** require a complement to complete the meaning of this sentence? (*Yes, No*)
173	174

Because	Every clause is used like a single word—like an *adverb,* an *adjective,* or a *noun.*
	Since no adverb, adjective, or noun makes sense by itself, it follows that no clause that is used like one of these words makes sense by itself either.
443	Only a (*clause, sentence*) makes sense by itself.
	444

No	**We raise** (*whatever we need*).
	If we omitted the noun clause, the sentence would lack a (*subject, direct object*).
713	714

Yes	An appositive phrase, because it is an "extra," should be set off from the rest of the sentence by commas. (*True, False*)
983	984

its rough coat covered with snow.	**Refugees wandered about aimlessly.** *Their homes were destroyed.*
	Refugees wandered about aimlessly, _____
	_____.
1253	1254

2–1–3 1–3–2	1. **clean your hands** 2. **after you paint** 3. **with turpentine** _____ _____ _____
1523	1524

except *from* his
or
his father's

1793

Next year we lose our best pitcher and hitter. (one person)

1794

Correct

2062

This is the finest stock car that *was* ever built. (Change **the finest stock car** to **one of the finest stock cars.**)

_____

2063

The iron had
been left on
all night.

2331

They *guarantee* these batteries for one year.

_____

_____

2332

---

themselves

2600

Do not use a reflexive pronoun in place of a simple pronoun like *I, he,* or *we*—especially in careful speech or in formal writing.

    a. *I* **went fishing.**   b. **Dad and *I* went fishing.**

In which sentence might you sometimes hear *myself* instead of *I?* _____

2601

May 28, 1934,
Callander,

2869

Yes we must realize my young friends that failure is often a steppingstone to success.

2870

French,
North

3138

Copy the words that require capitals:

There are americans of both the catholic and protestant faiths.

_____

3139

No 174	Here are two different *action verb* patterns: *Subject—Action Verb (S—V)* *Subject—Action Verb → Direct Object (S—V—DO)* **Several athletes from our school competed.** The pattern of this sentence is (*S—V, S—V—DO*). 175
sentence 444	In this lesson you will study **adverb clauses.** As its name suggests, an adverb clause is a clause that is used as an (*adjective, adverb*). 445
direct object 714	An *indirect* object precedes the *direct* object and shows *to whom* (or *to what*) or *for whom* (or *for what*) something is done. **She will pay the finder a reward.** The indirect object in the above sentence is the noun _____. 715
True 984	Lesson **26** The Process of Reduction [Frames 986–1021]
their homes destroyed. 1254	**Hundreds of persons work on each car.** *Each person performs one small operation.* **Hundreds of persons work on each car,** _____ _____. 1255
2–1–3 1–3–2 1524	1. **many people came** 2. **to see the game** 3. **from nearby towns** ____ ____ ____ 1525

Correct	**A dachshund's body is long and its legs very short.**
1794	1795

were	**The principal and the assistant principal** *attend* **every game.** (Change **and** to **or.**)
	_____
2063	2064

These batteries are guaranteed for one year.	**The voters** *will vote* **upon this proposal at the next election.**
	_____
	_____
2332	2333

	a. *I* **went fishing.**
	b. **Dad and** *I* **went fishing.**
b	Since you would never use *myself* in sentence *a,* it would seem just as unreasonable to use *myself* in sentence *b.*
	In both sentences, *I* is used as the _____ of
2601	the verb **went.** 2602

Yes, , my young friends,	**It is human failure not mechanical failure that is responsible as a matter of fact for most of the slaughter on our highways.**
.	
2870	2871

	3. Capitalize the entire names of organizations, companies, buildings, theaters, and institutions such as schools, clubs, churches, libraries, and hospitals.
Americans, Catholic, Protestant	a. **Evanston high school** b. **Evanston High School**
	Which is correctly capitalized? _____
3139	3140

Subject—Action Verb (S—V)
Subject—Action Verb → Direct Object (S—V—DO)

S—V

Anaïs Nin filled many diaries with her careful observations of people.

175

The pattern of this sentence is (*S—V, S—V—DO*).

176

An ordinary adverb modifies a verb by answering questions such as **When? Where?** or **How?** about its action.

Our sales increased *recently*.

adverb

The word *recently* is an adverb because it tells **when** about

the verb _____.

445

446

---

a. **She will pay the finder a reward.** ~~IDO~~

b. **She will pay whoever finds the dog a reward.**

finder

Write the four-word noun clause in sentence *b* that takes the place of the indirect object **finder** in sentence *a*. • *who has the*

Test - She will pay wh(ever) finds verb

715

716

When we substitute a simpler word group for a longer and more complicated word group, we say that we *reduce* the longer word group.

To reduce a word group means to (*simplify, complicate*) it.

986

In this and the following frames, eliminate the **and** by changing the italicized statement to a noun-participle phrase. (Rewrite the complete sentence.)

Their money was spent, **and the children left the carnival.**

**each person
performing one
small operation.**

_____

_____

1255

1256

**1—3—2
2—1—3
3—1—2**

1. **we gave the cookies**
2. **to the children**
3. **that had stuck to the pan**   ___ ___ ___

1525

1526

page 351

legs *are* very

1795

---

attends

2064

This proposal will be voted upon at the next election.

2333

---

subject

2602

, not mechanical failure,

, as a matter of fact,

2871

---

b

3140

Cathy's reason for breaking the date was she had a bad headache.

1796

Neither his hands nor his face *was* clean. (Reverse the positions of **hands** and **face**.)

_____

2065

Ronnie *had put* the letter in the wrong envelope.

_____

_____

2334

Do not use a reflexive pronoun unless the word it stands for appears earlier in the sentence.

Corey excused *himself* **and left early.**

The pronoun *himself* is correctly used because it stands for the noun _____ earlier in the sentence.

2603

The Liberty Bell cracked on July 8 1835 when it was tolled for the death of John Marshall Chief Justice of the United States.

2872

Copy and capitalize the words that require capitals:

The Rotary club made a donation to the Hillside children's hospital.

_____

3141

S—V—DO 176	a. **Our teacher will return in a few days.** b. **Our teacher will return the test papers.** Which sentence is in the *S—V—DO* pattern? _____ 177
increased 446	a. **Our sales increased** *recently.* b. **Our sales increased** *when we lowered our price.* Both the adverb clause in sentence *b* and the adverb *recently* in sentence *a* tell *(where, when, how)* about the verb **increased.** 447
whoever finds the dog 716	**She will pay** *whoever finds the dog* **a reward.** An indirect object is not an essential part of the sentence framework. If we omit the clause in the above sentence, does a complete sentence remain? *(Yes, No)* 717
simplify 986	In general, express your idea in the simplest word group you can without sacrificing clearness. A good sentence, like a good machine, has no useless parts. If you can express your idea in a prepositional phrase, don't use *(a sentence, an adjective).* 987
Their money spent, the children left the carnival. 1256	*No guides were available,* **and we had to depend on ourselves.** (Change *were* to *being.*) _____ _____ 1257

1-3-2
2-1-3

Lesson **42** Recognizing Dangling Word Groups

[Frames 1528-1560]

1526

was *that* she 1796	We can learn from almost everyone whom we come in contact. 1797
were 2065	This kind of rice *cooks* very fast. (Change **rice** to **beans**.) *= 1 unit count nour* _____ 2066
The letter had been put in the wrong envelope. 2334	Lesson **65** Review: Using Verbs Correctly [Frames 2336–2368]
Corey 2603	a. **The two brothers put** *themselves* **through college.** b. **Ralph and** *himself* **paid their own way through college.** In which sentence is the reflexive pronoun used correctly? _____ 2604
July 8, 1835, Marshall, 2872	Well the interview by the way lasted for over an hour. 2873
Club, Children's Hospital 3141	Such words as *company, building, theater, college, high school, church,* and *hospital* are not capitalized unless they are a part of a particular name. **a Baptist church** Is this the name of only one particular church at a particular location? (*Yes, No*) 3142

b

177

---

a. **The principal spoke a few words.**
b. **The principal spoke briefly.**

Which sentence is in the *S—V—DO* pattern? _____

178

---

when

447

---

a. **Our sales increased** *recently.*
b. **Our sales increased** *when we lowered our price.*

Because the clause in sentence *b* does the same job as the adverb in sentence *a*, it is an _____

clause.

448

Yes

717

---

a. **This is my** *recipe* **for fudge.**
b. **This is** *how I make fudge.*

Both the noun clause *how I make fudge* in sentence *b* and the noun *recipe* in sentence *a* complete the meaning of the linking verb **is.**

Both are used as (*subject complements, direct objects*).

718

---

a sentence

987

---

1. Sentence   3. Phrase (verbal, appositive, prepositional)
2. Clause   4. Single word (adjective, adverb)

As we proceed through this list from 1 to 4, the sentence elements become more (*simple, complicated*).

988

No guides being
available, we
had to depend
on ourselves.

1257

Mrs. Koss entered the store, and *her three children were trailing after her.*

_____

_____

1258

You have seen that it is a good idea, now and then, to begin a sentence with an introductory phrase or clause.

PRESENT PARTICIPIAL PHRASE: *Climbing the ladder,* . . .
ADVERB CLAUSE: *As Jan climbed the ladder,* . . .

The word group that doesn't tell **who** climbed the ladder is the (*phrase, clause*).

1528

Lesson 50 Making Logical Comparisons

[Frames 1799–1837]

Correct

Gambling *was* **his downfall. (Change gambling to horses.)**

_____

2066

2067

In this and the following frames, write the correct forms of the verbs in parentheses:

If the director had _____ (*give*) me a chance, I

would have _____ (*speak*).

2336

---

a

Underline the correct pronoun:

I hope that your parents and (*you, yourself*) can attend my commencement.

2604

2605

Well,
, by the way,

I wonder Phyllis if you ever see our old neighbors the Burgesses at church.

2873

2874

No

a. **a new Baptist church**   b. **Calvary Baptist church**

In which item should **church** be capitalized because it is part of the special name of a particular church? _____

3142

3143

a

178

In addition to a *direct* object, the *S—V—DO* sentence some-times contains an *indirect* object, which explains *to whom* (or *to what*) or *for whom* (or *for what*) something is done.

    a. **Mr. Harvey sold his stamp collection recently.**
    b. **Mr. Harvey sold my sister his stamp collection.**

Which sentence contains an indirect object? _____

179

---

adverb

448

Think of an adverb clause as a "stretched-out" adverb con-sisting of a number of words and having a *subject* and a

_____.

449

---

subject complements

718

This is (*how I make fudge*).

We cannot omit the noun clause because we should lose an essential part of the sentence framework. The part we would lose is the (*subject, direct object, subject complement*).

719

---

simple

988

The process of reducing a word group to a simpler word group is called **reduction.**

    a. Changing a sentence to an appositive phrase.
    b. Changing a single word to a clause.

Which is an example of reduction—*a* or *b?* _____

989

Mrs. Koss entered the store, her three children trailing after her.

1258

The artist came to the door, and *her hands were stained with paint.* (Insert the noun-participle phrase after **artist.**)

_____

_____

1259

---

phrase

1528

PAST PARTICIPIAL PHRASE: *Packed in straw, . . .*
ADVERB CLAUSE: *When this clock is packed in straw, . . .*

The word group that doesn't tell **what** was packed in straw is the (*phrase, clause*).

1529

Make comparisons only between things of the same class.

WRONG: **Tommy's** *vocabulary* **is like an** *adult*.

This comparison is faulty because Tommy's *vocabulary* is not like an *adult*. It is like an adult's _____.

1799

---

were

Potatoes *are* **our main crop.** (Reverse the positions of **potatoes** and **our main crop.**)

_____

2067

2068

---

given, spoken

The window was _____ (*break*) **when I** _____ (*see*) **it.**

2336

2337

---

you

DEMONSTRATIVE PRONOUNS

Demonstrative pronouns (or adjectives) are used to point out. There are only four demonstrative words:

this   that   these   those

Do you find the word *them* among these words? (*Yes, No*)

2605

2606

, Phyllis,
, the Burgesses,

Mr. Knox the principal pointed out that the boys after all were only children not adults.

2874

2875

---

b

a. **the Kirby oil company**
b. **a large oil company**

In which item should the words **oil company** be capitalized because they are part of the name of a particular company?

3143

_____

3144

b	**Mr. Harvey sold my sister his stamp collection.** The indirect object in this sentence is _____.
179	180

verb (*or* predicate)	**Our farm begins** *here.* The word *here* is an adverb because it tells **where** about the verb _____.
449	450

subject complement	**We were still ten miles from our** *destination.* The noun *destination* is the object of the preposition _____.
719	720

a	a. Changing a sentence to an appositive phrase. b. Changing a single word to a clause. Which change would be preferable in your writing? _____
989	990

The artist, her hands stained with paint, came to the door.	**Ten scouts stood on the stage,** *and each was holding a different flag.* (Insert the phrase after **scouts.**) _____ _____
1259	1260

phrase	PREPOSITIONAL GERUND PHRASE: *After biting six children, . . .* ADVERB CLAUSE: *After the dog had bitten six children, . . .* The phrase doesn't tell you **who** or **what** bit the children, but the clause tells you that it was a _____ .
1529	1530

vocabulary	a. **Tommy's** *vocabulary* **is like an** *adult.*
	b. **Tommy's** *vocabulary* **is like the** *vocabulary* **of an adult.**
	Which comparison is correct? _____
1799	1800

is	**One hour hardly** *seems* **enough time for this job.** (Change **One hour** to **Two hours.**)
	_____
2068	2069

broken, saw	**Bob might have** _____ (*become*) **ill from all the ice**
	water that he _____ (*drink*).
2337	2338

No	The word *them* is not a demonstrative pronoun. It is the (*objective, nominative*) form of the personal pronoun **they.**
2606	2607

, the principal, , after all, , not	**The Chinese Telephone Exchange 743 Washington Street San Francisco California 94103 welcomes visitors.**
2875	2876

	4. Capitalize the names of the days of the week, months, and holidays, but *not* the names of the seasons.
a	Wednesday Christmas spring
	February Memorial Day fall
	Copy the words that require capitals:
	In the autumn we look forward to thanksgiving day.
3144	3145

sister 180	**Mr. Harvey sold my sister his stamp collection.** When an indirect object is present, it always comes (*before*, *after*) the direct object. 181
begins 450	a. **Our farm begins** *here*. b. **Our farm begins** *where the road turns*. The adverb clause in sentence *b* does the same job as the adverb *here* in sentence *a*. Both tell (*where, when, how*) about the verb **begins.** 451
from 720	a. **We were still ten miles from our** *destination*. b. **We were still ten miles from** *where we were going*. In sentence *a*, the noun *destination* is the object of the preposition **from.** Write the noun clause in sentence *b* that is the object of the preposition **from.** _____ 721
a 990	When you reduce a word group, you generally improve your writing by using (*fewer, more*) words. 991
Ten scouts, each holding a different flag, stood on the stage. 1260	Lesson **34** Review: Devices for Sentence Variety [Frames 1262–1278]
dog 1530	INFINITIVE PHRASE: *To get more business, . . .* ADVERB CLAUSE: *If a company wants to get more business, . . .* The phrase doesn't tell you **who** or **what** is to get more business, but the clause tells you that it is a _____. 1531

b	a. **Tommy's** *vocabulary* **is like the** *vocabulary* **of an adult.** b. **Tommy's** *vocabulary* **is like** *that* **of an adult.** Each of these sentences is correct because *vocabulary* is compared with *vocabulary*. In sentence *b*, the word that stands for *vocabulary* is the pronoun _____.
1800	1801

Correct	**What color** *is* **its hair?** (Change **hair** to **eyes.**) _____
2069	2070

become, drank	**When Connie** _____ (*come*) **into the house, her ears were** _____ (*freeze*).
2338	2339

objective	Use the demonstrative pronoun (or adjective) *those,* not the personal pronoun *them,* to point out persons or things. a. *Them* **are good cookies. I like** *them* **cookies.** b. *Those* **are good cookies. I like** *those* **cookies.** The correct sentences follow the letter (*a, b*).
2607	2608

, 743 Washington Street, San Francisco, California 94103,	Lesson **80** Commas for Nonrestrictive Clauses [Frames 2878–2911]
2876	

Thanksgiving Day	a. **Our winter sale begins after New Year's.** b. **Our Winter sale begins after new year's.** Which sentence is correctly capitalized? _____
3145	3146

The charcoal gives the meat a tangy flavor.

The indirect object in this sentence is _____.

182

---

a. **Mr. Cruz spoke** *seriously.*
b. **Mr. Cruz spoke** *as if he meant business.*

Both the adverb clause in sentence *b* and the adverb *seriously* in sentence *a* tell (*when, where, how*) about the verb **spoke.**

452

We were still ten miles from (*where we were going*).

We cannot omit the noun clause because the preposition **from** would then be without an _____.

722

We have spent many frames on reducing sentences to subordinate word groups—to clauses and various kinds of phrases. Now we shall practice other types of reduction.

Ann stumbled *while she was coming down the stairs.*

Which two words can you omit from the adverb clause without changing the meaning? _____ _____

992

Each sentence lettered *a* represents one of the devices you have studied in this unit. Rewrite each sentence lettered *b*, putting it in the same arrangement as *a*.

a. **This fact no sensible person will deny.**
b. **The dog refused to eat these biscuits.**

_____

_____ 1262

CLAUSES: *As Jan climbed the ladder, . . .*
When this clock is packed in straw, . . .
After the dog had bitten six children, . . .
If a company wants to get more business, . . .

Do clauses have subjects that tell **whom** or **what** they are about? (*Yes, No*)

1532

Tommy's *vocabulary* is like an *adult's*.

that

This comparison is also correct because the possessive noun *adult's* implies an adult's _____.

1801

1802

This is the best fair that *was* ever held here. (Change **the best fair** to **one of the best fairs.**)

are

_____

2070

2071

---

came, frozen

Terry had _____ (*grow*) so much that you would hardly have _____ (*know*) him.

2339

2340

---

b

Underline the correct word:

Why don't we ask (*those, them*) **students to help us?**

2608

2609

Adjective clauses begin with the relative pronouns **who (whose, whom), which,** and **that.**

An adjective clause, like an adjective, modifies a noun or a

_____.

2878

---

5. Capitalize the brand names of particular products, but *not* the types of products that they identify.

Sunkist oranges   Chrysler car   Protecto paint

a

Copy the words that require capitals:

The makers of broadway shirts recommend that you use swish detergent. _____

3146

3147

meat

182

a. **Shirley read** *Cynthia* **her letter.**
b. **Shirley read her letter to** *Cynthia.*

In which sentence is *Cynthia* an indirect object? _____

183

---

how

452

Besides telling **when, where,** and **how** about verbs, as adverbs can do, adverb clauses can also tell **why.**

a. **We moved** *because our house was too small.*
b. **We moved** *where there were very few other houses.*

In which sentence does the adverb clause tell **why** about the verb **moved?** _____

453

---

object

722

An *appositive* is a noun or pronoun set after another noun or pronoun to explain it.

Our last hope, <u>*rescue*</u> *by the Marines,* **was soon to be realized.**

The appositive *rescue,* with its modifiers, follows and explains the noun _____.

723

---

she was

992

Ann stumbled *while (she was) coming down the stairs.*

The two words that we can omit from the adverb clause are the subject and a part of the _____.

993

These biscuits
the dog refused
to eat.

1262

a. **For a person of his age, such exercise seems much too strenuous.**
b. **Barbara Jordan held the interest of Congress from her first sentence.**

_____

_____

1263

Yes

1532

PHRASES: *Climbing the ladder, ...*
Packed in straw, ...
After biting six children, ...
To get more business, ...

Do phrases have subjects that tell whom or what they are about? (*Yes, No*)

1533

vocabulary 1802	a. **Tommy's vocabulary is like the vocabulary of an adult.** b. **Tommy's vocabulary is like that of an adult.** c. **Tommy's vocabulary is like an adult.** d. **Tommy's vocabulary is like an adult's.** The only incorrect comparison is in sentence _____. 1803
were 2071	There *was* **only one street between our house and the park.** (Change **one street** to **three streets**.) _____ 2072
grown, known 2340	I have _____ (*write*) **a letter to the company,** **complaining that the shirt has** _____ (*shrink*). 2341
those 2609	POSSESSIVE PRONOUNS Possessive pronouns show possession without the use of apostrophes. *Your's* or *our's* is just as incorrect as *hi's.* POSSESSIVE PRONOUNS: **yours, his, hers, its, ours, theirs** *Yours* **is just like** *ours.* Do the italicized pronouns require apostrophes? (*Yes, No*) 2610
pronoun 2878	To decide whether or not to set off an adjective clause with commas, ask yourself what purpose it serves. a. **all students** b. **all students** *who can typewrite* The adjective clause in *b* makes the noun **students** refer to (*more, fewer*) students. 2879
Broadway, Swish 3147	a. **Blue Star Gasoline** b. **Blue Star gasoline** Which item is correctly capitalized? _____ 3148

a

183

A linking verb can never by itself make a complete statement about its subject.

A linking verb must (*always, sometimes*) be completed by a subject complement that describes or identifies the subject of the sentence.

184

---

a

453

An adverb clause can also answer the question **On what condition?** or **Under what condition?** about the verb.

> a. **The engine will start** *if you push the car.*
> b. **The engine will start** *when you turn the key.*

In which sentence does the adverb clause tell **on what condition** the engine will start? _____

454

---

hope

723

---

a. **Our last hope,** *rescue by the Marines,* **was soon to be realized.**
b. **Our last hope,** *that the Marines would rescue us,* **was soon to be realized.**

The noun clause in sentence *b* does the same job as the appositive _____ in sentence *a*.

724

---

verb
(*or* predicate)

993

The word *elliptical* means "having words omitted." An adverb clause from which words have been omitted is an **elliptical clause.**

> **Ann stumbled** *while (she was) coming down the stairs.*

In the above sentence, using an elliptical clause eliminates _____ words. (How many?)

994

From her first
sentence,
Barbara Jordan
held the interest
of Congress.

---

a. **The land, dry and rocky, is useless for farming.**
b. **The old, dingy city hall was being remodeled.**

_____

1264

No

1533

Since a phrase leaves your reader in the dark, you must answer the question **Who?** or **What?** at the beginning of the main statement that follows.

> a. *Going up the ladder,* **a branch hit Jan's head.**
> b. *Going up the ladder,* **Jan hit her head on a branch.**

Which sentence answers the question **Who?** _____

1534

a. **Our customs are different from the customs of Mexico.**
b. **Our customs are different from Mexico.**
c. **Our customs are different from Mexico's.**
d. **Our customs are different from those of Mexico.**

The only incorrect comparison is in sentence _____.

1804

---

were

2072

UNIT **9: SOLVING YOUR VERB PROBLEMS**

Lesson **58** A Group of Similar
Three-Part Verbs

[Frames 2074–2109]

---

written, shrunk

2341

You would not have _____ (*eat*) **it if you had**
_____ (*see*) **it made.**

2342

No

2610

Because apostrophes are needed to make nouns possessive,
it is a natural and common mistake to use them with pronouns, too.

Underline the italicized word which requires an apostrophe
to show possession:

We parked *ours* **in** *Stanleys* **driveway.**

2611

---

fewer

2879

a. **people**
b. **people** *who fail to vote*

People means *all* people.

By adding the clause *who fail to vote,* we (*increase, limit*)
the number of people we are talking about.

2880

---

b

3148

6. Capitalize the names of governmental bodies, agencies,
departments, and offices.

Senate   **Board of Education**   **City Council**
Supreme Court **Treasury Department** **Department of Health**

Copy the words that require capitals:

The congress referred the matter to the state department.

3149

always

184

---

a. **are, were, seemed, became**
b. **ate, took, studied, listened**

Would you expect to find a subject complement after the words in group *a* or group *b?* _____

185

---

a

454

---

a. **Vern went to school** *because a test was scheduled.*
b. **Vern went to school** *although he had a bad cold.*

In which sentence does the adverb clause tell **under what condition** Vern went to school? _____

455

---

rescue

724

Our last hope, *that the Marines would rescue us,* **was soon to be realized.**

Our last hope . . . was soon to be realized.

When we omit the noun clause used as an appositive, does a complete sentence remain? (*Yes, No*)

725

---

two

994

Crackers will stay crisp *if they are kept in a tin box.*

Write the elliptical clause to which the italicized adverb clause can be reduced: _____.

995

The city hall,
old and dingy,
was being
remodeled.

1264

---

a. **The job would have been simple had I used the right tools.**
b. **Helen would have sung if we had urged her.**

(In revising sentence *b,* eliminate the adverb clause signal **if,** and keep the ideas in the same order.)

_____

_____

1265

---

b

1534

WRONG: *Going up the ladder,* **a branch hit Jan's head.**

Since there is no word for the italicized phrase to modify, it appears to modify the noun **branch.**

Is it the **branch** that is *going up the ladder?* (*Yes, No*)

1535

---

page 369

Always make sure that your comparisons are logical.

WRONG: **Montreal is larger than** *any city* **in Canada.**

Does *any city* include the city of Montreal? *(Yes, No)*

1805

The three basic forms of a verb from which all its various tenses are formed are called the **principal parts** of the verb.

PRESENT	PAST	PAST PARTICIPLE
talk	**talked**	**(have) talked**

Both the *past* and the *past participle* of this verb end with the two letters _____.

2074

When I _____ **(*run*) to the window, the car had already** _____ **(*drive*) away.**

2343

---

a. *Carols* **coat is newer than** *Virginias*.
b. *Yours* **is newer than** *hers*.

Which sentence is correct without apostrophes? _____

2612

To restrict means "to limit the number."

When we say the use of a parking lot is *restricted* to customers, we mean that its use is _____ to customers and that not everyone can park there.

2881

---

a. **Federal Bureau of Investigation**
b. **Federal bureau of investigation**

Which item is correctly capitalized? _____

3150

Subject—Linking Verb ← Subject Complement (S—LV—SC)

1————→2

a. **Larry lost his voice.**

1←————————1

b. **Larry became hoarse.**

Which sentence is in the *S—LV—SC* pattern? _____

186

Learn to recognize the clause signals that tell us that an adverb clause is beginning. They are grouped according to the kind of information that the clauses supply.

WHEN? **while, when, whenever, as, as soon as, before, after, since, until**

Look for adverb clauses (*before, after*) these words.

456

A noun clause is generally an essential part of the sentence framework and cannot be omitted. The only exceptions are noun clauses used as indirect objects or as appositives.

If a noun clause is used as a subject, direct object, subject complement, or object of a preposition, it (*can, cannot*) be omitted.

726

While he was looking for a job, **Ted had many disappointments.**

Write the elliptical clause to which the italicized adverb clause

can be reduced: _____.

996

Helen would
have sung had
we urged her.

1265

a. **Now that Eva has a driver's license, she wants to drive all the time.**
b. **I have a typewriter, and my work looks neater.**

_____

_____

1266

A phrase that has no word to modify or appears to modify the wrong word is a **dangling phrase.** It is like a plane circling in the air with no place to land.

   a. *Going up the ladder,* **Jan hit her head on a branch.**
   b. *Going up the ladder,* **a branch hit Jan's head.**

Which sentence contains a dangling phrase? _____

1536

Yes 1805	WRONG: **Montreal is larger than** *any city* **in Canada.** Since *any city* includes Montreal, this sentence states that Montreal is larger than itself. Therefore, this comparison is (*logical, illogical*). 1806
ed 2074	The past participle of a verb is the form we use in combination with any form of the helping verb **have** or **be**. PRESENT PAST PAST PARTICIPLE **talk** **talked** **(have) talked** In the case of the verb **talk,** is there any difference between the past and past participle form? (*Yes, No*) 2075
ran, driven 2343	Sue _____ (*give*) **the police a description of the bicycle that had been** _____ (*steal*). 2344

b
 	
2612
	No blunder is more common than confusing the possessive pronoun **its** (belonging to *it*) with the contraction **it's** (= *it is*).
	
	    RIGHT: *It's* (= *It is*) **waiting for** *its* (*possessive*) **meal.**
	
	Underline the correct words in the following sentence:
	
	    (*It's, Its*) **mother knows when** (*it's, its*) **hungry.**
	
	2613

limited 2881	A clause that restricts or limits the number of the word it modifies is called a **restrictive clause.** A restrictive clause makes the word it modifies mean (*less, more*) than it would mean without the clause. 2882
a 3150	In this and the following frames, copy only the words in each sentence to which capitals need to be added, according to the rules presented in this lesson: **Memorial day comes in the spring, not in the fall.** 3151

a. **Larry became a . . .**
b. **Larry found a . . .**

b

Which sentence would be completed by a subject comple-ment? _____

186

187

There are only two clause signals which can start adverb clauses that answer the question **Where?**

after

WHERE? **where, wherever**

        We hid the candy *where no one could find it.*

The adverb clause modifies the word (*hid, candy*).

456

457

---

cannot

A noun clause is a clause that is used in any way that a _____ can be used.

726

727

An adverb clause can often be reduced to a present parti-cipial phrase.

**While looking
for a job,**

        When I saw the child, **I put on the brakes.**
        Seeing the child, **I put on the brakes.**

This reduction eliminates _____ words. (How many?)

996

997

**Now that I have
a typewriter,
my work looks
neater.**

a. **Once a forest fire starts, it is hard to control.**
b. **After you play a card, you can't take it back.**

_____

_____

1266

1267

---

b

Going up the ladder, **Jan hit her head on a branch.**

Now the phrase no longer dangles because the question **Who?** is answered by the noun _____.

1536

1537

a. **Montreal is larger than** *any* **city in Canada.**
b. **Montreal is larger than** *any other* **city in Canada.**

Which comparison is correct? _____

1807

No

English verbs fall into two general classes: **regular** and **irregular** verbs. Verbs are classified as regular when both their past and past participle forms end with *-ed*.

PRESENT	PAST	PAST PARTICIPLE
talk	**talked**	**(have) talked**

The verb **talk** is (*regular, irregular*).

2075

2076

---

gave, stolen

The bell was _____ (*ring*) **just after Walter had**
_____ (*begin*) **his talk.**

2344

2345

Its, it's

Do not write the word **it's** unless you can put the words
_____ _____ in its place.

2613

2614

---

less

Students *who do failing work* **may not participate in sports.**

This sentence does not make a statement about *all* students.

It makes a statement only about those *who* _____

_____.

2882

2883

Day

The hurricane veered west on monday night and struck several states along the atlantic ocean.

(Does **west** indicate a direction, or does it name a geographical section of the country? See frame 3135, page 340.)

3151

3152

a
 	
187
	In one sentence, *are getting* is an action verb followed by a direct object; in the other, it is a linking verb followed by a subject complement.
	
	    a. **The boys** *are getting* **their own lunch.**
	    b. **The boys** *are getting* **hungry.**
	
	The verb *are getting* is a linking verb in sentence _____.
	                                          188

hid
 	
457
	Only two clause signals can start adverb clauses that answer the question **How?**
	
	HOW? **as if, as though**
	
	    a. **Mrs. Kay frowned** *as we told her our plan.*
	    b. **Mrs. Kay frowned** *as if she were doubtful.*
	
	The clause in sentence (*a, b*) tells **how** Mrs. Kay frowned.
	                                          458

noun
 	
727
	The words **that, whether, what, how,** and **why** are often used as clause signals to start noun clauses.
	
	    That anyone should believe this rumor **is absurd.**
	
	The noun clause begins with the word _____ and
	
	ends with the word _____.
	                                          728

two 997	Fill in the present participial phrase to which the adverb clause can be reduced: *Because I wanted experience,* **I fixed the radio myself.** _____, **I fixed the** **radio myself.** 998

Once you play
a card, you can't
take it back.
 	
1267
	a. **Good as the play was, many did not appreciate it.**
	    b. **The book was long, but it held my interest.**
	
	_____
	
	_____
	                                        1268

Jan 1537	*Packed in straw,* **you can ship this clock anywhere.** Is the introductory phrase followed closely by a word that tells **what** is *packed in straw?* (*Yes, No*) 1538

b 1807	WRONG: **Montreal is the largest of** *any other city* **in Canada.** The words *any other city* mean only *one* city. Can Montreal be the largest of *one* city? (*Yes, No*) 1808
regular 2076	Of the thousands of verbs in our language, fewer than 150 are irregular. A verb is classified as irregular when its past and past participle forms do not end with *-ed*. **work** **worked** **(have) worked** **drive** **drove** **(have) driven** The irregular verb is (*work, drive*). 2077
rung, begun 2345	Look at these memory rhymes once again: **"Yes-ter-day** **"In pain** **In bed he lay."** **he has lain."** In this and the following frames, underline the correct verbs: **The dog** (*lay, laid*) **down under the chair where Noreen was** (*sitting, setting*). 2346
it is 2614	Underline the correct words: (*It's, Its*) **not in** (*it's, its*) **usual place.** 2615
do failing work 2883	**Students** *who do failing work* **may not participate in sports.** Because the clause *who do failing work* restricts or limits the number of students we are talking about, it is a re_____ clause. 2884
Monday, Atlantic Ocean 3152	(Be sure to capitalize an entire name, not just a part of it.) **The Studio theater on Madison avenue features english, italian, and other foreign films.** 3153

b 188	**The boys are getting hungry.** The word **hungry** is a (*direct object, subject complement*). 189

b
 	
458
	Several clause signals can start adverb clauses that answer the question **Why?**
	
	WHY? **because, since, as, so that**
	    a. **I couldn't concentrate** *because of the noise.*
	    b. **I couldn't concentrate** *because the room was noisy.*
	
	In which sentence does *because* start a clause? _____ 459

That . . . rumor 728	*That anyone should believe this rumor* **is absurd.** The noun clause in the above sentence is used as the _____ of the verb **is.** 729

Wanting
experience,
 	
998
	An adverb clause that starts with the clause signal **so that** can often be reduced to an infinitive phrase.
	
	    I set the alarm *so that it would wake me at six.*
	    I set the alarm *to wake me at six.*
	
	This reduction eliminates _____ words. (How many?)
	
	999

Long as the book (it) was, it (the book) held my interest. 1268	a. **A lady asked me to baby-sit with her two children, neither of whom I had ever seen before.** b. **Ann applied to two colleges, and both of them accepted her.** _____ _____ 1269
No 1538	*Packed in straw,* **you can ship this clock anywhere.** The italicized phrase is a (*dangling, correct*) phrase. 1539

No	WRONG: **Montreal is the largest of all the** *other* **cities in Canada.**
	The words *all the other cities* exclude Montreal.
	Since Montreal is not among *all the other cities,* can it be the largest among them? (*Yes, No*)
1808	1809

drive	There is great variety among irregular verbs because they came into English from other languages and their forms have changed over the centuries without following any set pattern.
	drive **drove** **(have) driven**
	do **did** **(have) done**
	Are the forms of these two irregular verbs similar? (*Yes, No*)
2077	2078

lay, sitting	**When the curtain** (*raised, rose*), **a body was** (*lying, laying*) **on the floor of the living room.**
2346	2347

It's, its	In this and the following frames, underline the correct pronouns or, in some cases, the pronouns appropriate for formal usage:
	At a buffet dinner, the guests serve (*themselves, theirselves*).
2615	2616

restrictive	A sentence usually becomes untrue or absurd when you omit a restrictive clause.
	Because a restrictive clause is very essential to the meaning of a sentence, do *not* set it off with commas.
	Visitors *who stay too long* **are not welcome.**
	Does the italicized clause require commas? (*Yes, No*)
2884	2885

Theater, Avenue, English, Italian	**A crowd was gathered around a ford truck, where a man was giving away free samples of snowflake crackers.**
3153	3154

a. **The quality of the programs** *is* **excellent.**
b. **The quality of the programs** *is* **improving.**

subject
complement

In one of the sentences *is* serves as a helper to the main verb. In the other, it is a linking verb followed by a subject complement.

Which sentence contains a subject complement? _____

189   190

WHY? **because, since, as, so that**

b

    The man moved over . . . Doris and I could sit together.

The clause signal needed in this sentence would consist of (*one word, two words*).

459   460

    A lie detector shows *whether you are telling the truth.*

subject

The noun clause begins with the word _____

and ends with the word _____.

729   730

    He adjusted the carburetor *so that it would use less gas.*

three

Fill in the infinitive phrase to which the adverb clause can be reduced:

He adjusted the carburetor _____

999 _____.   1000

Ann applied to
two colleges,
both of which
accepted her.

a. **The union held a meeting, the outcome of which was not announced.**
b. **I was struck by a car, and the owner was not insured.**

_____

_____

1269   1270

---

a. *Packed in straw,* **you can ship this clock anywhere.**
b. *Packed in straw,* **this clock can be shipped anywhere.**

dangling

Which sentence is correct because the introductory phrase is followed closely by the word it modifies—the word that

answers the question **What?** _____

1539   1540

No 1809	WRONG: **Montreal is the largest of all the other cities in Canada.** To make this comparison logical, we must omit the word _____. 1810
No 2078	A small number of verbs such as **bet, hit, put,** and **shut** have only one form for all uses. These verbs that have reached the limit of simplification are called *one-part* verbs. **see** **saw** **(have) seen** **hit** **hit** **(have) hit** The one-part verb is (*see, hit*). 2079
rose, lying 2347	**I had** (*lain, laid*) **there reading for about an hour but then had** (*rose, risen*) **to answer the telephone.** 2348
themselves 2616	**Why did the clerk put** (*hisself, himself*) **in this embarrassing position?** 2617
No 2885	**A newspaper should not publish any news** *that has not been carefully checked.* Read this sentence again, omitting the italicized clause. Is the clause too important to the meaning of the sentence to be set off with a comma? (*Yes, No*) 2886
Ford, Snowflake 3154	**Our high school will open on september 5, the day after labor day.** _____ 3155

Gwen felt . . . about the tear in her jeans.

The missing word in this sentence would be a (*subject complement, direct object*).

191

---

two words
(so that)

460

Several clause signals can start adverb clauses that answer the question **On (*or* under) what condition?** These are **if, unless, though, although, provided that.**

The cake might burn *unless you watch it.*

The adverb clause explains **under what condition** the cake

_____ _____.

461

---

whether . . . truth

730

A lie detector shows *whether you are telling the truth.*

The noun clause is used as the _____
of the verb **shows.**

731

---

to use less gas.

1000

Adjective clauses, too, can often be reduced to the same kind of verbal phrases. See how we change an adjective clause to a present participial phrase:

   a. **The house was built on a hill** *that overlooked a lake.*
   b. **The house was built on a hill** *overlooking a lake.*

The present participle in sentence *b* is _____.

1001

I was struck
by a car, the
owner of which
was not insured.

1270

a. **The fact that Alfonso is good-natured makes him very popular.**
b. **Miss Daly has gray hair, but that doesn't make her old.**

_____

_____

1271

---

b

1540

After biting six children, **a police officer shot the dog.**

Since this introductory phrase is not followed by a word that sensibly answers the question **Who?** or **What?** it suggests that a _____ bit the children.

1541

other	a. **Montreal is the largest of any other city in Canada.** b. **Montreal is the largest of all the other cities in Canada.** c. **Montreal is the largest of all the cities in Canada.** Which comparison is correct? _____
1810	1811

hit	**burst** **burst** **(have) burst** **cost** **cost** **(have) cost** **find** **found** **(have) found** **hurt** **hurt** **(have) hurt** All the above verbs are one-part verbs except _____.
2079	2080

lain, risen	**We had** (*set, sat*) **a bench under a tree and had** (*lain, laid*) **our picnic baskets on it.**
2348	2349

himself	**Coach Fry told us that we might lose the game if we are too sure of** (*our selves, ourselves*).
2617	2618

Yes	Suppose that a druggist were to put a sign in the window to advertise for a salesperson.
	    a. **A salesperson is wanted.**
	    b. **A salesperson** *who has a car* **is wanted.**
	Which statement would restrict or limit the number of applicants for the job—*a* or *b*? _____

2886	2887

September, Labor Day	**Next fall Arlene plans to attend medical school in the east.** _____
3155	3156

subject complement	**We moved the . . . to the kitchen.**
	The missing word in this sentence would be a (*subject complement, direct object*).
191	192

	The adverb clause, just like the adverb it resembles, can generally be moved from one position to another in a sentence.
might burn	a. **Lucille changed her mind** *when she saw the price.*
	b. *When she saw the price,* **Lucille changed her mind.**
	The adverb clause comes first in sentence (*a, b*).
461	462

object *or* direct object	**You can depend on whatever he tells you.**
	The noun clause begins with the word _____
	and ends with the word _____.
731	732

	Books may be borrowed by anyone *who has a library card.*
	Fill in the present participial phrase to which the adjective clause can be reduced:
overlooking	**Books may be borrowed by anyone** _____
	_____.
1001	1002

The fact that Miss Daly has gray hair doesn't make her old.	a. **It was fortunate that the fire broke out after school.**
	b. **The child was traveling alone, and this seemed strange.**
	_____
	_____
1271	1272

	a. **After biting six children, the dog was shot by a police officer.**
	b. **After biting six children, a police officer shot the dog.**
police officer	Which sentence is wrong because it contains a dangling phrase? _____
1541	1542

c 1811	Now we shall look at another type of comparison. Supply the missing word that completes the comparison: **Laura earns** *as much* _____ **her brother.** 1812
find 2080	Many irregular verbs have the same form for both their past and past participles. These are called *two-part* verbs. **bring brought (have) brought** **spread spread (have) spread** One of the above verbs has one part; the other has two parts. The two-part verb is _____. 2081
set, laid 2349	**Herman moved to Appleton, where he** (*bought, buys*) **a small newspaper.** 2350
ourselves 2618	**Harvey and** (*you, yourself*) **can ride with us.** 2619
b 2887	**A salesperson** *who has a car* **is wanted.** Not anyone would apply for this job—only one *who has a car.* The clause *who has a car* is therefore a _____ clause. 2888
East 3156	**Surrounding Shady Grove park are an episcopal church, an elementary school, and a library.** _____ 3157

direct object 192	**The house seemed strangely empty without the children.** The word **empty** is a _____ _____. 193
b 462	a. **Lucille changed her mind** *when she saw the price.* b. *When she saw the price,* **Lucille changed her mind.** A comma is needed when the adverb clause comes (*before, after*) the main statement of the sentence. 463
whatever . . . you 732	**You can depend on whatever he tells you.** The noun clause is used as the object of a (*verb, preposition*). 733
having a library card. 1002	Now we shall reduce an adjective clause to a past participial phrase: **We bought some corn** *that was picked this morning.* Which two words in the adjective clause can be omitted without changing the meaning? _____ _____ 1003
It seemed strange that the child was traveling alone. 1272	a. **The article explains that, as time has gone on, football has become more complicated.** b. **Mother insisted that I had to invite Martha because she is my cousin.** (Insert the adverb clause after *that.*) _____ _____ 1273
b 1542	Of course, if your introductory word group has a subject to explain **whom** or **what** it is about, you do not need to explain this again in the main statement that follows it. a. **While I was pushing the car, I ripped my coat.** b. **While I was pushing the car, my coat ripped.** Are both sentences correct? (*Yes, No*) 1543

as	Supply the missing word that completes the comparison:
	Laura earns *more* _____ **her brother.**
1812	1813

	PRESENT	PAST	PAST PARTICIPLE
bring	bring	brought	(have) brought
	catch	caught	(have) caught
	swing	swung	(have) swung
2081	In two-part verbs, the past and _____ _____ forms are the same.		2082

bought	The play is about a woman who came to live with a family and (*tries, tried*) to take over.
2350	2351

you	The British and (*ourselves, we*) are united by the bond of a common language.
2619	2620

restrictive	Dictionaries *which are too small* are not very useful.
	Because a restrictive clause is essential to the meaning of a sentence, it (*should, should not*) be set off with commas.
2888	2889

Park, Episcopal	The Civil Aeronautics administration appealed to congress for new legislation.
3157	3158

subject complement 193	**A membership card gives one many privileges.** The indirect object in this sentence is the word _____. 194
before 463	a. **Although we were tired, we finished the job.** b. **We finished the job although we were tired.** The adverb clause comes first in sentence (*a, b*). 464
preposition 733	**This tiny spring is what powers the watch.** The noun clause begins with the word _____ and ends with the word _____. 734
that was 1003	**We bought some corn** *that was picked this morning.* Fill in the past participial phrase to which the adjective clause can be reduced: **We bought some corn** _____. 1004
Mother insisted that, because Martha is my cousin, I had to invite her. 1273	a. **No sooner had I turned in my test paper than I realized my mistake.** b. **It began to pour as soon as we stepped out of the house.** _____ _____ 1274
Yes 1543	Do you remember that an elliptical clause is an adverb clause from which the subject and part of the verb have been omitted? a. **While I was pushing the car, . . .** b. **While pushing the car, . . .** Which is an elliptical (incomplete) clause? _____ 1544

than 1813	WRONG: **Laura earns as much,** *if not more than,* **her brother.** Omit the italicized phrase and you will see what is wrong with the above sentence. The trouble is that **as much** is followed by *than* instead of by _____. 1814
past participle 2082	Most irregular verbs have a special form for the past participle. These are the *three-part* verbs that are responsible for most verb trouble. **see** **saw** **(have) seen** **catch** **caught** **(have) caught** The three-part verb is (*see, catch*). 2083
tried 2351	**Johnny couldn't understand why a fourth** (*was, is*) **larger than a fifth.** 2352
we 2620	(*Those, Them*) **dishes are exactly like** (*our's, ours*). 2621
should not 2889	Less frequently, an adjective clause is used merely to provide an additional fact about the word it modifies. Such a clause may be omitted without destroying the truth or accuracy of your statement. **Hale Smith,** *who composes music,* **is a professor.** Is this sentence true without the clause? (*Yes, No*) 2890
Administration, Congress 3158	**The program is sponsored jointly by the makers of zip soap and polar bear freezers.** (Brand names are treated somewhat differently from other names. See frame 3147, page 364.) 3159

Lesson 6 One-word Modifiers: Adjectives and Adverbs

[Frames 196–237]

---

a. **Although we were tired, we finished the job.**
b. **We finished the job although we were tired.**

A comma is needed when the adverb clause comes (*before, after*) the main statement.

a

464   465

This tiny spring is what powers the watch.

what . . . watch

The noun clause in this sentence completes the meaning of the linking verb **is** and is used as a (*subject complement, direct object*).

734   735

An adjective clause can sometimes be reduced to an infinitive phrase.

picked this
morning.

> **You need more facts** *that will prove your argument.*
> **You need more facts** *to prove your argument.*

In the second sentence we changed the verb *will prove* to

the infinitive _____.

1004   1005

---

a. **Not only did Marta pass the course, but she also received an A.**
b. **Phil borrowed my book, and he lost it.**

No sooner had
we stepped out
of the house
than it began
to pour.

_____ _____ _____

_____ _____ _____

1274   1275

---

a. **While I was pushing the car, . . .**
b. **While pushing the car, . . .**

b

After which clause would you need to tell **who** in order to

avoid a dangling word group? _____

1544   1545

as
 	
1814
	In combining an "as" and a "than" comparison, first complete the "as" comparison. Then add the "if" phrase at the end, where it need not be completed.
	
	  a. **Laura earns as much, if not more than, her brother.**
	  b. **Laura earns as much as her brother, if not more.**
	
	Which sentence is correct? _____ 1815

see 2083	The main danger with three-part verbs is confusing their two past forms—the simple past and the past participle. PRESENT PAST PAST PARTICIPLE **see** **saw** **(have) seen** The past form of the verb **see** that may be used by itself without a helping verb is (*saw, seen*). 2084
is 2352	**The doctor said that too much salt** (*is, was*) **bad for people.** 2353
Those, ours 2621	**Mrs. Kemp parked** (*hers, her's*) **next to** (*theirs, their's*). 2622
Yes 2890	a. **Any number** *which can be divided by two* **is an even number.** b. **Crater Lake,** *which is two thousand feet deep,* **has no inlet or outlet.** In which sentence can the clause be omitted without damaging the meaning of the sentence? _____ 2891
Zip, Polar Bear 3159	**The auditorium of the Utley high school is used for jewish religious services on saturdays and for christian services on sundays.** _____ 3160

Until this point, we have been dealing mainly with only the framework of sentences—subjects, verbs, and sometimes complements.

Brakes cause accidents.

Does this sentence contain any words that are not a part of its framework? (*Yes, No*)

196

---

before

465

a. **Children appreciate nothing if they are given too much.**
b. **If children are given too much they appreciate nothing.**

Which sentence requires a comma—*a* or *b?* _____

466

---

subject
complement

735

Some of the same clause signals that start adverb and adjective clauses can also start noun clauses; for example, **if, when, where, who,** and **which.**

If the clause is an essential part of the sentence that cannot be omitted, it is (*an adverb, an adjective, a noun*) clause.

736

---

to prove

1005

We are planning a program *that will stimulate an interest in science.*

Fill in the infinitive phrase to which the adjective clause can be reduced:

We are planning a program _____

_____ .

1006

Not only did Phil
borrow my book,
but he also
lost it.

1275

a. **The more one reads, the more interested one becomes in the characters.**
b. **As he argued more, he convinced me less.**

_____

_____

1276

---

b

1545

a. **While pushing the car, my coat ripped.**
b. **While pushing the car, I ripped my coat.**

Which sentence is wrong because it suggests that the coat

was pushing the car? _____

1546

b

1815

a. **The new school will be as large, if not larger, than ours.**
b. **The new school will be as large as ours, if not larger.**

Which sentence is correct? _____

1816

---

saw

2084

To avoid misusing the past and past participle forms of a verb, observe two rules:

1. Never use the past participle by itself without some form of the helping verb **have** or **be.**

    a. **I** *seen* **the accident.**   b. **I** *saw* **the accident.**

Which sentence is wrong? _____

2085

---

is

2353

Cooking is an art that always (*has appealed, appealed*) **to me.**

(*Note:* It still does.)

2354

---

hers, theirs

2622

(*Yours, Your's*) **must be in one of** (*those, them*) **drawers.**

2623

---

b

2891

A clause which merely adds a fact that is not essential to the meaning of the sentence is called a **nonrestrictive clause.**

A nonrestrictive clause is (*more, less*) important than a restrictive clause.

2892

High School,
Jewish,
Saturdays,
Christian,
Sundays

3160

Heroes of both the north and the south are buried in Arlington national cemetery.

3161

No 196	To supply additional information about the various parts of the sentence framework, we use *modifiers*. **Poor <u>brakes</u> <u>cause</u> many accidents.** This sentence contains two modifying words that are not part of its framework. These two words are: _____ and _____. 197
b 466	a. **Mr. Tate becomes hard-of-hearing, when anyone asks him for money.** b. **When anyone asks Mr. Tate for money, he becomes hard-of-hearing.** In which sentence should the comma be dropped? _____ 467
a noun 736	a. **The bus** *that the train delayed* **was an hour late.** b. **We found** *that a train had delayed the bus.* One clause is an adjective clause that can be omitted; the other is a noun clause that is an essential part of the sentence framework. Which sentence contains the noun clause? _____ 737
to stimulate an interest in science. 1006	By understanding the various types of subordinate word groups, you not only save words but also give more interesting variety to your sentences. If you had several adjective clauses close together, would it generally be a good idea to change one of them to a participial phrase? (*Yes, No*) 1007
The more he argued, the less he convinced me. 1276	a. **The nights being cold, we took along our sweaters.** b. **The inn was expensive, and we stayed only one day.** _____ _____ 1277
a 1546	a. **While pushing the car, my coat ripped.** b. **While pushing the car, I ripped my coat.** Which sentence is right because the elliptical clause is followed by a word that answers the question **Who?** _____ 1547

This is one of the best, *if not the best,* **hotel in town.**

Omit the italicized phrase and you will see what is wrong with the above sentence.

The trouble is that **one of the best** requires **hotels** (plural) and *the best* requires _____ (singular).

b

1816

1817

WRONG: **I** *seen* **the accident.**

This sentence is wrong because the past participle *seen* is used without the helping verb *have.*

Supply the correct form of **see:**

RIGHT: **I** _____ **the accident.**

a

2085

2086

---

has appealed

Uncle Raúl (*has smoked, smoked*) **for twenty years and then suddenly quit.**

2354

2355

Yours, those

(*It's, Its*) **looking for** (*it's, its*) **nest.**

2623

2624

---

less

Because a nonrestrictive clause is an "extra" that may be omitted—just like parenthetical expressions, appositives, and direct address—we set it off with commas.

Punctuate the following sentence:

My birthday *which is on Christmas* **receives very little attention.**

2892

2893

North, South,
National
Cemetery

The Union bank is in the Keystone building on the south side of Main street.

_____

3161

3162

Poor brakes cause many accidents.

Poor, many

The word **Poor** modifies the noun _____.

The word **many** modifies the noun _____.

197

198

---

a

The maple trees are still green *after the ash trees have shed their leaves.*

If you moved the adverb clause to the beginning of the sentence, would you put a comma after *leaves*? (*Yes, No*)

467

468

---

b

We found *that a train had delayed the bus.*

The noun clause cannot be omitted because it is the (*subject, direct object*) of the verb **found.**

737

738

Yes

If you thought that you had repeated the word *because* too many times, how could you change the adverb clause in the following sentence?

I threw away the box *because I thought it was empty.*

I threw away the box, _____ *it was empty.*

1007

1008

The inn being expensive, we stayed only one day.

a. **The two boys were playing together, their recent quarrel forgotten.**
b. **We looked up the old house, and its porch was still unrepaired.**

_____

_____

1277

1278

---

b

After an introductory word group that lacks a subject, do not use the possessive form of a noun or pronoun to answer the question **Who? or What?**

While standing in the crowd, *Pam's* **purse was stolen.**

This sentence is wrong because the person standing in the crowd was not *Pam's purse,* but _____.

1547

1548

hotel 1817	This is one of the best, if not the best, hotel in town. This is one of the best hotels in town, if not the best. We repaired this sentence as we did the others. We completed the first statement and then added the "if" phrase at the _____ of our sentence. 1818
saw 2086	2. Never use the simple past form of a three-part verb after any form of the helping verb **have** or **be**. PRESENT PAST PAST PARTICIPLE **write** **wrote** **(have) written** The form of **write** that must be used with the helping verb **have** is (*wrote, written*). 2087
smoked 2355	Electric home appliances (*have made, made*) the homemaker's chores much easier. 2356
It's, its 2624	(*It's, Its*) quills stiffen when (*it's, its*) frightened. 2625
birthday, Christmas, 2893	a. **Anyone** *who lives in Bedford* **knows Aunt May.** b. **Aunt May** *who lives in Bedford* **knows everyone in town.** In which sentence should the clause be set off with commas because it is not essential to the meaning of the sentence and is therefore nonrestrictive? _____ 2894
Bank, Building, Street 3162	Lesson **88** Further Uses of Capitals [Frames 3164–3201] *page 396*

(Poor) brakes (many) accidents 198	Words that modify *nouns* and *pronouns* are **adjectives.** Adjectives modify _____ different classes of words. (How many?) 199
Yes 468	**This book begins where the other leaves off.** The adverb clause in this sentence starts with the clause signal _____ and ends with the word _____. 469
direct object 738	a. *Where Captain Kidd buried his treasure* **remains a mystery.** b. **No one has yet discovered the place** *where Captain Kidd buried his treasure.* Which sentence contains a noun clause? _____ 739
thinking 1008	If you thought that you had used too many clauses begin- ning with "*When you . . . ,*" how could you change the adverb clause in the following sentence? *When you train a dog,* **always use the same commands.** *In* _____, **always use the same commands.** 1009
We looked up the old house, its porch still unrepaired. 1278	UNIT 6: RECOGNIZING THE SENTENCE UNIT Lesson **35** Some Typical Sentence Fragments: Clauses and Verbal Phrases [Frames 1280–1316]
Pam 1548	a. **While standing in the crowd, Pam's purse was stolen.** b. **While standing in the crowd, Pam had her purse stolen.** Which sentence is correct because the elliptical clause is followed by a word that answers the question **Who?** _____ 1549

end	a. **Cookie is one of the smartest dogs I know, if not the smartest.**
	b. **Cookie is one of the smartest, if not the smartest, dog I know.**
	Which sentence is correct? _____
1818	1819

written	PRESENT PAST PAST PARTICIPLE
	write **wrote** **(have) written**
	a. I *have wrote* **a letter.** b. I *have written* **a letter.**
	Which sentence is wrong? _____
2087	2088

have made	**We had hoped** (*to have visited, to visit*) **Williamsburg on our trip East last summer.**
2356	2357

Its, it's	Lesson **73** **Keeping Person and Number Consistent**
	[Frames 2627–2663]
2625	

b	a. **Rich people** *who pretend to be poor* **disgust me.**
	b. **Mr. Wetherby** *who pretends to be poor* **is really very rich.**
	Which sentence requires commas because the clause is nonrestrictive? _____
2894	2895

In this lesson we complete our study of capitals.

7. Capitalize titles that show a person's profession, rank, office, or family relationship *when they are used with personal names.*

     a. **the mayor of the city**   b. **for mayor Gibson**

Mayor should be capitalized in phrase (*a, b*).

3164

An **adjective** makes the meaning of a noun or pronoun more exact by telling *what kind, which one(s),* or *how many.* Underline the adjective that tells *what kind:*

these **roads** *wide* **roads** *three* **roads**

200

Fred looks tall until he stands beside his father.

The adverb clause in this sentence starts with the clause signal _____ and ends with the word _____.

470

Where Captain Kidd buried his treasure **remains a mystery.**

The noun clause is the _____ of the verb **remains.**

740

As I got off the bus, I saw fire engines.

After the above sentence, which of the following sentences would offer greater variety—*a* or *b?* _____

a. **As I looked down the street, I saw clouds of smoke.**
b. **Looking down the street, I saw clouds of smoke.**

1010

To be a sentence, a word group must pass two tests:

1. Does it have a subject and verb?
2. Does it make sense by itself?

If you change your mind

This word group fails to pass test (*1, 2*).

1280

---

a. **Raised in Georgia, Sally had a Southern accent.**
b. **Raised in Georgia, Sally's accent was Southern.**

Which sentence is correct? _____

1550

Do not omit words needed to prevent ambiguity (double meaning).

a. **Andy enjoys television more than his friends.**
b. **Andy enjoys television more than he enjoys his friends.**
c. **Andy enjoys television more than his friends enjoy it.**

Could sentence *a* mean either *b* or *c*? (*Yes, No*)

a

1819   1820

WRONG: I *have wrote* **a letter.**

This sentence is wrong because the simple past instead of the past participle is used with the helping verb *have.*

Supply the correct form of the verb **write:**

RIGHT: I *have* _____ **a letter.**

a

2088   2089

---

to visit

How could Gordon ever have expected (*to have memorized, to memorize*) **his speech in one evening?**

2357   2358

Personal pronouns show by their form whether they mean the person or persons *speaking, spoken to,* or *spoken about.*

The person *speaking* refers to himself as *I* and to his group as *we.* We say that these pronouns are in the **first person.**

Underline the two pronouns in the *first person:*

      you   I   he   we

2627

---

a. **It is against the law to use a stamp,** *which has been canceled.*
b. **Shakespeare died at fifty-two,** *which was considered an advanced age at that time.*

In which sentence should the comma be omitted because the clause is restrictive? _____

b

2895   2896

---

a. **Does superintendent Stern approve the plan?**
b. **A new superintendent will be selected.**

In which sentence should **superintendent** be capitalized because it is used with a personal name? _____

b

3164   3165

wide 200	Underline the adjective that points out *which one:* *comfortable* **chair** *one* **chair** *this* **chair** 201
until . . . father 470	**Poor sports do not enjoy games unless they can win.** The adverb clause in this sentence starts with the clause signal _____ and ends with the word _____. 471
subject 740	a. **The bike** *which I liked best* **was too expensive.** b. **I could not decide** *which I liked best.* Which sentence contains a noun clause? _____ 741
b 1010	In this and the following frames, reduce each italicized clause to the type of word group indicated in parentheses: *If they are overcooked,* **vegetables lose their flavor.** (elliptical clause) _____, **vegetables lose their flavor.** 1011

2
 	
1280
	Tests for a sentence:
	
	    1. Does it have a subject and verb?
	    2. Does it make sense by itself?
	
	A touchdown in the third quarter
	
	This word group fails to pass test (*1, 2, 1 and 2*). 1281

a 1550	In this and the following frames, circle the letter of the correct sentence—the one in which the introductory word group does *not* dangle: a. **Being barefooted, the stones cut our feet.** b. **Because we were barefooted, the stones cut our feet.** 1551

This sentence is also ambiguous:

The dealer made Dad a better offer than Ed.

Yes

Add the necessary words to mean that the dealer's offer to Dad was better than Ed's offer to Dad:

The dealer made Dad a better offer than _____ _____.

1820

1821

---

written

This and the following frames will present twenty-two three-part verbs whose past participles all end with -*n* or -*en*. Their similarity should help you to remember them. In each frame, fill in the correct forms of the verbs in parentheses. Be sure to use the past participle with any form of the helping verb **have** or **be**.   (*Turn to the next frame.*)

2089

2090

---

to memorize

Diana Nyad realized that she (*had reached, reached*) **the Florida coast.**

2358

2359

I, we

A pronoun in the **second person** is the one that the person *speaking* uses to address the person or persons *spoken to*.

Underline the one pronoun in the *second person:*

she   you   I   they

2627

2628

---

a

Occasionally, the same clause can be either restrictive or nonrestrictive, depending on what you mean to say.

Mr. Crump sold his land *which was unprofitable.*

If you mean that Mr. Crump sold only that part of his land *which was unprofitable,* you would make the clause restrictive by (*using, omitting*) a comma.

2896

2897

---

a

Wendy is staying with our Uncle Steve and Aunt Jane.

Would you capitalize **Uncle** and **Aunt** if you omitted the names **Steve** and **Jane?** (*Yes, No*)

3165

3166

this	Underline the adjective that tells *how many:*
	modern **houses** *these* **houses** *several* **houses**
201	202

	Donna seldom eats sweets although she enjoys them very much.
unless . . . win	The adverb clause in this sentence starts with the clause signal _____ and ends with the word
471	_____. 472

	When *that* starts an adjective clause, it is a relative pronoun. When *that* starts a noun clause, it is an "empty" word that merely signals the start of a noun clause.
b	a. **I have a tame crow** *that* (=*crow*) *can talk.*
	b. **Mother said** *that she was ready.*
741	Which sentence contains a noun clause? _____ 742

	A violin will deteriorate *if it is not played occasionally.* (elliptical clause)
If overcooked,	**A violin will deteriorate** _____
1011	_____. 1012

	1. Does it have a subject and verb?
	2. Does it make sense by itself?
1 and 2	If you cannot answer "Yes" to both questions, the word group is not a complete sentence but a **fragment.**
	A handle broken off a cup is to a cup what a fragment is
1281	to a _____. 1282

	Circle the letter of the correct sentence:
b	a. **Going down the drain, the chemical made a boiling sound.**
	b. **Going down the drain, I heard the chemical make a boiling sound.**
1551	1552

Ed made (*or* did) 1821	**The dealer made Dad a better offer than Ed.** Add the necessary words to mean that the dealer's offer to Dad was better than the dealer's offer to Ed: **The dealer made Dad a better offer than** _____. _____. 1822

2090
	PRESENT PAST PAST PARTICIPLE
	  blow **blew** **(have) blown**
	  tear **tore** **(have) torn**
	
	A gale had _____ (*blow*) **down our sign, and it**
	
	was badly _____ (*tear*).
	
	                                2091

had reached 2359	**The campers discovered that they** (*used, had used*) **their last match.** 2360

you
 	
2628
	You **are my best friend.**
	          You **are my three best friends.**
	
	Does the second-person pronoun **you** have different forms for singular and plural? (*Yes, No*)
	
	                                2629

omitting 2897	**Mr. Crump sold his land** *which was unprofitable.* If you mean that all of Mr. Crump's land was unprofitable and that he therefore sold all of it, you would make the clause nonrestrictive by (*using, omitting*) a comma. 2898

No
 	
3166
	a. **The flowers were from my Cousin.**
	    b. **The flowers were from my Cousin Manuel.**
	
	Cousin should not be capitalized in sentence (*a, b*).
	
	                                3167

several

202

This sentence contains three nouns:

Three *students* **received perfect** *scores* **on this** *test*.

How many adjectives does this sentence contain? _____

203

---

although . . .
much

472

The actor hesitated as though he had forgotten his lines.

The adverb clause starts with the two-word clause signal

_____ _____ and ends with the word _____.

473

---

b

742

The "empty" word *that*, which starts many noun clauses, is often omitted when the clause is a direct object.

I knew (*that*) *we would win*. **I hope** (*that*) *you can go*.

Is the clause signal *that* a relative pronoun that stands for any noun in the other part of the sentence? (*Yes, No*)

743

---

if not played
occasionally.

1012

As I walked through the tall grass, **I suddenly heard the rattle of a snake.** (present participial phrase)

_____ ,

I suddenly heard the rattle of a snake.

1013

---

sentence

1282

The various types of clauses and phrases you have used to subordinate ideas fail to meet the two tests of a sentence. If you detach them from the sentences with which they are grammatically connected, you have (*fragments, sentences*).

1283

---

a

1552

Circle the letter of the correct sentence:

a. **In opening the can, Amy's finger was badly cut.**
b. **In opening the can, Amy cut her finger badly.**

1553

he made (*or* did) to Ed 1822	**I know Sally better than Evelyn.** Add the necessary words to mean that you are better acquainted with Sally than you are with Evelyn: **I know Sally better than** _____. 1823

blown, torn
 	
2091
	PRESENT PAST PAST PARTICIPLE
	  give gave (have) given
	  fall fell (have) fallen
	
	The farmer _____ (*give*) **us the apples that had**
	
	_____ (*fall*) **from the tree.**
	
	2092

had used 2360	**If we** (*had offered, would have offered*) **Henry the nomination, he might have accepted.** 2361
No 2629	A pronoun in the **third person** indicates the person or persons *spoken about.* Underline three pronouns in the *third person:* he I she they you we 2630
using 2898	a. **Do not use string** *which is too weak.* b. **Do not use string,** *which is too weak.* Which sentence suggests that you avoid using only *certain* string—string which is too weak? _____ 2899
a 3167	**My grandmother speaks Cheyenne.** If you inserted the name **Whitedove** after **grandmother,** would you capitalize **grandmother?** (*Yes, No*) 3168

three (Three—perfect—this) 203	**Three students received perfect scores on this test.** Each adjective comes (*before, after*) the noun that it modifies. 204
as though . . . lines 473	**The dog chewed up the letter before we had read it.** The adverb clause in this sentence starts with the clause signal _____ and ends with the word _____. 474
No 743	Lesson **20** The *Who–Whom* Problem in Noun Clauses [Frames 745–784]
Walking through the tall grass, 1013	*Since I don't understand Spanish,* **I was at a serious disadvantage.** (present participial phrase) _____, **I was at a serious disadvantage.** 1014
fragments 1283	WRONG: **The class starts.** *When the bell rings.* *answers* *"When the bell rings"* is an adverb clause. Although it has a subject and verb, does it make sense by itself? (*Yes, No*) 1284
b 1553	Continue to circle the letter of the correct sentences: a. **If neatly written, more attention will be paid to your letter.** b. **If neatly written, your letter will get more attention.** 1554

I know (*or* do) Evelyn	**I know Sally better than Evelyn.**
	Add the necessary words to mean that Evelyn is not as well-acquainted with Sally as you are:
	I know Sally better than _____.
1823	1824

	PRESENT PAST PAST PARTICIPLE
gave, fallen	**fly** **flew** **(have) flown**
	drive **drove** **(have) driven**
	We have _____ (*fly*) **to Miami, and we have also**
2092	_____ (*drive*) **there.** 2093

had offered	**I would certainly have written to you from Hawaii if I** (*had remembered, would have remembered*) **your address.**
2361	2362

	The terms **first person, second person,** and **third person** apply to plural pronouns as well as to singular pronouns. Do not let this use of the term *person* confuse you.
he, she, they	*I* and *we* are both pronouns in the *first person.*
	He, she, and *they* are all pronouns in the _____ *person.*
2630	2631

	a. **Do not use string** *which is too weak.*
	b. **Do not use string,** *which is too weak.*
a	Which sentence suggests that you avoid using *all* string because *all* string is too weak for the purpose? _____
2899	2900

	As a mark of respect, the titles of high government officials are capitalized even when used without personal names.
Yes	a. **The President consulted the Secretary of State.**
	b. **The Corporal hoped to become a Sergeant.**
3168	The capitalization is correct in sentence (*a, b*). 3169

before 204	Besides coming right before the nouns they modify, adjectives are sometimes found in another position. **The car is blue. The eggs are fresh. The house looks new.** The adjectives in these sentences follow *linking verbs* and are therefore (*subject complements, direct objects*). 205
before . . . it 474	A sentence that contains a clause is called a **complex sentence.** It is more complex (or complicated) than a simple sentence. a. **My friend often telephones at dinnertime.** b. **My friend often telephones** *while we are eating dinner.* Which is a complex sentence—*a* or *b?* _____ 475
	Few people notice the *sign.* The noun *sign* is the direct object of the verb _____. 745
Not understanding Spanish, 1014	**We went to the lake** *so that we could escape the heat.* (infinitive phrase) **We went to the lake** _____. 1015
No 1284	SENTENCE: **The bell rings.** ADVERB CLAUSE: *When the bell rings* Which word in the clause makes the clause depend on something else for its full meaning? _____ 1285
b 1554	a. **To get an honor diploma, a student must maintain a B average or better.** b. **To get an honor diploma, a B average or better must be maintained** 1555

Evelyn knows her (Sally) *or* Evelyn does 1824	In this and the following frames, put a circle around the letter of the sentence which states the comparison logically: a. **Our traffic laws are different from Oregon's.** b. **Our traffic laws are different from Oregon.** 1825

flown, driven 2093	PRESENT PAST PAST PARTICIPLE **choose** **chose** **(have) chosen** **draw** **drew** **(have) drawn** **The design that was** _____ (*choose*) **by the judges** **was** _____ (*draw*) **by Vera.** 2094

had remembered 2362	**In a few more months, we** (*shall live, shall have lived*) **in our present house for twenty years.** 2363

third 2631	*I* or *we* (first person) speak to *you* (second person) about *him, her,* or *them* (third person). Write *first, second,* or *third* (but not in this order) in each blank to indicate the person of each italicized pronoun: *They* (_____ person) told *us* (_____ person) about *you* (_____ person). 2632

b 2900	Participial phrases, as well as adjective clauses, can be either restrictive or nonrestrictive. a. **All cars** *leaving Lewiston* **were stopped by the police.** b. **Maxine** *excusing herself politely* **went upstairs to study.** In which sentence would you use commas because the participial phrase is not essential to the meaning? _____ 2901

a 3169	**The courageous** *captain* **was decorated by the** *governor.* Which italicized word should be capitalized? _____ 3170

subject complements	The ca͡r is blue. The eg͡gs are fresh. The ho͡use looks new. When adjectives are subject complements, they come (*before*, *after*) the nouns they modify.
205	206

b	**My friend often telephones** *while we are eating dinner.* We know that this is a complex sentence because it contains a _____.
475	476

notice	a. **Few people notice the** *sign.* b. **Few people notice** *who directs a movie.* The clause *who directs a movie* in sentence *b* does the same job as the noun *sign* in sentence *a*. Both are _____ _____ of the verb **notice.**
745	746

to escape the heat.	**It is a tedious job** *which requires much patience.* (present participial phrase) **It is a tedious job** _____ _____.
1015	1016

When	WRONG: **The class starts.** *Promptly.* You would never think of separating the adverb *promptly* from the sentence that contains the word it modifies. **The class starts.** *When the bell rings.* Is it correct to separate an adverb clause from the sentence that contains the verb it modifies? (*Yes, No*)
1285	1286

a	a. **Questioned about her campaign, Miss Whitecloud's answers were very informative.** b. **Questioned about her campaign, Miss Whitecloud answered very informatively.**
1555	1556

a

1825

---

a. **We beat North High worse than Marshall Tech.**
b. **We beat North High worse than we beat Marshall Tech.**

1826

---

chosen, drawn

2094

PRESENT	PAST	PAST PARTICIPLE
freeze	**froze**	**(have) frozen**
wear	**wore**	**(have) worn**

If I had not _____ (_wear_) **my sweater, I would have** _____ (_freeze_).

2095

---

shall have lived

2363

By this time next year, you (_will have cast, will cast_) **your first vote.**

2364

They (third)
_us_ (first)
you (second)

2632

Write the word _first, second,_ or _third_ in each blank to indicate the person of the italicized pronouns:

You (_____ person) told _her_ (_____ person) to invite _me_ (_____ person).

2633

---

b

2901

In this and the following frames, supply the necessary commas. If the clause is restrictive because it is essential to the meaning of the sentence, add no commas and write _None_.

Willa Cather _who was born in Virginia_ **wrote stories about the American West.**

2902

Governor

3170

Copy the words that require capitals:

The chairman of the meeting sent a telegram of congratulation to senator Hayakawa and the president.

3171

---

after 206	a. **Melba Moore has an <u>excellent</u> voice.** b. **Melba Moore's voice is <u>excellent</u>.** Does the adjective **excellent** come after the noun it modifies in sentence *a* or *b*? _____ 207
clause *or* adverb clause 476	**I always drive as though everyone else were crazy.** Because this sentence contains a clause, it is called a _____ sentence. 477
direct objects 746	a. **Few people notice the** *sign.* b. **Few people notice** *who directs a movie.* Because the clause *who directs a movie* in sentence *b* is used just like the noun *sign* in sentence *a*, it is a _____ clause. 747
requiring much patience. 1016	**The union published a full-page advertisement** *which stated* *their viewpoint on the strike.* (present participial phrase) **The union published a full-page advertisement** _____ _____. 1017
No 1286	**The class starts** *when the bell rings.* Now the adverb clause makes sense because it is in the same sentence with the verb _____, which it modifies. 1287
b 1556	a. **After winning three games, the school keeps the trophy permanently.** b. **After winning three games, the trophy is kept permanently by the school.** 1557

b

1826

a. **Brazil has a greater area than any country in South America.**
b. **Brazil has a greater area than any other country in South America.**

(Can a country have a larger area than itself?)

1827

---

worn, frozen

2095

PRESENT	PAST	PAST PARTICIPLE
know	knew	(have) known
steal	stole	(have) stolen

The dealer must have _____ (*know*) that the car

was _____ (*steal*).

2096

---

will have cast

2364

Rewrite this sentence, changing the verb from passive to active:

The Segals' paper *had been left* at our door by mistake by the newsboy.

_____

_____

2365

You (second)
her (third)
me (first)

2633

She **and her** *dog* **were strolling down the street.**

Since a noun is something that you talk *about,* every noun—just like the pronouns *he, she, it,* and *them*—is ordinarily in the (*first, second, third*) person.

2634

Cather,
Virginia,

2902

It is the policy of our restaurant to serve no food *which we would not eat ourselves.*

2903

Senator,
President

3171

When a title is used alone, without a name, to refer to a particular person, it may be capitalized.

    a. **A** *principal* **has many responsibilities.**
    b. **The** *principal* **will address the parents' meeting.**

In which sentence would it be permissible to capitalize *principal?* _____

3172

b	Adjectives normally come before the nouns they modify except when they are _____ *complements.*
207	208

complex	Unlike a sentence, a clause (*does, does not*) make sense by itself.
477	478

noun	The choice between **who** and **whom,** when they start noun clauses, depends upon their use *within the clause.*
	who directs a movie
	The clause signal *who* is the subject of the verb _____.
747	748

stating their viewpoint on the strike.	**Every nail** *that was used in the old fort* **was made by hand.** (past participial phrase)
	Every nail _____ **was made by hand.**
1017	1018

starts	WRONG: **She went to Ohio.** *Leaving me in charge of the farm.*
	"Leaving me in charge of the farm" is a present participial phrase.
	Does it have a subject and verb, and does it make sense by itself? (*Yes, No*)
1287	1288

a	a. **When I was six years old, my aunt first took me sailing.**
	b. **When six years old, my aunt first took me sailing.**
1557	1558

b 1827	a. **Next year's team will be as good as this year's, if not better.** b. **Next year's team will be as good, if not better, than this year's team.** 1828
known, stolen 2096	PRESENT PAST PAST PARTICIPLE **grow** **grew** **(have) grown** **see** **saw** **(have) seen** **How Steve has** _____ (*grow*) **since I last** _____ (*see*) **him!** 2097
The newsboy (had) left the Segals' paper at our door by mistake. 2365	Rewrite this sentence, changing the verb from passive to active: **The star** *could be seen* **clearly by us through the telescope.** _____ _____ 2366
third 2634	Underline three words (nouns or pronouns) that are in the third person: **I team you it story we** 2635
None 2903	**Caffeine** *which is present in both tea and coffee* **stimulates the heart and raises blood pressure.** 2904
b 3172	When you use *mother, father, dad,* etc., in place of personal names, you may capitalize them or not—as you prefer. **Have I told you how Mother first met Dad?** **Have I told you how mother first met dad?** Are both sentences correct? (*Yes, No*) 3173

subject	**Most people are honest.**
	The two adjectives—**Most** and **honest**—modify the noun
	_____.
208	209

does not	An adverb clause is so called because it does the work of
	an _____.
478	479

	Use the subject form **who** for subjects and subject complements; use the object form **whom** for objects of verbs and prepositions.
directs	*who directs a movie*
	We use the subject form *who* because it is the (*subject, direct object*) of the verb *directs.*
748	749

used in the old fort	**Most of the articles** *that were advertised in the paper* **were sold out.** (past participial phrase)
	Most of the articles _____ **were sold out.**
1018	1019

No	RIGHT: **She went to Ohio,** *leaving me in charge of the farm.*
	The present participial phrase should be a part of the sentence containing the noun _____, which it modifies.
1288	1289

a	a. **Written in simple language, any child can enjoy this book.**
	b. **Written in simple language, this book can be enjoyed by any child.**
1558	1559

a 1828	Franklin D. Roosevelt served longer than *any* _____ American president. A president cannot serve longer than himself. To make this comparison logical, we must add the word _____. 1829

grown, saw
 	
2097
	PRESENT PAST PAST PARTICIPLE
	  take **took** **(have) taken**
	  throw **threw** **(have) thrown**
	
	Someone had _____ *(take)* **the letter and had**
	
	_____ *(throw)* **it away.**
	
	                                       2098

We could see the star clearly through the telescope.
 	
2366
	Change the verb from active to passive by eliminating the present subject:
	
	    My dad *had not paid* **our telephone bill.**
	
	_____
	
	_____
	
	                                       2367

team, it, story 2635	A shift in person confuses the viewpoint within a sentence. You begin by talking about one person and end up by talking about another. Underline the pronoun that continues the same viewpoint: **As we looked around us,** *(you, we)* **could see that spring was near.** 2636
Caffeine, coffee, 2904	**Pearl Buck** *who wrote many stories* **was one of the outstanding writers of her day.** 2905

Yes
 	
3173
	On the other hand, when you use *mother, father, dad,* etc., merely to show family relationship, always use small letters.
	
	    His *mother* **is a** *cousin* **of my** *father.*
	
	Should the italicized words be capitalized? *(Yes, No)*
	
	                                       3174

people 209	We very seldom use adjectives before pronouns as we do before nouns. We say "a *pretty* girl," but not "a *pretty* she"; "a *new* book," but not "a *new* it." **She looks very pretty. It is new.** In these sentences, the adjectives come (*before, after*) the pronouns they modify. 210
adverb 479	Any clause that modifies a verb is an _____ clause. 480
subject 749	**Few people notice** *who directs a movie.* Be careful to avoid the mistake of thinking that the clause signal is the direct object of the verb **notice** and therefore requires the object form *whom.* The direct object of the verb **notice** is not the clause signal but the entire noun _____. 750
advertised in the paper 1019	**Frank had little money** *that he could spend on entertainment.* (infinitive phrase) **Frank had little money** _____. 1020
She 1289	a. **She went to Ohio, leaving me in charge of the farm.** b. **She went to Ohio. She left me in charge of the farm.** c. **She went to Ohio. Leaving me in charge of the farm.** Which one of the above three items is incorrect? _____ 1290
b 1559	a. **Because the man was wearing a blue uniform, Dave mistook him for a police officer.** b. **Wearing a blue uniform, Dave mistook the man for a police officer.** 1560

other	a. **The Pacific is the largest of any other ocean in the world.** b. **The Pacific is the largest ocean in the world.**
1829	1830

taken, thrown	PRESENT PAST PAST PARTICIPLE **shake** **shook** **(had) shaken** **break** **broke** **(had) broken** **The collision had** _____ (*shake*) **up the box, and** **many dishes were** _____ (*break*).
2098	2099

Our telephone bill had not been paid.	Change the verb from active to passive by eliminating the present subject: **Bob Redwing** *delivers* **our mail around ten o'clock.** _____
2367	2368

we	SHIFT IN PERSON: *I* **liked this story because it kept** *you* **guessing until the very last page.** This sentence is faulty because *I* is in the first person and *you* is in the _____ person.
2636	2637

Buck, stories,	**We seldom interrupt a person** *who is praising us.*
2905	2906

No	When *father, mother, dad,* etc., are used with articles (*a, an, the*) or possessive pronouns (*my, his, your*), they show family relationship and should not be capitalized. **The** *mother* **of one of my friends knew my** *dad* **at college.** Should the italicized words be capitalized? (*Yes, No*)
3174	3175

after	We have seen that adjectives answer the questions *What kind? Which one(s)?* and *How many?* about nouns and
	_____.
210	211

adverb	Lesson **13** **Expressing the Exact Relationship**
	[Frames 482–523]
480	

clause	WRONG: **Few people notice** *whom directs a movie.*
	The object form *whom* is wrong because the clause signal is not the object of the verb **notice** but the subject of the verb _____ within the clause.
750	751

to spend on entertainment.	**We called a meeting** *so that we could elect officers.* (infinitive phrase)
	We called a meeting _____.
1020	1021

c	WRONG: **I sent for a free booklet.** *Advertised in a magazine.*
	"Advertised in a magazine" is a past participial phrase. Does it have a subject and verb, and does it make sense by itself? (*Yes, No*)
1290	1291

a	Lesson **43** **Repairing Dangling Word Groups**
	[Frames 1562–1586]
1560	

b 1830	In this and the following frames, cancel or add any words or letters that are necessary to make the comparisons logical: **Our way of life is very similar to Canada.** 1831

shaken, broken
 	
2099
	PRESENT PAST PAST PARTICIPLE
	   eat ate (have) eaten
	   ride rode (have) ridden
	If we had _____ (*eat*) our lunch, we would have
	_____ (*ride*) further.
	
	2100

Our mail is delivered around ten o'clock. 2368	UNIT **10: USING ADVERBS AND ADJECTIVES** Lesson **66** Using Adverbs to Describe Action [Frames 2370–2408]
second 2637	a. *I* **liked this story because it kept** *you* **guessing.** b. *I* **liked this story because it kept** *me* **guessing.** Which sentence is correct because the person of the pronouns is consistent? _____ 2638
None 2906	**One should be suspicious of any investment** *which offers an unusually high rate of return.* 2907
No 3175	**I want my** *dad* **and** *uncle* **Frank to meet your** *grandfather.* The only one of the italicized words that should be capitalized is _____. 3176

pronouns

211

We need another class of words to answer the questions that we might ask about the action of verbs.

George drove. *(When? Where? How? How much? How often?)*

Are the questions in parentheses about **George** or **drove?**

_____

212

In this lesson you will study **subordination** as a way of building sentences.

Subordinate means "of lower rank." A *clerk,* for example, is subordinate to a *manager.*

In the army, a *sergeant* is subordinate to a (*private, general*).

482

---

directs

751

Now we shall change the wording of our sentence:

Few people notice *who the director was.*

The direct object of the verb **notice** is not the clause signal *who* but the entire noun _____.

752

---

to elect officers.

1021

Lesson **27** Other Types of Reduction

[Frames 1023–1063]

No

1291

RIGHT: **I sent for a free booklet** *advertised in a magazine.*

The past participial phrase should be a part of the sentence containing the noun _____, which it modifies.

1292

Don't hesitate to start your sentences with word groups that do not tell **whom** or **what** they are about. They add interest to your writing. Just remember that you owe your reader this information (*somewhere in, at the beginning of*) the main statement that follows.

1562

Canada's.
or
that of Canada.
or
Canada's way
of life.
1831

The double bass is the largest of all the other members of the violin family.

1832

---

eaten, ridden

2100

PRESENT	PAST	PAST PARTICIPLE
swear	swore	(have) sworn
speak	spoke	(have) spoken

The witness _____ (*swear*) that he had never

_____ (*speak*) to the accused man.

2101

Adjectives can modify only nouns and pronouns—no other class of words.

Adverbs modify everything else that can be modified—verbs, adjectives, and other adverbs.

A word that modifies any word except a noun or a pronoun is

an _____.

2370

---

b

2638

SHIFT IN PERSON: **Whether** *you* **live in a big city or in the country, nature surrounds** *us.*

This sentence is faulty because *you* is in the second person

and *us* is in the _____ person.

2639

None

2907

It turned out that Shirley Smith *who was chosen Dairy Queen* is allergic to milk.

2908

---

uncle

3176

---

8. Capitalize the first word and all important words in titles of books, stories, movies, works of art, musical compositions, etc.

a. *Invisible Man*   b. *Invisible man*

Which title is correctly capitalized? _____

3177

George drove *safely.*

drove

Underline the question that the word *safely* answers:

When? Where? How? How much? How often?

212

213

---

general

In grammar, a subordinate word group is one that is *less than a sentence*—one that *does not make sense by itself.*

Phrases and clauses are examples of _____

word groups.

482

483

---

clause

who the director was

Within the noun clause, the subject of the linking verb *was* is not *who* but _____.

752

753

Reduction is the same principle as using a tack—and not a spike—to fasten a calendar to the wall.

If either a *clause* or a *phrase* says exactly the same thing, use the _____.

1023

---

booklet

a. **I sent for a free booklet. It was advertised in a magazine.**
b. **I sent for a free booklet. Advertised in a magazine.**
c. **I sent for a free booklet advertised in a magazine.**

Which one of the above three items is incorrect? _____

1292

1293

---

at the beginning of

When your introductory word group lacks a subject, tell **whom** or **what** it is about at the beginning of your main statement. Failure to supply this information results in an error

known as a _____ word group.

1562

1563

~~other~~ 1832	**Our gas bill was three dollars more than our neighbor.** 1833
swore, spoken 2101	Whenever you are doubtful about the past participle form of a verb, ask yourself, "Is there a form of this verb that ends with *-n* or *-en?*" If there is, use it after any form of **have** or **be**. Underline two verbs that have forms ending with *-n* or *-en:* **freeze** **think** **speak** **work** 2102
adverb 2370	Although a few adjectives end in *-ly* (*homely, manly, lonely*), the *-ly* ending usually signals an adverb. We can make an adverb of almost any adjective by adding *-ly* to it. Write the adverb form of each of the following adjectives: **sad** _____ **prompt** _____ **cheerful** _____ 2371
first 2639	a. **Whether** *you* **live in a big city or in the country, nature surrounds** *you.* b. **Whether** *you* **live in a big city or in the country, nature surrounds** *us.* Which sentence is correct? _____ 2640
Smith, Queen, 2908	**In our living room we don't have a single chair** *that is really comfortable.* 2909
a 3177	Do not capitalize the articles *a, an,* and *the* or short prepositions and conjunctions in a title except when they are the first word of the title. a. *Gone with the Wind* b. *Gone With The Wind* Which title is correctly capitalized? _____ 3178

How? 213	**George drove** *yesterday*. Underline the question that the word *yesterday* answers: **When? Where? How? How much? How often?** 214
subordinate 483	When we put an idea into a clause rather than into a sentence, we say that we *subordinate* it. When we subordinate an idea, we express it in a word group that is (*more, less*) than a sentence. 484
director 753	*who the director was* When we straighten out this clause by putting the subject first, we get: *the director was who* Since *who* completes the linking verb *was*, it is a (*subject complement, direct object*). 754
phrase 1023	If either a *phrase* or an *adverb* says exactly the same thing, use the _____. 1024
b 1293	WRONG: **Pat showed her bad manners.** *By laughing at my car.* "*By laughing at my car*" is a prepositional phrase with a gerund as the object of the preposition *By*. Can a prepositional phrase be written as a separate sentence? (*Yes, No*) 1294
dangling 1563	What is the difference between a *misplaced modifier* and a *dangling word group*? A *misplaced modifier* is not in its proper place with relation to the word it modifies. A *dangling word group,* on the other hand, often has no word at all to modify and therefore appears to modify the (*right, wrong*) word. 1564

neighbor's. *or* that of our neighbor. *or* neighbor's gas bill. 1833	**Death Valley, California, is hotter than any region on earth.** 1834
freeze, speak 2102	Even though you may make the mistake of saying **has broke, had spoke,** or **was froze,** you know that the words **broken, spoken,** and **frozen** exist. If there is a form of the verb ending with *-n* or *-en,* use it after any form of **have** or **be.** Underline two verbs that have forms ending with *-n* or *-en:* rang gave stole went 2103

sadly
promptly
cheerfully
 	
2371
	There are hundreds of modifiers that have both an adjective and an adverb form.
	
	  a. **bad** **rough** **noisy** **easy** **careful**
	  b. **badly** **roughly** **noisily** **easily** **carefully**
	
	Which group of words consists of adverbs? _____ 2372

a 2640	A pronoun should also agree with its antecedent in number. Use a singular pronoun to refer to a singular antecedent. Use a plural pronoun to refer to a _____ antecedent. 2641
None (*or* living room,) 2909	My parents *hearing of this opportunity* **moved our family to Oregon.** 2910
a 3178	Write the following title correctly: *the return of the native* _____ 3179

page 428

George drove *frequently.*

When?

Underline the question that the word *frequently* answers:

When?   Where?   How?   How much?   How often?

214

215

---

less

a. **The rain stopped.**
b. **when the rain stopped**

Which is a subordinate word group because it is less than

a sentence? _____

484

485

---

subject
complement

Few people notice (*who, whom*) *the director was.*

Because the clause signal is a subject complement, we use
the subject form (*who, whom*).

754

755

---

adverb

1. Sentence   3. Phrase (verbal, appositive, prepositional)
2. Clause   4. Single word (adjective, adverb)

As we move down this list from 1 to 4, the sentence elements
become (*simpler, more complicated*).

1024

1025

No

WRONG: **Pat showed her bad manners.** *By laughing at my
car.*

The prepositional phrase answers the question **How?** about

the verb _____ in the main statement.

1294

1295

---

wrong

To avoid a dangling word group, you must tell **who** or **what**
either (1) in the introductory word group itself or (2) at the
beginning of the main statement that follows it.

When a small baby, a bee stung me on the nose.

Does this sentence tell **who** in either place? (*Yes, No*)

1564

1565

other any ∧ region 1834	**The rat has been the most destructive of any other animal on this planet.** 1835
gave, stole 2103	In this and the following frames, supply the correct forms of the two verbs in parentheses. After any form of **have** or **be,** think whether the verb has an *-n* or *-en* form. If it has, use it. It _____ (*cost*) **ninety cents for the distance we had** _____ (*ride*). 2104
b 2372	The adverbs made by adding *-ly* to adjectives usually answer the question **How?** about the action of the verb. **Dean ate his soup** *noisily.* The adverb *noisily* answers the question **How?** about the action of the verb _____. 2373
plural 2641	SHIFT IN NUMBER: **You should train a** *dog* **before** *they* **get** **too old to learn.** This sentence is faulty because the plural pronoun *they* is used to refer to the singular noun _____. 2642
parents, opportunity, 2910	**This book will be valuable to anyone** *wanting to take better pictures.* 2911
The Return of the Native 3179	Write the following title correctly: *how to choose a vocation* _____ 3180

215

How often?

George drove *away.*

Underline the question that the word *away* answers:

When?   Where?   How?   How much?   How often?

216

---

b

a. **The rain stopped.**
b. **when the rain stopped**

We subordinated the idea in sentence *a* by adding the clause

signal _____.

485

486

---

who

WRONG: **Few people notice** *whom the director was.*

The object form *whom* is wrong because the clause signal is not the object of the verb **notice.**

The object of the verb **notice** is the entire _____

_____.

755

756

---

simpler

1. Sentence   3. Phrase (verbal, appositive, prepositional)
2. Clause   4. Single word (adjective, adverb)

When we reduce a word group, we move (*up, down*) the above list of sentence elements.

1025

1026

---

showed

a. **Pat showed her bad manners. By laughing at my car.**
b. **Pat showed her bad manners by laughing at my car.**

Which sentence is right because the prepositional phrase is in the same sentence as the verb **showed,** which it modifies?

_____

1295

1296

No

a. **When a small baby, I was stung on the nose by a bee.**
b. **When I was a small baby, a bee stung me on the nose.**

In which sentence is the question **Who?** answered sensibly

in the introductory word group? _____

1565

1566

page 431

most destructive of all the animals . . . *or* most destructive animal . . . 1835	Rewrite this sentence correctly: **I study as hard, if not harder, than Phil.** _____ _____ 1836
cost, ridden 2104	**Gilda was** _____ (*choose*) **because she has always** _____ (*drive*) **carefully.** 2105
ate 2373	The most common error in the use of adjectives and adverbs is failing to use the adverb (*-ly*) form to describe the action of a verb. The fact that *verb* is part of the word ad*verb* will remind you always to use an adverb to modify a _____. 2374
dog 2642	a. **You should train a** *dog* **before** *they* **get too old to learn.** b. **You should train a** *dog* **before** *it* **gets too old to learn.** Which sentence is correct? _____ 2643
None 2911	Lesson **81** Review: Uses of the Comma [Frames 2913–2932]
How to Choose a Vocation 3180	9. Capitalize the names of historical events, periods, and documents. **World War II** **Monroe Doctrine** **Bill of Rights** **Colonial Period** **Battle of Gettysburg** **Ten Commandments** Copy the words that require capitals: **The crusades took place during the middle ages.** _____ 3181

Where? 216	Words that modify verbs are called **adverbs.** The fact that the word ad*verb* contains the word *verb* will help you to remember that adverbs modify _____. 217
when 486	**when the rain stopped** Because this type of subordinate word group answers the question **When?**—like an ordinary adverb—it is classified as an _____ clause. 487
noun clause 756	Now we shall put the same idea in a different way: **Few people pay any attention to the** *director.* The noun *director* is the object of the preposition _____. 757
down 1026	a. **We play the game** *in a different way.* b. **We play the game** *differently.* When we reduce the prepositional phrase (4 words) in sentence *a* to the adverb *differently* in sentence *b*, do we change the meaning in any way? (*Yes, No*) 1027
b 1296	a. **Pat showed her bad manners. She laughed at my car.** b. **Pat showed her bad manners by laughing at my car.** c. **Pat showed her bad manners. By laughing at my car.** Which one of the above three items is incorrect? _____ 1297
b 1566	a. **When a small baby, I was stung on the nose by a bee.** b. **When I was a small baby, a bee stung me on the nose.** In which sentence is the question **Who?** answered in the main statement? _____ 1567

I study as hard
as Phil, if not
harder.

1836

Rewrite this sentence correctly:

This is one of the fastest, if not the fastest, car on the road.

_____

_____

1837

---

chosen, driven

2105

The suspect had _____ (_swear_) **that the car
was not** _____ (_steal_).

2106

---

verb

2374

The reward was divided (_equal, equally_) **between the two girls.**
To explain _how_ the reward **was divided,** use the adverb

_____.

2375

---

b

2643

a. **Most things are cheaper when you buy them in large
   quantities.**
b. **Most things are cheaper when you buy it in large quantities.**

Which sentence is correct? _____

2644

In this and the following frames, supply the necessary commas. If no commas are required, write _None_.

**Many years have passed since then and many changes of
course have taken place.**

2913

Crusades,
Middle Ages

3181

Copy the words that require capitals:

**Twenty years after the american revolution, the louisiana
purchase greatly increased the size of the new nation.**

_____

3182

verbs 217	Many adverbs—especially those that tell *how*—end with **-ly.** In fact, we form many adverbs by adding -ly to adjectives: **polite—politely, graceful—gracefully, fearless—fearlessly.** A *careful* **person drives** *carefully.* The adverb in this sentence is _____. 218
adverb 487	**We continued our game** *when the rain stopped.* The adverb clause *when the rain stopped* modifies the verb _____. 488
to 757	a. **Few people pay any attention to the** *director.* b. **Few people pay any attention to** *who directs a movie.* In sentence *a*, the object of the preposition **to** is the noun *director.* In sentence *b*, the object of the preposition **to** is the noun clause _____. 758
No 1027	By reduction we do not mean eliminating words that add to the meaning or interest of a sentence. When we reduce a word group, we make (*no, a slight*) change in the meaning. 1028
c 1297	WRONG: **The customer soon returned.** *To get his money back.* *"To get his money back"* is an infinitive phrase. It explains *why* about the verb _____ in the main statement. 1298
a 1567	If your introductory word group answers the question **Who?** or **What?** do you need to answer this question again at the beginning of your main statement? (*Yes, No*) 1568

Lesson 51 Removing Deadwood from Sentences

[Frames 1839–1861]

---

sworn, stolen

2106

Any food that is not _____ (*eat*) **will be** _____ (*throw*) **out.**

2107

---

equally

2375

Noel must have done (*poor, poorly*) **on his test.**

To explain *how* Noel **must have done** on his test, use the adverb _____.

2376

---

a

2644

You should use **he** or **she** when a statement applies equally either sex.

    A person should wash *his* **hands before** *he* **eats.**

What words would make the above sentence correct?

2645

---

then, changes, course,

2913

We had to wait for the principal was busy when we arrived at his office.

2914

American Revolution, Louisiana Purchase

3182

10. Capitalize all sacred names and religious titles:

    God   **Rabbi Lewis**   **the Reverend Smith**
    Lord   **Father Hobbs**   **Sister Iglesias**

Copy the words that require capitals:

The reverend Brown met with rabbi Barron early last week.

3183

carefully

218

We have seen that adjectives have a *fixed* position in the sentence—usually before the words they modify.

Most adverbs, by contrast, are very *movable*.

I finally finished the final chapter.

The word that can be shifted to another position is the (*adjective* **final**, *adverb* **finally**).

219

---

continued

488

We continued our game *when the rain stopped.*

Because the clause signal **when** starts a *subordinate* word group and also *connects* this word group with the sentence, we call it a **subordinating conjunction.**

The subordinating conjunction in the above sentence is

_____.

489

---

who directs
a movie

758

Few people pay any attention to who directs a movie.

Within the noun clause, the subject of the verb *directs* is the clause signal _____.

759

---

no

1028

In the previous lesson, we reduced clauses to phrases built on present and past participles, gerunds, and infinitives.

These word groups are simpler than clauses because they (*do, do not*) contain subjects and predicates.

1029

---

returned

1298

a. **The customer returned to get his money back.**
b. **The customer returned. To get his money back.**

Which sentence is right because the infinitive phrase is in the same sentence as the verb **returned,** which it modifies?

_____

1299

No

1568

If your introductory word group *does not* answer the question **Who?** or **What?** do you need to answer this question at the beginning of your main statement? (*Yes, No*)

1569

We remove deadwood from a tree because it contributes nothing to the life or productiveness of the tree. By "deadwood" in sentences, we mean empty words and phrases that add nothing to the meaning or to the interest.

Cross out two words that add nothing to the meaning of:

Mr. Lovett was an elderly man in age.

1839

---

eaten, thrown

2107

I would have _____ (*speak*) **to Mr. Price if I had** _____ (*see*) **him.**

2108

---

poorly

2376

WRONG: **Noel must have done** *poor* **on his test.**

This is wrong because the adjective *poor* cannot modify the

_____ **must have done.**

2377

---

or *her*
or *she*

2645

a. **Before a person votes, he or she should inform himself or herself about the candidates.**
b. **Before a person votes, he should inform himself about the candidates.**

Which sentence is better? _____

2646

---

wait,

2914

Before fireworks were prohibited hundreds of children were maimed blinded and killed every Fourth of July.

2915

Reverend,
Rabbi

3183

Too many capitals are as serious an error as too few. Do not capitalize—

FOODS: **spaghetti, hamburgers, brownies, angel food**

Copy the words that require capitals:

We ate chop suey at a chinese restaurant on Campus street.

3184

adverb *finally* 219	Our friends ∧ have ∧ come ∧ for dinner ∧. (often) Can the adverb **often** be inserted in the sentence at each point indicated by a caret (∧)? (*Yes, No*) 220
when 489	**We lost our way** *because we made a wrong turn.* The subordinating conjunction in the above sentence is _____. 490
who 759	WRONG: **Few people pay any attention to** *whom directs a movie.* The object form *whom* is wrong because the clause signal is not the object of the preposition **to** but the subject of the verb _____ within the clause. 760
do not 1029	Here is an adjective clause that can be reduced to something even simpler—a prepositional phrase. **The apples** *that were in the window* **looked larger.** **The apples** *in the window* **looked larger.** By reducing the adjective clause to a prepositional phrase, we eliminate _____ words. (How many?) 1030
a 1299	a. **The customer returned. He wanted his money back.** b. **The customer returned. To get his money back.** c. **The customer returned to get his money back.** Which one of the above three items is incorrect? _____ 1300
Yes 1569	*While peeling onions,* **my eyes always smart.** Does either the introductory word group or the main statement tell **who** is *peeling the onions?* (*Yes, No*) 1570

in age 1839	Some people try to impress others by using pretentious language, by repeating themselves, and by expressing themselves in a roundabout way. a. **Wilma Rudolph was one who was a determined person.** b. **Wilma Rudolph was a determined person.** The sentence containing "deadwood" is sentence (*a, b*). 1840
spoken, seen 2108	**The pipe had** _____ (*burst*) **because the water had** _____ (*freeze*). 2109
verb 2377	a. **The company is always quite . . . in handling complaints.** b. **The company always handles complaints quite . . . .** In which sentence would you use the adjective **prompt** because it would modify the noun **company?** 2378
a 2646	WRONG: **When a *student* plays football, *you* must keep in condition.** This sentence is wrong because the pronoun *you* disagrees with its antecedent in (*number, person*). 2647
prohibited, maimed, blinded(,) 2915	**A bank will not hire any person who is known to gamble.** 2916
Chinese, Street 3184	Do not capitalize— GAMES: baseball, hockey, checkers MUSICAL INSTRUMENTS: violin, piano, saxophone Copy the words that require capitals: **My cousin Lisa sees every colby football game because she plays the trumpet in the college band.** _____ 3185

Yes	Because adverbs are often movable, we frequently find them several words away from the verbs they modify.
	Aunt Mary talks about politics *continually*.
	The adverb *continually* modifies the verb _____.
220	221

because	The grammar term for the clause signals that start adverb clauses is *subordinating* _____.
490	491

	Few people pay any attention to *who directs a movie.*
directs	How do we know that the clause signal is not the object of the preposition **to?**
	If the clause signal *who(m)* were the object of the preposition **to**, the clause would have no (*subject, object*).
760	761

two	**This is a matter** *which is of great importance.*
	Reduce the italicized adjective clause to a prepositional phrase:
	This is a matter _____.
1030	1031

	Sentence fragments can result from splitting off a clause or a phrase from the beginning of a sentence, as well as from the end.
b	a. **I wandered among the crowd. Looking for a familiar face.**
	b. **Looking for a familiar face. I wandered among the crowd.**
	The sentence fragment comes first in (*a, b*). _____
1300	1301

	Sometimes it is difficult or awkward to tell **who** or **what** at the beginning of your main statement.
No	While peeling onions, _____?_____
	Since it would be difficult to continue this sentence, it would be best to tell **who** in the (*introductory word group, main statement*).
1570	1571

a 1840	The way to make a theme longer is to develop your thoughts and to add ideas. Don't pack it with empty words that waste your reader's time. _∧ **I think that the plot is weak.** To lengthen your theme, would it be a good idea to add the words **In my opinion** at the point indicated? (*Yes, No*) 1841
burst, frozen 2109	Lesson **59** Another Group of Three-Part Verbs [Frames 2111–2147]
a 2378	a. **The company is always quite . . . in handling complaints.** b. **The company always handles complaints quite . . . .** In which sentence would you use the adverb **promptly** because it would modify the verb **handles?** _____ 2379
person 2647	WRONG: **Always reread a** *letter* **before you mail** *them.* This sentence is wrong because the pronoun *them* disagrees with its antecedent in (*number, person*). 2648
None 2916	*Reminder:* After the first part of a date or an address, put a comma both before and after each additional part unless it ends the sentence. **We shall be at the Chippewa Motor Hotel 850 Laurel Street Brainerd Minnesota until Tuesday May 10.** 2917

Colby
 	
 3185
	Do not capitalize—
	     OCCUPATIONS: **engineer, artist, lawyer, minister**
	     DISEASES: **measles, mumps, flu, chicken pox, polio**
	 Copy the words that require capitals:
	 Just before easter our minister got pneumonia and was taken to the Oakfield hospital. _____
	
	 3186

talks 221	*Tomorrow* **my cousins will drive back to Springfield.** ? when The adverb *Tomorrow* modifies the verb _____. 222
conjunctions 491	You have had much practice in using the conjunctions **and, but,** and **or** to make compound sentences. These conjunctions, **and, but,** and **or,** are sometimes called **coordinating (co-** means *equal*) **conjunctions** because they connect words and word groups that are (*unequal, equal*) in rank. 492
subject 761	Now let us look at another sentence: **The producers must consider** *whom a movie might offend.* The pronoun *whom* cannot be the subject of the verb *might offend* because the verb already has a subject, the noun _____. 762

of great
importance.
 	
1031
	Sometimes you can do even better by reducing the adjective clause to a single adjective.
	
	    The plane carries a raft *that is made of rubber.*
	    The plane carries a *rubber* **raft.**
	
	Does the five-word adjective clause say any more than the one-word adjective *rubber*? (*Yes, No*)
	
	1032

b 1301	a. **Though I don't collect them. Stamps interest me.** b. **Stamps interest me. Though I don't collect them.** The sentence fragment comes first in (*a, b*). _____ 1302

introductory
word group
 	
1571
	When it is awkward to tell **who** or **what** in the main statement, change the introductory word group to a *complete adverb clause,* leaving the main statement as it is.
	
	    a. **While peeling onions, my eyes always smart.**
	    b. **While I peel onions, my eyes always smart.**
	
	Which sentence is correct? _____
	
	1572

1842

"Deadwood" also results from a lack of careful revision. Keep working at a sentence until you succeed in removing all useless words and roundabout expressions.

a. **There is a great deal of value connected with this book.**
b. **This book has great value.**

Which sentence is better? _____

1842

No

1841

2111

There are a number of irregular verbs that follow the pattern of the verb **ring.**

PRESENT	PAST	PAST PARTICIPLE
ring	**rang**	**(have) rung**

Underline the vowel in each of the above three forms of the verb **ring.** Vowels are *a, e, i, o, u.*

2111

2380

Underline the correct word:

My sunburn hurt (*bad, badly*) **for several days.**

2380

---

b

2379

2649

In this and the following frames, circle the *N* when the pronoun disagrees with its antecedent in *Number,* the *P* when it disagrees in *Person.* Then cross out the incorrect pronoun (and sometimes the verb, too), and write your correction above.

N   P   **A person is expected to keep their appointment.**

2649

---

number

2648

2918

The time will come however when nations will settle their differences around the conference table not on the battlefield.

2918

Hotel, Street, Brainerd, Minnesota, Tuesday,

2917

3187

Do not capitalize—

      TREES: **elm, maple, willow, pine, birch**
      FLOWERS: **rose, peony, orchid, dandelion**

Copy the words that require capitals:

The yellow chrysanthemums with the scarlet oak leaves make the display of the Meyer flower shop very colorful.

3187

Easter, Hospital

3186

---

will drive

222

---

a. **One of the windows** *occasionally* **sticks.**
b. **One of the windows sticks** *occasionally*.
c. *Occasionally* **one of the windows sticks.**

In which sentence is the adverb farthest away from the verb it modifies? _____

223

---

equal

492

Because the two parts of a compound sentence are equal in rank, they are connected by a (*coordinating, subordinating*) conjunction.

493

---

movie

762

---

whom a movie might offend

When we straighten out this clause, we get:

a movie might offend whom

The clause signal *whom* is the (*subject, direct object*) of the verb *might offend*.

763

No

1032

This is not a good book for people *who are nervous.*

Substitute a single adjective for the adjective clause:

This is not a good book for _____ **people.**

1033

---

a

1302

---

a. **Juan completely overhauls each motor. Before selling the car.**
b. **Before selling the car. Juan completely overhauls each motor.**

The sentence fragment comes first in (*a, b*). _____

1303

---

b

1572

Sitting on the step, **my foot fell asleep.**

The introductory word group is dangling because it was not the **foot** that was *sitting on the step,* but a person. It would be easier to correct this faulty sentence by answering the question **Who?** in the (*main statement, introductory word group*).

1573

b 1842	Some sentences remind us of a person who walks around the block to get to the house next door. The best sentence is one that—like an arrow—goes straight to the mark. **Before the realization of what had happened came to me, it was too late.** Could this sentence be improved by revision? (*Yes, No*) 1843
ring, rang, rung 2111	PRESENT PAST PAST PARTICIPLE **ring** **rang** **(have) rung** Does the vowel remain the same in any two forms of this verb? (*Yes, No*) 2112
badly 2380	Underline the correct word: **A family can live more** (*economical, economically*) **in a small town.** 2381
his or her N ~~their~~ 2649	*N P* **When people were in debt, you used to be put in prison.** (Punish the innocent for the crimes of the guilty?) 2650
come, however, table, 2918	**For the protection of small children matches drugs and sharp objects should be kept out of their reach.** 2919

Flower Shop
 	
3187
	Do not capitalize—
	  BIRDS: **robin, blue jay, crow, pheasant**
	  ANIMALS AND FISH: **terrier, spaniel, elephant, catfish**
	Copy the words that require capitals:
	We plan to take our collie with us to Moose lake, but we shall leave our canary with grandma Voss. _____
	
	3188

There are hundreds of adverbs that give information about verbs. In addition, there are some special adverbs that control the "power" of adjectives and other adverbs.

very **hot**	*somewhat* **hot** · *rather* **hot**	*so* **hot**
quite **hot**	*extremely* **hot**	*slightly* **hot**	*too* **hot**

The italicized adverbs modify the (*adjective, adverb*) **hot**.

c

223 | 224

---

coordinating

493

Conjunctions such as **because, when, if,** and **unless** are called **subordinating conjunctions** because they connect a word group of (*higher, lower*) rank than a sentence.

494

---

direct object

763

(who, whom) a movie might offend

Because the clause signal is the direct object of the verb *might offend*, we choose the object form _____.

764

---

nervous

1033

Often the single adjective to which we reduce an adjective clause is a present or past participle.

Milk is a necessity for any child *that is growing*.
Milk is a necessity for any *growing* **child**.

In the second sentence the adjective clause has been reduced to a (*present, past*) participle.

1034

---

b

1303

In this and the following frames, one of each pair of word groups is a sentence, and the other is a fragment. Draw a circle around the letter of the complete sentence.

a. **As soon as I realized my mistake.**
b. **I soon realized my mistake.**

1304

---

introductory word group

1573

a. **As I was sitting on the step, my foot fell asleep.**
b. **Sitting on the step, my foot fell asleep.**

Which sentence is correct? _____

1574

Yes 1843	a. **Before the realization of what had happened came to me, it was too late.** b. **Before I realized what had happened, it was too late.** How many useless words are eliminated by the revision of sentence *a?* _____ 1844
No 2112	PRESENT PAST PAST PARTICIPLE **ring** **rang** **(have) rung** Notice that the past and past participle are different. The vowel **a** in the past turns to _____ in the past participle. 2113
economically 2381	A few adverbs have two forms—one with -*ly* and another without; for example, **slow—slowly, quick—quickly, loud—loudly, fair—fairly, cheap—cheaply.** The shorter form is frequently used in brief commands and on traffic signs. a. **Drive . . . !** b. **I always eat my meals . . . .** In which sentence is the adverb **slow** acceptable? _____ 2382
they P ~~you~~ 2650	*N P* **When a person gets angry, they should count to ten.** 2651
children, matches, drugs(,) 2919	**Grace Hopper studied and improved computer programming and communication.** 2920

Lake, Grandma
 	
`3188
	11. Capitalize proper adjectives that modify common nouns.
	    Dutch apple pie **Swiss cheese** **Spanish moss**
	    Chinese checkers **Harvard beets** **American elm**
	Copy the words that require capitals:
	Our french poodle and siamese cat get along well together.
	
	3189

adjective 224	*very* **awkwardly** *rather* **awkwardly** *so* **awkwardly** *quite* **awkwardly** *somewhat* **awkwardly** *too* **awkwardly** All the italicized adverbs modify the (*adjective, adverb*) **awkwardly.** 225
lower 494	Because adverb clauses are of lower rank than the sentence to which they are attached, they are connected by (*coordinating, subordinating*) conjunctions. 495
whom 764	**The producer must consider** *whom a movie might offend.* We choose the object form *whom* because it is the direct object of the verb (*must consider, might offend*). 765
present 1034	**Nothing disgusts me more than a child** *that has been spoiled.* **Nothing disgusts me more than a** *spoiled* **child.** In the second sentence the adjective clause has been reduced to a (*present, past*) participle. 1035

b
 	
1304
	Continue to draw a circle around the letter of each complete sentence:
	
	    a. **I laughed until my sides ached.**
	    b. **Laughing until my sides ached.**
	
	1305

a 1574	In this and the following frames, correct the dangling word group by changing it to a complete adverb clause. Make no change in the main statement. **Being a rainy day, the outdoor track meet was postponed.** _____, **the** **outdoor track meet was postponed.** 1575

four 1844	a. **It tells how the American people conquered the wilderness.** b. **It tells of the American people and the way in which they conquered the wilderness.** Which sentence is better? _____ 1845
u 2113	Supply the missing forms of the verb **ring:** PRESENT PAST PAST PARTICIPLE **ring** _____ **(have)** _____ 2114
a 2382	a. **Play ... !** b. **The store treats all customers ....** Although both **fair** and **fairly** are adverbs, in which sentence should **fairly,** rather than **fair,** be used? _____ 2383
he or she N ~~they~~ 2651	*N P* **Can you really judge a person's character by their handwriting?** 2652
None 2920	**The newspaper praised Fran Kaslow the driver of the bus for her cool skillful handling of the emergency.** 2921
French, Siamese 3189	In this and the following frames, copy only the words in each sentence to which capitals need to be added: **Among the sponsors of the Good Will club are father Cole of Trinity church, mayor Morales, a judge, a doctor, and my uncle George.** 3190

adverb 225	**Too many people vote without sufficient information.** The adjective **many** modifies the noun **people.** What adverb modifies the adjective **many?** _____ 226
subordinating 495	A sentence that contains one or more subordinate clauses is called a **complex sentence.** Any sentence that contains an adverb clause is a (*complex, compound*) sentence. 496
might offend 765	To choose between **who** and **whom** in a noun clause, see how it is used *within the clause itself.* The way in which the entire noun clause is used in the full sentence has no bearing on your choice of **who** or **whom.** (*True, False*) 766

past
 	
1035
	Any adjective clause that identifies someone or something can be reduced to an appositive phrase very simply.
	
	    Corn, *which was our main crop,* **did poorly that year.**
	    Corn, *our main crop,* **did poorly that year.**
	
	This reduction eliminates two useless words: _____ and _____.
	
	1036

a 1305	a. **It was woven from discarded scraps of cloth.** b. **Woven from discarded scraps of cloth.** 1306
Because (Since, As) it was a rainy day, 1575	Continue to follow the directions for the previous frame. **Struggling through the underbrush, the hunter's clothes were badly torn.** _____, **the hunter's clothes were badly torn.** 1576

a 1845	Avoid repeating in the same sentence the meaning already stated by another word or group of words. Cross out two repetitious words: **The modern car of today is a complicated machine.** <div align="right">1846</div>
rang, (have) rung 2114	The next seven verbs that we study follow the **ring-rang-rung** pattern. One should help you to remember the others. Supply the missing forms: **ring**　　　　**rang**　　　　**(have) rung** **sing**　　　　**sang**　　　　**(have) _____** <div align="right">2115</div>
b 2383	When an adverb has two forms—one with *-ly* and another without—the longer form is preferred in formal usage. 　a. **Please come** *quick!* 　b. **A good executive can make important decisions** *quick.* In which sentence would it be advisable to change the adverb *quick* to *quickly?* _____ <div align="right">2384</div>
his or her N ~~their~~ 2652	*N P*　　**Once a player takes his hand off a checker, you can't take back the move.** <div align="right">2653</div>
Kaslow, bus, cool, 2921	**You know Ralph that any player who breaks the training rules is suspended for the season.** <div align="right">2922</div>
Club, Father, Church, Mayor, Uncle 3190	**Perhaps grandma Wiles will spend easter with my aunt in the east.** _____ <div align="right">3191</div>

Too 226	**Lois speaks French very fluently.** The adverb **fluently** modifies the verb **speaks.** What adverb modifies the adverb **fluently?** _____ 227
complex 496	In every complex sentence that contains an adverb clause, you can expect to find a (*coordinating, subordinating*) conjunction. 497
True 766	To decide whether to use the pronoun **who** or **whom**, you need to look only (*inside, outside*) the clause. 767
which, was 1036	**The next event,** *which was a tug of war,* **was won by the freshmen.** Write in the appositive phrase to which the italicized clause can be reduced: **The next event,** _____**, was won by the freshmen.** 1037
a 1306	a. **Although the movie finally came to a happy ending.** b. **The movie finally came to a happy ending.** 1307
While (As) he struggled through tho underbrush, 1576	**Unless thoroughly cooked, a person should not eat pork.** _____ _____**, a person should not eat pork.** 1577

of today 1846	Reduce the following wordy sentence to only four words: **John's attitude toward his parents was that he had respect for them.** _____ 1847

sung
 	
2115
	Supply the missing forms:
	
	PRESENT PAST PAST PARTICIPLE
	  ring **rang** **(have) rung**
	  sink _____ **(have) sunk**
	  shrink **shrank** **(have)** _____
	
	2116

b 2384	Although we frequently hear **sure** (instead of **surely**) used as an adverb in informal conversation, to many people it sounds slangy and slipshod. **He** _surely_ **gave our suggestion his careful consideration.** The adverb _surely_ is required because it modifies the verb _____. 2385
he or she P ~~you~~ 2653	_N P_ **It's exciting to hook a sailfish because they put up a big fight.** 2654
know, Ralph, 2922	In the remaining frames, put circles around any commas that should be omitted. If all the commas in any sentence are necessary, write _Correct_. **When we finally reached the stadium, we drove around, and looked for a place to park.** 2923
Grandma, Easter, East 3191	**My dad often says that he married my mother because she was born on the fourth of July, and he therefore would not run the risk of forgetting her birthday.** _____ 3192

very

227

The lake was slightly rough.

The adverb **slightly** modifies the _____ **rough.**

228

---

subordinating

497

---

a. **when, as, since, where, after, as if, because, unless, so that, although,** *etc.*
b. **and, but, or**

Which one of the above groups consists of subordinating conjunctions—*a* or *b*? _____

498

---

inside

767

If the clause signal is the subject or subject complement within the clause, use the subject form (*who, whom*).

768

---

a tug of war

1037

Do you remember that a gerund is a noun formed by adding *-ing* to a verb and that a gerund can be used in any way that a noun is used?

The women raised money *by selling books.*

Here the gerund phrase *selling books* is the object of the preposition _____.

1038

---

b

1307

---

a. **He gave no signal to the car behind him.**
b. **Giving no signal to the car behind him.**

1308

Unless it (the pork) has been thoroughly cooked,

1577

Used for only a short time, the Sibleys expect a good price for their car.

_____

_____, **the Sibleys expect a good price for their car.**

1578

John respected his parents.	In this and the following frames, improve each sentence by crossing out the number of useless words indicated in the parentheses:
	It would do more harm than it would do good to your car. (3)
1847	1848

	Supply the missing forms:

	PRESENT	PAST	PAST PARTICIPLE
sank, (have) shrunk	**ring**	**rang**	**(have) rung**
	spring	————	**(have) sprung**
	swim	**swam**	**(have)** ————
2116			2117

	Underline the correct word:
gave	**Young people** (*sure, surely*) **appreciate a parent's interest in their activities and problems.**
2385	2386

it puts	
N ~~they put~~	*N P* **The less exercise one takes, the less food you need.**
2654	2655

around⊙	**Films, slides, and models, make a science course, for example, much more interesting.**
2923	2924

Fourth	**The president urged full support of the United nations.**
	————————————————————————
3192	3193

adjective (*or* subject complement) 228	**Jack can type quite rapidly.** The adverb **quite** modifies the _____ **rapidly.** 229
a 498	a. **A serious fire broke out, and the building was empty.** b. **A serious fire broke out while the building was empty.** One sentence merely adds one fact to another. The other sentence explains *how* the two facts are related. Which sentence brings out more clearly the *relationship* between the two ideas—*a* or *b?* _____ 499
who 768	If the clause signal is the object of a verb or preposition within the clause, use the object form (*who, whom*). 769
by 1038	An adverb clause can often be reduced to a prepositional phrase with a gerund phrase as the object of the preposition (*by, for, on, in, before, after,* etc.). *Because we took a short cut,* **we saved five miles.** *By taking a short cut,* **we saved five miles.** The gerund phrase is the object of the preposition _____. 1039
a 1308	a. **Which makes her look much taller than she is.** b. **It makes her look much taller than she is.** 1309
Because (Since, As) it (the car) was used for only a short time, 1578	**Seeing a large crowd around the car, our curiosity was aroused.** _____ _____, **our curiosity was aroused.** 1579

it would do	The dashboard on the inside of the car has also been improved. (3)
1848	1849

sprang, (have) swum	Supply the missing forms, following the **ring-rang-rung** pattern:
	PRESENT PAST PAST PARTICIPLE
	begin _____ **(have)** _____
	drink _____ **(have)** _____
2117	2118

surely	If using **surely** sounds stiff and unnatural to you, you can use the adverb **certainly** in its place.
	Supply an adverb with the same meaning as **surely**:
	We _____ **saved money by painting the house ourselves.**
2386	2387

one (he or she) needs P ~~you need~~	*N P* Before you take medicine, a person should always read the label.
	(*Note:* In this frame you need to cross out a noun rather than a pronoun.)
2655	2656

models⊙	We are supposed to memorize, not read, our parts in the play.
2924	2925

President, Nations	Our assignment was to write an interpretation of "the Death of the Hired man" by Robert Frost, the new england poet.
3193	3194

adverb 229	You have now seen that adverbs can modify *three* different classes of words. Besides modifying verbs, adverbs can also modify other modifiers. By "other modifiers" we mean adjectives and _____. 230
b 499	a. **A serious fire broke out, and the building was empty.** b. **A serious fire broke out while the building was empty.** Which sentence is a complex sentence because it contains a subordinating conjunction? _____ 500
whom 769	When a noun clause begins with **whoever** or **whomever,** we make our choice in exactly the same way as we did with **who** and **whom.** Underline the correct word: **Mrs. Torrey tells** (*whoever, whomever*) *will listen* **about her travels.** 770
By 1039	*When he saw his final grade,* **Ron leaped with joy.** Complete the following sentence by supplying a gerund phrase as the object of the preposition *On:* *On* _____, **Ron leaped with joy.** 1040
b 1309	In this and the following frames, write an *S* for each word group that is a *Sentence,* and an *F* for each word group that is a *Fragment.* Write your answers on the two lines in the same order as the word groups. **This article recommends electing our Presidents. By a direct** **vote of the people.** _____ _____ 1310
Because (Since, As) we saw a large crowd around the car, 1579	**While writing my summary of *Macbeth,* my baby sister kept interrupting me.** _____ _____, **my baby sister kept interrupting me.** 1580

on the inside 1849	We weighed the meat on a scale in order to see if we had been cheated. (5) 1850
began, (have) begun drank, (have) drunk 2118	a. **rang, sang, sank, shrank, sprang, swam, began, drank** b. **rung, sung, sunk, shrunk, sprung, swum, begun, drunk** Which group consists of simple past verbs that you would use *without* the forms of the helping verb **have** or **be?** ——— 2119
certainly 2387	Use **really,** not **real,** as an adverb meaning **very.** Underline the correct word: **Dorothy Hamill is** (*real, really*) **serious about skating.** 2388
you P ~~a person~~ 2656	From here on, supply a pronoun that agrees in number and person with its antecedent: **If a person overparks, the police tow _____ car away.** 2657
Correct 2925	**No, I should not like to meet Mr. Parker, when he is angry.** 2926
"The . . . Man," New England 3194	**Among the exhibits of the Library of congress are the original declaration of independence and the constitution.** _____ _____ 3195

adverbs 230	In this and the following frames, the position of the periods should tell you whether the missing word would be an adjective or an adverb. **Our hotel room was very . . .** The missing word (such as *small, shabby,* or *comfortable*) would be an (*adjective, adverb*). 231
b 500	a. **A serious fire broke out, and the building was empty.** b. **A serious fire broke out while the building was empty.** The relationship between the two facts is brought out more clearly by the (*complex, compound*) sentence. 501
whoever 770	**Mrs. Torrey tells** *whoever will listen* **about her travels.** *Whoever* is correct because it is the (*subject, object*) of the verb *will listen* within the clause. 771
seeing his final grade, 1040	**You can often frighten away wild animals** *if you will hit two stones together.* Supply a gerund phrase as the object of the preposition *by:* **You can often frighten away wild animals** *by* _____ _____ . 1041
S F 1310	Write an *S* (for *Sentence*) or an *F* (for *Fragment*) for each of the two word groups: **Thinking that the gun was empty. He jokingly pointed it at his friend.** ____ ____ 1311
While (As, When) I was writing my summary of *Macbeth,* 1580	From here on, correct each sentence by answering the question **Who?** or **What?** at the beginning of the main statement. Make no change in the introductory word group. **Having studied hard, my test score disappointed me.** **Having studied hard,** _____ _____ . 1581

on a scale
in order

1850

After the time that our family moved to Argyle, I did not see Uncle John very frequently from then on. (6)

1851

---

a

2119

a. **rang, sang, sank, shrank, sprang, swam, began, drank**
b. **rung, sung, sunk, shrunk, sprung, swum, begun, drunk**

Which group consists of past participles that you would use

with the forms of the helping verb **have** or **be?** _____

2120

---

really

2388

a. **The test was *real* difficult.**
b. **The party was a *real* success.**

The word *real* should be changed to *really* in sentence _____.

2389

---

his or her

2657

The poster shows a person how _____ should put on a life preserver.

2658

Mr. Parker⊙

2926

Not a thing was broken, or lost, or mislaid as a result of our moving.

(Note that there are two *or*'s in this series.)

2927

Congress,
Declaration,
Independence,
Constitution

3195

At various times we have owned a collie, a police dog, an irish terrier, and a persian cat.

_____

_____

3196

adjective 231	**We . . . find Skippy in a neighbor's yard.** The missing word (such as *often,* *usually,* or *sometimes*) would be an (*adjective, adverb*). 232
complex 501	a. **The dog won't eat, and it seems to be hungry.** b. **The dog won't eat although it seems to be hungry.** The relationship between the two facts is brought out more clearly by the (*compound, complex*) sentence. 502
subject 771	Underline the correct word: (*Whoever, Whomever*) *the country elects* **will face serious problems.** 772
hitting two stones together. 1041	*Before I joined the club,* **I attended several meetings.** Supply a gerund phrase as the object of the preposition *Before:* *Before* _____, **I attended several meetings.** 1042
F S 1311	Write an *S* (for *Sentence*) or an *F* (for *Fragment*) for each of the two word groups: **Although the dog is friendly to the family. It is very unfriendly to others.** _____ _____ 1312
I was disappointed in my test score. 1581	**When inflated with air, six people can be carried on this raft.** **When inflated with air,** _____ _____. 1582

the time that,
from then on

1851

Shirley had unusual self-confidence in herself when she went shopping to buy something for herself or someone else. (5)

1852

---

b

2120

Underline three verbs that follow the **ring-rang-rung** pattern:

think   sing   sink   wink   spring

2121

---

a

2389

Although -*ly* is used mainly to change adjectives to adverbs, it is also used to change a few nouns to adjectives; for example, **friend-ly, neighbor-ly, father-ly, order-ly.**

Our new neighbors are unusually *friendly.*

The word *friendly* is an adjective because it modifies the noun _____.

2390

---

he or she

2658

Why don't you boys help _____ to some lunch?

2659

---

broken⊙
lost⊙

2927

The alligator has a thick, tough, leathery, hide.

2928

Irish, Persian

3196

The members of our latin class sent Alva an african violet after her operation for appendicitis at the Bennett hospital.

3197

adverb 232	**The fair will last for . . . days.** The missing word would be an (*adjective, adverb*). <div align="right">233</div>
complex 502	SUBORDINATING CONJUNCTIONS **when, as, since, where, after, as if, because, unless, so that, although,** *etc.* COORDINATING CONJUNCTIONS **and, but, or** The conjunctions that show *more specifically* the relationship between the two facts or ideas that they connect are the (*subordinating, coordinating*) conjunctions.<div align="right">503</div>
Whomever 772	*Whomever the country elects* **will face serious problems.** *Whomever* is correct because it is the (*subject, object*) of the verb *elects* within the clause. <div align="right">773</div>
joining the club, 1042	Here is an adjective clause, too, that can be reduced in the same way: **We have a plan** *that would improve the bus service.* Supply a gerund phrase as the object of the preposition *for:* **We have a plan** *for* _____ _____.<div align="right">1043</div>
F S 1312	Sara Teasdale admired Christina Rossetti. Who wrote imaginative poetry. ____ ____ <div align="right">1313</div>
this raft can carry six people. 1582	**Reaching for the sugar, the cream pitcher was overturned by my dad.** **Reaching for the sugar,** _____ _____.<div align="right">1583</div>

in herself, to buy something	**Of all the hunter's articles of equipment that he uses, his rifle is the most important to him. (7)**
1852	1853

sing, sink, spring	Underline three verbs that follow the **ring-rang-rung** pattern: **swim fling skin begin drink**
2121	2122

neighbors	Since words such as **neighborly, fatherly,** and **orderly** are adjectives, they cannot be used to modify verbs. WRONG: **Mr. Momaday discusses literature** *scholarly.* This sentence is wrong because the adjective *scholarly* cannot modify the verb _____.
2390	2391

yourselves	**Some of the customers made it difficult for the clerk by rushing** _____.
2659	2660

leathery⊙	**To tell the truth, I tried to be friendly, but Bob didn't respond.**
2928	2929

Latin, African, Hospital	**Dr. Carver, the great black agricultural chemist, refused money for his discoveries because he felt that he was doing god's work.**
3197	3198

adjective 233	**We studied the road map . . . carefully.** The missing word would be an (*adjective, adverb*). 234
subordinating 503	We can give a sentence many different meanings merely by changing the subordinating conjunction. **I shall not tell Ruth . . . I see her.** Underline the only subordinating conjunction that does *not* fit into the above sentence: **when until so that if unless although** 504
object 773	Underline the correct word: **I have great admiration for** (*whoever, whomever*) **wrote this article.** 774
improving the bus service. 1043	**The French class has a new tape recorder** *on which they listen to their pronunciation.* Change the adjective clause to a prepositional phrase with a gerund: **The French class has a new tape recorder** _____ _____ *to their pronunciation.* 1044
S F 1313	**Situated at the southern tip of Florida. Everglades Park is a vast wilderness of plants, birds, and animals.** _____ _____ 1314
my dad overturned the cream pitcher. 1583	**Rolled very thin, you can make five dozen cookies from this dough.** **Rolled very thin,** _____. 1584

articles of, that he uses, to him 1853	The reporter spent a week in the town of Belding in order to observe the differences that exist between city life and small-town life. (7) 1854
swim, begin, drink 2122	In this and the following frames, supply the correct forms of the verb in parentheses. All follow the **ring-rang-rung** pattern. **After the bell had _____ three times, it _____ once again.** (*ring*) 2123
discusses 2391	**neighborly fatherly scholarly lovely** Since these adjectives already end in *-ly,* can we make adverbs of them by adding another *-ly?* (*Yes, No*) 2392
him 2660	**Don't judge a person entirely by _____ clothes.** 2661
Correct 2929	**When we hit the wet, and slippery pavement, our car skidded badly.** 2930
Black, God's 3198	**A boys' chorus from Ralph Bunche high school sang "Joy to the world" and several french christmas carols at the december meeting.** _____ _____ 3199

adverb 234	**The room looks very . . . without the piano.** The missing word would be an (*adjective, adverb*). 235
so that 504	Think of the meaning of each sentence before you select the clause signal. **The boys greeted each other . . .** *nothing had happened.* Underline the clause signal you would use to explain **how** the boys greeted each other: **unless as if although so that** 505
whoever 774	Underline the correct word: **Scholars have argued about** (*who, whom*) **wrote Shakespeare's plays.** 775
for listening 1044	A prepositional phrase can sometimes be replaced by a single adjective or adverb. **The cashier looked at the check** *in a suspicious way.* Substitute an adverb for the italicized prepositional phrase: **The cashier looked at the check** _____. 1045
F S 1314	**I have more than two thousand stamps. All of which are different.** _____ _____ 1315
this dough will (can) make five dozen cookies. 1584	**While waiting for a bus, a passing car splashed me.** **While waiting for a bus,** _____ _____. 1585

the town of, in order, that exist 1854	When he had his examination, it showed that he needed dental work to be done in his mouth by a dentist. (13) 1855
rung, rang 2123	The shirt _____ more than it should have _____. (*shrink*) 2124
No 2392	lovely neighborly fatherly scholarly To make adverbial modifiers of these -*ly* adjectives, we must put them in prepositional phrases that can modify verbs: for example, **in a fatherly way, in an orderly manner.** **Mr. Momaday discusses literature** *in a scholarly manner.* The italicized phrase modifies the verb _____. 2393
his or her 2661	Once a customer has worn a dress,_____ cannot return it. 2662
wet⊙ 2930	The Springfield Electric Company, which employs many young people, will not hire anyone, who has not completed high school. 2931
High School, World, French, Christmas, December 3199	Our pastor told about the four chaplains of the catholic, jewish, and protestant faiths who went down with linked arms when their ship was sunk by the germans in world war II. _____ _____ 3200

adjective

235

It is . . . hot at the equator.

The missing word would be an (*adjective, adverb*).

236

---

as if

505

Bob studies at night . . . *he completes his work in the afternoon.*

Underline the clause signal you would use to explain **on what condition** Bob studies at night:

until   although   because   unless

506

---

who

775

No preposition
No D.O.

Underline the correct word:

The jury could not decide (*who, whom*) **they could believe.**

776

---

suspiciously.

1045

You can buy a film at the store *on the corner.*

Substitute an adjective for the italicized prepositional phrase:

You can buy a film at the _____ store.

1046

S   F

1315

Many college students help to pay their expenses. By doing odd jobs in their spare time. _____ _____

1316

I was splashed
by a passing
car

1585

By sitting around and talking, our work will never get done.

By sitting around and talking, _____

_____.

1586

When he had, it, to be done in his mouth by a dentist 1855	My handicap that I have is in not being able to pronounce the sound of new words that I am not familiar with. (13) 1856
shrank, shrunk 2124	All of us _____ more cider than we should have _____. (*drink*) 2125
discusses 2393	WRONG: **Mr. Dale spoke to Earl** *fatherly*. This sentence is wrong because the adjective *fatherly* cannot modify the verb **spoke**. Supply a prepositional phrase that will include the adjective *fatherly*: **Mr. Dale spoke to Earl** _____. 2394
she 2662	The graduate should choose a college that is outstanding in the field of _____ choice. 2663
anyone ⊙ 2931	Don't yawn, or look at your watch, when you are entertaining guests. 2932
Catholic, Jewish, Protestant, Germans, World War 3200	The zinnias bloom in august, but the asters do not bloom until fall. _____ 3201

adverb 236	An adjective can modify only two classes of words: nouns and pronouns. An adverb, however, can modify _____ classes of words. (How many?) 237
unless 506	**María applied for the job . . .** *she read the advertisement in the newspaper.* Underline the clause signal you would use to explain **when** María applied for the job: **if** **as soon as** **although** **where** 507
whom 776	Underline the correct word: **The jury could not decide** (*who, whom*) **was telling the truth.** 777
corner 1046	In this and the following frames, reduce each italicized word group to the construction indicated in parentheses: **The author** *who wrote this story* **knows a lot about sports.** (prepositional phrase) **The author** _____ **knows a lot about sports.** 1047
S F 1316	Lesson **36** Other Types of Sentence Fragments [Frames 1318–1355]
we will never get our work done. *or* we will never finish our work. 1586	Lesson **44** Parallel Construction for Parallel Ideas [Frames 1588–1618]

that I have, in,
the sound of,
that I am not
familiar with

1856

In the remaining frames, rewrite each sentence to express the idea more directly. (If your answer differs from that in the key, count your answer right if you have eliminated useless words.)

The meal that I receive the most enjoyment out of is breakfast. _____

1857

---

drank, drunk

2125

We _____ **where we had never** _____

before. (*swim*)

2126

---

in a fatherly
way (manner).

2394

Correct the following sentence:

Mrs. Cornelius, our grocer, treats all her customers very *neighborly*.

Mrs. Cornelius, our grocer, treats all her customers _____

_____.

2395

---

his or her

2663

Lesson **74** Pronouns That Mean One

[Frames 2665–2703]

---

yawn⊙
watch⊙

2932

Lesson **82** How to Use Semicolons, Colons, and Dashes

[Frames 2934–2974]

August

3201

Lesson **89** Review: The Principles of Graphics

[Frames 3203–3232]

Lesson 7 The Prepositional Phrase as a Modifier

[Frames 239–282]

---

as soon as

507

Our guide tied the canoe to a tree . . . *it would not drift away.*

Underline the clause signal you would use to explain **why** the guide tied the canoe to a tree:

    as if   **where**   **since**   **so that**

508

---

who

777

Underline the correct word:

(*Who, Whom*) **contributed this money is a deep and dark secret.**

778

---

of this story

1047

The employee must state the reason *why he was absel*
(prepositional phrase)

The employee must state the reason _____

_____.

1048

Don't let an appositive phrase become a fragment.

WRONG: **The home run was hit by Baker.** *The first man at bat.*

"The first man at bat" is an appositive phrase.

Does the appositive phrase have a subject and a verb?
(*Yes, No*)

1318

When you dress in the morning, you may select any shoes you please as long as they make a matching pair.

Similarly, when you express two or more similar ideas, you may use any type of word group you wish as long as they (*match, differ*).

1588

I enjoy (my) breakfast most.	**Judy started going with another boy, and this boy that she started going with was very popular.**
	_____
	_____
1857	1858

swam, swum	**The game had already _____ when it _____ to rain.** (*begin*)
2126	2127

in a very neighborly way (manner).	Do not use **kind of** and **sort of** as adverbial modifiers meaning **rather** or **somewhat** except in relaxed conversation. They are out of place in formal writing or speaking. a. **I felt** *kind of* **embarrassed about my mistake.** b. **The public is** *kind of* **dubious about campaign promises.** In which sentence is *kind of* inappropriate? _____
2395	2396

	The pronouns **everyone** and **everybody** are peculiar words. They are often singular and plural at the same time. They are singular in form because they are built upon the words **one** and **body,** which are (*singular, plural*).
	2665

	SEMICOLONS **His car was out of gas, and mine had two flat tires.** This is a compound sentence. Its two main clauses are connected by the conjunction _____.
	2934

	a. **Bert pulled over to the side of the road, and the oil truck passed him.** b. **Bert pulled over to the side of the road, and let the oil truck pass.** Omit the comma in sentence (*a, b*).
	3203

The picture . . . the cover is amusing.

Is the **picture** *on, in, near, over,* or *behind* the **cover?**

We need a word to show the *relationship* between the noun **cover** and the noun _____.

239

---

so that

Mr. Hart put in a pinch of grass seed . . . *he pulled out a weed.*

Underline the clause signal you would use to explain **where** Mr. Hart put in grass seed:

> **after**   **so that**   **if**   **wherever**

508

509

Who

Underline the correct word:

The newspaper would not reveal (*who, whom*) **their inform-ant was.**

(*Note:* Take into account that the subject of the linking verb **was** is **informant.** If you are puzzled, look back to frame 754, page 427.)

778

779

---

for his absence.

The article offers many suggestions *that are practical.* (adjective)

The article offers many _____ **suggestions.**

1048

1049

No

The home run was hit by Baker. *The first man at bat.*

Does the appositive phrase make sense by itself? (*Yes, No*)

1318

1319

---

match

The principle of expressing similar ideas in a similar or parallel way is known as **parallel construction.**

This principle means that if you put one idea into a prepo-sitional phrase, you should also put a parallel idea into (*a prepositional phrase, an adverb clause*).

1588

1589

Judy started
going with
another boy who
was very popular.

1858

The reason that I got up early was that I had work that
needed to be done.

_____

_____

1859

---

begun, began

2127

The chorus _____ the same numbers that they had

_____ at their spring concert. (*sing*)

2128

---

b

2396

In more formal speech and writing, use the adverb **rather** or
somewhat instead of **kind of** or **sort of**.
Correct the following sentence:
The public is *kind of* **dubious about campaign promises.**

The public is _____ **dubious about campaign
promises.**

2397

---

singular

2665

Everyone *is* **ready.**   **Everybody** *was* **impatient.**

Do the pronouns **Everyone** and **Everybody** take singular or

plural verbs? _____

2666

---

and

2934

A semicolon may be used in place of the conjunction **and,
but,** or **or** to connect the main clauses in a compound
sentence.

His car was out of gas; mine had two flat tires.

The two main clauses of this compound sentence are not

connected by a conjunction but by a _____. 2935

---

b

3203

You may omit the comma and the conjunction in a compound

sentence and replace them with a _____.

3204

The picture *on* the cover is amusing.

picture

The word that now shows the relationship between **cover** and **picture** is _____.

239

240

---

wherever

Fear is good . . . *it leads you to protect yourself.*

Underline the clause signal you would use to explain **under what condition** fear is good:

though   **if**   **although**   **unless**

509

510

---

who

Underline the correct word:

The orchestra extends an invitation to *(whoever, whomever)* **can play a musical instrument.**

779

780

---

practical

People *who are irritable* **do not make good clerks.** (adjective)

_____ **people do not make good clerks.**

1049

1050

No

The home run was hit by Baker, *the first man at bat.*

Now the appositive phrase makes sense because it is in the same sentence with the noun _____, which it explains.

1319

1320

---

a prepositional phrase

If you put one idea into an infinitive phrase, you should also put a parallel idea into *(a participial, an infinitive)* phrase.

1589

1590

I got up early because I had work to do.

1859

I sent a defective pen to you approximately a month or so ago to have a repair job done on it for me.

_____

_____

1860

---

sang, sung

2128

The ship _____ where several other ships had _____ before. (*sink*)

2129

---

rather *or* somewhat

2397

---

a. It made us *sort of* sad to leave the old farm.
b. Jefferson was *sort of* fearful of centralized government.

In which sentence is *sort of* inappropriate? _____

2398

---

singular

2666

Everyone *is* ready.   Everybody *was* impatient.

Although **everyone** and **everybody** are singular in form and always take singular verbs, we tend to think of them as meaning a number of persons, rather than a single person.

Although **everyone** and **everybody** are *singular* in form, they are somewhat _____ in meaning.

2667

---

semicolon

2935

I tried to explain; he was too angry to listen.

In this compound sentence the semicolon takes the place of the conjunction (*and, but*).

2936

---

semicolon

3204

Fortunately the tornado missed our town.
Occasionally Mr. Baxter forgot to give an assignment.

Putting commas after the italicized adverbs would give them (*more, less*) emphasis.

3205

Jerry strolled . . . the park.

Did Jerry stroll *through, past, around,* or *toward* the park?

We need a word to show the *relationship* between the noun

park and the verb _____.

See how simple it is to combine two sentences by using an adverb clause.

As

∧ *The man came closer.* **I noticed a scar on his cheek.**

We change the italicized sentence to an adverb clause by adding the subordinating conjunction **As.** Then we change

the period after the first sentence to a _____.

Underline the correct word:

Margaret Mead, the famous anthropologist, became a friend to (*whoever, whomever*) **she studied.**

These toys were made of materials *which had been discarded.* (past participle)

These toys were made of _____ materials.

---

a. **The home run was hit by Baker. He was the first man at bat.**
b. **The home run was hit by Baker. The first man at bat.**
c. **The home run was hit by Baker, the first man at bat.**

Which one of the above three arrangements is incorrect—

a, b, or *c?* ____

Bert's parents promised *to buy a new car.*

In the above sentence, what Bert's parents promised is expressed in an (*infinitive phrase, adverb clause*).

I sent you a pen approximately a month ago for repair. 1860	**The reason for my having been absent is that my chemistry class visited a factory where they make glass.** _____ _____ 1861
sank, sunk 2129	The five common irregular verbs that follow often cause errors that give the impression of uneducated speech. PRESENT　　　　'　PAST　　　　　PAST PARTICIPLE 　**do**　　　　　　**did** (not **done**)　　　(have) **done** Fill in the correct forms of **do**: I _____ **what anyone else would have** _____. 2130
b 2398	Correct the following sentence: **Jefferson was** *sort of* **fearful of centralized government.** **Jefferson was** _____ **fearful of centralized government.** 2399
plural 2667	**everyone　　　everybody** Shall we use singular pronouns to refer to these words because of their singular form, or shall we use plural pronouns because of their plural meaning? Those who consider form more important than meaning would use (*singular, plural*) pronouns. 2668
but 2936	A semicolon can also take the place of the clause signal **because** in a complex sentence. 　　　a.　**The bird couldn't fly; its wing was broken.** 　　　b.　**The streets were icy; traffic moved slowly.** In which sentence does the semicolon take the place of the clause signal **because?** _____ 2937
more 3205	a.　*For the first time in many years* **we won every game of the season.** b.　*For the first time* **we won every game of the season.** Because of the length of the introductory expression, a comma would more commonly be used in sentence (*a, b*). 3206

strolled 241	Jerry strolled *through* the park. The word that now shows the relationship between **park** and **strolled** is _____. 242
comma 511	**The man came closer. I noticed a scar on his cheek.** *As the man came closer,* **I noticed a scar on his cheek.** We have combined the two sentences by making a (*compound, complex*) sentence. 512
whomever 781	Underline the correct word: (*Whoever, Whomever*) **wrote this courageous editorial deserves a lot of admiration.** 782
discarded 1051	**I was kept awake by the faucet** *that was dripping.* (present participle) **I was kept awake by the** _____ **faucet.** 1052
b 1321	Now look at another cause of sentence fragments—the sentence with a compound predicate. **We climbed the tower and looked at the scenery.** The above sentence has a compound predicate that makes (*one, two*) statement(s) about the subject **We** in the first word group. 1322
infinitive phrase 1591	**Bert's parents promised** *to buy a new car.* *To buy a new car* is an infinitive phrase. If you wanted to state a second promise that Bert's parents made, it would be better, for the sake of parallel construction, to use an (*adverb clause, infinitive phrase*). 1592

I was absent
because my
chemistry class
visited a glass
factory.
1861

Lesson 52 Review: Problems of Sentence Construction

[Frames 1863–1883]

---

did, done	PRESENT PAST PAST PARTICIPLE **go** **went** **(have) gone** (not *went*) Fill in the correct forms of **go:** **Joan** _____ **to say good-by to Iris, but Iris had** **already** _____.
2130	2131

---

rather *or* somewhat	In this and the following frames, underline the correct modifier or, in some cases, the word appropriate for formal usage: **Clarence types fast but not very** (*accurate, accurately*).
2399	2400

---

singular	**Nearly everyone** *likes* **to see** *his or her* **name in print.** In this sentence, both the verb and the pronouns that refer to **everyone** are (*singular, plural*).
2668	2669

---

a	A comma by itself cannot connect two main clauses. Only a semicolon has the power to hold main clauses together without the help of the conjunction **and, but,** or **or.** a. **I shook the branches, the apples came tumbling down.** b. **I shook the branches; the apples came tumbling down.** Which sentence is correct? _____
2937	2938

---

a	a. **Before we bought our new car, we got prices from several dealers.** b. **We got prices from several dealers, before we bought our new car.** Omit the comma in sentence (*a, b*).
3206	3207

page 484

through 242	A word that shows the relationship of the noun or pronoun that follows it to some other word in the sentence is called a **preposition**. A preposition shows _____ ship. 243
complex 512	**The man came closer, and I noticed a scar on his cheek.** *As the man came closer,* **I noticed a scar on his cheek.** The relationship between the two facts is brought out more clearly by the (*compound, complex*) sentence. 513
Whoever 782	In conversational English, **who** and **whoever** are often used in place of the object forms. In formal speech or writing, however, **whom** and **whomever** are the correct object forms. a. INFORMAL: **I wonder ... Peggy will invite.** b. FORMAL: **The public wonders ... the mayor will blame.** The pronoun **who** would be considered an error in (*a, b*). 783
dripping 1052	**Dr. Rosalyn Yalow,** *who was the winner of the Nobel Prize for Medicine,* **is a renowned physicist.** (appositive phrase) **Dr. Rosalyn Yalow,** _____, **is a renowned physicist.** 1053
two 1322	A careless writer sometimes creates a fragment by cutting off the last part of a compound predicate. WRONG: **We climbed the tower.** *And looked at the scenery.* The italicized word group lacks a (*subject, verb*). 1323
infinitive phrase 1592	a. **My parents promised** *to buy a new car* **and** *that they would let me drive it.* b. **My parents promised** *to buy a new car* **and** *to let me drive it.* ———— 1593

Here is a letter written by a father to his son's camp counselors at Camp Michiwaki. Each sentence contains one of the errors studied in this unit. At the top of each frame, circle the letter of the error found in that frame. Then revise the sentence correctly.   (*Turn to the next frame.*)

1863

---

went, gone

2131

PRESENT   PAST   PAST PARTICIPLE
   run   **ran**   **(have) run**

Fill in the correct forms of **run:**

Cathy _____ **for the same office for which her**

mother had _____.

2132

---

accurately

2400

Ron (*sure, surely*) **understood that I needed this money** (*badly, bad*).

2401

---

singular

2669

When the pronoun that refers to **everyone** or **everybody** is possessive (*his, her*), the singular pronoun sounds sensible and is preferred in formal writing and speaking.

Underline the pronoun preferred in formal usage:

Everybody **has the right to state** (*his or her, their*) **mind.**

2670

---

b

2938

When there are other commas in a compound sentence, the important comma that breaks the sentence into two parts gets lost among the others.

My Cousin Nan was popular, good-looking, and athletic, and, to tell the truth, I was a little jealous of her.

The *compound sentence* comma follows the word _____.

2939

---

b

3207

a. **While we discuss the teacher sits among the class and listens.**
b. **While we eat we often listen to the TV evening news program.**

To avoid misunderstanding, it would be advisable to use a comma after the short introductory clause in sentence (*a, b*).

3208

relationship

243

Many prepositions show relationships in **position.**

POSITION: *in, on, by, under, below, beneath, above, over, beside, behind, across, against,* etc.

Underline the preposition that shows position:

box of crackers   man from Mars   car behind us

244

---

complex

513

Combine each pair of sentences by changing the italicized sentence to an adverb clause. Write the full sentence, keeping the ideas in the same order.

Veal is not my favorite meat. **I sometimes eat it.**

_____

_____

514

---

b

783

a. **The Senate is likely to approve . . . the President appoints.**
b. **You can vote for . . . you want.**

In which sentence would **whoever** be more acceptable as conversational usage? _____

784

---

winner of the Nobel Prize for Medicine

1053

Steve's General Store, *which is the only store in the village,* **sells everything from lollipops to washing machines.** (appositive phrase)

Steve's General Store, _____

_____ **, sells everything from lollipops to washing machines.**

1054

---

subject

1323

We climbed the tower. *And looked at the scenery.*

"And looked at the scenery" is a predicate that makes a statement about the subject _____ of the first word group.

1324

---

b

1593

The company wants a driver *who knows the city.*

In the above sentence the qualification for the driver is expressed in (*a prepositional phrase, an adjective clause*).

1594

a. dangling word group   b. faulty pronoun reference
c. faulty comparison

Never having been away from home before, we hope that you will give our son special attention.

_____,

we hope that you will give him special attention.

1864

---

ran, run

PRESENT	PAST	PAST PARTICIPLE
come	**came** (not **come**)	(have) **come**

Fill in the correct forms of **come:**

Earl _____ **home an hour ago, but Allen hasn't**

_____ **home yet.**

2132

2133

---

surely, badly

No teacher could have been more (_patient, patiently_) **than Annie Sullivan, Helen Keller's teacher.**

2401

2402

---

his or her

Though we hear the plural pronoun _their_ widely used to refer to **everyone** and **everybody** in informal English, it is likely to be criticized in formal writing or speaking.

Has _everybody_ **turned in** _their_ **paper?**

This sentence is acceptable as (_informal, formal_) usage.

2670

2671

---

athletic

When other commas are present, it is a good idea to change the _compound sentence_ comma to a semicolon.

My Cousin Nan was popular, good-looking, and athletic; and, to tell the truth, I was a little jealous of her.

Using a semicolon instead of a comma after **athletic** makes the main break in the sentence (_more, less_) conspicuous.

2939

2940

---

a

When people are at home, do they strew papers, tin cans, and bottles, around their yards?

Omit the comma after the word _____.

3208

3209

behind

244

Some prepositions show **direction**.

DIRECTION: *to, from, toward, down, up, at*

The rock rolled down the mountain.

The preposition **down** shows the _____ in which the rock rolled.

245

Although veal is not my favorite meat, I sometimes eat it.

514

Follow the directions given in the previous frame:

Skippy hid under the sofa. *He was afraid of the storm.*

_____

_____

515

---

b

784

UNIT 4: OTHER DEVICES OF SUBORDINATION

Lesson **21** Subordination by Present Participles

[Frames 786–827]

---

the only store in the village

1054

After he had saved all this money, **Jones lost it.** (prepositional phrase with gerund)

_____, **Jones lost it.**

1055

We

1324

We climbed the tower and looked at the scenery.

This sentence is right because a predicate belongs in the same sentence with its _____.

1325

---

an adjective clause

1594

The company wants a driver *who knows the city.*

Who knows the city is an adjective clause.

If you want to state a second qualification for the driver, it would be better, for the sake of parallel construction, to use (*an adjective clause, a prepositional phrase*).

1595

a Since (Because, As) our son has never been away from home before, 1864	a. misplaced modifier b. nonparallel construction c. incorrect omission of words **We will telephone daily to inquire whether he is happy, comfortable, and his health is good.** **We will telephone daily to inquire whether he is** _____ _____. 1865
came, come 2133	PRESENT PAST PAST PARTICIPLE **come** **came** **(have) come** **run** **ran** **(have) run** To avoid a very common error, notice that **come** and **run** are two-part, not one-part, verbs. The form that is different from the other two is the _____ form. 2134
patient 2402	**In those days people lived** (*simpler, more simply*) **than they do today.** 2403
informal 2671	a. *Everyone* **should wash** *their* **hands before touching food.** b. *Everyone* **should wash** *his or her* **hands before touching food.** Which sentence would be more acceptable in formal speech or writing? _____
more 2940	**The mature reader enjoys a novel for its ideas, its portrayal of character, and its literary style, but the youthful reader, generally speaking, looks for excitement, suspense, and sudden surprises.** To make the sentence break more conspicuous, substitute a semicolon for the comma after the word _____. 2941
bottles 3209	**An old sailor and his dog and his cat lived in this lonely weather-beaten shack.** One comma is required after the word _____. 3210

direction
 	
245
	A few prepositions show relationships in **time**.
	
	TIME: *before, during, after, until, till*
	
	    a. **Brush your teeth . . . meals.**
	    b. **Park your car . . . the corner.**
	
	Which sentence requires a preposition that will show a *time* relationship? _____
	
	246

Skippy hid under the sofa because (since, as) he was afraid of the storm. 515	*You are the oldest.* **It was your responsibility.** _____ _____ (*Note:* Count your sentence right if it makes good sense, even if you did not use the same clause signal given in the answer.) 516
	In this unit we study other useful devices for subordination that will help us to write more mature sentences. When we subordinate a fact or an idea, we express it in a word group that is (*more, less*) than a sentence. 786
After saving all this money, 1055	*If you will make notes of important facts,* **you will make reviewing easier.** (prepositional phrase with gerund) _____ _____, **you will make reviewing easier.** 1056

subject
 	
1325
	a. **We climbed the tower. We looked at the scenery.**
	    b. **We climbed the tower and looked at the scenery.**
	    c. **We climbed the tower. And looked at the scenery.**
	
	Which one of the above three arrangements is incorrect—*a, b,* or *c?* _____
	
	1326

an adjective clause 1595	a. **The company wants a driver** *who knows the city* **and** *who has a good safety record.* b. **The company wants a driver** *who knows the city* **and** *with a good safety record.* In which sentence are the italicized word groups parallel? _____ 1596

b
happy,
comfortable,
and healthy.

1865

Do not force him to eat salad, which he never has and never will eat.

Do not force him to eat salad, _____

_____ .

1866

PRESENT	PAST	PAST PARTICIPLE
come	**came**	**(have) come**
run	**ran**	**(have) run**

past

2134

The past forms of **come** and **run** are _____ and

_____ .

2135

---

more simply

2403

It was (*rather, kind of*) **surprising that the public accepted the news so** (*calm, calmly*).

2404

---

b

2672

So far we have been dealing with the possessive pronoun *his*.

The situation is somewhat different when we use the nominative pronoun *he* or *she* or the _____ pronoun *him* or *her*.

2673

---

style

2941

COLONS

A colon says to the reader, "Look ahead. Here it comes," and directs his or her attention to what follows.

a. **I am taking five courses.**
b. **I am taking five courses:**

You expect the courses to be listed after (*a, b*).

2942

---

lonely

3210

Gwendolyn Brooks, a Black writer, won the Pulitzer Prize for Poetry, on May 1, 1950.

Omit the comma after the word _____ .

3211

246 / a

Still other prepositions, such as *of, for, about, with, except,* and *but* (when it means *except*), show many different kinds of relationships between the words they relate.

EXAMPLES: **a pound <u>of</u> tea**   **a story <u>about</u> war**
           a letter <u>for</u> me   **a cake <u>with</u> frosting**

Each of the underlined words is a _____.

247

---

516 / Since you are the oldest, it was your responsibility.

Mr. Doyle decided to buy our car. *We had already sold it.*

(In other words, Mr. Doyle made up his mind too late.)

_____

_____

517

---

786 / less

Prepositional phrases and adverb, adjective, and noun clauses are **subordinate** word groups because they (*do, do not*) make complete sense apart from a sentence.

787

1056 / By making notes of important facts,

There seemed to be no way *in which we could reduce our expenses.* (prepositional phrase with gerund)

There seemed to be no way _____

_____.

1057

1326 / c

A noun-participle (absolute) phrase consists of a noun followed by a present or past participle that modifies it.

              a. **Dripping with rain**
              b. **His raincoat dripping**

Which item is a noun-participle phrase? _____

1327

1596 / a

a. **It was cruel** *to catch the bird* **and** *keeping it in a cage.*
b. **It was cruel** *to catch the bird* **and** *to keep it in a cage.*

Which sentence is better? _____

1597

c which he never has eaten and never will eat. 1866	**Also, if there is any skin on chicken, he will refuse to eat it.** **Also, he will refuse** _____ _____. 1867
came, ran 2135	Notice the similarity between **come** and **become**: PRESENT PAST PAST PARTICIPLE **come** **came** **(have) come** **become** **became** **(have) become** Fill in the correct forms of **become**: **Howard** _____ **a draftsman although he could** 2136 **have** _____ **an engineer.**
rather, calmly 2404	**In spite of the customer's bad manners, the clerk conducted himself** (_gentlemanly, in a gentlemanly manner_). 2405
objective 2673	When the pronoun that refers to **everyone** or **everybody** is nominative (_he, she_) or objective (_him, her_), we are often forced to use the plural pronoun _their_ (or _them_) to prevent absurdity. _Everybody_ **had warned me, but I didn't believe** _him or her._ Do the singular pronouns _him or her_ make good sense in this sentence? (_Yes, No_) 2674

b
 	
2942
	Use a colon (:) before an item or a series of items introduced by a statement that is grammatically complete.
	
	    a. **My favorite courses are . . .**
	    b. **These are my favorite courses . . .**
	
	After which statement would you use a colon because the statement is grammatically complete? _____
	
	2943

Poetry 3211	A _restrictive_ clause is essential to the meaning of a sentence. A _nonrestrictive_ clause merely adds a fact that is unessential to the meaning of a sentence. The clause that should be set off with commas from the rest of the sentence is the (_restrictive, nonrestrictive_) clause. 3212

preposition 247	The noun or pronoun that follows a preposition is called its **object**. **The man in the next seat was a doctor.** The preposition is **in**; the object of the preposition is the noun _____. 248
Mr. Doyle decided to buy our car after we had already sold it. 517	_Peaches are plentiful._ **They are very poor.** (_Note:_ **Because** or **when** would not make good sense here.) 518
do not 787	**Verbals** are also useful devices for subordination. A **verbal** is a verb that has crossed the boundary line and become another class of word without completely losing its identity as a verb. A word that functions as both a verb and an adjective would be classified as a _____. 788
of reducing our expenses. 1057	**Unfortunately, the family has never been fully responsible** _in financial matters._ (adverb) **Unfortunately, the family has never been fully responsible** _____. 1058

b
 	
1327
	A noun-participle phrase is often mistaken for a complete sentence.
	
	    a. **His raincoat** dripped.
	    b. **His raincoat** _dripping._
	
	Which item is a complete sentence? _____
	
	1328

b 1597	a. **Ammonia is used** _for softening water_ **and** _for dissolving grease._ b. **Ammonia is used** _for softening water_ **and** _to dissolve grease._ Which sentence is better? _____ 1598

c
to eat chicken if there is any skin on it. *or* to eat any skin that is . . .
 	
1867
	a. misplaced modifier b. *is when* or *is where* error
	           c. faulty comparison
	Be especially careful not to serve any food to our child that is spoiled.
	Be especially careful not to serve _____
	
	_____ .
	
	                                            1868

became, become 2136	In this and the following frames, supply the correct forms of the verbs in parentheses. Be sure to use the past participle after any form of **have** or **be.** Several verbs follow the **ring-rang-rung** pattern. **Miss Doyle had** _____ (*go*) **to the office to see why the bell had been** _____ (*ring*). 2137
in a gentlemanly manner 2405	**Some of the umpire's decisions** (*sure, certainly*) **seemed** (*unfair, unfairly*) **to most of the fans.** 2406
No 2674	a. **We hope** *everyone* **will attend, but** *he* **never does.** b. **We hope** *everyone* **will bring** *his or her* **parents.** In both sentences, a singular pronoun is used, according to rule, to refer to *everyone.* In which sentence does following the rule result in absurdity? _____ 2675

b
 	
2943
	You would not write—
	                My favorite course is: math.
	So don't make the same mistake by writing—
	                My favorite courses are: math, history, and biology.
	Colons should not be used after statements that are grammatically (*complete, incomplete*).
	                                              2944

nonrestrictive 3212	a. **The Presidents** *who accomplished most* **were the most severely criticized.** b. **My mother** *who used to be a track star* **gave me valuable advice.** The italicized clause should be set off with commas in sentence (*a, b*). 3213

<table>
<tr><td>

seat

248

</td><td>

A group of words that begins with a preposition and ends with its object is a **prepositional phrase.**

> The cause ⸨of this sudden explosion⸩ remains a mystery.

The prepositional phrase begins with the preposition **of** and

ends with its object _____.

249

</td></tr>

<tr><td>

Although
peaches are
plentiful, they
are very poor.

518

</td><td>

In this and the following frames, convert each *compound* sentence to a *complex* sentence by changing the italicized statement to an adverb clause:

> *I opened the cabinet,* **and a jar fell out.**

_____

_____

519

</td></tr>

<tr><td>

verbal

788

</td><td>

The three kinds of verbals that we study in this unit are all "double-duty" words that have some of the characteristics of both a verb and another class of words—sometimes a noun, sometimes an adverb or an adjective.

Look at the word *verbal.* As its name suggests, every verbal

is formed from a _____.

789

</td></tr>

<tr><td>

financially.

1058

</td><td>

Some children have unusual talent *in music.* (adjective)

Some children have unusual _____ **talent.**

1059

</td></tr>

<tr><td>

a

1328

</td><td>

> a. **His raincoat** *dripped.*
> b. **His raincoat** *dripping.*

Which item is *not* a sentence because it contains a present

participle rather than a verb? _____

1329

</td></tr>

<tr><td>

a

1598

</td><td>

When similar ideas are expressed in a similar way, we say

that the construction is _____.

1599

</td></tr>
</table>

a (to) our child any food that is spoiled. 1868	a. dangling word group b. nonparallel construction c. incorrect omission of words **While eating his meals, no one should hurry him.** ————————————————————————, **no one should hurry him.** 1869
gone, rung 2137	**We quickly** _____ (_do_) **the dishes and** _____ (_run_) **up to our room.** 2138
certainly, unfair 2406	**Three can sit very** (_comfortably, comfortable_) **in the front seat.** 2407
a 2675	When following the rule does not lead to absurdity, it is better —especially in formal usage—to refer to **everyone** or **everybody** with a (_singular, plural_) pronoun. 2676
incomplete 2944	The statements that require colons often contain the words _following, as follows, these,_ or _there are._ a. **The ingredients of waffles are: flour, milk, eggs. . . .** b. **Waffles contain the following ingredients: flour, milk, eggs. . . .** The colon is used correctly in sentence (_a, b_). 2945
b 3213	**The child feared many things; for example, electrical storms and the dark.** Instead of using the semicolon, you could use (_a dash, a period followed by a capital letter_). 3214

explosion
 	
249
	We need prepositional phrases to express meanings that cannot be expressed by a single adjective or adverb.
	
	    a glass *for water* a *water* glass
	    a glass *for milk* a *milky* glass
	
	Which adjective is not the equivalent of the corresponding prepositional phrase—*water* or *milky?* _____
	
	250

When I opened the cabinet, a jar fell out. 519	Follow the directions given in the previous frame: **Jim insisted on changing the tire, and** *he had on his best suit.* _____ _____ 520
verb 789	**a** *cold* **wind** Because the word *cold* modifies the noun **wind,** it is an _____ . 790
musical 1059	**Mr. Hollis listens** *in a patient way* **to all complaints.** (adverb) **Mr. Hollis listens** _____ **to all complaints.** 1060
b 1329	**His raincoat** *dripping.* Does a present participle by itself have the power to make a complete statement about a subject? (*Yes, No*) 1330
parallel 1599	Suppose that we should wish to enumerate the various duties of office secretaries: **The duties of secretaries are** *to receive visitors, opening the mail,* **and** *they type letters.* Is each of the three duties expressed in the same type of word group? (*Yes, No*) 1600

a While he is eating his meals, 1869	a. dangling word group b. nonparallel construction c. faulty comparison **Eating slowly is better for him than not to eat at all.** **Eating slowly is better for him than** _____ _____. 1870
did, ran 2138	**Water** _____ (_become_) **a serious problem after the well had** _____ (_run_) **dry.** 2139
comfortably 2407	**It was** (_somewhat, sort of_) **surprising that the strike should end as** (_sudden, suddenly_) **as it began.** 2408
singular 2676	Underline the pronoun that would be more appropriate in formal writing and speaking: **Under a democracy, everybody has the right to express** (_his or her, their_) **opinions.** 2677
b 2945	a. **These are the primary colors: red, blue, yellow.** b. **The primary colors are as follows: red, blue, yellow.** c. **The primary colors are: red, blue, yellow.** d. **The following are the primary colors: red, blue, yellow.** In which sentence is the colon incorrect because it does not follow a grammatically complete statement? _____ 2946
a dash 3214	**We have many aunts, uncles, and cousins, and all, of course, must be invited to the wedding.** To make the main break in this compound sentence more conspicuous, change the comma after the word **cousins** to a _____. 3215

We walked *with care.*   **We walked** *carefully.*
We traveled *by train.*   **We traveled** *trainly.*

milky

The adverb *carefully* can be substituted for the prepositional phrase *with care.*

Is there a proper adverb that can take the place of the phrase *by train?* (Yes, No)

250   251

Jim insisted on changing the tire although he had on his best suit.

You wait long enough, **and everything comes back into style again.**

_____

_____

520   521

---

adjective

a *stinging* **wind**

Because the word *stinging* modifies the noun **wind**, it is also an _____.

790   791

---

patiently

Remember not to leave things such as mops and pails on the stairs *to the basement.* **(adjective)**

Remember not to leave things such as mops and pails on the _____ **stairs.**

1060   1061

---

a. **His raincoat** *dripping.*
b. **His raincoat** *was dripping.*

No

In sentence *b*, we have made the present participle part of a verb by adding to it the helping verb _____.

1330   1331

---

a. **The duties of secretaries are** *to receive visitors, opening the mail,* **and** *they type letters.*
b. **The duties of the secretary are** *to receive visitors, to open the mail,* **and** *to type letters.*

No

Which sentence is correct because the italicized word groups match? _____

1600   1601

b not eating at all. 1870	a. misplaced modifier b. nonparallel construction c. faulty comparison **Do not force him to play childish games, because his interests are just like a grownup.** **Do not force him to play childish games, because his interests are just like** _____. 1871

became, run 2139	**When my sweater** _____ (*come*) **back from the cleaner, I noticed that it had** _____ (*shrink*) **a great deal.** 2140

somewhat, suddenly 2408	**Lesson 67 Choosing Modifiers After Sense Verbs** [Frames 2410–2446]

his or her 2677	**anyone anybody each** **someone somebody each one** **no one nobody either** Can these pronouns mean either a boy or a girl, a man or a woman? (*Yes, No*) 2678

c 2946	a. **The rent includes the following items: gas, electricity, and water.** b. **The rent includes: gas, electricity, and water.** In which sentence is the colon used correctly? _____ 2947

semicolon 3215	a. **The three basic rights mentioned in the Declaration of Independence are: life, liberty, and the pursuit of happiness.** b. **The Declaration of Independence mentions three human rights: life, liberty, and the pursuit of happiness.** The colon is correctly used in sentence (*a, b*). 3216

No 251	Most prepositional phrases are used as modifiers—either as an adjective or as an adverb. A prepositional phrase which—like an adjective—modifies a noun or pronoun is called an **adjective phrase.** An adjective phrase does the work of an _____. 252
If you wait long enough, everything comes back into style again. 521	**I'll set the alarm, and** *I'll be sure to get up early.* (Keep the word groups in the same order.) _____ _____ 522
adjective 791	**a** *cold, stinging* **wind** Which adjective was formed from a verb—*cold* or *stinging?* _____. 792
basement 1061	a. *There are curtains in the kitchen.* **They need washing.** b. **The curtains** *that are in the kitchen* **need washing.** c. **The curtains** *hanging in the kitchen* **need washing.** d. **The curtains** *in the kitchen* **need washing.** e. **The** *kitchen* **curtains need washing.** Which sentence states the idea in the fewest words? _____ 1062
was 1331	To serve as a verb, a present participle must be combined with some form of the verb *be.* a. **His raincoat was dripping.** b. **His raincoat dripping.** Which item is a sentence because the present participle is combined with a form of *be?* _____ 1332
b 1601	a. **The duties of secretaries are** *to receive visitors, to open the mail,* **and** *to type letters.* b. **The duties of secretaries are** *receiving visitors, opening the mail,* **and** *typing letters.* Are both sentences correct? (*Yes, No*) 1602

c a grownup's. *or* those of a grownup. *or* a grownup's interests. 1871	a. nonparallel construction b. faulty pronoun reference c. faulty comparison **He has, by the way, read more books than any boy or girl in his class.** **He has, by the way, read more books than** _____ _____. 1872
came, shrunk 2140	**We had** _____ (*sing*) **only a few songs when the** **lights** _____ (*begin*) **to flicker.** 2141

	look smell taste feel hear (sound)
	These verbs that relate to our senses have two different meanings. One requires an adverb, the other an adjective.
	
	    a. **Joey** *looked* **at the cake.**
	    b. **The cake** *looked* **delicious.**
	
	Looked means an action of the eyes in sentence (*a, b*).
	
	2410

Yes 2678	Since a pronoun such as **anyone, anybody, someone, somebody** can mean either sex, we use the pronouns *his or her, he or she,* or *him or her* to refer to such pronouns. *Anyone* **who never changes** *his or her* **mind is stubborn.** Does this statement, as it is worded, apply to either sex? (*Yes, No*) 2679
a 2947	a. **Scandinavia consists of three countries: Norway, Sweden, and Denmark.** b. **Scandinavia consists of: Norway, Sweden, and Denmark.** The colon is used incorrectly in sentence (*a, b*). 2948
b 3216	**Many of Bach's relatives,** *brothers, uncles, and cousins,* **were also musicians.** To make it clear that the italicized nouns are used as appositives, change the commas after **relatives** and *cousins* to (*semicolons, colons, dashes*). 3217

adjective

252

the *corner* **house**

Because *corner* modifies the noun **house,** it is an *adjective.*

the house *on the corner*

Because the prepositional phrase *on the corner* also modifies the noun **house,** it is an _____ *phrase.*

253

I'll set the alarm so that I'll be sure to get up early.

522

Sally smells roses, **and she begins to sneeze.**

_____

_____

523

---

stinging

792

a *stinging* **wind**

The adjective *stinging* was formed by adding _____ to the verb *sting.*

793

---

e

1062

a. *There are curtains in the kitchen.* **They need washing.**
b. **The curtains** *that are in the kitchen* **need washing.**
c. **The curtains** *hanging in the kitchen* **need washing.**
d. **The curtains** *in the kitchen* **need washing.**
e. **The** *kitchen* **curtains need washing.**

These sentences illustrate the process of _____.

1063

---

a

1332

a. **Columbo walked into the living room. His raincoat was dripping.**
b. **Columbo walked into the living room. His raincoat dripping.**

The noun-participle phrase which is written as a fragment is found in (*a, b*).

1333

Yes

1602

The basic idea of parallel construction is this:

If your first item begins with a participle, then all should begin with participles.

If your first item is a clause, then all the others should be

_____.

1603

c

any other boy
or girl in his
class.

1872

a. *is when* or *is where* error   b. faulty pronoun reference
c. faulty comparison

Our son plans to become a scientist because it is his greatest interest.

Our son plans to become a scientist because _____

_____ .

1873

---

sung, began

2141

The bone had _____ (*spring*) **back into place**

before the doctor _____ (*come*).

2142

---

a

2410

a. **The water** *felt* **cold.**
b. **The customer** *felt* **the material.**

In which sentence does *felt* mean an action of the hands?

_____

2411

Yes

2679

It is generally better to use the pronouns *his or her* to refer to both sexes than to use just *his* or *her*.

a. **Somebody has forgotten** *his or her* **paper.**
b. **Somebody has forgotten** *his* **paper.**

Which sentence is preferable? _____

2680

---

b

2948

A colon may be used before a single item that is introduced by a complete statement.

Only one thing stopped me from going: my lack of money.

    a. **Eva had only one ambition: to win the music prize.**
    b. **Eva's only ambition was: to win the music prize.**

The colon is used correctly in sentence (*a, b*).

2949

---

dashes

3217

Dad predicted that I would change my mind, and I did.

To make the end of this sentence more forceful, change the

comma to a _____ .

3218

adjective

253

the *corner* house
the house *on the corner*

The *adjective* comes before the noun it modifies.

The *adjective phrase* comes (*before, after*) the noun it modifies.

254

Whenever (*or* when) Sally smells roses, she begins to sneeze.

523

Lesson **14** Understanding Adjective Clauses

[Frames 525–564]

---

ing

793

An adjective that is formed by adding *-ing* to a verb is called a **present participle.** We can turn any verb into a present participle by adding *-ing* to it (sometimes making a minor change in the spelling).

The present participle form of the verb *lose* is _____.

794

---

reduction

1063

UNIT 5: ACHIEVING SENTENCE VARIETY

Lesson **28** Shifting Word Order in the Sentence

[Frames 1065–1098]

---

b

1333

His knee bandaged,

This noun-participle phrase contains a (*present, past*) participle.

1334

---

clauses

1603

If your first item is an adjective, then all the others should be _____.

1604

b
science is his
greatest
interest.

1873

---

a. misplaced modifier   b. *is when* or *is where* error
c. faulty comparison

**Do not let him watch violent television shows before he goes
to bed, which are likely to give him nightmares.**

_____

_____.

1874

---

sprung, came

2142

The *Titanic* **had** _____ (*run*) **into an iceberg and
had** _____ (*sink*).

2143

---

b

2411

---

a. **The cook** *tasted* **the soup.**
b. **The medicine** *tasted* **bitter.**

In which sentence does *tasted* mean an action performed by
the subject's tongue? _____

2412

---

a

2680

Because some people feel uncomfortable in using the pronouns *his or her* in statements to refer to both sexes, they
fall back on the plural pronoun *their*, which is acceptable
as informal usage.

      If *anyone* **should call, take** *their* **number.**

This sentence is acceptable as (*informal, formal*) usage.

2681

---

a

2949

DASHES

The dash is not a general punctuation mark that may be used
for all purposes. Its uses are just as exact as those of any
other punctuation mark.

May a dash be used to take the place of any comma or period?
(*Yes, No*)

2950

---

dash

3218

---

a. **The coach said, "This is our last chance to win."**
b. **The coach said, "this is our last chance to win."**

Which sentence is correct? _____

3219

Adjective phrases—just like adjectives—are often used after linking verbs as subject complements.

    a. **The lilacs are beautiful.**
    b. **The lilacs are in full bloom.**

In which sentence is an adjective phrase used as a subject complement? _____

We have just studied adverb clauses—clauses that are used as adverbs.

Now we turn our attention to the **adjective clause.**

As its name suggests, an adjective clause is a clause that is used as an _____.

The present participle form of the verb *win* is _____.

Sentences are usually parts of a paragraph—with other sentences before and after them. In a particular position, one sentence pattern might suit your purpose much better than another. Should the pattern of any preceding sentences influence a sentence that you might, at the moment, be writing? (*Yes, No*)

---

    a. **His knee bandaged.**
    b. **His knee was bandaged.**

Which item is *not* a sentence because it contains a past participle rather than a verb? _____

In expressing parallel ideas, it doesn't matter which pattern you use at the beginning so long as you follow through with (*the same, a different*) pattern.

a Before he goes to bed, do not . . . shows, which are likely to give him nightmares. 1874	a. dangling word group b. nonparallel construction c. incorrect omission of words **Please look in, now and then, during the night to keep him covered and seeing that he doesn't fall out of bed.** **Please look in, now and then, during the night to keep him covered and** _____ _____ . 1875
run, sunk 2143	The police had _____ (*become*) **suspicious when the boy** _____ (*run*) **away from home.** 2144
a 2412	**look smell taste feel hear (sound)** When these verbs mean actions of the body, use adverbs to describe these actions—just as you use adverbs to describe any other actions. Underline the correct word: **We smelled gas very** (*distinct, distinctly*) **in the kitchen.** 2413
informal 2681	Although you may use in conversation whatever forms seem natural to you, use only singular pronouns to refer to antecedents such as **anyone, anybody, someone,** and **somebody** in all careful speech and formal writing. Underline the proper pronoun for formal usage: **Nobody can escape the results of** (*his or her, their*) **actions.** 2682
No 2950	To some extent dashes are used like commas, but they are stronger, more forceful marks that interrupt a sentence more abruptly. a. **Rice's hit, a line drive to center field, won the game.** b. **Rice's hit—a line drive to center field—won the game.** Which sentence makes the appositive more forceful? _____ 2951
a 3219	a. **"Is anybody hurt?" asked the police officer.** b. **"Is anybody hurt," asked the police officer?** Which sentence is correct? _____ 3220

b 255	In all but one of these sentences, the linking verb is followed by an adjective phrase used as a subject complement. a. **The plane** *was* **on time.** c. **The crops** *were* **dry.** b. **The piano** *seems* **in tune.** d. **The ring** *is* **of no value.** The one sentence in which the linking verb is not completed by an adjective phrase is sentence _____. <div align="right">256</div>
adjective 525	An adjective modifies a noun or pronoun. <div align="center">**I just read an** *interesting* **article.**</div> The word *interesting* is an adjective because it modifies the noun _____. <div align="right">526</div>
winning 795	<div align="center">a. **We have a** *good* **team.** b. **We have a** *winning* **team.**</div> In which sentence does a present participle modify the noun **team?** _____ <div align="right">796</div>
Yes 1065	You may wish to avoid repeating a word or a sentence pattern. You may consider that one pattern sounds better than another in a particular situation, or that it gives an idea more needed emphasis. Could a sentence be good in itself but poor at a particular point in a paragraph? (*Yes, No*) <div align="right">1066</div>
a 1335	<div align="center">a. **His knee bandaged.** b. **His knee was bandaged.**</div> In sentence *b,* we have made the past participle part of the verb by adding it to the helping verb _____. <div align="right">1336</div>
the same 1605	In the following exercise, each sentence contains three parallel ideas arranged in columns to make comparison easier. You will find that one of the ideas does not match the other two. Your job is to rewrite this "misfit" so as to bring it in line with the other two ideas, thus making the construction _____. <div align="right">1606</div>

b to see that he doesn't fall out of bed. 1875	a. misplaced modifier b. dangling word group c. incorrect omission of words **If he coughs, sneezes, or any other symptom of a cold, wire us at once.** **If he coughs, sneezes, _____** **_____, wire us at once.** 1876
become, ran 2144	**We had _____ (_swim_) for only a few minutes** **when it _____ (_begin_) to rain.** 2145
distinctly 2413	a. **Our costumes _looked_ rather curious.** b. **Everyone _looked_ at our costumes curiously.** In which sentence does _looked_ mean an action of the eyes? _____ 2414
his or her 2682	a. **If that is _someone_ for me, ask _them_ to wait.** b. **If _someone_ is falsely accused, _they_ have the right to defend _themselves_.** In which sentence would the use of the plural pronoun(s) be acceptable because the situation is informal? _____ 2683
b 2951	a. **This horse—high-spirited and nervous—was hard to control.** b. **This horse, high-spirited and nervous, was hard to control.** Which sentence makes the adjectives more forceful? _____ 2952
a 3220	a. **"People matter," said Eleanor Roosevelt, "we are here to help one another."** b. **"People matter," said Eleanor Roosevelt. "We are here to help one another."** Because the quotation consists of two separate sentences, which is correctly punctuated—_a_ or _b_? _____ 3221

c 256	A prepositional phrase can also be used as an adverb. **spoke** *proudly* Because *proudly* modifies the verb **spoke,** it is an *adverb.* **spoke** *with pride* Because the phrase *with pride* also modifies the verb **spoke,** it is an _____ *phrase.* 257
article 526	a. **I just read an** *interesting* **article.** b. **I just read an article** *which interested me.* The clause in sentence *b* does the same job as the adjective *interesting* in sentence *a.* The clause *which interested me* is therefore called an _____ *clause.* 527
b 796	Besides being formed from a verb, a present participle resembles a verb in still another way: It may take a direct object or a subject complement, as no ordinary adjective can do. **I found Roy** *reading a magazine.* (Roy read a magazine.) The present participle *reading* is completed by the direct object _____. 797
Yes 1066	In furnishing a room, you can't say whether a particular chair is good or bad without considering the other furnishings with which it must fit in. Can the same be said of a particular sentence pattern? (*Yes, No*) 1067
was 1336	a. **Namath returned to the game, his knee bandaged.** b. **Namath returned to the game. His knee bandaged.** Which arrangement is correct? _____ 1337
parallel 1606	Rewrite only the "misfit" on the corresponding line at the side to make it parallel with the other two: **The new cars are tested for** a. **speed,** _____ b. **comfort, and** _____ c. **if they are safe.** _____ 1607

c or shows (has, develops) any other symptom of a cold 1876	a. dangling word group b. faulty pronoun reference c. *is when* or *is where* error **In your camp bulletin, it says that parents may not visit during the first two weeks.** _____ **that** **parents may not visit during the first two weeks.** 1877
swum, began 2145	**When Dick** _____ (*come*) **over, Earl had already** _____ (*go*) **to bed.** 2146
b 2414	**Everyone** *looked* **at our costumes (curious, curiously).** In this sentence, *looked* means an action of the eyes. To describe this action, we should choose the adverb (*curious, curiously*). 2415
a 2683	Underline the proper pronoun for formal usage: *Anyone* **who fails to report a crime is shirking** (*his or her, their*) **moral duty.** 2684
a 2952	A dash gives more force to an added idea than a comma. a. **Only one person knew the combination to the safe, and he was out of town.** b. **Only one person knew the combination to the safe—and he was out of town.** Which sentence is more forceful? _____ 2953
b 3221	a. **"Where all men think alike," said Walter Lippmann, "no one thinks very much."** b. **"Where all men think alike," said Walter Lippmann, "No one thinks very much."** Which sentence is correct? _____ 3222

adverb 257	Like the adverbs they resemble, adverb phrases answer the questions *When? Where?* and *How?* about verbs. **The car turned** *at the next intersection.* Underline the question that the adverb phrase answers: **When?** **Where?** **How?** <div align="right">258</div>
adjective 527	**I just read an article** *which interested me.* Now look at just the adjective clause. Does it have a subject and a verb? (*Yes, No*) <div align="right">528</div>
magazine 797	**I found Roy** *feeling lonesome.* (Roy felt lonesome.) The present participle *feeling* is completed by the subject complement _____. <div align="right">798</div>

Yes
 	
1067
	Because English is a subject-first language, we naturally begin most of our sentences with the subject.
	
	    a. **The whole pile of dishes went down.**
	    b. **Down went the whole pile of dishes.**
	
	In which sentence does the subject come first? _____
	
	<div align="right">1068</div>

a
 	
1337
	a. **Our engine was repaired. We continued on our way.**
	    b. **Our engine repaired, we continued on our way.**
	    c. **Our engine repaired. We continued on our way.**
	
	Which one of the above three arrangements is incorrect?
	
	_____
	
	<div align="right">1338</div>

c. safety. 1607	**Rick's theme was not accepted because** a. **of its lateness,** _____ b. **it was too short, and** _____ c. **it was written in pencil.** _____ <div align="right">1608</div>

b Your camp bulletin says 1877	a. nonparallel construction b. faulty pronoun reference c. faulty comparison **Therefore, if he gets homesick or any special food is wanted, tell him to telephone us immediately.** **Therefore, _____** **_____, tell him to telephone us immediately.** 1878
came, gone 2146	**Walter _____ (*drink*) the milk that his little brother should have _____ (*drink*).** 2147
curiously 2415	a. **I *felt* my pocket . . . to see if my wallet was there.** b. **I *felt* very . . . about my test score.** In which sentence would you use the adverb **anxiously** because *felt* means an action and the adverb **anxiously** would describe this action? _____ 2416
his or her 2684	The same problem arises when you use the words **a person** or **any person** to make a statement that applies to either sex. INFORMAL: **Can *any person* park *their* car here?** FORMAL: **Any person can improve *his or her* speech.** Formal usage requires a *(singular, plural)* pronoun. 2685
b 2953	Supply a missing punctuation mark that will give more force to the added idea: **Ann said that nothing could stop her from going to college and she meant it.** 2954
a 3222	Insert any necessary apostrophes: **Myra hurts peoples feelings and then wonders why she isnt popular.** (*Note:* The feelings belong to the **people,** not to the **peoples.**) 3223

Where? 258	*During the night* **it snowed.** Underline the question that the adverb phrase answers: **When?** **Where?** **How?** <div align="right">259</div>
Yes 528	**I just read an article** *which interested me.* Although the adjective clause has a subject and a verb, does it make sense by itself apart from the sentence? (*Yes, No*) <div align="right">529</div>
lonesome 798	Like the verb from which it is made, a present participle may be modified by an adverb. **The lawyer defended her client,** *believing firmly in his innocence.* The present participle *believing* is modified by the adverb _____.<div align="right">799</div>
a 1068	Another way of achieving sentence variety is to begin a sentence, now and then, with an adverbial modifier—an adverb, an adverb phrase, or an adverb clause. Underline the adverb phrase that can be put ahead of the subject: **I never trusted ladders after that experience.** <div align="right">1069</div>
c 1338	a. **Tuesday being Election Day. The banks will be closed.** b. **Tuesday is Election Day. The banks will be closed.** c. **Tuesday being Election Day, the banks will be closed.** Which one of the above three arrangements is incorrect? _____<div align="right">1339</div>
a. it was late, 1608	**In cooking class, we learned** a. **to prepare meat,** _____ b. **baking cakes, and** _____ c. **to make salads.** _____ <div align="right">1609</div>

a. misplaced modifier   b. faulty comparison
c. faulty pronoun reference

Be sure that they don't tease him, for he often develops temper tantrums.

————————————————————————————,

for he often develops temper tantrums.

1879

---

drank, drunk

2147

60 Lesson **Three Tricky Pairs of Verbs:**
Lie–Lay, Sit–Set, Rise–Raise

[Frames 2149–2191]

---

look   smell   taste   feel   hear (sound)

Much more commonly, these same verbs are used as *linking* verbs that express no action at all. They link an adjective in the predicate with the subject it describes.

The cake looked *delicious.*

The adjective *delicious* modifies the subject ——————.

a

2416

2417

---

singular

2685

Underline the proper pronoun for formal usage:

Any person **can train** (*him- or herself, themselves*) **to concentrate.**

2686

---

college—and

2954

The three women, Walker, Wheatley, and Giovanni, are all well-known poets.

Is it possible to interpret the subject of this sentence as meaning either *three* or *six* people? (*Yes, No*)

2955

---

people's, isn't

3223

Remember that possessive pronouns show possession without the use of apostrophes.

a. *Yours* **is the same color as** *theirs.*
b. **The** *Dunns* **car is the same color as the** *Clarks.*

Apostrophes are required only in sentence (*a, b*).

3224

When?

259

We mended the picture *with paste.*

Underline the question that the adverb phrase answers:

When?   Where?   How?

260

No

529

a. **A tree surgeon removed the** *dead* **branches.**
b. **A tree surgeon removed the branches** *that were dead.*

Both the adjective *dead* in sentence *a* and the adjective clause *that were dead* in sentence *b* modify the noun

_____.

530

---

firmly

799

Participles—with their related words—form useful phrases known as **participial phrases.** These phrases are used as adjectives to modify nouns and pronouns.

The dog, *shivering with cold,* **came into the house.**

The participial phrase modifies the noun _____.

800

---

after that
experience

1069

a. **I never trusted ladders after that experience.**
b. **After that experience, I never trusted ladders.**

Which sentence would it be better to use after you had

written a number of subject-first sentences? _____

1070

---

a

1339

If both word groups are sentences, add a period and a capital, or a semicolon. If one word group is a fragment, make no change except to add a comma if needed. Write only the word before and after the space between the word groups.

The lake was choppy   no small boats ventured out.

_____

1340

---

b. to bake
cakes, and

1609

All our neighbors are

a. **kind,**   _____

b. **friendly, and**   _____

c. **give help.**   _____

1610

a. nonparallel construction   b. *is when* or *is where* error
c. faulty comparison

A temper tantrum, as you know, is when a child holds his breath and turns blue from anger.

In a temper tantrum, as you know, _____

_____.

1880

To lie means "to rest in a flat position" or "to be in place."

To lay means "to put (down) or to place something."

Underline the correct word or words:

You ought (*to lie, to lay*) **down and rest for a while.**

2149

cake

2417

When used as linking verbs, "sense" verbs serve much the same purpose as the linking verb **be** (*is, am, are—was, were, been*).

The water *felt* (= *was*) **cold.**

The verb *felt* serves as a linking verb—like *was*—to show that the adjective **cold** modifies the subject _____.

2418

him- or herself

2686

Underline the proper pronoun for formal usage:

A person **should have the courage of** (*their, his or her*) **convictions.**

2687

Yes

2955

Use dashes to set off a series of appositives that might be confused with the nouns they explain.

The three women—Walker, Wheatley, and Giovanni—are all well-known poets.

The dashes make it clear that you are talking about (*three, six*) people.

2956

b

3224

Insert any necessary apostrophes:

Freds injuries were slight, but hers were more serious.

3225

An adverb phrase can also answer the question *Why?* about a verb.

    a. **I often read science fiction** *for a change.*
    b. **I often read science fiction** *for a few days.*

In which sentence does the adverb phrase explain *Why?* in regard to the verb? _____

261

---

    a. **A tree surgeon removed the** *dead* **branches.**
    b. **A tree surgeon removed the branches** *that were dead.*

The adjective *dead* in sentence *a* comes *before* the noun it modifies.

The adjective clause *that were dead* comes (*before, after*) the noun it modifies.

531

A participial phrase can often be shifted about.

    Shivering with cold, **the dog came into the house.**
    The dog, *shivering with cold,* **came into the house.**
    The dog came into the house, *shivering with cold.*

Can a participial phrase be some distance away from the noun it modifies? (*Yes, No*)

801

Underline the adverb clause that you could put ahead of the subject:

    Our sales increased as soon as we lowered our price.

1071

Continue to follow the directions for the previous frame:

    The lake was choppy   no small boats venturing out.

    _____

1341

Iris spent the afternoon

a. **lying on the sofa,** _____

b. **reading a novel, and** _____

c. **she ate chocolates.** _____

1611

a child holds his
breath and turns
blue from anger.

1880

---

a. dangling word group b. nonparallel construction
c. faulty pronoun reference

Please remind him to write us every day and that he should brush his teeth after every meal.

Please remind him to write us every day and _____

_____.

1881

---

to lie

2149

Of the two verbs **lie** and **lay, lie** causes most of the trouble.

PRESENT	PAST	PAST PARTICIPLE
lie (to rest)	**lay**	**(have) lain**

Notice especially that the past form of **lie** is _____.

2150

---

water

2418

Whenever a "sense" verb is used as a linking verb, you can generally put a form of **be** in its place.

a. **The sky** *looks* **cloudy.**
b. **The sailor** *looks* **at the sky.**

In which sentence is *looks* used as a linking verb because you can put *is* in its place? _____

2419

---

his or her

2687

---

anyone	anybody	each
someone	**somebody**	**each one**
no one	**nobody**	**either**

In formal writing or speaking, refer to these words by using (*singular, plural*) pronouns.

2688

---

three

2956

Supply the missing punctuation:

Several pieces of equipment   a file, a typewriter, and a duplicator   were contributed by the Men's Club.

2957

Fred's

3225

Insert three necessary apostrophes. (This is a high-error frame. Be sure to put each apostrophe after the noun or the part of the noun that names the owner or owners.)

This girls job is to check the mens and ladies wraps.

3226

An adverb phrase—just like an adverb—can often be moved from one position to another in the sentence.

My friend takes a nap *after dinner.*
After dinner **my friend takes a nap.**

The fact that a prepositional phrase can be moved shows

that it is an _____ *phrase.*

262

It is easy to see why an adjective clause must come *after* the word it modifies.

A tree surgeon removed the branches *that were dead.*

If we put the adjective clause before the noun *branches,* which it modifies, the sentence would be very (*smooth, clumsy*).

532

The train roared past, *leaving a trail of smoke.*

The participial phrase is separated by several words from the word it modifies, the noun _____.

802

---

a. **The fish jumped the hook** *as I pulled in my line.*
b. *As I pulled in my line,* **the fish jumped the hook.**

Which sentence arouses more suspense by keeping you

guessing until the end? _____

1072

Our job was to watch for forest fires   and report any sign of smoke.

(Do you recall that no comma is used before the conjunction when it connects the two parts of a compound predicate?)

_____

1342

We traded in our car because

a. **the engine burned oil,** _____

b. **the smooth tires, and** _____

c. **the body was rusty.** _____

1612

We would appreciate your keeping a watchful eye on the companions whom he associates.

We would appreciate your keeping a watchful eye on _____

_____.

b (to) brush his teeth after every meal. 1881	1882

	PRESENT	PAST	PAST PARTICIPLE
	lie (to rest)	**lay**	**(have) lain**

Use these rhymes to remember the forms of this verb:

"Yes-ter-day	**"In pain**
In bed he lay."	**He has lain."**

lay	The past participle of **lie** is _____.
2150	2151

---

	look smell taste feel sound
a	When these verbs show no action but are used as linking verbs, they are followed by adjectives that describe the subject. Underline the correct word: **Our garden looks** (*beautiful, beautifully*) **in the spring.**
2419	2420

---

singular 2688	In this and the following frames, underline the pronoun (and sometimes the verb, too) that is appropriate for formal writing or speaking. Watch out for one sentence in which the sense makes the use of a plural pronoun necessary to refer to *everyone* or *everybody*. **A person cannot select** (*their, his or her*) **ancestors.** 2689

---

equipment— duplicator— 2957	Use a dash to indicate hesitation in speech or a broken-off sentence. a. **"She—she broke my wagon," sobbed little Linda.** b. **"If he ever asks to borrow my car again—"** In which sentence does the dash indicate hesitation in speech? _____ 2958

---

girl's, men's, ladies' 3226	Copy the correct words: (*They're, Their*) **testing** (*it's, its*) **engines before taking off.** 3227

a. **They have improved the design** *of the car.*
b. **A crowd was standing** *around the car.*

adverb

In one sentence the phrase can be moved; in the other it can't.

Which sentence contains an adverb phrase? _____

263

---

clumsy

In a previous lesson, you saw that an *adverb clause* can often be shifted from one position to another.

I watched television *after I studied.*

Can the adverb clause *after I studied* be moved to another position? (*Yes, No*)

532

533

---

train

We have now become acquainted with three kinds of word groups that are used like adjectives to modify nouns.

ADJECTIVE PHRASE: **a girl** *with a dog*
ADJECTIVE CLAUSE: **a girl** *who was walking her dog*
PARTICIPIAL PHRASE: **a girl** *walking her dog*

All three word groups modify the noun _____.

802

803

---

b

Putting an adverbial modifier, now and then, ahead of the subject adds variety to your writing. It also creates a greater feeling of (*suspense, confusion*).

1072

1073

---

fires and

The circus is a national institution   a part of our national tradition.

_____

1342

1343

---

b. the tires
were smooth, and

Fish jump out of the water

a. **to shake off parasites,**   _____

b. **to catch flies, and**   _____

c. **escaping enemies.**   _____

1612

1613

c
the companions
with whom he
associates. *or*
... whom he
associates with.

1882

---

a. dangling word group   b. nonparallel construction
c. faulty comparison

We trust that you will find her one of the best, if not the best, camper at Michiwaki.

We trust that you will find him one of the best _____

_____

1883

(have) lain

2151

Complete these memory rhymes:

"Yes-ter-day   "In pain

In bed he _____."   He has _____."

2152

---

beautiful

2420

A field of sweet clover *smells* **very pleasant.**

In this sentence, the "sense" verb *smells* is used as (*an action, a linking*) verb.

2421

---

his or her

2689

I believe that everyone should set a reasonable goal for (*themselves, him- or herself*).

2690

---

a

2958

Use a dash to indicate a sudden turn in the thought before an idea is completed.

"We stopped at—what was the name of that town?"

Supply the missing punctuation:

"That car   well, I just can't describe it."

2959

They're, its

3227

Copy the correct words:

(*Your, You're*) **the only one** (*who's, whose*) **not going.**

3228

b 263	An adverb phrase can usually be shifted about. Therefore it can be several words away from the verb it modifies. a. *On the first automobiles,* **solid rubber tires were used.** b. **Solid rubber tires were used** *on the first automobiles.* The adverb phrase is farthest from the verb it modifies in sentence _____. 264
Yes 533	**The teacher scolded the little girl** *who wandered away from the group.* Can the adjective clause *who wandered away from the group* be moved to another position? (*Yes, No*) 534
girl 803	To change a sentence to a participial phrase is simple. (*We*) *heard a loud crash.* **We rushed to the window.** ↓ *Hearing a loud crash,* **we rushed to the window.** To change the italicized sentence to a participial phrase, drop the subject *We* and change the verb *heard* to the present participle _____. 804
suspense 1073	Another reason for departing from the usual subject-first word order is to give emphasis to a particular idea. On entering your room, you would be more likely to notice a piece of furniture if it (*were, were not*) in its usual position. 1074
institution, a 1343	**You can't change your face you can change your expression.** _____ 1344
c. to escape enemies. 1613	**Rosemary does her work** a. **with willingness,** _____ b. **quickly, and** _____ c. **accurately.** _____ 1614

c
campers at
Michiwaki, if not
the best.

1883

Lesson 53 Keeping Your Mind on the Subject

[Frames 1885–1927]

---

lay, lain

2152

PRESENT: *Lie* **down. Don't** *lie* **in the sun. The rug** *lies* **on the floor. Your letter is** *lying* **on the desk.**

Fill in the correct words:

I asked Mother to _____ **down, but she was already**

_____ **down.**.

2153

---

a linking

2421

A field of sweet clover *smells* **very pleasant.**

Because *smells* is used as a linking verb, it is followed by the (*adjective, adverb*) **pleasant.**

2422

---

him- or herself

2690

No one must be made to feel that (*he or she is, they are*) **forced to contribute.**

2691

---

car—well

2959

Use dashes to set off a sharp interruption in the thought of a sentence.

Once—and once was enough—I investigated a hornet's nest.

Insert the sentence **that's our dog** on the blank line, and punctuate it:

Patty _____ **first noticed the flames.**

2960

You're, who's

3228

In each of the remaining frames, you will find four phrases, in one of which the capitalization is incorrect. Copy this *one* phrase only, making the necessary corrections.

a. **her new spring outfit**   c. **read "the thing in the pond"**
b. **in a Buick car**   d. **at the Overton High School**

3229

A pot *of stew* **was simmering** *on the stove.*

This sentence contains both an adjective phrase and an adverb phrase.

The adverb phrase is the (*first, second*) phrase.

a

264

265

No

An adjective clause must always follow the noun or pronoun it modifies.

Can an adjective clause ever come at the very beginning of a sentence? (*Yes, No*)

534

535

---

hearing

I picked up the hot pan. (*I*) *thought it was cold.*

↓

I picked up the hot pan,   *thinking it was cold.*

To change the italicized sentence to a participial phrase, drop the subject *I* and change the verb *thought* to the present participle _____.

804

805

---

were not

In the very same way, a word that has been moved from its usual position attracts more attention.

The normal word order of an English sentence is—

Subject—Verb—Complement

If we put the complement first, it would attract (*more, less*) attention.

1074

1075

---

face. You
or
face; you

Suspected of being a spy   the man was shadowed day and night.

_____

1344

1345

---

a. willingly,

Curt Flood has spent time

a. **playing ball,**   _____

b. **a business was run, and** _____

c. **broadcasting.**   _____

1614

1615

A singular subject requires a singular verb; a plural subject requires a plural verb. This is what we mean when we say that the subject and verb must agree in number.

We Washes Cars

This sign, seen on a garage, looks absurd because the subject **We** is plural, but the verb **Washes** is _____.

1885

---

lie, lying

2153

PAST: **Yesterday I** *lay* **in bed until noon. Dad** *lay* **back in his chair and took a nap. The food** *lay* **on the table all day.**

Lay is the past form of the verb _____.

2154

---

adjective

2422

Underline the correct word:

The old house smells (*musty, mustily*).

2423

---

he or she is

2691

Each girl is encouraged to join a club of (*their, her*) **own choice.**

2692

—that's our dog—

2960

Use either a dash or a semicolon before the words **for example** when they follow a complete statement.

Many words imitate sounds—for example, *crash, bang, splash.*

Would a semicolon serve equally as well as a dash in this sentence? (*Yes, No*)

2961

---

c. read "The Thing in the Pond"

3229

a. **a great author**   c. **my father's uncle**
b. **a shot for the Flu**   d. **at Niagara Falls**

_____

3230

second 265	**We saw** *through the telescope* **the outline** *of a ship.* The adverb phrase is the (*first, second*) phrase. 266
No 535	a. **The chair collapsed** *when I sat down.* b. **I sat on a chair** *which was broken.* In which sentence can the clause *not* be moved to another position? _____ 536
thinking 805	(*Bob*) *needed a haircut.* **He looked for a barber shop.** ↓ *Needing a haircut,* **he looked for a barber shop.** In changing the italicized sentence to a participial phrase, we lost the subject _____. 806
more 1075	**Terry would not accept this money.** The noun **money** is the (*subject complement, direct object*) of the verb **would accept.** 1076
spy, the 1345	**Telephone operators wear headsets leaving their hands free** **to operate the switchboard.** _____ 1346
b. running a business, and 1615	**The Owens want a house** a. **with a fireplace,** _____ b. **having a garage, and** _____ c. **with a screened porch.** _____ 1616

singular 1885	If all agreement errors sounded as bad as **"We Washes Cars,"** we would have no problem. However, we cannot always trust our ears in selecting a verb to match the subject. Without stopping to think, underline the verb which sounds right to your ear. (Don't score your answer right or wrong.) **One of you** (*is, are*) **always teasing the other.** 1886
lie 2154	PAST PARTICIPLE: **She** *has lain* **in bed most of the day. The dog must** *have lain* **down in the mud. This rug** *has lain* **there for years.** The past participle of **lie** that should be used after any form of **have** or **be** is _____. 2155
musty 2423	**The old house smells** *musty*. The adjective *musty* is correct because it modifies the noun _____. 2424
her 2692	**We should elect someone who can give all** (*his or her, their*) **time to the organization.** 2693
Yes 2961	a. **Our dog has several bad habits for example, chasing cars.** b. **Our dog has several bad habits for example, chasing cars.** In each sentence, insert a different punctuation mark before **for example.** 2962
b. a shot for the flu 3230	a. **for Mother's Day** c. **south of the park** b. **a college football star** d. **a school in the south** _____ 3231

first	When we have two (or more) prepositional phrases in a row, each phrase can modify a different word.
	We put a drop of water under the microscope.
	The phrase **of water** modifies the noun **drop.**
	Which word does the adverb phrase **under the microscope**
266	modify? _____ 267

b	a. **The chair collapsed** *when I sat down.*
	b. **I sat on a chair** *which was broken.*
	Which sentence contains an adjective clause? _____
536	537

Bob	*(Bob) needed a haircut.* **He looked for a barber shop.**
	Bob
	Needing a haircut, ~~he~~ **looked for a barber shop.**
	To let the reader know the name of the person you're writing about, you must substitute **Bob** for the pronoun _____
806	in the main statement. 807

direct object	a. **Terry would not accept this money.**
	b. **This money Terry would not accept.**
	Which sentence gives greater emphasis to the direct object
	money? _____
1076	1077

headsets, leaving	**The textile mill closing hundreds of employees were thrown out of work.**
	_____
1346	1347

b. with a garage, and	**We shall need a board**
	a. **six feet in length,** _____
	b. **two feet wide, and** _____
	c. **one inch thick.** _____
1616	1617

If *are* (wrong) sounded right, you will see why you can't always trust your ear.	a. **One is stuck.**
	b. **One (of the wheels) is stuck.**
	Sentence *a* doesn't indicate whether **One** means a key, a window, a seat, or a wheel. We therefore add the prepositional phrase **of the wheels** to make our meaning clear.
1886	The subject in both *a* and *b* is the pronoun _____.
	1887

lain	Fill in the missing forms of **lie**:

PRESENT	PAST	PAST PARTICIPLE
lie (to rest)	_____	**(have)** _____

2155   2156

house	When a sentence states that something has a certain *look, taste, smell, feel,* or *sound,* the "sense" verb is then used as (*an action, a linking*) verb.
2424	2425

his or her	**Any girls interested in this job should see Miss Cruz as soon as** (*they, she*) **can.**
2693	2694

a. ; *or* —	The frames that complete this lesson provide good opportunities for using semicolons, colons, and dashes effectively. In several sentences, either one of two marks would be considered correct. Do not add any commas.
b. — *or* ;	**Before retirement, María worked steadily after retirement, she traveled around the world.**
2962	2963

d. a school in the South	a. **the Hale drug company** c. **a French horn**
	b. **next Tuesday night** d. **his idea of God**
3231	3232

put

267

Two (or more) prepositional phrases can also modify the same word.

Dad flew to Houston on Friday.

The phrase **to Houston** modifies the verb **flew**.

Which word does the phrase **on Friday** modify? _____

268

---

b

537

a. **The bank discharged the employee** *who gambled.*
b. **The bank discharged the employee** *because he gambled.*

In one sentence the clause can be shifted; in the other, it can't.

Which sentence contains the adjective clause? _____

538

---

he

807

If you lose a noun when making a participial phrase, put this noun back at the *beginning* of your main statement.

Aunt Mae lives alone. **She is often lonesome for company.**

Fill in the blank space:

Living alone, _____ **is often lonesome for company.**

808

---

b

1077

Jackie Robinson certainly was a hero.

The noun **hero** follows the linking verb **was** and is therefore a (*subject complement, direct object*).

1078

---

closing, hundreds

1347

The water level was dropping   all danger of a flood was past.

_____

1348

---

a. six feet long,

1617

A real friend is

a. **considerate,**   _____

b. **helpful, and**   _____

c. **sympathizes with you.** _____

1618

One

1887

One of the wheels **is** stuck.

The noun **wheels** is not the subject of the above sentence.

It is the object of the preposition _____.

1888

---

lay, (have) lain

2156

To lay means "to put down or to place something."

You *lay* a book on the table, money on the counter, a package on the floor.

PRESENT	PAST	PAST PARTICIPLE
lay (to put)	**laid**	**(have) laid**

The past and past participle forms are (*alike, different*). 2157

---

a linking

2425

The use of **badly,** instead of **bad,** after the linking verb **feel** is widespread in informal usage, even though it violates our general rule.

I feel (*bad, badly*) **about it.**

Since **feel** is used as a linking verb in this sentence, the adjective (*bad, badly*) is correct in formal writing or speaking.

2426

---

they

2694

Every applicant is asked whether (*they have, he or she has*) **had any experience.**

2695

---

steadily;

2963

Their lemon chiffon pie   well, I just can't find words to describe it.

2964

---

a. the Hale Drug Company

3232

flew 268	A prepositional phrase can modify the object of the preceding prepositional phrase. **The family lived on the edge of a great forest.** The phrase **on the edge** modifies the verb **lived**. Which word does the phrase **of a great forest** modify? _____ 269
a 538	There are only a small number of *clause signals* that generally start adjective clauses: **who (whose, whom), which, that** These adjective clause signals are (*the same as, different from*) those that start adverb clauses. 539
Aunt Mae 808	Which of two sentences you subordinate depends on which idea you prefer to put in the background of the sentence. a. *Reaching for the sugar,* **I knocked over a glass.** b. **I reached for the sugar,** *knocking over a glass.* Which of the two sentences emphasizes the accident that occurred? _____ 809
subject complement 1078	a. **A hero Jackie Robinson certainly was.** b. **Jackie Robinson certainly was a hero.** Which sentence gives greater emphasis to the subject complement **hero**? _____ 1079
dropping. All *or* dropping; all 1348	**Ellen gets angry over trifles but forgives and forgets quickly.** _____ 1349
c. sympathetic. 1618	Lesson **45** Putting Sentences into Parallel Construction [Frames 1620–1647]

of	**One of these steaks . . . enough for a meal.**
	The verb has been omitted from this sentence.
	The verb we choose should agree in number with the word (*One, steaks*).
1888	CONTINUED ON PAGE 2 1889

	PRESENT	PAST	PAST PARTICIPLE
	lay (to put)	laid	(have) laid

Use the verb **lay** only when the sentence tells *what* was **laid** (put) somewhere.

alike

George *had laid* **his cards on the table.**

What *was laid* on the table? _____

2157 CONTINUED ON PAGE 2 2158

---

bad

We feel *unhappy* **about losing the game.**
We feel *bad* **about losing the game.**

In both sentences the verb **feel** is followed by an adjective.

Are both sentences correct? (*Yes, No*)

2426 CONTINUED ON PAGE 2 2427

---

he or she has

Everybody was happy, and I didn't want to spoil (*their, his or her*) **fun.**

2695 CONTINUED ON PAGE 2 2696

---

pie—

Campers are expected to supply the following items   sheets, blankets, pillowcases, and towels.

2964 CONTINUED ON PAGE 2 2965

edge

269

Remember—

A prepositional phrase that modifies a noun or a pronoun is called an *adjective phrase.*

A prepositional phrase that modifies a verb is called an

_____ *phrase.*

CONTINUED ON PAGE 1 270

---

different from

539

a. **while, when, as if, because, unless, although,** etc.
b. **who (whose, whom), which, that**

In which group are the clause signals that are used to start

adjective clauses? _____

CONTINUED ON PAGE 1 540

---

a

809

a. *Reaching for the sugar,* **I knocked over a glass.**
b. **I reached for the sugar,** *knocking over a glass.*

Which sentence emphasizes the action that led to the accident? _____

CONTINUED ON PAGE 1 810

---

a

1079

His *strong, calloused* **hands were no strangers to work.**

The most common position of adjectives is (*before, after*) the nouns they modify.

CONTINUED ON PAGE 1 1080

---

trifles but

1349

Cheap paper is made from wood pulp   high-grade paper is made from rags.

_____

CONTINUED ON PAGE 1 1350

Parallel construction is a way of streamlining your writing— of giving your sentences smooth, clean lines. It is based on a very simple idea: Say similar things in a (*different, similar*) way.

CONTINUED ON PAGE 2 1620

WRITING APPLICATIONS

Contents

The Writing Process

The first part of this textbook presented a step-by-step program, or process, that enabled you to review grammar, sentence-building, usage, and punctuation. You were first given a bit of information in a frame; then you tried to apply it. If you did not get the correct answer the first time, you were given another opportunity to get the correct answer in another frame. You completed entire sections of this book using this process. When you write, you can also use a process that will give you additional opportunities to improve your writing. This process is called the **writing process.**[1] In this section of your textbook, you will be introduced to the six basic stages of the writing process. Once you have mastered these stages, you should be able to apply them in any writing task.

WHY STUDY THE WRITING PROCESS?

You will be able to communicate more easily, meaningfully, and effectively by using the writing process. Since an important part of the writing process is evaluating and revising, you always have several opportunities to analyze and improve your writing before you prepare the final version.

Following this introduction (pages 543–548), you will find writing applications that correspond to each of the units in the first part of this book. The applications are designed to give you practice in applying the principles of grammar, sentence-building, usage, and punctuation that you reviewed and practiced in the first part of this textbook. They will also enable you to practice the writing process and to improve your writing skills. In addition, you may find that they help you organize your thoughts and give you practice in analyzing information.

HOW TO USE THIS SECTION OF THE BOOK

After you read this section, refer to it to help you complete the writing applications. Use the basic models presented here whenever you need help composing. In this section, you will learn about and practice the six stages of the writing process. These six stages are (1) prewriting, (2) writing the first draft, (3) evaluating, (4) revising, (5) proofreading, and (6) writing the final version.

Prewriting

The prewriting stage enables you to formulate ideas before you write. During this thinking and planning stage, you will answer five important questions: Why am I writing? For whom am I writing? What will I write about? What will I say? How will I say it? More specifically, you will determine your purpose; identify your audience; choose and limit your topic; establish your tone; and gather, classify, and arrange information.

[1] Adapted from pp. 3–34 in *English Composition and Grammar,* Benchmark Edition, Complete Course, by John E. Warriner. Copyright © 1988 by Harcourt Brace Jovanovich, Inc. Reprinted by permission of Harcourt Brace Jovanovich, Inc.

SELECTING A PURPOSE

Before you begin writing, you should have in mind a clear purpose. Your purpose will guide your writing and help determine the content and language you use. There are four basic purposes for writing: to tell a story or relate a series of events; to inform or explain; to describe a person, place, or thing; or to persuade or convince. Writing to tell a story is called **narrative** writing. Writing to inform or explain is called **expository** writing. Writing to describe a person, place, or thing is called **descriptive** writing. Finally, writing that attempts to persuade or convince is called **persuasive** writing.

DETERMINING YOUR AUDIENCE

You will always write for an audience, but audiences may vary widely in age, background, and opinion. Like purpose, your audience will help guide your writing since you do not write the same way for all people. Determine carefully who your reading audience will be. Then decide whether they will need background information and whether your subject will interest them. Also, decide how simple or difficult the language you use should be.

CHOOSING AND LIMITING A SUBJECT

Before you write, choose a subject that is interesting to you and your audience and is neither too complex nor too simple. Then limit your subject so that you can write about it adequately in the time and space you have. To limit your subject, consider your purpose and the form of writing you have chosen. A broad, general subject that has been limited is called a **topic.**

ESTABLISHING TONE

Determine your attitude, or point of view, toward your topic to help you establish your tone. Tone is the expression of your attitude; for example, happiness, anger, or seriousness. You express your tone through the details and language you use in your writing.

GATHERING INFORMATION

Gather information to include in your writing that is appropriate to your purpose. For example, if your purpose is to describe someone famous, you may want to gather facts about that person's life, appearance, and mannerisms. You can use several methods in gathering information. A few that are described here include brainstorming, clustering, asking the 5 W-How? questions, and asking point-of-view questions.

Brainstorming. In brainstorming, you generate information by writing down ideas that come freely to mind. First, write your topic at the top of a sheet of paper. Then, think about your topic, listing any ideas that you associate with your topic. Do not worry if some of the ideas seem silly or incomplete. You will be able to eliminate or expand these ideas later.

EXAMPLE   *Topic:* December vacation in San Francisco Bay area

Ideas: Took weekend vacation with Mom and Dad during winter break
Arrived in San Francisco to 60° weather—green grass, lush
vines, and palms
Visited several popular tourist sites: Ghirardelli Square,
Fisherman's Wharf, and Stanford University
Saw Alcatraz from Fisherman's Wharf
Ate delicious seafood while there
Disappointed that did not see Chinatown, Nob Hill, and Golden
Gate Park
Will fly out there again next winter break

Clustering.   Clustering is like brainstorming in that you write down ideas as
they come freely to mind. In clustering, however, you arrange the ideas in
groups, or clusters. To begin clustering ideas, write your topic in the center of
your paper and circle it. Then begin thinking about ideas that relate to the topic.
Write down and circle these ideas also. Draw lines to connect ideas to the topic.

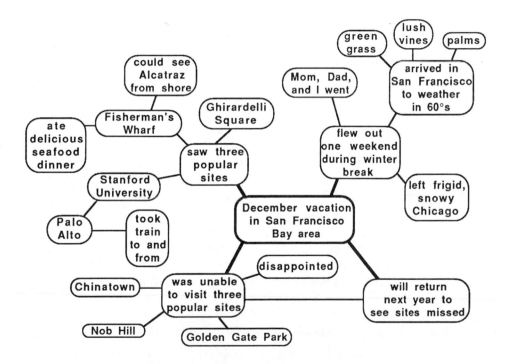

Asking the 5 W-How? Questions.   Another technique for gathering information is asking the *5 W-How?* questions. The *5 W-How?* questions are *Who?*
What? When? Where? Why? and *How?* Ask yourself these questions to find out
specific details about your topic. You may not be able to use every question with
every topic, but you will always be able to use at least several of the questions.

EXAMPLE   *Topic:* December vacation in San Francisco Bay area
             Who went? (Mom, Dad, and I)
             What did we do? (flew out to San Francisco Bay area)
             When in December did we take this vacation? (one week during winter
                break)
             Where did we go in the San Francisco area? (Ghirardelli Square,
                Fisherman's Wharf, and Stanford University)
             Why did we fly to San Francisco? (to rest, to enjoy a change of
                weather and scenery, and to visit a city we had never seen before)
             How did we travel to California? (flew in from Chicago)

Asking Point-of-View Questions.   Still another technique that can be used
to gather information is to look at a topic from three different points of view. To
determine the point of view, ask these three questions: (1) What is it? (2) How
does it change or vary? (3) What are its relationships?

EXAMPLE   *Topic:* December vacation in San Francisco Bay area

    1. What is a December vacation in San Francisco? (a winter break
       from school and work; a change of scenery and weather)

    2. How did our trip start? (We flew in from frigid, snowy Chicago;
       we arrived to find 60° weather and greenery everywhere.)

       How did our trip progress? (visited Ghirardelli Square, Fisherman's
       Wharf, and Stanford University)

       How did our trip end? (ate delicious seafood at Fisherman's Wharf
       before leaving for airport to fly home)

    3. What sites or events did we enjoy most? (All were exciting, but the
       biggest thrill was the change in landscape.)

       What experiences were unpleasant? (none, other than not having
       time to visit Chinatown, Nob Hill, and Golden Gate Park)

CLASSIFYING INFORMATION

   The next step in the writing process is to classify, or sort, your ideas and
information into related groups. Classifying helps you organize your information
for writing. One of the simplest ways to classify information is to look for
similarities and differences. Another way is to determine which ideas are more
important than others. The more important ideas may become the main ideas of
your paragraphs. The less important ideas are likely to become supporting
details.

EXAMPLE   *Topic:* December vacation in San Francisco Bay area

Time	Weather	Pleasant Memories	Unpleasant Memories
December during winter break	60° in San Francisco frigid, snowy in Chicago	Visiting Ghirardelli Square, Fisherman's Wharf, and Stanford University Greenery everywhere	Not having time to visit Chinatown, Nob Hill, and Golden Gate Park

ARRANGING INFORMATION

The last step in the prewriting process is to arrange the ideas you have classified into some logical order or sequence. Often your purpose will determine your order. For example, if you are writing a narrative paragraph, you will write your paragraph in chronological order. Sometimes, however, your purpose will not dictate an exact order. In these cases, you should present your information in any way that will be most interesting and clear to your audience.

EXAMPLE   *Topic:* December vacation in San Francisco Bay area
            Purpose: Narrative, to tell a story
            Order: Chronological
            1. Mom, Dad, and I flew out of frigid Chicago during my winter break.
            2. We arrived in San Francisco to 60° weather and greenery.
            3. We visited Ghirardelli Square, Fisherman's Wharf, and Stanford University.
            4. Before flying home, we ate a delicious seafood dinner at Fisherman's Wharf.
            5. We flew home, disappointed not to have seen Chinatown, Nob Hill, and Golden Gate Park.
            6. We plan to return next year.

Writing a First Draft

The next stage of the writing process is to write a first draft based on the information you prepared in the prewriting stage. In this stage, you put your ideas into sentences and paragraphs. Remember that this draft will not be your final one. Therefore, you should evaluate and revise your writing as many times as you need. Keep your prewriting notes in front of you as you write, and write freely.

Evaluating

Evaluating is the third stage of the writing process. In this stage, you review your first draft for content, organization, and style. You determine your weaknesses and decide what works and what does not. Use the following checklist to help you evaluate your writing.

1. Do the ideas help to achieve a main purpose: to explain, to describe, to persuade, or to tell a story?
2. Are the topic and details suitable and interesting for the audience?
3. Are enough details provided so that the topic can be easily understood? Is any information unnecessary?
4. Does the order of the information make the main ideas clear?
5. Are sentences smoothly joined by connecting words?
6. Is the choice of words appropriate for the audience? Does the writing sound serious without sounding angry? Is the tone used light enough, or is it too light?
7. Are the words used specific and precise rather than vague?

Revising

Once you have evaluated your writing and have determined its weaknesses, you are ready to revise it. Revising your writing means making changes to it to improve it. Four basic techniques are used when revising: adding, cutting, replacing, and reordering. Note how this paragraph has been revised using these techniques.

EXAMPLE   One of my most exciting vacations was a ~~short~~ *weekend* trip to the San

Francisco Bay area during winter break this year. Mom, Dad, and I

flew out ~~to California from a Chicago that was~~ *of snow-covered Chicago* frigid, overcast, and

~~snowy,~~ to arrive several hours later in beautiful *green* San Francisco. ~~We were~~

~~fortunate to see several interesting sites.~~ The temperature was in the

60°s ~~the entire time we were there.~~ *every day* While we were ~~there,~~ *in California,* we visited

Ghirardelli Square and Fisherman's Wharf. In addition, we took the

train to Palo Alto and toured Stanford University. ~~Unfortunately, we did~~ *Although we enjoyed*

the weather and the sightseeing, we were disappointed ~~not~~ to have seen

~~not have the chance to see~~ Chinatown, ~~the cable cars,~~ Nob Hill, ~~or~~

and Golden Gate Park. *However,* ~~We~~ plan to return next winter. *to see these popular sights*

Proofreading

In the proofreading stage of the writing process, you reread your revised draft one last time to find and correct errors. Proofreading means finding and correcting mistakes in grammar, usage, and mechanics (spelling, capitalization, and punctuation). Special standardized marks called revising and proofreading symbols are used in making the corrections. You will find a complete list of these marks on the inside back cover of this textbook.

Writing the Final Version

Writing the final version is the last step of the writing process. This step includes preparing a clean copy of your revised and proofread paper. Although your teacher will provide you with specific directions, you can use these general guidelines when completing any of the writing applications.

1. Write on lined 8½ × 11-inch composition paper. If you are typing your composition, use 8½ × 11-inch white paper.
2. Write or type on only one side of each sheet of paper.
3. Write in blue or black ink, or type your composition using double-spacing.
4. Leave top, bottom, and side margins of one inch.
5. Indent the first line of each paragraph about one-half inch.

UNIT 1 Patterns of the Simple Sentence

WRITING APPLICATION A: Using Vivid Action Verbs

Have you ever had to reread a paragraph because it was so dull you could not remember what it said? Perhaps the writing seemed dull because the writer did not use vivid, precise verbs to describe actions. In your own writing, always try to use lively, precise action verbs to help your reader form a clear picture of what you are describing. Note how the second sentence in each of the examples below creates a clearer picture simply by using a more vivid action verb.

EXAMPLES   1. The reporters *came* into the crowded auditorium.
             The reporters *rushed* into the crowded auditorium.

           2. The two candidates *talked* for more than an hour.
             The two candidates *argued* for more than an hour.

Writing Assignment: On a separate sheet of paper, write about a current event that is particularly interesting to you.

Evaluation Checklist: After you write your first draft, use these guidelines to help you evaluate your paragraph.

____ My information is accurate.
____ I have used vivid action verbs in my writing.
____ My writing contains each of the points found on the checklist on page 547.

Revising, Proofreading, and Writing the Final Version: Revise your first draft carefully. If you have used vivid action verbs, your reader will be able to picture clearly the action you are describing. Proofread your revised draft. Then write your final version.

WRITING APPLICATION B: Varying Sentence Patterns and Lengths

How would you like to attend a variety show only to see the same act performed over and over again? You would probably lose interest quickly and leave. In a similar way, if you use the same sentence patterns and lengths over and over again in your writing, your reader may lose interest in your message and stop reading. Use a variety of sentence patterns and lengths to maintain interest.

NO VARIETY   The magician wore a tuxedo and a top hat. He introduced his five pet rabbits. He pulled them out of his hat. He then made the rabbits disappear. He did this merely by snapping his fingers. His act was, all in all, well received by the audience.

VARIETY   The magician wore a tuxedo and top hat, and he introduced his five pet rabbits by pulling them out of his hat. Then he made the rabbits disappear merely by snapping his fingers. All in all, his act was well received by the audience.

Writing Assignment: On a separate sheet of paper, write about a special function that you have attended. Describe some of the things you did or people you saw there. Include a topic sentence and supporting sentences in each paragraph you write.

Evaluation Checklist: After you write your first draft, use these guidelines to help you evaluate your paragraph.

____ I have used a variety of sentence patterns and lengths in my writing.

____ I have included a topic sentence and supporting sentences in each paragraph I have written.

____ My writing contains each of the points found on the checklist on page 547.

Revising, Proofreading, and Writing the Final Version: Revise your first draft carefully. Proofread your revised draft. Then write your final version.

WRITING APPLICATION C: Using Descriptive Adjectives

To prepare a meal that is both flavorful and appealing to the eye, you need to use foods that are fresh and colorful. In a similar way, to make your writing appeal to your reader, you need to use adjectives that are fresh, colorful, and descriptive. Adjectives give life and feeling to your sentences; however, using too many of them may overpower your writing. Choose your adjectives carefully as you write. You need not use them before every noun.

EXAMPLES
1. The *fluffy little* puppy with the *big, bright* eyes nipped at Judy's stockings.
2. Elise was welcomed by *thunderous* applause as she approached the stage.
3. The *soft, powdery* snow created a *winter* wonderland for the children that year.
4. The *shiny red* convertible cruised slowly down the *deserted* avenue.
5. The *cool autumn* wind rustles and twirls *multicolored* leaves.

Writing Assignment: On a separate sheet of paper, write about your favorite season. Describe some of the things you do during that time that help make the season particularly special for you. Remember that you can use adjectives that add color and feeling to your writing.

Evaluation Checklist: After you write your first draft, use these guidelines to help you evaluate your paragraph.

____ I have used adjectives that add color and feeling to my writing.

____ I have not used too many adjectives in my writing.

____ My writing contains each of the points found on the checklist on page 547.

Revising, Proofreading, and Writing the Final Version: Revise your first draft carefully. Check that your adjectives add sufficient color and feeling to your writing. Proofread your revised draft. Then write your final version.

UNIT 2 The Process of Compounding

WRITING APPLICATION A: Writing Compound Sentences

Just as paper clips hold together sheets of paper, conjunctions hold together sentences and parts of sentences. Sentences that are joined by a conjunction are called compound sentences. In compound sentences, a comma is used before the conjunction.

EXAMPLES
1. Ray Bradbury has written many science-fiction novels, *but* he has also written plays and screenplays.
2. The meeting had to take place in that room, *or* it could not take place at all.
3. I won the first-place award, *and* my brother Mark received an honorable mention.

Writing Assignment: On a separate sheet of paper, write a narrative about a special experience in your life. Try to use compound sentences to help you express your ideas.

Evaluation Checklist: After you write your first draft, use these guidelines to help you evaluate your paragraph.

____ I have used compound sentences in my writing.
____ I have inserted a comma before the conjunction in compound sentences.
____ My writing follows a logical order.
____ My writing contains each of the points found on the checklist on page 547.

Revising, Proofreading, and Writing the Final Version: Revise your first draft carefully. Proofread your revised draft. Then write your final version.

WRITING APPLICATION B: Writing Compound Predicates

College students who live in dormitories can usually save money by sharing a room. In writing, you can save words and writing space by using compound predicates in your sentences. Compound predicates share the same subject and are connected by a conjunction. Since two or more predicates refer to the same subject, a comma is not used before the conjunction.

TWO SENTENCES	I hope to visit Paris someday. I want to see the Eiffel Tower.
ONE SENTENCE WITH COMPOUND PREDICATE	I hope to visit Paris someday and see the Eiffel Tower.

Writing Assignment: On a separate sheet of paper, write about a place you hope to visit someday. Describe interesting landmarks you would like to see there. Use compound predicates to help you combine ideas.

Evaluation Checklist: After you write your first draft, use these guidelines to help you evaluate your writing.

____ I have used compound predicates in my sentences to help me combine ideas.

____ I have not used a comma before the conjunction in sentences having compound predicates.

____ I have included a topic sentence and supporting sentences in each of my paragraphs.

____ My writing contains each of the points found on the checklist on page 547.

Revising, Proofreading, and Writing the Final Version: Revise your first draft carefully. Make sure your compound predicates share the same subject. Proofread your revised draft. Then write your final version.

WRITING APPLICATION C: Connecting Sentences with Semicolons

In high school sports, an alternate is a player who substitutes for a regular team member who cannot play. Similarly, in writing, a semicolon used between sentences may be thought of as an alternate for a period. Although a period is normally used between sentences, a semicolon may be used when the sentences are close in thought. When using a semicolon between sentences, lowercase the first letter of the word following the semicolon, unless that word is a proper noun.

TWO SENTENCES	Louisa saved for six years to go to Italy to study Italian. She deserves to study there.
ONE SENTENCE WITH SEMICOLON	Louisa saved for six years to go to Italy to study Italian; she deserves to study there.

Writing Assignment: On a separate sheet of paper, write about a time when you worked hard to accomplish or obtain something you really wanted. Use semicolons to connect some sentences that are close in thought.

Evaluation Checklist: After you write your first draft, use these guidelines to help you evaluate your writing.

____ I have used a semicolon between sentences I have written that are close in thought.

____ I have lowercased the first word following a semicolon if that word is not a proper noun.

____ My writing contains each of the points found on the checklist on page 547.

Revising, Proofreading, and Writing the Final Version: Revise your first draft carefully. Check that you have not used semicolons between too many of your sentences or between sentences that are not close in thought. Proofread your revised draft. Then write your final version.

The Complex Sentence to Show Relationship

WRITING APPLICATION A: Using Adverb Clauses

A good watch is made up of complex parts that work well together. Similarly, a good paragraph is often made up of complex sentences in combination with other types of sentences. Complex sentences frequently contain adverb clauses, which always begin with subordinating conjunctions, such as *when, whenever, while, as, as soon as, before, after, since,* and *until.*

EXAMPLE   *Although Sam was an artist,* he never painted a picture or sculpted a statue. Sam was a flutist who lived directly above us in an apartment in Boston. He played with the Boston Pops for several years *before moving to New York City three years ago. While I was growing up,* I would hear him practicing early every morning. He used to drive my mother crazy, but I liked his music. To this day, *whenever I hear the* "William Tell Overture," I think fondly of Sam.

Writing Assignment: On a separate sheet of paper, write about someone you remember fondly but no longer see. Describe some of the characteristics of this person. Use adverb clauses in your writing.

Evaluation Checklist: After you write your first draft, use these guidelines to help you evaluate your paragraph.

____ I have used adverb clauses in my writing.

____ Each of my paragraphs contains a topic sentence and supporting sentences.

____ My writing contains each of the points found on the checklist on page 547.

Revising, Proofreading, and Writing the Final Version: Revise your first draft carefully. You should have a subordinating conjunction in any sentence you think has an adverb clause. Proofread your revised draft. Then write your final version.

WRITING APPLICATION B: Writing Adjective Clauses

Just as a caboose never comes at the beginning of a train, an adjective clause never comes at the beginning of a sentence. An adjective clause must always follow the noun or pronoun it modifies. This rule is helpful to know if you have trouble distinguishing adverb clauses from adjective clauses. Note in the examples below how the adjective clause cannot be moved to the beginning of the sentence and still make sense.

EXAMPLES   1. The project manager is the person *who makes budget decisions.*
2. The new word processor has the program *that he prefers to use.*
3. Maria is a landscape painter *whose work has sold extremely well.*

Writing Assignment: Write a short paper explaining the responsibilities that various people have in a club or social group to which you belong. Use some adjective clauses in your writing.

Evaluation Checklist: After you write your first draft, use these guidelines to help you evaluate your writing.

____ I have used adjective clauses in my writing.

____ My writing contains each of the points found on the checklist on page 547.

Revising, Proofreading, and Writing the Final Version: Revise your first draft carefully. Proofread your revised draft. Then write your final version.

WRITING APPLICATION C: Using *Who* and *Whom*

Using a shortcut when you travel can be an invaluable timesaver. Using a shortcut when you need to decide whether to use *who* or *whom* in a sentence can also be an invaluable timesaver. To determine quickly which word you should use, mentally substitute the word *him* for *whom* and the word *he* for *who*. If *him* fits, you should be using *whom*. If *he* fits, you should be using *who*. In some cases, you will need to rearrange the sentence slightly to test the word.

EXAMPLE   (*Who, Whom*) is going to make the presentation to the board of directors?

TEST *WHOM*   *Him* is going to make the presentation to the board of directors? (*Him* does not fit.)

TEST *WHO*   *He* is going to make the presentation to the board of directors? (*He* fits.)

SOLUTION   *Who* is going to make the presentation to the board of directors?

Writing Assignment: On a separate sheet of paper, write a paragraph for a business letter, requesting the names of three people who will be able to give you information about a product or service for which you are interested. Use *who* or *whom* at least three times in your writing.

Evaluation Checklist: After you write your first draft, use these guidelines to help you evaluate your paragraph.

____ I have used *who* and *whom* correctly in my sentences.

____ My paragraph contains each of the points found on the checklist on page 547.

Revising, Proofreading, and Writing the Final Version: Revise your first draft carefully. Make sure your request has a courteous tone suitable for a business letter. Proofread your revised draft. Then write your final version.

UNIT 4 Other Devices of Subordination

WRITING APPLICATION A: Avoiding Dangling Participles

Although you may purposely want to end a story so that it leaves your readers hanging, you never want to leave your sentences dangling. A dangling participle is a participle that modifies a word it cannot logically modify in a sentence. If you are not careful when you write, you may accidently write participles that dangle in your sentences.

INCORRECT   Swinging with ease through the air, I watched the trapeze artist.
            (*Swinging through the air* modifies *trapeze artist,* not *I.*)
CORRECT   I watched the trapeze artist swinging through the air with ease.

Writing Assignment: On a separate sheet of paper, describe an interesting event you have watched as a spectator. Examples of events are a circus, a baseball game, or an air show. Use present or past participles in your writing. Be careful not to use dangling participles.

Evaluation Checklist: After you write your first draft, use these guidelines to help you evaluate your writing.

____ I have included present or past participles in my writing.
____ I have not used dangling participles in my writing.
____ My writing contains each of the points found on the checklist on page 547.

Revising, Proofreading, and Writing the Final Version: Revise the first draft carefully. If you have used participles correctly, they will logically modify specific words in your sentences. Proofread your revised draft. Then write your final version.

WRITING APPLICATION B: Using Appositives to Explain

Have you ever had to add a postscript to the end of a letter because you forgot to include important information in the body? In a way, an appositive in a sentence is like a postscript in a letter. An appositive explains or adds information about a noun or pronoun in a sentence. It is usually set off with commas.

EXAMPLES   1. Their son Paul, *a law student,* will graduate from college in June.
            2. Clara Barton, *a battlefield nurse,* founded the American Red Cross more than 100 years ago.
            3. George Washington Carver, *a chemist and an inventor,* became famous for his agricultural research.

Writing Assignment: On a separate sheet of paper, write about someone famous that you have admired. Explain some of the things this person has done to earn your admiration. Use some appositives in your writing.

Evaluation Checklist: After you write your first draft, use these guidelines to help you evaluate your writing.

____ I have used appositives in my writing to explain or add information about a noun or pronoun in a sentence.

____ I have set off appositives with commas.

____ My writing contains each of the points found on the checklist on page 547.

Revising, Proofreading, and Writing the Final Version: Revise your first draft carefully. Proofread your revised draft. Then write your final version.

WRITING APPLICATION C: Using Reduction for Conciseness

To many people, reducing means losing weight to improve one's health or appearance. In writing, reducing means expressing your ideas in the fewest words possible without sacrificing clarity. The process of reducing a word group to a simpler word group is called reduction. In the examples below, note how entire word groups, shown in parentheses, can be omitted from the sentences without changing the meaning.

EXAMPLES
1. George whistled while (he was) building the house near the edge of the hill.
2. Impatiens, pansies, and begonias grow well in indirect light if (they are) watered daily.
3. While (she was) working on the report, Elena was constantly interrupted by her secretary.
4. Mr. Hollins arrived at the theater early (so that he would be able) to get a good seat.
5. We have already hung all the birthday decorations (that were) delivered this morning.

Writing Assignment: On a separate sheet of paper, write about something for which you planned carefully, such as a party, a dance, special lessons, a class or family reunion, or a vacation. Describe some of the many things you had to do to make that event successful.

Evaluation Checklist: After you write your first draft, use these guidelines to help you evaluate your writing.

____ My writing follows a logical order.

____ I have used reduction to help eliminate all excess words from my writing.

____ My writing contains each of the points found on the checklist on page 547.

Revising, Proofreading, and Writing the Final Version: Revise your first draft carefully. Eliminate any remaining unnecessary words that you find in your sentences. Proofread your revised draft. Then write your final version.

UNIT **5** Achieving Sentence Variety

WRITING APPLICATION A: Using Adjective Clauses

To single out a person in a crowd, you might call out that person's name. In a similar way, when you write, you can use adjective clauses to single out items in a group. Adjective clauses can help emphasize specific information about people, places, or things that are part of a larger group.

EXAMPLES
1. Ryan has three cousins, *two of whom are older than 25.*
2. The gymnast completed four routines, *one of which received a perfect score from the judges.*
3. Megan collects seashells, *many of which she found in California and Florida.*

Writing Assignment: On a separate sheet of paper, write about something you collect. Use adjective clauses to describe specific items in your collection.

Evaluation Checklist: After you write your first draft, use these guidelines to help you evaluate your writing.

____ I have used adjective clauses in my writing.
____ I have used the pronoun *whom* in adjective clauses when I am referring to people.
____ My writing contains each of the points found on the checklist on page 547.

Revising, Proofreading, and Writing the Final Version: Revise your first draft carefully. Proofread your revised draft. Then write your final version.

WRITING APPLICATION B: Using Effective Sentence Devices

Knowing how to use electrical devices such as hair dryers, computers, and washing machines makes life much easier for many people. In a similar way, knowing how to use a variety of sentence devices can make your writing tasks easier. The three sentence devices you practiced in the first part of this book were (1) "no sooner . . . than," (2) "not only . . . but also," and (3) "the more . . . the more" or "the more . . . the less." Knowing how to use these devices will enable you to provide special emphasis in your sentences.

EXAMPLES
1. When we arrived at the barber shop, Johnny wanted to leave.
   No sooner had we arrived at the barber shop *than* Johnny wanted to leave.
2. Johnny wanted to leave and go back to his old barber.
   Not only did Johnny want to leave, *but* he *also* wanted to go back to his old barber.
3. As I tried to calm Johnny down, he just fretted more and more.
   The more I tried to calm Johnny down, *the more* he fretted.

Writing Assignment: On a separate sheet of paper, write a narrative about a visit to a dentist's office, a doctor's office, a hair salon, or a barber shop. Try to use all three sentence devices in your writing to explain what happened.

Evaluation Checklist: After you write your first draft, use these guidelines to help you evaluate your writing.

____ I have used three sentence devices in my writing.
____ My writing follows chronological order.
____ My writing contains each of the points found on the checklist on page 547.

Revising, Proofreading, and Writing the Final Version: Revise your first draft carefully. Check that you have properly used all three sentence devices in your writing and that your writing follows a logical order. Proofread your revised draft. Then write your final version.

WRITING APPLICATION C: Writing Noun-Participle Phrases

A person who is independent is one who is not affected or influenced by others. In writing, a specific word group called a noun-participle phrase is independent and does not refer to any other word in a sentence. Since this type of phrase stands on its own, it can be moved anywhere in a sentence without changing the meaning.

EXAMPLES
1. *His hands trembling,* John opened the old, creaky basement door slowly.
2. John, *his hands trembling,* opened the old, creaky basement door slowly.
3. John opened the old, creaky basement door slowly, *his hands trembling.*
4. *The car's left-rear tire becoming suddenly flat,* Sarah put on her signal to exit the freeway.
5. Sarah put on her signal to exit the freeway, *the car's left-rear tire becoming suddenly flat.*

Writing Assignment: On a separate sheet of paper, write about a frightening experience you once had. Check that your writing follows a logical order. Use some noun-participle phrases to help you express your ideas.

Evaluation Checklist: After you write your first draft, use these guidelines to help you evaluate your writing.

____ I have used noun-participle phrases in my writing.
____ My writing contains each of the points found on the checklist on page 547.

Revising, Proofreading, and Writing the Final Version: Revise your first draft carefully. Proofread your revised draft. Then write your final version.

WRITING APPLICATION A: Avoiding Sentence Fragments

Just as you must pass tests in your classes to be promoted to the next grade or to graduate, so must the word groups you use in your writing pass tests to be considered sentences. To test your sentences for completeness, ask these two questions: (1) Does the word group have a subject and a verb? (2) Does the word group make sense by itself? If you cannot answer yes to both questions, the word group is a fragment rather than a sentence. One of the most common fragment errors is made when an adverb clause is punctuated as a sentence rather than as a clause within a sentence. You can usually correct this error by joining the clause to another sentence.

INCORRECT   When I finally found a seat. I realized I had taken the wrong bus.

CORRECT   When I finally found a seat, I realized I had taken the wrong bus.

Writing Assignment: On a separate sheet of paper, write about an interesting experience you had your first year of high school. Begin several of your sentences with adverb clauses. Make sure all your sentences are complete.

Evaluation Checklist: After you write your first draft, use these guidelines to help you evaluate your writing.

____ I have punctuated each of my sentences correctly.
____ I have used adverb clauses correctly in my writing.
____ My writing contains each of the points found on the checklist on page 547.

Revising, Proofreading, and Writing the Final Version: Revise your first draft carefully. Make sure you have used correct punctuation in sentences that have clauses. Proofread your revised draft. Then write your final version.

WRITING APPLICATION B: Writing Complete Sentences

The distance you travel on vacation does not determine whether you will enjoy that vacation. Similarly, when you write, the length of a word group you use does not determine whether the words make up a sentence. A sentence can be as short as one word or it can go on for pages. A sentence ends only when the last grammatically connected idea has been expressed completely.

COMPLETE   Listen. (The subject *you* is understood.)

INCOMPLETE   In the spring in Michigan, if you get up fairly early in the morning and hear the sweet, high-pitched song of a robin, which is also that state's bird, you may find that you want to listen to this morning melody for. (This sentence could be made complete by inserting a noun after the word *for,* or it could continue on and end later.)

Writing Assignment: On a separate sheet of paper, write about a vacation you have particularly enjoyed. Use sensory details of sight, hearing, touch, and smell in your writing. Write complete sentences.

Evaluation Checklist: After you write your first draft, use these guidelines to help you evaluate your writing.

____ Each of my sentences is complete.
____ I have punctuated each of my sentences correctly.
____ I have used sensory details in my writing.
____ My writing contains each of the points found on the checklist on page 547.

Revising, Proofreading, and Writing the Final Version: Revise your first draft carefully. Proofread your revised draft. Then write your final version.

WRITING APPLICATION C: Stopping Run-on Sentences

Running head-on into another person or object can be a physically painful experience. In a similar manner, writing sentences that run into one another can be a mentally painful experience for a reader. When sentences run on, the reader becomes confused because the writing makes little sense. As you write, avoid run-on sentences by punctuating them in one of four ways: (1) Add a period between sentences. (2) Add a semicolon between sentences. (3) Add a comma and a conjunction between two sentences. (4) Make one part of a sentence dependent on the other, and add a comma if necessary.

RUN-ON SENTENCE	My younger sister likes to get up before dawn I prefer to sleep late.
COMPLETE SENTENCES	1. My younger sister likes to get up before dawn. I prefer to sleep late.
	2. My younger sister likes to get up before dawn; I prefer to sleep late.
	3. My younger sister likes to get up before dawn, but I prefer to sleep late.
	4. Although my younger sister likes to get up before dawn, I prefer to sleep late.

Writing Assignment: On a separate sheet of paper, write about what you believe would be the perfect weekend. Describe when you would get up in the morning, what you would do during the day and evening, where you would go, and what the weather would be like.

Evaluation Checklist: After you write your first draft, use these guidelines to help you evaluate your writing.

____ Each of my sentences is complete and correctly punctuated.
____ My writing follows a logical order.
____ My writing contains each of the points found on the checklist on page 547.

Revising, Proofreading, and Writing the Final Version: Revise your first draft carefully. Correct any run-on sentences you have found in your writing. Proofread your revised draft. Then write your final version.

UNIT 7 The Smooth-Running Sentence

WRITING APPLICATION A: Avoiding Misplaced Modifiers

Have you ever misplaced your keys just as you were about to leave your house? If you were unable to find the keys quickly, you probably became quite frustrated. In a similar way, when you write, you will frustrate your readers if you misplace modifiers in your sentences. Your readers will not easily be able to make sense of your sentences and may become confused. In most cases, you can correct misplaced modifiers by moving the modifiers to their correct position.

MISPLACED MODIFIER	We sold the car to our neighbor *with the blue upholstery.*
CORRECTLY PLACED MODIFIER	We sold the car *with the blue upholstery* to our neighbor.
MISPLACED MODIFIER	The package is in your room *that the courier delivered.*
CORRECTLY PLACED MODIFIER	The package *that the courier delivered* is in your room.

Writing Assignment: On a separate sheet of paper, write about a special gift you have given or received. Use modifiers in your writing.

Evaluation Checklist: After you write your first draft, use these guidelines to help you evaluate your writing.

____ I have correctly placed modifiers in my sentences.
____ My writing contains each of the points found on the checklist on page 547.

Revising, Proofreading, and Writing the Final Version: Revise your first draft carefully so that your modifiers are correctly placed. Proofread your revised draft. Then write your final version.

WRITING APPLICATION B: Using Parallel Construction

To ski down a snow-covered hill without falling, you need to keep your skis parallel. When you write, you need to express ideas in a similar or parallel way to make your sentences read smoothly. If you put one idea in a sentence into an infinitive phrase, you should also put any parallel idea in the same sentence into an infinitive phrase. If you express an idea using a gerund, you should express a parallel idea using a gerund. Apply this rule when using any part of speech.

NONPARALLEL	I enjoy *planning* schedules much more than *to follow* them.
PARALLEL	I enjoy *planning* schedules much more than *following* them.

NONPARALLEL	*Making* two or three of your own outfits can sometimes be less expensive than *to buy* one outfit.
PARALLEL	*Making* two or three of your own outfits can sometimes be less expensive than *buying* one outfit.

Writing Assignment: On a separate sheet of paper, write about a method you have used to simplify a task or to save yourself time.

Evaluation Checklist: After you write your first draft, use these guidelines to help you evaluate your writing.

____ I have used parallel construction in my sentences.

____ My writing contains each of the points found on the checklist on page 547.

Revising, Proofreading, and Writing the Final Version: Revise your first draft carefully. Look for ways to use parallel structure to clarify your ideas. Proofread your revised draft. Then write your final version.

WRITING APPLICATION C: Making Logical Comparisons

Comparing people, places, and things in your writing will always be like comparing apples to oranges if you make illogical comparisons. When you are writing and want to compare one thing with a group of which it is part, include the word *other* or *else*. When comparing one thing with another using an "as" and "than" comparison, first complete the "as" comparison. Then add the "if" phrase at the end.

ILLOGICAL	Los Angeles is larger than *any city* in California.
LOGICAL	Los Angeles is larger than *any other city* in California.

ILLOGICAL	Tanya studies as much, *if not more than,* her brother Richard.
LOGICAL	Tanya studies as much as her brother Richard, *if not more*.

Writing Assignment: On a separate sheet of paper, write about two of your favorite cities. Compare their size, facilities, and physical characteristics. Make logical comparisons in your sentences.

Evaluation Checklist: After you write your first draft, use these guidelines to help you evaluate your writing.

____ I have used correct forms of comparison in my writing.

____ My writing contains each of the points found on the checklist on page 547.

Revising, Proofreading, and Writing the Final Version: Revise your first draft carefully. Reread your sentences carefully to make sure you have made only logical comparisons. Proofread your revised draft carefully. Then write your final version.

UNIT 8 Making Subject and Verb Agree

WRITING APPLICATION A: Recognizing Singular Subjects

When a group of people is "in agreement," its members agree with each other on at least one point. When a sentence is in agreement, its subject agrees in number with its verb. The words *each, each one, either, either one, neither, any one,* and *every one* are singular because they refer to only one person or thing at a time. These words always require a singular verb, whether the words that follow them are singular or plural.

EXAMPLES
1. *One* of the witnesses *was* subpoenaed nearly two weeks ago.
2. *Either* applicant *has* the right credentials for the position.
3. *Any one* of those rings *is* available for sale.

Writing Assignment: On a separate sheet of paper, write about a particular item you hope to own someday. Compare that item to other items that are similar in some way. Use the words *one of, each,* and *any one* in your writing.

Evaluation Checklist: After you write your first draft, use these guidelines to help you evaluate your paragraph.

____ I have used correct subject-verb agreement in all my sentences.
____ My writing contains each of the points found on the checklist on page 547.

Revising, Proofreading, and Writing the Final Version: Revise your first draft carefully. If any sentence lacks subject-verb agreement, change the number of the verb to agree with the number of the subject. Proofread your revised draft. Then write your final version.

WRITING APPLICATION B: Using Combined Subjects

An architect walking past a building might see hundreds of structural details. Another person walking past the same building may see only a single structure. Whether a person sees one thing or many will depend on that person's interests and inclinations. In writing, whether a combined subject in a sentence is considered singular or plural will depend on the writer's intended meaning. If you join subjects with the conjunction *and,* determine whether you are writing about one combined subject or several subjects. When you join two singular subjects with *and* to refer to the same person or thing, use a singular verb. When you join two singular subjects with *and* to refer to different persons or things, use a plural verb.

EXAMPLES
1. The *valedictorian and the recipient* of the Rosen Scholarship *are* to be announced at tonight's banquet. (The valedictorian and the scholarship recipient are thought of as two separate people.)
2. The *valedictorian and recipient* of the Rosen Scholarship *is* Anthony Orr. (Anthony is both valedictorian and scholarship recipient.)

Writing Assignment: On a separate sheet of paper, write about someone you know who has more than one title or occupation. The person may be a relative, a friend, an acquaintance, or someone famous. Discuss that person's background and responsibilities. Use correct subject-verb agreement in your writing.

Evaluation Checklist: After you write your first draft, use these guidelines to help you evaluate your writing.

_____ I have used a singular verb with combined subjects when my subject is one and the same person.

_____ I have used a plural verb with combined subjects when my subjects are different people.

_____ My writing contains each of the points found on the checklist on page 547.

Revising, Proofreading, and Writing the Final Version: Revise your first draft carefully. Proofread your revised draft. Then write your final version.

WRITING APPLICATION C: Using Collective Nouns

A collection can be thought of as a number of items that are similar in some way, or it can be thought of as a single entity. Similarly, a collective noun refers to a collection of people, animals, or things that can be thought of as singular or plural. A collective noun takes a singular verb when the group acts together as a single unit. It takes a plural verb when the members of the group act individually. Examples of collective nouns are *audience, couple, family, flock, group, team, crowd, committee, class,* and *jury*. It is sometimes difficult to decide whether a group is acting as a single unit or as individuals. Whatever you decide, be sure to keep the pronouns you use consistent with your verbs.

EXAMPLES   1. The history *class was* (singular) ready for *its* (singular) test.
            2. The *couple were* (plural) married early last year in *their* (plural) hometown.
            3. The *committee agree* (plural) that *their* (plural) bylaws need rewriting.
            4. Rose Marie's *family want* (plural) to sell *their* (plural) house as soon as possible.
            5. The *team was* (singular) anxious to receive *its* (singular) equipment.

Writing Assignment: On a separate sheet of paper, write about a field trip you once took that left a lasting impression. Describe some of the things your class saw and did. Use the collective nouns *class* and *group* in your writing.

Evaluation Checklist: After you write your first draft, use these guidelines to help you evaluate your writing.

_____ I have used the collective nouns *group* and *class* in my writing.

_____ Any pronouns I have used are consistent with my verbs.

_____ My writing contains each of the points found on the checklist on page 547.

Revising, Proofreading, and Writing the Final Version: Revise your first draft carefully. Proofread your revised draft. Then write your final version.

WRITING APPLICATION A: Selecting Irregular Verb Forms

To teach a person how to do something well, you need to give good directions. To give good directions, you need to tell exactly *when* and *how* to complete specific steps. You also need to use correct wording so that your directions are not misunderstood. Three frequently used pairs of words that are often used in directions but are confused or misused in writing are *lie* and *lay, sit* and *set,* and *rise* and *raise.* Knowing the correct meaning and forms of these irregular verbs will help you write clearer directions.

Present	Past	Past Participle
lie (to rest)	lay	(have) lain
lay (to put)	laid	(have) laid
sit (sitting position)	sat	(have) sat
set (to place)	set	(have) set
rise (to get up)	rose	(have) risen
raise (to lift)	raised	(have) raised

Writing Assignment: Think of something you know how to make or do well. Then, on a separate sheet of paper, write directions for a classmate. Use at least three verbs from the irregular verb pairs shown above. Write your directions in a step-by-step order.

Evaluation Checklist: After you write your first draft, use these guidelines to help you evaluate your writing.

____ I have used irregular verb forms correctly in my writing.
____ I have used at least three verbs from the irregular verb pairs shown.
____ My directions follow a step-by-step order.
____ My writing contains each of the points found on the checklist on page 547.

Revising, Proofreading, and Writing the Final Version: Revise your first draft carefully. Check that your directions are accurate, complete, and in correct order. Proofread your revised draft. Then write your final version.

WRITING APPLICATION B: Using the Present Perfect Tense

An Olympic diver must have perfect timing to complete a series of somersaults in midair and then enter the water a moment later in a vertical position. When you write, you can use tenses called the perfect tenses to help you describe actions that continue into another time period. For example, you can use the present perfect tense to describe an action that began in the past but that continues, or whose effect continues, into the present.

| PAST | We *waited* a long time for them to arrive. (We are no longer waiting.) |
| PRESENT PERFECT | We *have waited* a long time for them to arrive. (We are still waiting.) |

Writing Assignment: On a separate sheet of paper, write about something interesting you have done that you continue to do even today. Use the present perfect tense in your writing.

Evaluation Checklist: After you write your first draft, use these guidelines to help you evaluate your writing.

____ I have used the present perfect tense in my writing.

____ I have used logical order in my writing.

____ My writing contains each of the points found on the checklist on page 547.

Revising, Proofreading, and Writing the Final Version: Revise your first draft carefully. Check that you have used the present perfect tense correctly. Proofread your revised draft. Then write your final version.

WRITING APPLICATION C: Using the Active Voice

The difference between acting in a play and watching one is similar to the difference between writing in the active voice and writing in the passive voice. An actor participates directly in a play, while a person watching a play merely observes the action. The audience is the bystander rather than the center of attention. Similarly, a sentence written in the active voice has a subject that is doing or being something, while a sentence written in the passive voice has a subject that is merely receiving the action. In general, you should use the active voice when you write, because doing so will make your sentences more effective.

| ACTIVE | The new batter smashed the ball into left field. |
| PASSIVE | The ball was smashed into left field by the new batter. |

Writing Assignment: On a separate sheet of paper, write about a game or a sports activity in which you played particularly well. Use the active voice in your writing.

Evaluation Checklist: After you write your first draft, use these guidelines to help you evaluate your writing.

____ I have primarily used the active voice in my writing.

____ I have used logical order in my writing.

____ My writing contains each of the points found on the checklist on page 547.

Revising, Proofreading, and Writing the Final Version: Revise your first draft carefully. Check carefully that you have used the active voice rather than the passive voice in most of your sentences. Proofread your revised draft. Then write your final version.

UNIT 10 Using Adverbs and Adjectives

WRITING APPLICATION A: Selecting Adverb Forms

Using an adjective in a sentence where you should be using an adverb is a little like using salt in a recipe that calls for sugar. Three of the adjective and adverb forms that are commonly confused by inexperienced writers are *bad* and *badly*, *real* and *really*, and *sure* and *surely*. *Bad, real,* and *sure* are adjectives that can modify only nouns and pronouns. *Badly, really,* and *surely* are adverbs that modify verbs, adjectives, and other adverbs.

EXAMPLES
1. The soprano's singing was *bad* at last night's performance.
2. Colt's fractured finger hurt *badly* for hours after the construction accident.
3. Each of his concerns is *real* and requires immediate attention.
4. Additional seating in the stadium would *really* improve concession sales.
5. Joanna's appointment as director of marketing and sales seemed a *sure* thing.
6. The owners of the building will *surely* need to repair the air conditioner before summer.

Writing Assignment: On a separate sheet of paper, write an argument to persuade your classmates that a much-needed improvement to your school or community should be completed as soon as possible. Give at least three reasons for your argument and support those reasons with evidence. As you write, try to use a few of the commonly confused adverbs described above.

Evaluation Checklist: After you write your first draft, use these guidelines to help you evaluate your writing.

____ I have used the adjectives *bad, sure,* and *real* correctly in my writing.
____ I have used the adverbs *badly, surely,* and *really* correctly in my writing.
____ My writing contains each of the points found on the checklist on page 547.

Revising, Proofreading, and Writing the Final Version: Revise your first draft carefully. Check that you have correctly used adjective and adverb forms in your writing. In addition, make sure your argument is serious but does not have an angry tone. Remember that your argument should be supported with evidence. Proofread your revised draft. Then write your final version.

WRITING APPLICATION B: Using Sense with Adverbs

Knowing when to use an adverb form in your writing is often a matter of using good sense. Sensory verbs that directly relate a person's experiences to sight, smell, taste, touch, and hearing require adverbs rather than adjectives to help describe actions.

EXAMPLES   1. Darrell could hear *distinctly* the crackle of the burning wood in the next room.
2. Irene looked *curiously* at each person's unusual makeup.
3. I *carefully* felt the coarse texture of the rough-hewn wood.
4. Joe *suddenly* smelled smoke coming from the shed behind the barn.
5. We *quickly* tasted each of the colorful cheeses on the plate.

Writing Assignment: On a separate sheet of paper, describe a favorite food to your classmates, using sensory details of sight, smell, taste, touch, and hearing. Include adverbs in your writing.

Evaluation Checklist: After you write your first draft, use these guidelines to help you evaluate your writing.

____ I have included sensory details in my writing.
____ I have used adverbs correctly in my sentences.
____ My writing contains each of the points found on the checklist on page 547.

Revising, Proofreading, and Writing the Final Version: Revise your first draft carefully. Proofread your revised draft. Then write your final version.

WRITING APPLICATION C: Using Adjectives with Linking Verbs

Links in a chain make connections that hold the entire chain together. Similarly, in writing, linking verbs connect a subject in a sentence with an adjective to hold a sentence together. As you have read in the first part of this textbook, adverbs should never be used with linking verbs. When you are unsure whether a verb is a linking verb, mentally substitute a form of *seem,* which is always a linking verb. If the substitution does not greatly change the meaning of the sentence, the verb is a linking verb and should be followed by an adjective rather than an adverb.

EXAMPLES   1. Leon's forehead felt (seemed) *hot.*
2. The itinerary for Margie's trip to Europe looked (seemed) *wonderful.*
3. The broccoli quiche cooling near the window smelled (seemed) *delicious.*
4. The water from the hose tasted (seemed) *cool* and *sweet.*

Writing Assignment: On a separate sheet of paper, write about the sights, sounds, and smells of your favorite place. Examples of places might include a library, a sports arena, a movie theater, or a fishing dock. Use linking verbs and adjectives in your writing.

Evaluation Checklist: After you write your first draft, use these guidelines to help you evaluate your writing.

____ I have used sensory details in my writing.
____ I have used adjectives with linking verbs.
____ My writing contains each of the points found on the checklist on page 547.

Revising, Proofreading, and Writing the Final Version: Revise your first draft carefully. Proofread your revised draft. Then write your final version.

UNIT 11 Solving Your Pronoun Problems

WRITING APPLICATION A: Choosing the Correct Pronoun

How would you like to arrive at school one morning and discover you are wearing two different color shoes? Chances are that you would feel quite embarrassed. Similarly, in writing, using the incorrect form of a pronoun with another pronoun or noun in a sentence is a little like wearing shoes that do not match. In sentences in which you have a conjunction connecting two pronouns or a noun and a pronoun, your choice of pronouns may at times seem confusing. However, you can easily choose the correct pronoun by quickly testing each one alone in the sentence. The pronoun that makes the best sense in the sentence is the correct one.

SENTENCE	Brett and (*her, she*) arrived early at the auditorium.
TEST 1	*Her* arrived early at the auditorium. (makes poor sense)
TEST 2	*She* arrived early at the auditorium. (makes sense)
SOLUTION	Brett and *she* arrived early at the auditorium.

Writing Assignment: On a separate sheet of paper, write about a special function you have attended with a friend or relative. Describe some of the things you did together. Use pronouns in your writing.

Evaluation Checklist: After you write your first draft, use these guidelines to help you evaluate your writing.

____ Each of my pronouns is in the correct form.

____ My writing contains each of the points found on the checklist on page 547.

Revising, Proofreading, and Writing the Final Version: Revise your first draft carefully. Proofread your revised draft. Then write your final version.

WRITING APPLICATION B: Using Pronouns in Comparisons

To imply means to hint at or to suggest. In writing, for the sake of brevity, words are frequently implied rather than written out. For example, in sentences in which the word *than* or *as* is used in making a comparison, unnecessary words are often implied rather than written out. To decide which pronoun should follow the word *than* or *as* in these comparisons, think of the missing words in the sentence, and you will have no trouble deciding which case of the pronoun to use.

EXAMPLES
1. Bob can draw much better than *I* (can draw).
2. Paulette gave Ralph just as good a review as (she gave) *me*.
3. They think more of her than *I* (think of her).
4. They think more of him than (they think of) *me*.
5. The Steinbergs have a better garden than *we* (have).

Writing Assignment: On a separate sheet of paper, write about and compare two of your favorite movies, books, or records. Use pronouns in your comparisons.

Evaluation Checklist: After you write your first draft, use these guidelines to help you evaluate your writing. Check that you have used the correct pronoun forms in your sentences by mentally inserting any missing words.

_____ I have made comparisons using pronouns.
_____ I have used pronouns correctly in my comparisons.
_____ My writing contains each of the points found on the checklist on page 547.

Revising, Proofreading, and Writing the Final Version: Revise your first draft carefully, changing any pronouns that you have used incorrectly. Proofread your revised draft. Then write your final version.

WRITING APPLICATION C: Using Possessive Pronouns

A possessive person may cling so tightly to another person or object that he or she leaves no room for other people or experiences. In a similar fashion, possessive personal pronouns have specific forms that include no room for apostrophes. Examples of possessive personal pronouns are _his, hers, ours, theirs,_ and _its._ One of the most common errors made in writing is confusing the possessive pronoun _its_ with _it's. It's_ is always a contraction that means _it is._

EXAMPLES
1. The common parakeet, which is native to Australia, is known for _its_ colorful plumage.
2. Joseph could hardly contain _his_ excitement about attending the circus.
3. _Yours_ is the beige leather coat on the left.
4. All the books in the new reference library are _theirs._
5. The report delivered to _his_ office by mistake was actually _hers._

Writing Assignment: On a separate sheet of paper, use the pronoun _it,_ the possessive pronoun _its,_ and the contraction _it's_ to describe an object in your classroom. Provide details that will enable your classmates to easily guess what you are describing.

Evaluation Checklist: After you write your first draft, use these guidelines to help you evaluate your writing.

_____ I have used _its_ as a possessive personal pronoun.
_____ I have used _it's_ only as a contraction.
_____ I have written all other possessive pronouns correctly.
_____ My writing contains each of the points found on the checklist on page 547.

Revising, Proofreading, and Writing the Final Version: Revise your first draft carefully. Proofread your revised draft, checking that you have written possessive pronouns correctly. Then write your final version.

WRITING APPLICATION A: Inserting Introductory Commas

Everyday items that many people take for granted are sorely missed when they are needed but are not around. Similarly, introductory commas in sentences often seem unnecessary but become quite useful in sentences that would otherwise be misread. Note how the following sentences are improved when a comma is inserted after the introductory phrase or clause.

EXAMPLES   1. To advertise the circus owners need only fill out a short form.
                  To advertise, the circus owners need only fill out a short form.
           2. According to Robert Joe Christmas was one of William Faulkner's most interesting characters.
                  According to Robert, Joe Christmas was one of William Faulkner's most interesting characters.

Writing Assignment: On a separate sheet of paper, write about the opinions of someone with whom you may not agree but nonetheless respect. Use introductory commas after introductory phrases that might be misread.

Evaluation Checklist: After you write your first draft, use these guidelines to help you evaluate your writing.

____ I have used a comma after each introductory phrase or clause that might otherwise be misread.
____ My writing contains each of the points found on the checklist on page 547.

Revising, Proofreading, and Writing the Final Version: Revise your first draft carefully. Check that you have used all punctuation correctly in addition to commas. Proofread your revised draft. Then write your final version.

WRITING APPLICATION B: Using Colons

The table of contents in a book prepares readers for what follows. Similarly, in a sentence, a colon prepares readers for one or more items that follow in the sentence. However, a colon may be used only when the statement preceding the item or items is grammatically complete.

EXAMPLES   1. Ethan has only one goal: to become a landscape architect.
           2. The painting used only three colors: red, blue, and black.
           3. Alicia planned to visit the following cities in Massachusetts: Springfield, Cambridge, Worcester, and Boston.

Writing Assignment: On a separate sheet of paper, write about the variety of materials you have used in making or assembling something. Ideas might include ingredients in a recipe, materials for a mobile, parts for a car or a piece of furniture, or materials for clothing. When you introduce a list, use a colon.

Evaluation Checklist: After you write your first draft, use these guidelines to help you evaluate your writing.

___ I have used a colon only before an item or a series of items introduced by a grammatically complete statement.

___ My writing contains each of the points found on the checklist on page 547.

Revising, Proofreading, and Writing the Final Version: Revise your first draft carefully. Proofread your revised draft. Then write your final version.

WRITING APPLICATION C: Using Quotation Marks

Footprints in the sand serve as reminders that someone or something actually walked along a beach. Similarly, in writing, quotation marks serve to remind readers that the words between the marks are actually those of the speaker. When using quotation marks in your writing, insert a comma as a separator between the quotation and the expression used by the speaker (such as, *he said*). If you are only reporting indirectly what someone else has said, you do not need to enclose the words in quotation marks.

EXAMPLES 1. The electrician said, "I will stop by the house tomorrow."
The electrician said that she would stop by the house tomorrow.
2. "My vacation was so wonderful and action-packed," said Marshall, "that it would take me hours to describe everything that happened." Marshall said his vacation was so wonderful and action-packed that it would take hours to describe everything that happened.

Writing Assignment: On a separate sheet of paper, write about a compliment you have received that especially pleased you. Use a direct and an indirect quotation to identify what the other person said about you.

Evaluation Checklist: After you write your first draft, use these guidelines to help you evaluate your writing.

___ I have enclosed all direct quotes in quotation marks.

___ I have used a comma as a separator in direct quotations.

___ My writing contains each of the points found on the checklist on page 547.

Revising, Proofreading, and Writing the Final Version: Revise your first draft carefully. Proofread your revised draft, checking that you have used quotation marks correctly with other punctuation marks. Then write your final version.

FRAME INDEX

Each entry is indexed by frame number, followed by the page number, in parentheses, on which the frame appears. The frames indexed here are definitive, illustrative, or pivotal. Additional information and related exercises may be found in the frames preceding and following those listed. Complete review exercises for major topics are listed in the table of contents.

absolute phrase, 1237 (313)
action verbs, 84–86 (167–171)
active verb(s):
  defined, 2301 (286)
  followed by *well*, 2428 (2)
  subject of, 2304 (292)
  use of, in sentence, 2310 (304)
addresses, punctuation of, 2860 (328), 2863 (334)
adjective(s):
  adjective clause reduced to, 1032 (443)
  capitalization of, 3137 (334), 3189 (448)
  comma between, 2822 (252), 2825 (258), 2828 (264)
  defined, 199 (397), 200 (399)
  demonstrative, 2606 (358)
  -er with *the more, the less*, 1225 (289)
  formed from nouns, 2390 (464)
  function of, 200 (399), 526 (511), 2370 (424)
  kind of, sort of, misused, 2396 (476)
  -ly, as adverb sign, 2393 (470)
  misused as adverbs, 2374 (432)
  as modifiers, 200 (399), 526 (511), 2370 (424), 2418 (520)
  after noun, for emphasis, 1082 (3)
  positions of, 204–205 (407–409), 208 (415), 210 (419)
  prepositional phrase reduced to, 1045 (469)
  with pronouns, 210 (419)
  after sense verbs, 2417 (518)
  as subject complement, 205 (409), 2418 (520)
  well as, 2431 (8)
adjective clause(s):
  comma with, 2893 (394), 2897 (402)
  in complex sentence, 644 (207)
  defined, 525 (509)
  distinguished from appositive clause, 964 (307)
  to express explanatory fact, 638 (195)
  formed from compound sentence, 666 (251)
  formed from simple sentence, 657 (233)
  function of, 526–527 (511–513)
  introduced by preposition, 567 (53)
  introduced by pronoun, 542 (3), 544 (7)
  omission of relative pronoun in, 578 (75)
  with *one of, the only one of*, 1978–1979 (178–180), 1984–1985 (190–192)
  position of, 532 (523), 535 (529), 1499 (297)
  recognition of unsignaled, 579 (77), 581 (81)
  reduced to appositive, 1036 (451)
  reduced to infinitive phrase, 1005 (389)
  reduced to participle, 1034–1035 (447–449)
  reduced to preposition and gerund, 1043 (465)
  reduced to prepositional phrase, 1030 (439)
  reduced to present participial phrase, 1001 (381), 1003 (385)
  reduced to single adjective, 1032 (443)

relation of, to main statement, 644 (207)
signals for, 539 (537), 542 (3), 554 (27)
verb agreement with *who, which, that* in, 1971 (164), 1977 (176), 1978–1979 (178–180), 1984–1985 (190–192)
with *whose*, 1156 (151)
adjective phrase(s):
  defined, 252 (503), 270 (539)
  function of, 270 (539)
  position of, 254 (507)
adverb(s):
  as adjective and adverb modifiers, 224 (447)
  conjunctive, 1436–1438 (171–175)
  adverb clause signaled by, 456–461 (371–381)
  to begin sentence, 426 (311), 1069 (517), 1073 (525)
  defined, 217 (433)
  forms of, 218 (435), 2371 (426), 2382 (448)
  function of, 212 (423)
  mistaken for conjunctions, 419 (297)
  mobility of, 219–221 (437–441)
  modifying sense verbs, 2413 (510)
  noun clause signaled by, 736 (391)
  position of, 57 (113), 1492 (283)
  prepositional phrase reduced to, 1045 (469)
  use of, without *-ly*, 2382 (448), 2384 (452)
  as verb modifiers, 56 (111), 212 (423), 446 (351), 2370 (424), 2382 (448), 2384 (452)
adverb clause(s):
  although omitted from, 1127 (93) to begin sentence, 1069 (517), 1073 (525), 1089 (17)
  beginning with adjective, 1127 (93)
  comma with, 463 (385), 2775 (158), 2780 (168), 2783 (174)
  in complex sentence, 496 (451)
  connected by subordinating conjunction, 495 (449)
  to correct dangling word group, 1572 (443)
  defined, 445 (349)
  elliptical, 994 (367)
  with *for*, 2780 (168)
  with *if*, 1100 (39)
  to modify verb, 453–454 (365–367)
  after noun-clause signal, 1189 (217)
  with *now that*, 1120 (79)
  with *once*, 1115 (69)
  position of, 462 (383)
  reduced to elliptical clause, 994 (367)
  reduced to infinitive phrase, 999 (377)
  reduced to prepositional phrase and gerund, 1039 (457)
  reduced to present participial phrase, 997 (373)
  relation of, to main statement, 499 (457), 501 (461), 503 (465)
  shift of, for clear meaning, 1507 (313)

adverb clause(s) (*continued*)
  signals for, 456–461 (371–381), 999 (377), 1100 (39),
    1115 (63), 1120 (79), 2780 (168)
  with *so that,* 999 (377)
adverb phrase(s):
  to begin sentence, 1069 (517), 1073 (525)
  defined, 257 (513), 270 (539)
  function of, 258 (515), 261 (521)
  position of, 262 (523), 1510 (319)
agreement of pronouns:
  in number, 2641 (428)
  in person, 2636 (418)
agreement of subject and verb:
  with collective nouns, 2025 (272)
  with *Here is, Here are,* 2009 (240), 2012 (246)
  in interrogative sentences, 2016 (254)
  with *neither . . . nor,* 1951 (124), 1953 (128)
  in number, 1885 (530)
  with *one of the things that,* 1991 (204)
  with *one of those who,* 1978 (178)
  with plural units of measurement, 2031 (284)
  with subject complement, 1912 (46)
  with singular subjects joined by *and,* 1937 (96),
    1939–1940 (100–102)
  with subjects joined by *or, nor,* 1945 (112)
  with *There is, There are,* 2009 (240), 2012 (246)
  with *There was, There were, There has been, There
    have been,* 2014 (250)
  with verb ending in *-s,* 1897 (16), 1898 (18)
  with verb separated from subject, 1891 (4)
  in *who, which, that* clauses, 71 (164)
  See *also* number
  all the other in comparisons, 1809 (378)
also omitted from *not only . . .
  but also,* 1214–1215 (267–269)
although clause, substitute for, 1127 (93), 1132 (103)
and:
  in compound sentences, 293 (45), 305 (69), 678 (275),
    684–685 (287–289)
  to join singular subjects, 1937 (96), 1939 (100)
  to join two ideas, 352 (163), 678 (275)
  for parallel construction, 1621 (2)
antecedent:
  defined, 1684 (128)
  introductory *It* used without, 1170–1171 (179–181),
    1697–1698 (154–156)
  number of, in *who, which, that* clauses, 1971 (164)
  pronoun agreement with, 2636 (418), 2641 (428)
  required, 1689 (138)
  of *you,* 1706 (172)
any one, with singular verb, 1929 (80)
any other, in comparisons, 1807 (374), 1808 (376)
apostrophe:
  in contractions, 3096 (262), 3097 (264)
  with nouns, 2611 (368), 3055–3056 (180–182)
  of phrase as substitute for, 3077 (224)
  with plurals, 3126 (322)
  with pronouns, 2611 (368), 3106 (282)
  to show ownership, 3054–3056 (178–182), 3062 (194)
appear, as linking verb, 151 (301)
appositive clause, 724 (367)
appositive phrase:
  defined, 955 (289)
  distinguished from adjective clause, 964 (307)
  as fragment, 3138 (475)
  formed from sentence, 959 (289)
  punctuation of, 967 (313), 2853 (314)
  to reduce adjective clause, 1036 (451)
appositive(s):
  with dashes, 2956 (520)

defined, 723 (365), 946 (271)
  in *let's you and me,* 2567 (280)
  modifiers of, 953 (285)
  position of, 946 (271)
  pronouns as, 2560 (266)
  the fact that clause as, 1180 (199)
article:
  omission of, 1769–1770 (298–300)
  repetition of, for clarity, 1772 (304)
  use of indefinite, 1769 (298)
as, as well as, parallel construction with, in comparisons,
    1625 (10)
  as or *than,* case of pronoun after, 2550 (246)
  as much as . . . if not more than, 1815 (390)
  auxiliary verbs, see helping verb(s)

badly, used with *feel,* 2426 (536)
be:
  forms of, 138 (275), 148 (295)
  as helping verb, 148 (295)
  as linking verb, 137 (273)
  nominative case after, 2503 (152)
  objective case after, 2512 (170)
  omission of, in forming participial phrases, 845–846
    (69–71)
  omission of *that* after, 1781 (322)
  with past participle, 2308 (300)
  with present participle, 1332 (503)
  as substitute for sense verb, 2419 (522)
  as test for linking verb, 154 (507)
become, as linking verb, 151 (301)
because:
  replaced by *for,* 2780 (168)
  replaced by *now that,* 1120 (79)
  replaced by semicolon, 402 (263), 2937 (482)
besides:
  as cause of run-on sentences, 1442 (183)
  as conjunctive adverb, 1436 (171)
but:
  in compound sentences, 293 (45), 301 (61), 305 (69)
  to contrast ideas, 352 (163)
  for parallel construction, 1621 (2)
  as preposition, 247 (493)
but, but also with *not only,* 1210 (259), 1214–1215
    (267–269)

capitalization:
  to begin direct quotation, 2979 (28)
  of brand names, 3147 (364)
  of days, months, holidays, 3145 (360)
  of family names, 3173–3174 (416–418)
  of geographical names, 3132 (334), 3135 (340)
  of governmental bodies, 3149 (368)
  of historical events, periods, documents, 3181 (432)
  of institutions, 3140 (350), 3142 (354)
  in interrupted quotation, 2988 (46), 2994 (58)
  of languages, 3137 (344)
  of nationalities, 3137 (344)
  of organizations, 3140 (350), 3142 (354)
  of proper adjectives, 3189 (448)
  of proper nouns, 3131 (332)
  of races, 3137 (344) '
  of sacred names, 3183 (436)
  of seasons, 3145 (360)
  of titles (of books, etc.), 3177–3178 (424–426)
  of titles used alone, 3169 (408), 3172 (414), 3173–
    3174 (416–418)
  of titles used with names, 3164 (398)

quotation marks (*continued*)
  with uninterrupted quotation, 3001 (72)
  See also direct quotation(s)
question:
  in direct quotation, 3026 (122)
  in indirect quotation, 3019–3020 (108–110)
  position of subject in, 64 (127)
  signal for, 64 (127)

really meaning *very*, 2388 (460)
reduction:
  of adjective clause, *see* adjective clause(s)
  of adverb clause, *see* adverb clause(s)
  of compound sentence, 666 (251), 896 (171), 1256
    (351)
  defined, 986 (351), 989 (357)
  list of sentence elements for, 988 (355), 1026 (431)
  omission of words for, 994 (367)
  of prepositional phrase, 1045 (469)
  of simple sentence, *see* simple sentence
  by substituting *whose* for *of which*, 1156 (151)
reference of pronouns:
  ambiguous, 1725 (210), 1726–1728 (212–216), 1730
    (220), 1741–1742 (242–244)
  to antecedent, 2029 (280)
  defined, 1721 (202)
  to people, 597 (113), 600 (119), 1157 (153)
  to things and animals, 598 (115), 600 (119), 1157
    (153)
reflexive pronouns:
  defined, 2588 (322)
  formal usage of, 2601 (348), 2603 (352)
  list of, 2592 (330)
regular verb, defined, 2076 (374)
relative pronoun(s):
  defined, 544 (7)
  list of, 566 (51), 596 (111)
  in *of whom, of which* clauses, 1140 (119)
  omission of, 578 (75)
  to refer to people, 597 (113), 600 (119), 1157 (153)
  to refer to things and animals, 598 (115), 600 (119),
    1157 (153)
restrictive clause(s):
  defined, 2882 (372)
  no comma with, 2885 (378)
ring, rang, rung pattern of verbs, 2111–2118 (444–458)
rise-raise, 2175–2176 (34–36)
run-on sentence(s):
  with comma, 1391 (81), 1394 (87), 2812 (232)
  with conjunctive adverbs, 1437 (173), 1442 (183)
  correction of, 1408–1411 (115–121)
  defined, 1389 (77)
  with *it*, 1401 (101)

s for singular verb, 1893 (8), 1897 (16)
seem, as linking verb, 151 (301)
semicolon:
  in compound sentence, 396–397 (251–253), 402
    (263), 406 (271), 415 (289), 1393 (185), 2935 (478),
    2938 (484), 2940 (488)
  with coordinating conjunction, 2940 (488)
  to correct run-on sentences, 1410 (119)
  for force in construction, 410 (279)
  before *for example*, 2961 (530)
  to replace *because*, 402 (263), 2937 (482)
sense verb(s):
  badly used with, 2426 (536)

be as substitute for, 2419 (522)
  as linking verbs, 2417 (518), 2420 (524)
  list of, 2410 (504)
  modified by adverbs, 2413 (510)
sentence(s):
  begun with pronouns, 1401–1402 (101–103)
  completeness of, test for, 1280 (399)
  complex, *see* complex sentence
  compound, *see* compound sentence
  defined, 2 (3)
  determining end of, 1364–1365 (27–29)
  essentials of, 4 (7), 1280 (399)
  fragment, *see* fragment
  as part of paragraph, 1065–1067 (509–513)
  patterns, *see* sentence patterns
  run-on, *see* run-on sentence(s)
  simple, *see* simple sentence(s)
  word order in, *see* word order in sentence
sentence patterns:
  I, 89 (177), 106 (211)
  II, 100 (199), 106 (211)
  III, 146 (291)
series:
  of appositives with dashes, 2956 (520)
  colon before, 2943 (494)
  comma omitted in, 2819 (246)
  comma with, 2806 (220), 2812 (232), 2816 (240)
  defined, 2803 (214)
simple sentence(s):
  compound sentence formed from, 293 (45)
  defined, 289 (37)
  reduced to adjective clause, 638 (195), 641 (201), 657
    (233)
  reduced to adverb clause, 511 (481)
  reduced to appositive, 959 (297)
  reduced to infinitive phrase, 929 (237)
  reduced to noun clause, 1177 (193)
  reduced to noun-participle phrase, 1239 (317), 1244
    (327)
  reduced to participial phrase, 804 (527), 845 (69)
simple subject, 8 (15)
simple tenses, list of, 2233 (150)
sit-set, 2168 (20), 2170 (24)
sort, type, kind, with *this, that*, 2021 (264)
sort of:
  formal substitute for, 2397 (478)
  misused as adverbial, 2396 (476)
so that clause, reduction of, 999 (377)
subject(s):
  with active verb, 2301 (286)
  agreement of, with verb, *see* agreement of subject and
    verb
  defined, 8 (15)
  delayed, 1698 (156)
  with *It*, 1698 (156)
  joined by *and*, 1937 (96), 1939 (100)
  joined by *neither . . . nor*, 1951 (124), 1953 (128)
  joined by *or, nor*, 1945 (112), 1953 (128)
  in nominative case, 2482 (110)
  with passive verb, 2303 (290)
  phrase mistaken for, 1941 (104)
  relation of, to subject complement, 160 (319)
  separated from verb, 1891 (4)
subject complement:
  defined, 145 (289)
  after linking verb, 205 (409)
  omission of *that* in, 1781 (322)
  in pattern III, 146 (291)
  plural, after singular verb, 1912 (46)

Harcourt College Publishers

Where Learning Comes to Life

TECHNOLOGY
Technology is changing the learning experience, by increasing the power of your textbook and other learning materials; by allowing you to access more information, more quickly; and by bringing a wider array of choices in your course and content information sources.

Harcourt College Publishers has developed the most comprehensive Web sites, e-books, and electronic learning materials on the market to help you use technology to achieve your goals.

PARTNERS IN LEARNING
Harcourt partners with other companies to make technology work for you and to supply the learning resources you want and need. More importantly, Harcourt and its partners provide avenues to help you reduce your research time of numerous information sources.

Harcourt College Publishers and its partners offer increased opportunities to enhance your learning resources and address your learning style. With quick access to chapter-specific Web sites and e-books . . . from interactive study materials to quizzing, testing, and career advice . . . Harcourt and its partners bring learning to life.

Harcourt's partnership with Digital:Convergence™ brings :CRQ™ technology and the :CueCat™ reader to you and allows Harcourt to provide you with a complete and dynamic list of resources designed to help you achieve your learning goals. Just swipe the cue to view a list of Harcourt's partners and Harcourt's print and electronic learning solutions.

http://www.harcourtcollege.com/partners/